The Wines of Greece

FABER BOOKS ON WINE
General Editor: Julian Jeffs

Bordeaux (new edition) by David Peppercorn
Burgundy by Anthony Hanson
French Country Wines by Rosemary George
Port by George Robertson
Sherry by Julian Jeffs
Spirits and Liqueurs by Peter Hallgarten
The Wines of Portugal (new edition) by Jan Read
The Wines of the Rhône by John Livingstone-Learmonth and Melvyn C. H. Master
The Wines of Spain (new edition) by Jan Read
The Wines of Australia by Oliver Mayo
Drilling for Wine by Robin Yapp

THE WINES OF GREECE

MILES LAMBERT-GÓCS

faber and faber
LONDON · BOSTON

First published in 1990
by Faber and Faber Limited
3 Queen Square London WC1N 3AU

Phototypeset by Input Typesetting Ltd, London
Printed in Great Britain by
Clays Ltd, St Ives plc

British Library Cataloguing in Publication Data is available

ISBN 0–571–15387–9
ISBN 0–571–15388–7 (pbk)

For my friend,
Elias ('Louie') Sotirhos
of Seattle, Washington

It is thanks to Louie that I know that even in their
most ordinary condition the modern Greeks have
kept alive that special spark of the ancients. I learned
it one day as we walked in a heavily forested and
nearly deserted park half a world away from his
native village below Parnassos. When I commented
to Louie on the beauty of the place, he responded
without a moment's hesitation, 'But no people
today. The people is the beautiful.'

Ποτές μήν πιάνεσαι ἀπ'τά κλωνιά,
Πιάσου ἀπ'τόν κορμό

Never hold on by the shoots;
take hold of the stock.

proverb heard at Arakhova,
Central Greece

Contents

CONTENTS

Appendices

Illustrations

———

1 Samos (Eastern Sporades). Terraced vineyards of *moskháto áspro* in the north-central semi-mountainous zone.
2 Samos. A rainbow of muscat wine – from young dry wine from fresh grapes on the left, to aged sweet wine from partially raisined grapes on the right: Samian rosē is second from left.
3 Rhodes (Dodecanese). Plantings of *athíri* on the flanks of Mt Ataviros by Embonas.
4 Santorini (Cyclades). Vineyards on the island's inclined plateau, looking north from Fira.
5 Naousa (Macedonia). Rows of *xynómavro* at Yiannakokhori.
6 Rapsani (Thessaly). Vintage-time on the spines of Mt Kissavos, the Ossa of the ancients.
7 Nemea (Peloponnesos). *Ayioryítiko* ripening in 'the deep valley of Nemea' (Pindar, *The Nemean Odes*)
8 Cephalonia (Ionian Islands). View southwest towards the island capital of Argostoli, from *robóla* vineyards in the appellation zone near Dilinata.

Maps

─────

Author's Preface

———

I hope this book will be a useful guide and valued companion to Greek wine. The wines of Greece are as multifarious and fascinating as its geography, and well worth knowing and watching, especially now that more and more unique vintages are becoming available in bottle. Other wine countries have banked on an interested, informed, and appreciative foreign audience in updating their production of wine, and wine lovers the world over should want to help urge Greek producers to do their very best, to coax more wine-growers into bottling, and to bring about an upturn for wine at places not presently heard from because of unfortunate circumstances in recent times.

I have aimed to present the regional and local traditions in Greek wine so that wine lovers abroad can know what to expect and ask of places and producers. Furthermore, because individual producers and labels may come and go over the decades, it is particularly worth understanding the traditions they represent since those are a continuum by which faithful replacements can be recognized and encouraged.

While contemporary Greek wine is my focus, it has been hardly possible to avoid altogether Greece's ancient past in wine. For one thing, certain things seen and heard in Greek vineyards and cellars today are distinctly reminiscent of passages found in ancient literature and make them germane to an acquaintance with the background of contemporary wine. I have devoted a section to 'Classical Reflections' in each of the eleven regional chapters, as well as a chapter to what I think is a vital and relevant picture of Greek wine in antiquity. Since this chapter is an overview and the Classical Reflections sections are discussions of narrower topics suggested to me by the respective regions or their wines, readers with a special interest in wine history might find it particularly rewarding to read the chapter on wine and the Greeks during antiquity first and then to re-read it at the finish, even at the risk of allowing the larger-than-life ancients to commandeer the story of Greek wine, as can happen all too easily. I might draw special attention, too, to the Lexicon, largely intended as an exploration of the sensory language of the ancient Greeks, and which I believe has the merit of providing new perspectives on ancient wine, and also on our own language of wine appreciation.

Miles Lambert-Gócs
Alexandria, Virginia
October 1989

Acknowledgements

It would not have been possible to assemble the information I wanted about Greek wines without the cooperation of those who make them, and so I am very much indebted to all the producers who took the time to discuss their wine-making with me. However, I must single out Count Nikolaos Comoutos of Zakynthos for his extra effort in aiding my research.

Other persons in the Greek wine industry to whom I wish to express my appreciation are Dr Ulysses Davides, Professor Emeritus of the Department of Ampelology at the Superior College of Agriculture of Athens; Dr Stavroula Kourakou-Dragona, former Director of the Greek Wine Institute; Yiannis Boutaris, President of the Association of Greek Wine and Beverage Industries (SEVOP); and Dimitrios Kavour, General Director of the Central Union of Wine-producing Cooperative Organizations of Greece (KEOSOE).

Among the numerous individuals in various walks of life who facilitated my acquaintance with Greek wine regions, I would like to make special mention of Evangelos Katevenis of Samos; Pantelis Kefalas of Khios; Panayiotis Koritos of Arakhova, Central Greece; Yeoryios Itzkaras of Naousa, Macedonia; and John Ternas of Queens, New York.

For their help in arranging a variety of matters in support of this book, I also owe thanks to Nikolaos Efstathiadis, former Agricultural Counsellor of the Embassy of Greece in Washington, DC; Charalambos Machairidis, Greek Commercial Counsellor, Washington, DC, and Yiannis Papadimitriou, Greek Commercial Counsellor, New York, NY. In addition, I am grateful to Theresa Papademetriou of the Library of Congress, Washington, DC, for always taking the time to help me with my research no matter how small the point in question.

ACKNOWLEDGEMENTS

I feel honoured that Gerald Asher agreed to write the introduction, and could hardly have been more pleased. I do not think another writer on wine could better appreciate the task. I am indebted to Julian Jeffs, editor of Faber and Faber's wine series, for his great patience in preparing the manuscript for the printer.

Finally, in another vein altogether, I would like to thank my friends Gary Laden, Jon Nowick, Kevin Lanagan, Marie Winfrey Bernegger, and Hal McNitt for their encouragement. I believe I may rightly call them 'salt and bean friends', from Plutarch's description of 'friends who are so close to us as to be content to dine with us on salt and a bean', although I have never known any of my group to stop there.

Excerpts from the translations of ancient Greek texts are reprinted by permission of The Loeb Classical Library and Harvard University Press.

Foreword

In *The Hill of Kronos*, his autobiographical chronicle of wandering through Greece with a knapsack at various times in his life, Peter Levi, the Oxford classicist and poet, describes an encounter in the 1960s with a priest in a remote village: 'He gave me lunch, an enormous lunch at half past three in the afternoon, fried eggs from [his] Byzantine hens, and a wine that tasted of rocks and bushes.'

With those few words Levi plunges us into a Greek universe where wine is robust and elemental. Made from ancient, indigenous vine varieties, Greek wines were and are prized for their individuality. The character of each is sacred, to be preserved, protected, and, above all, appreciated.

Stavroula Kourakou, the formidable director of the Greek Wine Institute until her recent retirement, began more than twenty years ago a campaign further to protect the originality and quality of Greek wines. In the face of Greek entry into the European Common Market, she proposed and won approval of a system of controlled appellations in which indigenous Greek vine varieties would be matched to those areas in which the best Greek wines had traditionally been produced. At the same time, new standards of viticulture and wine-making were imposed for those appellations to raise quality levels.

It would be perverse to deny the need for the imposition of controlled appellations, because by the 1960s the resin jar had come close to eradicating the distinctions and the quality of Greek wines. This was not because all wines were resinated, but because resin – too conveniently to hand, a veil ready to be drawn over error whenever necessary – had become a disincentive to careful, distinctive wine-making.

Change was wrought with discretion. By enhancing those characteristics that made a Greek wine inherently Greek, a new generation of enologists, though trained mostly in France and Germany, began to uncover one forgotten wine after another, as if removing accumulated grime from a picture and revealing detail that had lain long neglected behind it. I felt this stir of activity when I spent a few days in Athens in the mid-1970s and encountered for the first time, not only the labels of unfamiliar producers, but the names of grape varieties and of entire wine regions I hardly knew existed.

At a dinner in his Alexandria apartment not long after (Alexandria, Virginia, that is, not the city of Athenaeus), Miles Lambert-Gócs let me ramble on before starting to pull from cartons and closets wines from Crete, from Santorini, from Naousa, from Rapsani. Since then, my rediscovery of Greek wine – largely with his help – has been a constant pleasure to me. I might not yet have met Peter Levi's wine, tasting of rocks and bushes, but I have found others, impeccably made, with the stamp of place and time that, in wine, has ever been the hallmark of quality and distinction. Why else do we talk of appellations and vintages?

Lambert-Gócs tempers his enthusiasm with scholarship, writing of Greek wine objectively, while drawing on vast personal experience and relying on his own sure judgment. He tells us that Greek wines, from grape varieties unfamiliar in the West, and produced in distinctive environments, do not lend themselves to comparison with others. But then neither does this book. It is a richly engaging survey of men and wines, of islands, mountains and vineyards, of food and folklore, of past and present. Its pages illuminate brilliantly not only Greek viticulture, but Greece itself.

Gerald Asher
San Francisco
July 1989

Introduction:
Greek Wine in Modern Times

Athenaeus's outstanding third-century AD account of gastronomy in the ancient world, *The Deipnosophists*, provides evidence of the continued production of wine at Greek places famed for wine during antiquity, as that era came to a close. Fragments of information from the Byzantine centuries that followed indicate the further survival of wine-growing at many of the individual locales. Usually the evidence consists of cadastral or tax notations, but sometimes archaeological finds as well, and occasionally even a morsel more palatable to a latter-day Athenaeus, such as the twelfth-century Byzantine poem 'The Abbot's Table', in which the author, Theodoros Prodromos, boasts of having managed four goblets of Khian (Chian) wine, one of the most prized of Aegean vintages during antiquity, and clearly as highly thought of as late as Prodromos's day. Documents from places later ruled by the Venetians, and travelogues of still later Western visitors to the Greece of Ottoman times, attest to more recent perpetuation of the Greek tradition in wine at particular places.

The continuity of wine-growing at the remarkable, environmentally idiosyncratic sites of antiquity would in turn have favoured the retention of previously acclimatized grape varieties, at least in so far as those varieties had not been valued only in conjunction with certain archaic wine-making practices, such as the use of particular flavouring substances, that were discontinued as a result of the technological developments that took place subsequent to the ancient era. In that regard, it ought to be noted that in the earliest record of modern Greek grape varieties, a poem of 1601 (see page 207), the thirty-four varietal names mentioned must have been commonly known for a long time before. Furthermore, they refer to varieties mostly having characteristics typical of vines of the Eastern Mediter-

ranean and Black Sea areas, rather than Western Europe. Nevertheless, in spite of the continuity of Greek wine tradition as tied to place
of production, changes between the ancient and modern eras would
have taken place following accommodation to wine-making innovations. Most notably, the gradual switch-over from earthenware
jars to wooden barrels, which began to occur in Greece sometime
after Strabo's seemingly bemused mention of 'wooden jars' being
used along Italy's central Adriatic coast in the first century AD, would
probably have entailed alterations in practices and occasioned some
changes in wine characteristics.

A gradual degradation in Greek wine tradition as concerns quality
began in the late Middle Ages, as the Byzantine administration
started to deteriorate. Feudalism spread on the Greek mainland, and
increasingly obliged the peasants to deliver work and produce to
their landlords. Viticulture took on a special importance for the
peasants, since it was the one sphere of endeavour in which they were
allowed some independence of action, although a tax had to be paid
for the privilege. Vineyards could usually be freely created and
transferred, and records from some places indicate that peasants
often held several vineyard plots, typically dispersed ones, and
sometimes even in different villages, their aim being possibly to offset
the negative effects of less favourable seasonal conditions on one plot
by resort to another. By the early fourteenth century, family economic
well-being in parts of the mainland had become so heavily vested in
vineyards that fragmentation of holdings brought about by customary law pertaining to inheritance and dowries, as well as by sales of
vineyard plots to enable the economic survival of families, added to
the impoverishment of the peasantry stemming from other causes.
Lack of funds spelled decreased capacity for the input necessary to
produce the best wine possible from the vineyards that remained in
private possession, while activity by the small category of merchants
involved with wine production was generally too limited to counteract the effect of the evolution in landholding patterns.

With the decline of wine quality at the level of peasant production,
the best of local wine traditions gradually became concentrated in
monastic communities. Monasteries often took over ownership of
vineyards which peasants had been forced to sell and in that way
also garnered the best vineyard lands. Because of their financial
endowments, the religious communities also possessed outstanding

facilities for wine-making, remarked upon even centuries later by Western visitors to Greek monasteries:

> The cellar [of the monastery of Mega Spilion, at Kalavryta in the Peloponnesos] was not far off. A large . . . indenture in the cavern, Polypheneus-looking, wide and broad, and particularly lofty, constituted as fine a repository for the purpose as the most numerous community could desire. Huge wine-barrels, of Heidelberg pretensions, lay ranged in imposing order, according to their seniority, which, as we passed along, was carefully noted. The different contributing 'ἀμπέλια' [ambélia], or vineyards, were also duly and variously honoured, as their vintage held a higher or lower place in the estimate of the fraternity.
>
> (Thomas Wyse, *An Excursion in the Peloponnesus*, 1865)

Later, under the Ottomans, the monasteries generally lost their claim on financial resources they possessed at distant places under other jurisdictions, but were granted tax-exempt status.

The Ottoman occupation of the Greek lands began in the fourteenth century, that is, even before the fall of Constantinople (Istanbul) in 1453. In the early centuries of its rule, the Ottoman administration generally made no attempt to curtail wine-growing among the indigenous population. On the contrary, local Ottoman officials, thrown on their own resources to generate income, were usually anxious to protect wine-growing, which could be an outstanding source of revenue if the place concerned were a viable commercial producer and no other more lucrative crop could compete. The number of merchants dealing in wine consequently increased at not a few mainland towns. Furthermore, the lands at the disposal of the Ottoman officials often included vineyards, and the officials might also enjoy the privilege of a monopoly on sales of must to traders – whom they might then proceed to tax – for periods of up to two months after the vintage, thereby assuring themselves premium prices. The Ottomans did not seek to curtail the drinking of wine either, and not only because the infidels' consumption was in the officials' pecuniary interest. The fact is that not all Moslems on Greek territory heeded the Prophet's strictures against wine drinking, especially not converts from Christianity, whose number was by no means negligible in some areas of the mainland and on Crete. Indeed, no Western visitor who spent much time in Ottoman Europe could fail to make humorous note of laxity in that matter:

One cadi [Moslem village elder] who was a great *amateur* told me . . . that if Mohammed had known this wine, he would have made a verse expressly to prescribe its usage, the creator not having given such a drink only for the pleasure of Christians.

(François Pouqueville, *Voyage de la Grèce*, 1826)

Negative influences on wine-growing were compounded in the course of the Ottoman centuries, however. The more persistent and deleterious effects emanated from taxation, although even in that respect, the Ottoman system varied from place to place and time to time. On the whole, more accessible places were taxed harder than more remote ones, a circumstance usually favouring the Archipelago, which the Turks generally seem to have avoided as a habitation, and out-of-the-way mountainous places on the mainland. Also, the circumstances under which a place had come under Ottoman control, that is, whether 'voluntarily' or not, was another determining factor, which again usually favoured the islands, since most of them had acquiesced in the takeover because of the impossibility of effective armed resistance. Conversely mountainous places on the mainland sometimes did not acquiesce, but were effectively left 'free' anyway, simply because the resistance they could mount made their moles-tation not worth the bother from the Ottoman standpoint, provided some token arrangement of overlordship could be worked out. Usually, the Ottoman administrators were content to let previous local custom govern the rate of taxation on wine production, as if deferring to the Byzantine experience as to how much could be extracted without causing the peasants to neglect their vineyards altogether. The local inhabitants, for their part, were most satisfied if the resident Ottoman officials were strangers to their place and customs.

The taxation system began to break down under pressure from a nascent capitalism that grew in mainland towns as from the fifteenth century. The towns attracted inhabitants from the more heavily oppressed countryside, to such an extent that by the end of the eighteenth century the French visitor Félix Beaujour found what he reckoned to be half of arable Macedonia uncultivated. The population shift caused a decline in the revenues of rural Ottoman officials, and spurred them on to heavy tax depredations when the Porte began losing control over its provincial representatives in the eighteenth century. As Ottoman rule began to collapse, both the frequency and cupidity of tax collection grew, and in cases where the tax on wine production was assessed against a village as a whole, a larger assessment on the peasantry had to compensate for the tax-exempt status of monasteries. In the late eighteenth and nineteenth centuries, some local potentates turned very nasty in their dealings with wine-growers. Some were known to prevent the transport of harvested grapes from the vineyards until the arbitrary tax had been paid, thus causing the grapes to deteriorate in the meantime. Or they might turn their animals loose in the vineyards for free grazing, just to show who could exert the really big crush at vintage. In order to complete the vintage as soon as possible, before untoward interference by the authorities, wine-growers found it expedient to gather the fruit of their dispersed parcels of land all at once, irrespective of the state of ripeness of the grapes, to the detriment of wine quality. In a few rare cases (one possible instance is mentioned on page 210), that practice, which has yet to disappear entirely, may have originated in a traditional type of wine deliberately made from a must of under-ripe and over-ripe grapes.

The Ottomans were forced to withdraw piecemeal from Greek territory between 1829 and 1913. As a result of the Greek War of Independence, fought during 1821–9, the Ottomans relinquished somewhat less than half of Greece's present territory, mostly on the southern mainland (Central Greece and the Peloponnesos). Open commercial enterprise thus became possible in free Greece, but wine-growers in most places were in no position to benefit. In a pattern that would be repeated as the rest of Greece was freed, the Ottomans had uprooted or burned vineyards in many places – one Greek reporter of the day noted that the greater part of mainland vineyards suffered that fate – either as part of military operations, or merely as a rearguard reprisal. Even liberated islands, notably among the Cyclades, that were unscathed during the war, and could otherwise have been expected to profit from the new economic climate, were unable to take advantage, since they had expended their financial resources on the struggle for independence. Those areas of Greece that remained under the Turks continued to suffer throughout the decline of Ottoman rule, and in some cases became immersed in increasing violence and warfare that sapped resources of all sorts.

Greek wine-growing took a long time to recover from nearly five centuries of Ottoman occupation. In the decades immediately following the War of Independence, free Greece had little incentive to expand or upgrade commercial wine-making. Towns were rather few and small, and many town-dwellers owned vineyards, or had relatives who did, in their native area, through which they largely kept themselves supplied with wine. Consequently, the domestic market for surplus wine production, though never absent, was limited. Incentive for wine-growers came in the second half of the nineteenth century, but in the form of demand by a Western clientele seeking wine for blending during the pan-European period of vineyard afflictions. The wine-blending trade sustained interest in viticulture in some areas, but generally encouraged a sacrifice of quality for quantity. In free Greece in particular, the virtually guaranteed market for blending-wine resulted in the expedient planting of currant vines, whose fresh fruit could be vinified if the price proved more attractive, all across the northern Peloponnesos: here the acreage in currants rose from 4,350 hectares in 1878 to 56,400 hectares in 1905, and came to comprise 35 per cent of the vineyards of free Greece.

Greece itself did not escape the diseases and pests that had descended on European vineyards. Phylloxera was by far the most destructive, but its course in Greece was distinguished from all its other manifestations in Europe by the extremely slow rate at which the pest progressed through the country (see the accompanying map). Phylloxera first appeared on the north-eastern mainland and some of the northerly Aegean islands in the late nineteenth century, but in most of Greece it arrived later. Its advance was slowed in some cases by natural barriers – it may be usefully recalled that Greece has ever comprised an assemblage of very distinct geographic units – and in other cases by large gaps in vineyard areas that were occasioned by earlier depopulation and destruction. Some parts of continental Greece were not hit by phylloxera until the 1950s, 1960s, and 1970s; indeed, a large part of the country still remains untouched by the pest. Consequently Greece has had a late recovery from phylloxera, and even where the process of replanting was begun relatively early it was delayed by hostilities, beginning with the Balkan Wars of 1912–13 and ending only with the Greek Civil War of 1947–9, and by emigration, which has plagued numerous Greek wine locales from early in this century until the present day.

For a long time the government of the modern Greek state remained aloof from wine-growing and other such mundane matters, being preoccupied with more central matters of state. The onset of phylloxera, however, forced the Greek government into active involvement. A task force led by the French viticulturalist Pierre Viala was commissioned to report on the phylloxera situation in Greece, and its findings, drafted in 1914, became the basis for setting up a network of government stations to supply new rootstock material to Greek wine-growers. Ampelographic studies were also commissioned. Legislation included the abolishing of taxes on vines, and the halting of the spread of currant vines over the Peloponnesos. When the viability of Greek wine production was generally threatened by world wine gluts during the two decades between the First and Second World Wars, the government urged the establishment of cooperatives, through which growers might join forces and survive. In the island of Samos, for example, the establishment of a cooperative was imposed by the government by legislation of 1934, in order to defuse a highly charged local situation brought about by the gluts.

For most of the twentieth century, Greece's internal underdevelopment and external dependence combined to confine commercial wine-making mostly to bulk sales of blending-wine. Nevertheless, bottled wine gradually gained ground in response to the growth of towns, coming into its own after the Second World War, with the burgeoning of the cities of Athens, Thessaloniki and Patras, and the steady rise in the number of tourists – over 8 million annually in the 1980s – from abroad. The immediate goal in bottled wine generally was the rather modest one of producing stable wines of standardized type, for wide consumption. Although the results were not of the kind to attract international attention, the way was opened to the production of superior bottled wines. The requirements of standardized wine production necessitated the instruction of growers through commercial agents and government agronomists, and made grower follow-through worthwhile financially, while the standardized wines largely broke down lingering Greek consumer resistance to bottled wines, which was in part a legacy of the times when families made and drank their own wine, or that of a relative or special family friend, and did not have confidence in wines sold by just any merchant.

A new plateau in modern Greek wine history was reached in 1969, with the adoption of legislation establishing a national framework for authorizing qualifying wines to bear certain geographic place-names, either in the form of a 'controlled appellation of origin' (*onomasía proeléfseos elenkhoméni*), or an 'appellation of origin of superior quality' (*onomasía proeléfseos anotéras piótitos*)): see page

12 for further explanation of these terms. The step was taken with a view towards Greece's accession to the European Economic Community (EEC), and was therefore designed to conform with the EEC's system of appellative regulation. Legislation of 1971 and 1972 conferred appellation status on certain wines of twenty-one locales, and in the 1980s four further locales were awarded the distinction. The Ministry of Agriculture's Wine Institute (*Institoúton Ínou* [*Oinou*]), founded in 1937, but effectively engaged only since 1952, has been the prime mover in the process of establishing appellative zones, and instrumental as well in formulating the details of the technical requirements (yields per hectare, alcohol content, etc.) to be met by qualifying wines in each recognized zone. The Institute fully expects other appellation zones to be added in coming years, and is currently developing a conceptual framework for inaugurating legislation pertaining to the awarding of *vin de pays*/'country wine' (*topikós ínos* [*oinos*]) status.

At present, the outlook for the future of commercial Greek wine is more favourable than it has been for many centuries. Large private wineries are leading the way in introducing contemporary technology. Cooperative wineries, whose potential in some of the appellation of origin areas is very considerable, are gradually resolving, sometimes with the aid of EEC funding, financial constraints that have held them back from achieving their best in bottled wine. Small individual growers are returning to the Greek bottled-wine market after a long lapse of interest, usually adopting new technology as their resources permit, as well as employing the services of enologists on a seasonal basis. The results of these developments are to be seen in new bottled wines that have appeared in Greece with increased frequency since the mid-1970s. Quality may not as yet be representative of the best traditions of the places concerned in each instance, but the varied work of the Wine Institute is devoted to determining the precise conditions for high-quality wine at the various locales, and to balancing the best in local traditions with the demands of the world market. Throughout the spectrum of the Greek wine industry it is fervently believed that in achieving that balance Greece will in the twenty-first century regain the reputation in wine it first earned in ancient times.

NOTES ON GAINING FAMILIARITY
WITH GREEK WINE

Greece remains the most difficult of wine countries to become acquainted with, and its wines continue to confound enophiles. One would like to see a concerted effort on the part of the Greek industry – large firms, cooperatives, small private producers – to improve the situation, but they remain hamstrung by jealousies, mutual suspicions and secretiveness that recall the ancients, at their worst, and inhibit action for the common good. In these circumstances, non-Greeks are left largely on their own, and how they fare is too often utterly a matter of chance, all of which may be in order according to the eternal Greek way of thinking, but not infrequently damaging for the reputation of Greek wine.

Somewhat stagnant economic conditions mean that numerous noteworthy or even outstanding Greek wine-growing areas remain confined to artisanal production, entirely outside the sphere of bottling. One must sometimes spend days at such places in order to comprehend the nature, logic and worthiness of the sounder of their traditions and practices in wine-making. As for bottled Greek wines, one ought to be aware that few of the better ones have been exported at all, even fewer are exported on an ongoing basis, and still fewer are ever distributed abroad outside Greek ethnic channels. Bottled wines of limited production can be difficult to locate even in Greece.

Nor, as yet, does satisfaction necessarily follow upon finding a Greek wine that one has sought out, unless one is lucky enough to have the opportunity of meeting Greeks who own a home cellar – their number has been multiplying in recent years with improvements in income and living standards. In Greek retail shops and restaurants, however, one will not encounter bottles of cellarable wine that have been laid down for several years, and so the wine may not be 'ready'. Furthermore, storage facilities in commercial establishments are rarely of the standard required for a successful outcome in laying wine aside for improvement in bottle. Indeed storage conditions generally are so poor in retail shops that even a well-made wine may sometimes embarrass its producers through no fault of theirs. Nevertheless, in Athens and at some of the major resort areas there are shops where wines may be bought with a good deal of confidence. Major supermarket chains have also become most reliable sources of supply, and are stocking a more than adequate variety, sometimes including limited-production wines.

The customer buying Greek wine can usually ensure avoiding an unhappy purchase by one means or another. For example, many Greek wines are still put in clear glass bottles, and can be examined for signs of brownish colour, which in all but a few instances indicates a deteriorated condition. Also, vintage dates are increasingly appearing on Greek wines of quality; by law, Greek wines with a vintage indication must be produced from the specified vintage in an amount of at least 85 per cent. In the case of appellation of origin wines, whether or not vintage-dated, a Ministry of Agriculture banderole across the mouth of the bottle will display the last two digits of the year the bottle was released from the winery, behind the slash after the initials of the appellation region. For vintage-dated appellation wines, any overage between the release date and the maturation times mentioned in this book for specific wines may be taken to represent time spent in bottle at the winery. In the case of wines from cooperatives, it is often desirable that any such discrepancy should be minimal, since their capacity for safely storing bottles is typically not up to accommodating production volume. It still happens that cooperatives will release a once satisfying wine on to the market when it is already at the upper limit of its qualitative potential, with the result that some bottles start going flat in a short time. An ocean voyage can cause them to arrive in that condition on overseas markets, where the reputation of Greek wine can hardly afford such occurrences. More prudent stock management will necessarily be part of the solution.

On the other hand, one can shift too much of the onus of responsibility for ensuring satisfaction with Greek wine on to the wines themselves. Sometimes that tendency takes the form of holding contemporary Greek wines to an exaggerated standard derived from the ancient record. At other times, irrelevant foreign models are imposed as the standard of quality. In the latter regard, it ought to be kept in mind that Greek wines are typically the products of distinctive environments and grape varieties unfamiliar to Western enophiles. Consequently, the colours, bouquets and flavours of Greek wines – and not least in the very best of them – for the most part do not lend themselves to direct comparison with wines of other more familiar, and perhaps more popular, places. Familiarity with Greek wine therefore demands an extra fund of experience, including such matters as cellaring time and serving temperature, in addition to all the other factors more directly pertaining to wine appreciation.

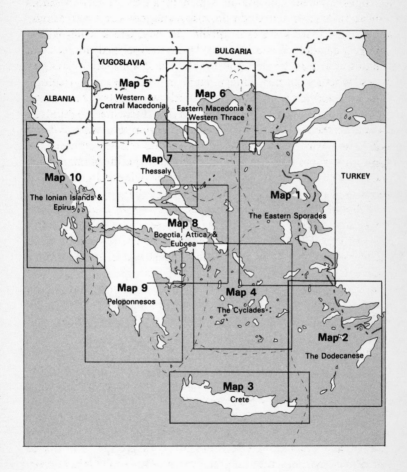

Greek Appellations of Origin

The Greek appellation of origin system is meant to ensure that wines bearing the stated appellation have been made in accordance with sound regional practice for the production of quality wine. An appellation regulation requires the use of choice grape varieties, delineates the areas having appropriate soils for the production of quality wine from those varieties, specifies the system of cultivation, and sets a maximum level of vine yields and a minimum level of sugar content in the grape must. Additionally, in the case of 'controlled' appellations of origin, more detailed reporting as regards such matters as varietal composition of vineyards, vine age, new plantings, and quantities of wines made and in stock is required, in order to monitor development of the region itself. Thus far, the 'controlled appellation' system has been applied only to liqueur wines. The appellation system is administered by the Central Committee for the Protection of Wine Production (KEPO), under the Ministry of Agriculture. It should be noted, however, that the appellation system is not meant as a guarantee of the quality of a particular wine.

To date, the following appellations of origin have been authorized. Wines authorized to bear an appellation of origin are issued numbered banderoles that must be affixed over the mouth of each bottle. In the case of a 'controlled appellation of origin', the banderole is blue and white; in the case of a 'appellation of origin of superior quality', the banderole is red and white. The appellation initials, as they appear on the banderoles, are noted in parentheses below.

Controlled Appellations of Origin *(Onomasía Proeléfseos Elenkhoméni)*

Mavrodaphne of Cephalonia (MK)

Muscat of Patras (ΜΠ)

Mavrodaphne of Patras (ΜΠ)

Muscat of Rhodes (MP)

Muscat of Cephalonia (MK)

Muscat of Rion of Patras (MP)

Muscat of Limnos (ΛΜ)

Samos (ΣΜ)

Appellations of Origin of Superior Quality *(Onomasía Proeléfseos Anotéras Piótitos*

Amyntaion (AM)	Limnos (ΛΜ)	Playies Melitona (ΠΜ)
Ankhialos (AX)	Mantinia (MN)	Peza (ΠZ)
Arkhanes (AP)	Naousa (ΝΣ)	Rapsani (PΨ)
Dafnes (ΔΦ)	Nemea (NM)	Rhodes (PΔ)
Goumenissa (ΓΜ)	Paros (ΠΡ)	Robola of Cephalonia (PK)
Kantza (KN)	Patras (ΠΤ)	Santorini (ΣΝ)
		Sitia (ΣΤ)

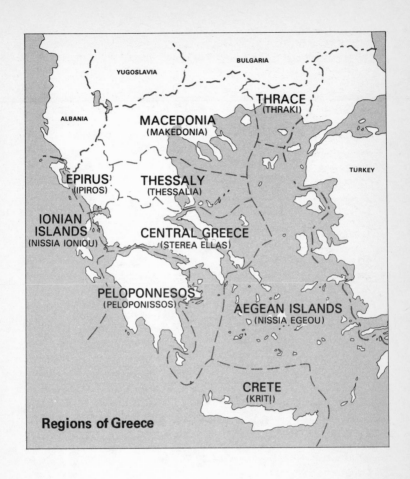

YUGOSLAVIA

BULGARIA

THRACE
(THRAKI)

ALBANIA

MACEDONIA
(MAKEDONIA)

TURKEY

EPIRUS
(IPIROS)

THESSALY
(THESSALIA)

IONIAN
ISLANDS
(NISSIA IONIOU)

CENTRAL GREECE
(STEREA ELLAS)

PELOPONNESOS
(PELOPONISSOS)

AEGEAN ISLANDS
(NISSIA EGEOU)

CRETE
(KRITI)

Regions of Greece

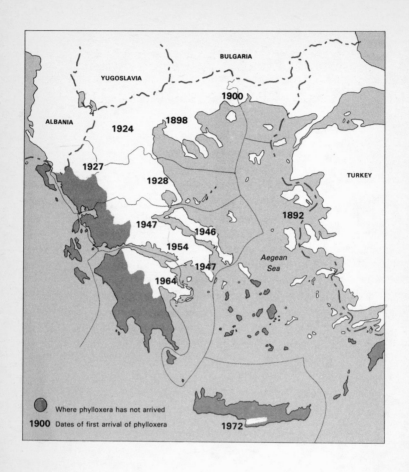

BULGARIA

YUGOSLAVIA

1900

ALBANIA

1924

1898

TURKEY

1927

1928

1892

1947

1946

1954

Aegean
Sea

1947

1964

Where phylloxera has not arrived

1900 Dates of first arrival of phylloxera

1972

PART I
THE AEGEAN ISLANDS

I

Samos and the Eastern Sporades

The wines [of Samos] are in large part muscats and more white than red. Far from meriting the reproaches which were formerly addressed to them . . . by Strabo and Apuleius, they are, on the contrary, now justly renowned among all those of the Archipelago, and if they are not deserving of being placed in the first rank, they can occupy the second without much handicap.

(Victor Guérin, French traveller, *Description de l'île de Patmos et de l'île de Samos*, 1856)

SAMOS

By far the most widely known place-name in Greek wine over the past several centuries has been Samos. Samos is a lofty island – its very name is thought to come from the Phoenician word for 'heights' – lying just off the mainland of Asia Minor, in the east-central Aegean. Early Aegean wine-growers observed that superior elevation tends to aid wine quality, which may explain why Samos sported vineyards even in times before it became a centre of the Ionian civilization spawned along the littoral. None the less, the ancients would doubtless be surprised by Samos's recent success with wine. In their era, Samian wines ranked far below a host of other Aegean wines, while the geographer Strabo stated that everything grown on Samos *except* wine was of excellent quality. The discrepancy in opinion between ancient and modern times is not attributable to a deterioration in quality standards or a change in taste generally, but to a shift in Samiote wine tradition which occurred during the intervening centuries.

One detects in Strabo's mention of Samos's felicitous environment for agriculture some surprise as to why only the grape-vine should be so disfavoured. Later history indicates the reason to have been

17

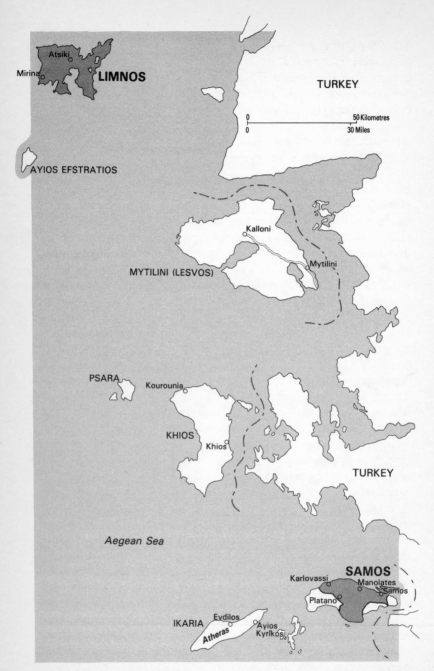

The Eastern Sporades

that during antiquity Samos did not acquire grape varieties capable of bringing out its potential for viticulture. Right up to the fifteenth century AD, Samos seems to have been known in the Greek world only as a producer and trader of red wine, and that was probably dry rather than sweet. The retreat of the red began fortuitously with a near depopulation of the island that occurred around 1475, when most inhabitants departed for Khios after several decades of constant harassment by pirates seeking refuge on Samos's wooded shores. Towards the end of the sixteenth century, piracy began to abate, and the Ottoman sultan offered privileges, including land grants, tax alleviations and a measure of home rule, to encourage resettlement. By the early seventeenth century, Samos was once again densely populated. Its vineyards were flourishing too, but with the difference that the variety called *moskháto áspro* (white muscat), or just *moskháto*, had become characteristic of the island.

The *moskháto áspro* is so widespread in Greece, especially insular Greece, that it must almost certainly have been grown in the Aegean islands during antiquity. Some classicists have regarded the varietal family described in Latin as *apiana* by Pliny in his *Natural History* to have been the muscats, primarily because the name signified that bees (*apis*) liked it, much as the modern name *muscatello* may indicate the same about flies (*musca*). Although *muscatello* was more likely derived from the Greek term *moskháto*, and therefore from the Persian term *moushk* (musk), the possibility of a muscat/*apiana* identity nevertheless merits consideration, since the *apiana* varieties were associated with sweet wines. Pliny stated that those wines had 'a peculiar flavour which is not that of wine', by which he may have been alluding to the characteristic muscat scent that causes the varietal family to be termed 'aromatic'. We might note here his mention of the fact that the Greeks called *apiana* vines 'psithian' (*psíthios*). The word 'psithian' probably came from the name for wormwood, or *apsínthion*, a plant valued for its special aromatic character – and therefore sometimes used as a perfume in wine-making – different though that character is from the scent of muscat grapes. Or does the *psíthios* name therefore refute the identity of the *apiana* and the muscats?

Greek ampelographers think that the *moskháto áspro* originated in Asia Minor, but there is no record of the *moskháto áspro* on Samos until the late sixteenth century, and the island is not known to have been associated with 'psithian' wine during antiquity. Possibly first introduced only during the resettlement, the *moskháto áspro* gained predominance on Samos as the export of muscat wine increased. By the time Joseph Georgirenes wrote the first modern description of Samos, in 1678, the trade in muscat was quite brisk. That commercial success inevitably caused other grape varieties to recede in importance. Nevertheless, red Samian wine continued to be produced in considerable quantity for over two centuries more, as borne out by visitors' reports, and remained a typical island wine until it was dealt a sudden and serious setback during a second replanting of Samos, which followed the arrival of phylloxera in 1892. The island's trade in muscat had thrived while Western Europe's vineyards were recovering from the effects of the pest, and consequently Samian growers thought their future very largely dependent on muscat.

The primacy of the *moskháto áspro* was secured in 1934. At that time, national legislation presaging the later appellation of origin framework was enacted to protect Samian wine-growing, and provided that only the *moskháto áspro* could be used for wine entitled to bear the Samos name commercially. The Union of Vinicultural Cooperatives of Samos (EOSS), was also set up and put under obligation to buy all muscat grapes offered. By thus rendering superfluous any function red wine might have had as a financial cushion in periods of slow sales of muscat, and in effect transferring that advantage to muscat grapes, the legislation effectively banished most of the dark-skinned varieties from the island vineyards, in favour of the more profitable and secure *moskháto*. Today, of the approximately 2,000 hectares of vineyards on Samos, or nearly one-tenth of the cultivated area, about 95 per cent is planted in that variety.

The legislation of 1934 was motivated by the Greek government's desire to bring a halt to deteriorating economic and social conditions on Samos. A world wine glut had taken its toll on grower income, prompting wine-growers to form an organization to protect their interests *vis-à-vis* the more than two dozen wine traders on Samos, who had organized themselves into a union. The two groups cooperated for a time and made contractual arrangements, but as the world market continued to deteriorate the traders' union discontinued contracting and the organization of growers responded by marketing their product on their own, underselling the traders. A great deal of antagonism was fomented on Samos, growers on the one side, and traders and their employees on the other. Further, the very low prices asked by the growers' organization reduced foreign exchange earnings, and threatened the reputation of Samian wine.

To forestall violence and prevent lasting damage, the Greek government ultimately stepped in to reorder the commercial framework of wine-growing on Samos. The production and trade functions for Samian wine were fused in one organization, EOSS, which has no counterpart elsewhere in Greece. It is an 'obligatory' system of cooperatives, whereby growers must sell all of their grapes to EOSS, except for amounts allowed for household use, while the Union, for its part, is obliged to purchase all grapes offered to it by growers. Furthermore, EOSS has exclusive authority to produce Samian wine for commercial sale, although it may sell wine to other, off-island bottlers for marketing under their own label, with the Samos appellation, if the wine qualifies.

Given its 'obligatory' nature, EOSS has to contend with a certain added threat to wine quality. To ward off the potential negative effects of the system in that respect, various measures are taken, beginning with a detailed specification of where vines may and may not be planted. Moreover, no increase in the total authorized area will be permitted. The vineyards of Samos are located in most parts of the island, but mainly on the northern side between the ports of Karlovassi and Samos, respectively on the west and east, where EOSS has its two wineries. Variation in elevation is considerable, ranging from practically sea level at some points to 800 metres above it. Soil varies in chemical consistency, but is pebbly, calcareous, and well drained at most vineyard sites. The intense insolation everywhere is tempered by sea breezes, which blow so strongly that short pruning of the vines is required, if sporadically at the risk of some rotting when grape clusters brush the ground (the latter condition, by the way, was apparently that in which bees preferred to have *apiana* grapes, if *apiana* was indeed muscat). Having observed the performance of Samos's vineyards for decades, EOSS has a decided view as to the very best vineyard areas, most of which are found in the semi-mountainous zone. But while it would like to take advantage of its experience in that regard, to produce even single vineyard wines, commercial demand generally has not warranted EOSS's moving in that direction.

Owing to the variation in vineyard exposure and altitude, grapes are delivered to EOSS between July and September, and sometimes into October from the terraces at higher altitudes. A year's output of must usually falls between 80,000 and 100,000 hectolitres, though even in the eastern Aegean an exceptionally poor vintage can occur. In processing the raw material, EOSS employs several means to reserve the best Samian grapes for sweet wine. Between 6 and 10 per cent of a year's must is required to be distilled, and quantities of must, as well as industrial wine for vermouth, are exported. EOSS also makes its own vermouth. Furthermore, about one-quarter of the must is vinified for dry wine for bottled sales. As a result of those measures, only about three-fifths of a year's must goes to produce sweet muscat wines. A further stipulation protecting wine quality, as well as ensuring authenticity, is that Samos is closed to the landing of must or wine in barrel. Yet the most direct and important factor in maintaining the quality of Samos's sweet muscat wine is the observance of the traditional differentiation among the island's several varieties of it.

In recommending in an article of 1914 that Samian wine production should be converted to a cooperative basis, the Greek agronomist G. Palamiotis expressed his concern that under the marketing pressures of the day the operations of the island's private traders would result in the loss of the Samian tradition in wine-making. He was particularly disturbed that at that time almost no sweet muscat wine was being produced commercially. What was exported as Samos Muscat was actually mistelle, unfermented must to which grape spirits are added. Alcohol content was simply brought to 12–15° by the addition, leaving sugar concentration at about 230–60 grams per litre. Traditionally, Samian sweet muscat wine was produced by any of four methods, all involving fermentation, and resulting in five individual types of wine. Palamiotis believed that the Samian tradition of muscat was in the best long-run interest of all the island's inhabitants, and today EOSS is maintaining the variety at the heart of that tradition.

Un-Aged Sweet Wines from Fresh Grapes

Two kinds of Samos muscat wine are made from fresh grapes harvested at peak maturation. The grapes may come from any area of the island authorized for *moskháto áspro*, as long as their must attains a minimum sugar content of 260 grams per litre. Both wines are ready for bottling within months of the vintage. They are of a deep golden colour, and while they exhibit 'only' varietal aroma, it can be of such penetrating and quintessentially muscat quality that one might be excused for musing about the *apiana*/muscat question and recalling that Columella (*De Re Rustica*) included *apiana* with the vines 'most renowned for their precious flavours', even if Pliny described these as somewhat 'peculiar' for wine.

SAMOS GLYKO (OR SAMOS DOUX)

The major wine of Samos, and the one that originally formed the basis of Samos's trade in wine after the repopulation, is a kind produced by crushing the grapes, removing the skins immediately, and arresting fermentation with grape spirits of 95–96° once fermentation has brought natural sugar content down to 160 grams per litre. Alcohol is left at 13.5°. It was fortification and stabilization of that sort that made it feasible to ship wine of Glyko type far and wide in earlier centuries. It was surely the sort of Samian wine that the wine writer André Jullien had in mind in 1816 when he assigned Samos to his third rank of wines.

The bright colour and intense, spiced apricot aroma of Samos Glyko attract people to it like flies, but some are afterwards put off by its rather unctuous texture, and are unable to get beyond the initial flavour, as the wine livens up. Others dislike the aromatic flavour, which is virtually the same as that of Samian muscat grapes; I must suppose they would not enjoy those either. Perhaps a few others are put off by the fact that such plainly good sweet wine should be so affordably available. Still others, however, never stop going back for more of it throughout their years of wine drinking, even after they have become acquainted with dessert wines – not the least of which may also be Samian – that they might concede to be better in certain respects. For the faithful, only the words of Marguerite Yourcenar adequately capture the virtues of Samos Glyko:

> a cup of Samos drunk at noon in the heat of the sun or, on the contrary, absorbed of a winter evening when fatigue makes the warm current be felt at once in the hollow of the diaphragm and the sure and burning dispersion spreads along our arteries, such a drink provides a sensation which is almost sacred, and is sometimes too strong for the human head. No feeling so pure comes from

the vintage-numbered cellars of Rome; the pedantry of great connoisseurs of wine wearies me.

(Memoirs of Hadrian, 1962)

SAMOS IMIGLYKO (OR SAMOS DEMI-DOUX)

Grapes from the same vineyards and with the same composition as for Samos Glyko are used to produce a must that undergoes a natural fermentation, that is, one which comes to a halt without the introduction of grape spirits, the traditional method used by islanders who make sweet wine for themselves. The skins are left in the must for the first forty hours of fermentation, so that aroma will be sufficient for what is appropriate to Samos Muscat wine. Longer contact with the skins poses the risk of the wine contracting tannins and related substances that would have a negative influence on flavour; that problem can sometimes be encountered in home-made wines. The colour and aromatic features of Samos Imiglyko are virtually identical to those of Samos Glyko, but at 15° alcohol and only about 55 grams of sugar per litre, divergence in the feel of the wine is to be expected. In particular, it is less unctuous in texture.

In 1982 EOSS began producing a special Imiglyko on commercial order from abroad. A quantity of it was also put out to celebrate the fiftieth anniversary of EOSS in 1984. Called Grands Crus Imiglyko, it is produced from selected grapes from areas known for superior quality. Its advantage over standard Samos Imiglyko is marked in the persistence of its aromatic flavour. Would there were the economic incentive for EOSS to do more along this line!

Aged Sweet Wines from Partially Dried Grapes

Other sweet muscat wines are produced on Samos from selected over-ripened grapes, or from fully ripened ones that have been spread in the sun for seven to eight days following picking; without trying to influence the course of debate over the possibility of an *apiana*/muscat identity, it might be noted, by way of demonstrating that the Greeks have a long habit of doing so with grapes of 'peculiar' character, that Pliny specifically associated 'psithian' wine with raisin wines. In an average year, about 10 per cent of the Samian grape harvest is destined for concentration of sweetness by those methods. The resultant wines are given a more or less lengthy maturation in oak, and can be readily distinguished from Samos Glyko and Samos Imiglyko by their darker colours, which overlap orange and brown, and even hint at reddishness in the ultimate instance. They are also distinguishable by their developed bouquet. It was certainly his acquaintance with at least one of these wines that caused Guérin to challenge Jullien's rating of Samos Muscat; that Jullien did not know of them is clear from his statement that Samian wines would be better 'if they were kept'. Those who wish to drink aged Samian sweet wine, or to put some away for maturation in bottle, should choose from among the following wines, rather than lay down bottles of Samos Glyko or Samos Imiglyko, neither of which has anything to gain from bottle-aging.

SAMOS ANTHEMIS

Apparently known to Guérin, this sort of wine was referred to by him as *anthosmie*, the gallicized rendering of Greek *anthosmía*, or 'flower-smell', that is, 'bouquet'. The term, rather than the particular type of wine, dates back to the ancient Greeks, who applied it generally to the smell of sound older wines, and also had a wine which they produced by a particular technique and called *anthosmías*. EOSS has in this case altered the name for marketing purposes, while otherwise leaving the tradition of Samian *anthosmía* intact. Samos Anthemis is fortified, with grape spirits being added to stop fermentation at about 140 grams of sugar per litre, while alcohol is brought to 15°. It is then matured in oak for three to four years before being bottled, picking up its *anthosmía* in the meantime ('Now even uncompounded substances have certain odours, which men endeavour to assist by artificial means, even as they assist nature in producing palatable tastes': Theophrastus, *Concerning Odours*).

Samos Anthemis offers a smooth gradation of colour from amberish-orange and brown at the centre, to a honey-coloured gold, to a yellowish-gold, and finally to a greenish-yellow at the rim. The greenishness is nascent even further inward, as is true of the orange heading outward. Of course, with accumulated bottle-age, the amber tendency deepens and becomes quite dominant. Anthemis projects a bouquet typical of Samos Glyko, but overlaid by a toasty, slightly toffee-like aroma that becomes more apparent in the mouth. Sweetness and acidity are integrated, forestalling any cloying impression in the course of a mouthful. A vaguely astringent sensation chimes in to enhance the wine's long, firm finish on the tongue.

SAMOS NECTAR

As Glyko is paralleled by Anthemis in being fortified, so Imiglyko is paralleled by Samos Nectar in being the product of a natural fermentation. Since the sugar content of the must in this case is quite elevated, at 500 grams per litre, the fermentation is the most difficult one undergone by any Samian wine, and lasts about three months. Fermentation stops when sugar is at about 100 grams per litre and alcohol at 14–15°. The wine is then aged in oak for four to five years prior to bottling, making it quite unusual among unfortified muscats.

Samos Nectar is of a lustrous orangish colour, and distinguishes itself among muscat wines by the finesse with which it presents the sensations of a very considerable fatness. Its nose might be thought of as an extension of that found on Samos Glyko: there is apricot dominating, but it is now the concentrated essence of it, as in the dried fruit, while smells related to butterscotch also participate. In the mouth, the wine is so concentrated aromatically that the mouth-coating sweetness which keeps aroma pouring out is actually masked in part by it. The aromatic flavour is so intense and persistent that I have never been able to notice any particular sharpness in feel, although as in any wine, it must be a high decree of acidity, intertwined with alcohol and the rest, that provides the backbone to allay any cloying feel. ('This is heaven, let me tell you, and, as I said just now, our drink is nectar': Zeus, in Lucian's *Dialogues of the Gods*.)

PALAIO NECTAR

Writing in 1813, the English visitor John Galt intimated that Samian sweet wines of very advanced age were to be had on the island. Perhaps they were an inadvertent offshoot of early wine gluts, such as the one Galt mentioned. EOSS produces a wine called Palaio Nectar (Old Nectar) by setting aside exceptional wine of Nectar type for additional maturation in barrel, for eight to ten years altogether. By then, Palaio Nectar acquires an almost pinkish shading over a yellowish-brown base, and a dominance of toffee-like smells in bouquet and aromatic flavour. Ordinarily, it would perhaps not be preferred over Samos Nectar, or even the other Samian sweet wines, but Palaio Nectar does stand as something of a rebuke to challengers of Samos, no other unfortified *moskháto áspro* wines having proved up to bearing the sort of maturation it receives without loss of their essential character as muscat wine. Although it is not a commercial wine at present, a bottle of Palaio Nectar is not impossible to acquire from EOSS.

When Byron called for Samian wine, he no doubt had sweet muscat in mind, for this was what Samos generally exported to Athens, where the bard placed his order. A bowl of it might seem a tall order in these calorie-conscious times, and I would therefore suggest a mere glass of it, to be taken at times other than at the conclusion of a major Levantine meal. The middle of a lazy afternoon is a perfect moment, for example.

I am prepared to accept that Samos Glyko is not the wine for everyone. Corresponding in a liquid way to *baklavá* and other such sweet pastries, Glyko might still stir in some of us that very abhorrence *baklavá* once did in Western visitors to the Balkans and beyond:

> There before us, on the table, was a large Baklava cake, compounded of wafer-like paste fried in oil, drenched in syrup, interleaved with walnut mash, and crowned with cream. It was a climax of sweetness, stickiness, oiliness, and indigestibility, and we stood before it struck dumb with horror and surfeit.
>
> (Jan and Cora Gordon, *Two Vagabonds in Albania*, 1927)

Having witnessed in my own time, however, the widespread acceptance of *baklavá* by Westerners, some of whom even have the temerity to distinguish 'better' from 'good', I think there might be some reason to expect that most of us potentially can fathom the harmonies of Samos Glyko. And for those who do, my first recommendation for accompanying it will always be . . . *baklavá*! In the middle of a lazy afternoon, to be sure. That sweet, whether or not 'crowned with cream', is one of those with which we are told no wine can cope, much less agree, yet there is Samos Glyko to do both, and in both the aromatic and tactile spheres of flavour sensation. I would also like to mention how good I have found Glyko with French toast dusted with cinnamon and drizzled with maple syrup. I would drink Samos Imiglyko in quite the same way as I would Glyko, but with less sweet things, such as *finíkia* cookies. If I had my choice, I would take Samos Nectar with *galaktoboúreko* and with creams flavoured with vanilla or caramel, such as *crème caramel*. I find that Samos Anthemis tolerates sharper flavours in desserts than do its brethren: both Anthemis and Palaio Nectar seem to me to offer some resistance to chocolate. However, the thing to do with Palaio Nectar in EOSS's view seems to be to dunk *friganiés* in it, at least in mid-morning. *Friganiés* are browned, oven-dried slices of bread, and the stranger reluctant to join in this use of the vinous rarity might encourage himself by reviewing Athenaeus's long discussion of breads, wherein he mentions a 'brazier bread' (*eskharítin*) intended to be 'dipped in sweet wine', and thus softened before eating.

Samiotes, by the way, urge a bowl of sweet muscat as a morning tonic. I could think their motive base, what with their stocks of muscat wine, but Athenaeus's quotation from Epicharinus's *The Sirens* suggests a very old tradition that is possibly still at work: 'Early in the morning, with the first coming of dawn, we would put on the fire some plump small fry, the roasted flesh of a pig, and some polyps; then we would wash them all down with sweet wine.' Having given the experience several trials, I might say that twentieth-century technological man is sorely in need of the habit. More soberly, I would not recommend more than a decilitre to any but those who are either at their leisure, or else unusually enthusiastic about their employment. Even in that case, however, Epicharinus's suggestion of a bed of food for the wine to fall into upon the drinkers rising from theirs is well worth following ('We at least, belonging neither to the class of those who drink too much nor to those who get drunk in the morning, resort to these erudite symposia': Athenaeus, *The Deipnosophists*).

I should conclude my advice for visitors to Samos first of all by assuring them that the Samiotes do not loll about all day sipping sweet wine in between frolicking on the beach. Actually, one rarely sees a Samiote wine-grower there: 'They bathe only in their own sweat,' a local joked when I naively suggested the non-income benefits of existence as a Samiote grape-grower. In the island villages, people mostly drink resinated dry muscat of their own making, a habit that was introduced on Samos at least as early as the repopulation, when people from the southern mainland, those real heirs to resination, came to settle. A grower up in the village of Platano, one of the island's superb vineyard locales, says he resinates because the wine then seems less sweet (*glykó*), and he prefers it this way as a mealtime beverage. Be that as it may, the joining of muscat aroma with pininess is frowned on by Greek enologists, because the varietal aroma is thus neutralized. Nevertheless, even EOSS makes and bottles its Retsina, which has a good market on Samos and other islands of the eastern Aegean. More *un*resinated dry muscat is made, though. It sells under the Samena label, which can be either 'white' or 'black', denoting respectively the better and the lesser. Both are at 12–13°. White-label Samena would probably qualify for appellation of origin status, were the Samos entitlement extended to dry muscats. However, that step is unlikely because the Greek government fears it would result in a cutback in the production of the ultimately more lucrative, though more slowly sold off, sweet wines.

EOSS also offer a rosé wine called Fokianos, a 12° wine made from the red grape of that name. The *fokianós* carries the name of the ancient Ionian (Asia Minor) city of Phocaea, and is a relic of bygone centuries when Samos made red wines. It occupies nearly the entire 5 per cent of Samos's vineyard land that is not planted with *moskháto áspro*. Assuming that Samian red wine was indeed 'nothing much', the goodness of Fokianos rosé may come as a surprise.

THE EASTERN SPORADES

Samos can be loosely grouped geographically with the rather far-flung islands of the north-eastern Aegean, which are sometimes called the Eastern Sporades. Most of these islands are relatively large and have histories telling of exceptional suitability for vine cultivation in some areas. The only island in the group that at present has any significance in wine, however, is Limnos, the most northerly. An island of low topographic profile, Limnos has its vineyards primarily alongside the shallow valleys of its north-western hill country, extending west from around Atsikí. About 1,000 hectares are planted, of which nearly 700 are in *moskháto alexandrías* (muscat of Alexandria), a variety not generally esteemed for wine-making, but which succeeds unusually well on Limnos and has therefore been entitled to an appellation of origin since 1971. Unlike the case of Samos, both sweet and dry Limniote muscats may qualify for the appellation, and both are produced by the Union of Agricultural Cooperatives of Limnos, the only bottler on the island. The sweet muscat, which is similar to Samos Glyko in flavour and quality, though with more of an alcohol smack it has seemed to me, is usually produced as a fortified wine of 15° alcohol, but may also be found unfortified.

As at Samos, red wine was the dominant type of wine on Limnos in the past. Several Western visitors in recent centuries remarked on finding good dark reds there. However, the profitability of Limniote muscat wine occasioned the spread of the *moskháto alexandrías* subsequent to phylloxera, at the expense of interest in other varieties. The big loser was the indigenous *limnió* – also called *kalabáki* locally – which is the ancient *limnía* variety mentioned by Polydeuctes in the second century AD. The Union bottles an attractive, bright-coloured, light dry red wine from *limnió*, which, like its other wines, is marketed under the Limnos label.

Sizeable Mytilini (Lesvos), south-east of Limnos, grows mostly *limnió*, though no longer in any great quantity. It may be our loss, for in 1553 Pierre Belon advised that Mytilini's wines 'were reputedly the best in the Aegean' at the time. William Turner reported in 1820 that the island's 'black wine [has] some body and a sweet taste, but not enough to be disagreeable'. The semi-sweet red wine of the medieval village of Kalloni retains a particular reputation for excellence, but is made from the black *kalloniátiko* variety. I have found no mention of this variety in Greek ampelographies, which leads me to wonder whether the *kalloniátiko* may actually be a more widely planted Aegean variety generally known by another name, but so-called on Mytilini because there it is planted mostly at Kalloni.

One of the Eastern Sporades of outstanding historical interest is Khios (Chios), directly south of Mytilini. It is with the past foremost in mind, too, with regard to wine, that one has to go there, since nowadays less than 1,000 hectolitres are produced in a year's vintage on all of this sizeable island. The wine pilgrim's destination is in the upper north-western part of Khios, between the Pelinaion and Amoni mountains, in the vicinity of the contemporary villages of Kourounia, Nenitouria and Keramos. It is a rugged and calcareous area, and one subject to somewhat peculiar climatic influences due to the particularly high elevations on its eastward side, together with Khios's broadside position *vis-à-vis* the mainland of Asia Minor just further east. Pausanias related that the island's name comes from the Greek for snow, and an elderly native living in New York has told me of winters in north-western Khios in his youth when sheep lay dead all about, frozen in snow that reached to a man's thighs. This curious area was formerly known as Ariousia, a name that is one of the most illustrious in the annals of wine. For 1500 years its name rang in the ears of Aegean enophiles much as Bordeaux has in ours for the past 150.

Accounts given by numerous Western visitors stopping at Khios between the sixteenth and nineteenth centuries suggest that the tradition of Ariousian wine had remained intact until then, if at a depressed level of production in later years. In 1822, however, the Ottomans effectively laid waste to Khios – as commemorated in words by Victor Hugo and pictures by Delacroix – in retaliation for the Greek uprising of 1821. They wantonly destroyed the vineyards of Ariousia, completing the work of their previous attempt on them at the beginning of the eighteenth century, which had already cut back the region's wine trade. Without a widespread sprinkling of apprised and caring wine lovers who could provide financial support, few vineyards were replanted, and such little recovery as was achieved was practically wiped out by phylloxera and emigration in the early twentieth century. The remnants of Ariousia, such as they are, consist of the paltry 10 hectares of vineyards scattered from 50 to 500 metres above the Aegean at Kourounia, where hundreds of hectares of vines once crowded these steeply inclined slopes. Gone, too, is the name *Arioúsios ínos* (*oinos*). Now it is Kourounia, named for the pigs (*gouroúnia*) once raised in numbers thereabouts, that gives its name to the wine, *kourouniótiko krasí*. Still, it appears that there is a lick of the Ariousian tradition left.

Athenaeus mentioned 'three kinds of [Ariousian wine]: one dry, another rather sweet; the third, a mean between these two in taste'. *Kourouniótiko* comes in two kinds: one is a dry *rozé* (rosé), made like a red wine, but from the lightly coloured *rozakiá, soultaní* and *bigléri* grapes, plus the darker *ayianítes* (or *ayianiótiko*); the other is a rather sweet *mávro* (black) made from the grape called by the simple but most venerable name *krasostáfylo* (wine grape), which according to what I have been able to learn is apparently the widespread Aegean variety generally called *mandilariá*, though possibly of a clone unto itself. The *rozé*, I gather, is relatively new to Kourounia, probably having been introduced after phylloxera. The *mávro*, on the other hand, is believed by the Kourouniotes to be virtually as old as their area, and it is difficult to dispute it. The grapes are dried in the sun for about a week before crushing, a method of concentrating sweetness that has been commonplace throughout the Aegean since early times:

But when Orion and Sirius are carried into mid-heaven, and rosy-fingered dawn sees Arcturus [September], then cut off all the grape-clusters, Perses, and bring them home. Show them to the sun ten days and ten nights: then cover them over for five, and on the sixth day draw off into vessels the gifts of joyful Dionysus.

(Hesiod, *Works and Days*, 7th century BC)

Some of the ancients thought Khios the first place where 'black' wine was made, which, even if unlikely, affirms a very long tradition of red wine. But no matter the pedigree of Kourounia's *mávro*, visiting wine lovers ought to be sure to remove their caps while there, for the lesson of the place is solemn: we never know when our own favourite wine, one we hope future generations will also know and appreciate, will be on the block, the victim of circumstances beyond its control.

South of Khios and just west of Samos, Ikaria rises out of the Aegean as a veritable block of granite, looking inhospitable and barely habitable. Yet inhabited it has been since before Homer. It is not an entirely stark place either, despite its wholly mountainous nature. Parts of the interior surprise with splurges of dark green woods, the landscape around Rakhes prompting the author Spiros Leotsakos, an Athenian admirer of Ikaria, to call it 'a piece of Switzerland in the middle of the Aegean'. Many visitors arrive for the island's curing, radium-charged thermal waters, rather than for the scenery, but there is also good reason for the enophile to begin his odyssey in the Aegean there, for Ikaria's claim to vinous fame is in its possession of what is not only one of the oldest known geographical designations in wine, but also the oldest in continuous use, Pramnian.

A settlement named Oinoi (Oenoe) prospered on Ikaria in ancient times, in the vicinity of today's community of Evdilos, near the north-central coast. Its earliest vineyards were south of there, close by what ancient writers mentioned as the *Prámni pétra* (Pramnos rock) which present-day villagers in the area point out as identical to the site they call *ta Bra*. The Pramnos name would seem to have been attached because of proximity to a more prominent topographical feature earlier named Pramnos. That name had a connection with the crest of mountains, gentle to the north, steep to the south, that runs parallel to Ikaria's southern coast. Now called Atheras, that mountainous span may have been known as Pramnos in ancient times. Or the name may have been applied to a peak or section about midway

32

along Atheras; a local tradition claims that the mountain divide today called Prioni is the spot anciently identified as Pramnos. In any case, the Ikariotes, by a perfectly comprehensible logic, began exporting their surplus wine under the Pramnian name.

As Pramnian gained name recognition, other wine-producing areas of the Aegean also began using the Pramnos 'appellation' – it continued for so many hundreds of years that the misappropriation of certain wine place-names in modern times pales in comparison – with the eventual result that considerable confusion spread as to just what the name signified. By the time of Dioscorides, in the first century AD, the Pramnian name had become totally separated from the concept of geographic origin, for he associated it only with a generic kind of wine, the so-called *prótropon*, produced from the juice extracted by the weight of the grapes themselves, a type of wine which probably had no similarity to any grown on Ikaria. Athenaeus, in the third century AD, quoted the writer Eparhides, believed to have been an Ikariote of the early second century BC, rather as if to substantiate the Ikariote origin of the Pramnian name. Eparhides had described Pramnian as 'neither sweet nor fat, but dry, hard and of extraordinary strength', which recalls Aristophanes' earlier comment that Pramnian wines 'contract the eyebrows as well as the bowels'.

The Ikariotes apparently lost their stake in the Pramnian name at an early date. In the sixth century BC, Ikaria was plundered for its timber, another source of island wealth, by the autocrat Polycrates of Samos, to use for a fleet which he was having constructed. He also took the Ikariotes as slaves, especially to man his ships. It was the first in a long series of downturns in Ikaria's fortunes that had a bad effect on wine-growing. Already by the first century AD, Strabo found the island scarcely populated, and used mostly for cattle-grazing by the Samiotes. Over the centuries, the Ikariotes became homing seafarers for whom agriculture was a quite secondary activity. Although viticulture remained the island's main domestic activity until the end of the nineteenth century, it was sustained mostly by the market for Ikaria's black raisins. Around the turn of the century, nearly 900 hectares of vines were still producing, but the arrival of phylloxera in 1910 drastically reduced that area, and subsequent ideas of replanting have been perennially thwarted by incessant emigration. The island has under 100 hectares in vineyards now and, with some still producing grapes for raisins, Ikaria today has very little wine to its name, and no name in wine, not even within Greece.

The thought of Ikariote wine ever being bottled, let alone in the running for an appellation of origin, seems absolutely preposterous, notwithstanding its staggering credentials.

Vines on Ikaria are cultivated mostly on terraces flanking Atheras. The black varieties *koundoúra (mandilariá)* and *fokianí (fokianós)* – the latter also used for raisins – as well as the white *kolokitháto* and *rozakiá*, are grown. Today's *prámnio*, as some Ikariotes call it, is mostly dry red wine, and I suppose we are bound to wonder whether any of it could possibly bear any resemblance to ancient Pramnian. I cannot truly offer any advice on that, beyond referring to the ancient descriptions. I should mention the fact that the Ikariotes, by reason of their poverty and isolation, have retained some antique habits. Writing in 1678, Georgirenes mentioned that the Ikariotes were the only islanders of the Aegean who by that time were still unacquainted with barrels. Instead they stored their wine in earthen jars, which they routinely buried, completely covered, in the ground. At least one old man was doing just that a mere decade ago, to give the wine what to him remained a proper maturation. Furthermore, I am told by a recent Ikariote emigrant, totally unfamiliar with Athenaeus and Eparhides, of a special kind of aged red wine, produced in very minor quantity by just a few growers, that 'takes your head off after just a small glass of it'. Perhaps it is the buried kind. I can already see streams of wine buffs, spade in hand, setting off to dig up long jars in Ikariote fields!

CLASSICAL REFLECTIONS

Among the passages most likely to tickle the enophile perusing old books about the Aegean is one from Georgirenes concerning wine habits on hoary Ikaria. It might leave one wondering whether the Ikariotes could have been of the same stuff as ourselves:

> Their Wine is always made with a third part Water, and so very weak and small. When they drink it, so much as is thought sufficient is put into one large Bowl, and so passes round.
> (*A Description of the Present State of Samos, Nicaria, Patmos, and Mount Athos, 1678*)

Making a connection that might explain our interminable if urbane tableside disputes about 'best' wines, Leotsakos notes that even today the Ikariotes 'are neither friends of wine, nor of quarrelling'. The subject of the mingling of water and wine in any case makes one wonder about wine during antiquity.

The French viticulturalist Pierre Viala called Greece 'the country *par excellence* of sobriety'. Perhaps that is so, although Guérin earlier reported much backsliding on wine-deluged Samos in his day, but it must be supposed that a great deal of sobering experience accounts for it. How else, after all, could Aristotle have had sufficient opportunity to observe and conclude that wine lands the over-indulgent drinker face down, whereas barley beer causes him to pass out belly up? For that matter, it is most likely that Dionysus was converted in the first instance from a god of vegetative growth into the god of the vine and wine because the attribution to him of phenomena in plant life, particularly annual regeneration, or 'rebirth', made him seem responsible for the 'altered state' to which wine could transport man: *ékstasis* (rising out of one's ordinary state), *enthousiasmós* (achieving spiritual union with the gods), *manía* (yielding one's self-will to attractions emanating from outside one's self) all became integral to Dionysian worship. In order to tame wine, or rather to gain mastery over it, people learned to weaken its power by diluting it with water. Indeed, Athenaeus mentioned that people had had no appreciation of water before acquaintance with wine, whereas afterwards it was regarded as an ally of sorts. He went so far as to express his opinion that the watering of wine commercially, a practice already regarded as a ruse long before his time, may have originated not in profit-making, but out of 'forethought for the purchaser' (*The Deipnosophists*).

Although Aristotle noted that the particular pleasure of a wine's bouquet was spoiled through mixture with water (*Problems*), the two liquids were none the less regarded as compatible because they are not wholly alien to one another; the physician Galen observed that the capacity of two substances to mix and assimilate to one another was in fact a proof of their 'affinity' (*On the Natural Faculties*). Plato actually called wine a kind of water that had coursed through the plants of the earth (*Timaeus*), a notion which comported well with the sense of the ancient Greek term for wine, *ínos* (*oinos*), which was linked etymologically to a part of the vine, as befitted the early Greek wine drinkers' understanding of Dionysus's role. Athenaeus indicated that quite a few compositional overlaps were possible between waters and wines, as manifest mostly in similarities of feel, but sometimes also in physiological effect, with an occasional water even sparking a giddiness he likened to intoxication. The ancients therefore spoke of some waters as being *inódis* (*oinodes*), that is, winy or vinous. By the same token, some wines participated more than others in the nature of water (*ýdor*) and could on that account be mentioned as *ydatódis*, or watery.

The goal in mixing must generally have been as stated by Aristotle, who wrote that 'well-mixed wine obscures all perception of water, and only gives a sensation of soft wine' (*Problems*). Consequently, practices pertaining to the mixture of water and wine usually varied according to the specific water and wine at hand. For example, Hippocrates, in speaking of the virtues of 'light' waters of altitudinous places, noted that 'the wine they can stand is but little' (*Ancient Medicine*). Sometimes, however, circumstantial factors may also have influenced mixing, perchance even more in favour of the water than the wine:

> Five, indeed, is in the ratio 3:2, three parts of water being mixed with two parts of wine: three is in the ratio 2:1, two parts of water being mixed with one of wine; and four – three parts of water being poured into one of wine – this is a ratio of 4:3, a drink for some group of sensible magistrates in the prytaneion, or logicians, their brows contracted as they meditate upon syllogistic conversion, a sober and feeble mixture.
>
> (Aristion, in Plutarch's *Moralia*: 'Table-talk'; 'No one attacked Aristion's remarks for clearly his talk was play.')

No unmixed wine was poured at symposia in particular, yet even in more ordinary circumstances mixture was so much the general rule that the drinking of unmixed wine, *ákratos*, became conspicuous, and thereby lent its name to the morning meal, *akrátisma*, at which its use remained common, if mostly as a liquid medium in which to take solid foods, or else just to moisten them. Mixed wine, *kekraménos ínos* (*oinos*), was prepared in the vessel called *krátir* (mixing bowl), a procedure called *krásis* (mixing). It was from this terminology that wine acquired a colloquial name that has come down to the modern Greeks as *krasí*, and has supplanted *ínos* (*oinos*) in ordinary speech.

GASTRONOMIC NOTES

I do not believe it should detract from the epicurean allure of the
Eastern Sporades to observe that they do not rank in culinary stature
as they did when Ionia was at its acme and Khios, reportedly the first
Greek place to use purchased slaves, had freed itself from drudgery
and earned a mention by Timocles as being 'by far the best in inventing
dainty dishes' (Athenaeus, *The Deipnosophists*). I remember with
special pleasure enjoying on Samos, at an apparently unnamed
tavérna to which I was taken, situated up a flight of stairs in
Paleokastro, what was quite simply the best seafood meal I have
ever had, in spite of the resinated Samian muscat poured to accompany it.

> My poor Lucius used to amuse himself by concocting delicacies
> for me; his pheasant pasties with their skilful blending of ham and
> spice bore witness to an art which is as exacting as that of a musician
> or painter, but I could not help regretting the unadulterated flesh
> of the fine bird. Greece knew better about such things: her resin-
> steeped wine, her bread sprinkled with sesame seed, fish grilled at
> the very edge of the sea and unevenly blackened by the fire, or
> seasoned here and there by the grit of sand, all satisfied the appetite
> alone without surrounding by too many complications
> this simplest of our joys. In the merest hole of a place in Aegina or
> Phaleron I have tasted food so fresh that it remained divinely clean
> despite the dirty fingers of the tavern waiter.
>
> (Marguerite Yourcenar, *Memoirs of Hadrian*)

I concede, though, that one is usually better off being invited into a
native's home, even a wine-grower's humble abode, than having to
be confined to a *tavérna* perspective.

The high point of Eastern Sporadic cuisine today is probably
the mushrooms that spring up plentifully in the dense forests of
Samos and Ikaria. Numerous sorts of mushrooms, called *manitária*
generally in Greek, are to be found there, and each edible variety,
graced with its own name, is prepared in a way, or ways, deemed
particularly suitable to it. The subject so absorbed one official of the
Agricultural Bank of Greece on Samos whom I met, that he had
developed an amateur ethnographical interest in it. Once, as we sat
in the café of the high-altitude first-rank muscat village of Manolates,
drawing the puzzled attention of the regulars, he played me what

seemed an endless tape-recording of Samiote villagers describing their myriad habits of collecting and preparing mushrooms. It was too much for me to digest in a single sitting, and I am consequently scarcely less ignorant on the subject now than I was then. Unfortunately, in looking over the standard *tavérna* menu, one might never guess that Samos and Ikaria are the centre of Greek mycology.

The list of special foodstuffs from the Eastern Sporades includes several kinds of table olives and cheese. Khios has a most distinctive sort of olive, as peculiar in appearance as it is in taste. Of a nutty flavour, with a more or less gritty texture, these olives appear wrinkled and brown, hence their name *khourmádes* (dates). Traditionally, they are collected following hard rains and high winds that knock them off the trees. Samos offers a rather round, brownish-green olive that is well regarded in Greece. Cheeses are headed by *Khiakí kopanistí* (Khian pounded), a somewhat malleable, though not quite soft, sheep's-milk cheese, made by kneading every few days over a two- to three-month period until a fungus forms, giving it an idiosyncratic flavour akin to that of very ripe blue cheeses: in fact it is sometimes referred to as Khian Roquefort. However, as there is very little of the genuine article, ersatz versions, usually called just *kopanistí*, are more commonly sold in Greece. They may or may not be entirely of sheep's milk, and they owe their sharpness to the addition of capsicum, rather than to the original *kopanistí* technique. On Samos, goat cheeses are particularly good. Natives sometimes eat them while sipping sweet muscat of Glyko or Imiglyko type; the taste contrast parallels that of *prosciutto* with melon. Mytilini, whose olive oil is touted as the best of the Eastern Sporades, is a major producer and exporter of *ladotýri* (oil-cheese), a hard sheep's-milk cheese that acquires a special flavour and texture by curing in olive oil.

Two distilled drinks from the eastern islands have a considerable reputation in Greece. One is Mytilini's *oúzo*, the aniseed-flavoured spirit now associated with Greece nearly worldwide. A very great deal of *oúzo* is produced and bottled by the Distillers' Union of Mytilene (*sic*), or EPOM, which also exports abroad. On Mytilini, the excellent local sardines (*sardélles*) are highly thought of as a *mezé*, or tidbit, to accompany the *oúzo*. The other drink comes from Khios and is a close relative of *oúzo*. It is *mastíkha*, which is flavoured with mastic in addition to aniseed. The world's mastic production is wholly concentrated in the southernmost part of the island, in the *mastikokhóra*, or mastic country. The bushy little trees, which require considerable expert care, yield their valuable sap drop by drop on to the ground, where it hardens, to be collected later for cleaning and eventual dispatch to world markets for chewing-gum. For reasons I have never quite been able to fathom, unless it is that in the days before toothpaste mastic was appreciated as a breath-freshener in Ottoman harems, *mastíkha* is considered rather a lady's drink, or at any rate something of a feminine version of *oúzo*. I am reminded of Aristotle's comment on the difference between wine and barley beer. Anyway, mastic may also be taken as a 'spoon sweet' (*glykó tou koutalioú*), in which case it is referred to as *ypovrýkhio* (submarine), because instead of sipping the water that is always served with spoon sweets, the habit in this case alone is to dip a spoonful into the glass.

2

Rhodes and the Dodecanese

In the greater part of [Rhodes] the coast inclines imperceptibly. . . . Most of the slopes are covered with thorny bushes or bramble. Some of them afford vineyards which still produce the perfumed wine sought by the ancients. It is of a very pleasant taste and leaves an exquisite flavour [bouquet] in the mouth . . . It would be easy to multiply [the vineyards], and cover with them hills of a great extent, which are lying without cultivation.

(Claude Savary, French traveller, *Letters on Greece*, 1788)

RHODES (RODOS)

South of Samos and Ikaria the Aegean grows thicker with islands. Beginning at Patmos an almost linearly arranged string of them appears on the horizon at regular intervals. Collectively called the Dodecanese, or the 'Twelve Isles', the group curves slightly to the south-east, as though following the south-western coast of Asia Minor. Nowadays they seem a very remote and minor outpost of the Greek state, but during antiquity their position so close to the Asian mainland enabled certain of the Dodecanese to gain a significance in the Greek world out of all proportion to their size. The natural centre of the group is Rhodes, which is quite the largest member, and just about the easternmost of them. By reason of its forward position to the south-east, Rhodes was a major contact point between the Greeks and other civilizations to the east, and earlier had actually been settled by the Phoenicians. The island might therefore have been among the earliest spots in the Aegean to receive the vine and vinify its fruit, and was a major trader in wine by the seventh century BC. Its maritime prowess, which perhaps was acquired in no little part through its wine trade, later encouraged Rhodes to undertake a

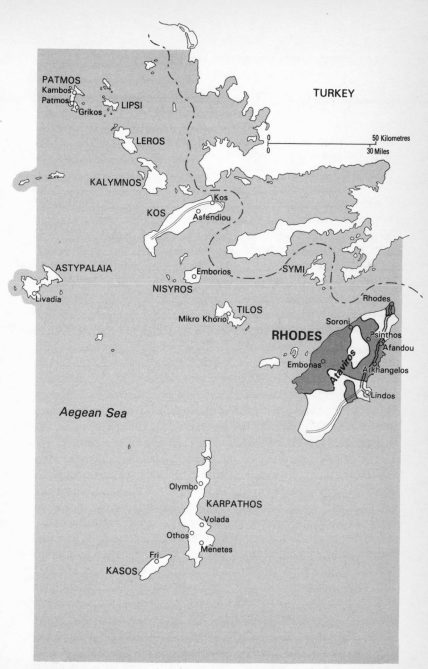

PATMOS
Kambos
Patmos
Grikos
LIPSI

LEROS

KALYMNOS

KOS
Kos
Asféndiou

ASTYPALAIA

Livadia

NISYROS
Emborios

TILOS
Mikro Khorio

TURKEY

50 Kilometres
0
0
30 Miles

SYMI

Rhodes
Soroni
Psinthos
Afandou
RHODES
Atáviros
Arkhangelos
Embonas
Lindos

Aegean Sea

Olymbo

KARPATHOS

Volada

Othos
Menetes

Fri

KASOS

The Dodecanese

voluminous transit trade in grain, which brought it unparalleled wealth. It was around that time, in the third century BC, that the short-lived Colossus of Rhodes spanned the harbour entrance. Rhodes's own products were apparently pulled along by the impetus of its transit trade, and reached as many and as distant places as did its grain transhipments. Foremost among the native goods traded was wine, carried off in amphoras marked specifically as Rhodian, fragments of which have been unearthed virtually throughout the ancient world.

Later wine-growers of Rhodes also prospered. While under the administration of the crusading Knights of St John, who established themselves on the island in 1309 to avail themselves of its strategic location, the local farmers benefited from the opportunity of provisioning the chevaliers with both food and drink. It was in that period too that Rhodes began participating in the lucrative malmsey trade. As late as the mid-eighteenth century the visiting Lord Charlemont found what seemed to him 'a very great quantity of excellent wine'. However, by that time Rhodes was firmly under Ottoman control, and it was only the attraction of revenues from the malmsey trade that kept the local rulers from choking off wine production. Rhodian farmers, including producers of table wines, generally faced only disincentives under the Ottomans, because when the Knights of St John surrendered the island in 1522, after resisting the Ottoman siege for 177 days, the new rulers punished Rhodes by granting it none of the privileges enjoyed by others of the Dodecanese that had acquiesced in Ottoman rule.

Just a few decades after Lord Charlemont's visit, Savary found Rhodian agriculture in distress ('And with the destruction of agriculture goes also the destruction of all arts and crafts which she initiates and for which she supplies the basis and the material' : Plutarch, *Moralia*, 'Dinner of the Seven Wise Men'). The ruling pasha of the day would do nothing to stimulate farming, for reasons which were transparent. Enjoying a monopoly on trade, the pasha was more than satisfied to keep output low and prices high, and had no desire to invest revenues rather than consume them, knowing that only his successor – who, under the Ottoman system, would not be a hereditary one – would reap the rewards of enhancing the island's agricultural potential. Subsequent rulers, ever more independent of the Porte, and proportionately less concerned about the future of the land in their charge, only exacerbated the situation Savary had found.

Thus, by the middle of the nineteenth century Rhodian wine-growing reached its nadir:

> well made . . . the red wines of Rhodes would be excellent *vins de table* which would not lack having an outlet in Europe; but this culture is little diffused and in most of the villages is even unknown.
>
> (Guérin, *Étude sur l'île de Rhodes*, 1856)

The occasion of deliverance for the Dodecanese was the Italo-Turkish War of 1912. As a result of its victory, Italy acquired the group. Italian rule was not without its failings. Animosity was stirred by efforts at administrative Italianization, including the undoing of local landholding customs, which the Ottomans had left intact. Many inhabitants of the Dodecanese departed in frustration and protest. None the less, the Italians were aware of the squandering of economic resources under the Ottomans, and took a special interest in upgrading agriculture, especially on the main island of Rhodes, where an Italian agricultural colony was established, rather in the nature of a model farming community. Improvement of vineyard cultivation and wine-making figured prominently in Italian visions of the development of Rhodes, and the task was eased by the circumstance that Rhodes had been, and still is, spared phylloxera.

A most significant development for Rhodian wine occurred in 1928, when a private society called CAIR, the Agricultural and Industrial Company of Rhodes, was formed by a group of foreign entrepreneurs for the purpose of processing agricultural goods, including wine. Although the Dodecanese passed out of Italian control in 1943, to be incorporated by Greece in 1947, CAIR lives on as the wine-production arm of the Union of Agricultural Cooperatives of the Dodecanese. Headquartered in the town of Rhodes, CAIR buys over 90 per cent of all grapes marketed on the island, and turns out about 90,000 hectolitres of wine annually. Thanks to its vigorous marketing programme throughout Greece, and on export markets as well, CAIR has kept viticulture profitable for Rhodite growers. Indeed Rhodes was among the few areas of Greece that experienced an extension of vineyard land in the post-Second World War years. CAIR may also be largely credited with having put Rhodes in a position to gain appellation of origin rights, which it did in 1971, for qualifying dry white, dry red, and sweet muscat wines.

More fundamental than CAIR to recent Rhodian success in wine is the same factor that worked to the island's advantage in antiquity: its natural environment. Rhodes is singularly blessed for viticulture. It has the longest season of summery weather in Greece – which keeps the droves of tourists coming – and enjoys a particularly high level of insolation. More sunny days and fewer rainy ones occur there than anywhere else in the Aegean, and threats to grape quality are parried by exposition, air currents, and moisture. The most esteemed fruit for quality dry wine is grown mostly on north-facing sites along the north-western side of the Mount Ataviros range that bisects the island from north-east to south-west, which to a large extent forestalls the potentially harmful effects of the insolation on sugar-acid balance in the grapes. The considerable threat of excessive soil temperature in particular is allayed by sea breezes that cool the land twice a day during the May to September ripening period. Also, owing to the influence of the highlands of Asia Minor, a concentrated period of rainfall occurs in between tourist seasons, such that more rain falls on Rhodes annually than in most of the southern Aegean. The island gets twice as much rain as Attica, and it takes a long while to trickle down through Ataviros.

Varietal make-up goes a long way towards bringing to fruition the potential for grape quality offered by the environment of Rhodes. The island is among the most varietally uniform of the archipelago, which is especially remarkable if its size is considered. The two main grape varieties are the white *athíri* and the red *mandilariá*, which together account for over 90 per cent of the approximately 2,000 hectares of vineyards. Both varieties are found widely in the southern Aegean, but rarely adapted so well as to be able to yield dry varietal wines of quality, and nowhere on the scale of Rhodes. Rhodes is in fact likely to remain the only place that produces any varietal *athíri* wine, and also the only one to be granted appellation rights for dry varietal *mandilariá* wine. At present, nearly 1,100 hectares of *athíri* and 600 hectares of *mandilariá* are cultivated in their respective appellative zones, which overlap considerably, at least as regards the villages included in them. In elevation, the vineyards whose fruit qualifies for appellation white or red dry wines differ markedly, the *athíri* occupying the high ground, and the *mandilariá* the lower.

The *athíri* is of particular interest for its apparent antiquity; indeed it may have begun its accommodation to Rhodian conditions a very long time ago, very likely with the variety which the ancients knew as *thiriakí*, so called after the island of Thira, or Santorini; it has been

supposed that the name would have evolved as *thíraia* . . . *thíri* . . .
athíri. The *thiriakí* seems to have been generally associated with
sweet wine in ancient times, and indeed this is the sort of wine for
which the *athíri* has mostly been used in the southern Aegean in the
modern era. On Rhodes, the variety succeeds best in the range of
300–800 metres above sea level in the north-western area, where
ample acidity is assured in the resultant wines. CAIR produces
annually nearly 30,000 hectolitres of 12° dry *athíri* wine that qualifies
for the Rhodes appellation, using grapes from the villages of
Embonas, Ayios Isidoros, Kritinia, Siana, Monolithos and Apollona,
all of which are places specified by the appellative regulation. Of
them, Embonas has the best reputation for white wine.

CAIR uses contemporary technology in making its white appellation wine, which it bottles under the Ilios label. (Ilios was formerly
called Lindos, a name still encountered in some wine and travel books.
The earlier name was changed because it gave a false impression of
the area of the island from which the wine hails.) In a healthy
state, Ilios is of a lustrous, pale straw colour, and should appear
substantially so through the clear glass bottle. In my experience, the
vintage-dated Ilios offers little reward for being kept, not even when
laid down, much less when standing upright several years as it might
in a Greek neighbourhood grocery, but the maxim 'age before beauty'
is refuted by Ilios's scent. I might call it a mild blend of herby and
floral smells, but they defy individual analysis, instead comprising a
whole that might truly be identified only as what it is . . . *athíri* of
Rhodes. 'Sweating glass' serving temperatures intended to simulate
crispness through coolness neutralize the light but clear aroma of
Ilios, and more generally upset a balance of flavour features pertaining
to impressions of both delicacy and strength.

Its various characteristics recommend Ilios as an aperitif wine,
especially when appetizers to be served are substantial, though
bitterish or aromatically pungent ones can distract. The *khourmádes*
olives of Khios might be appropriate, and, among cheeses, the cow's-
milk types, especially milder ones, including Syrian/Armenian 'string'
cheese. Grilled mushroom caps stuffed with savoury fillings can also
win friends for Ilios. It is also a good accompaniment for main
courses, and I might suggest the Greek version of stuffed cabbage
(*lakhanodolmádes*) with minced lamb in the filling and *avgolémono*
(egg-lemon) sauce. Meatless stuffed tomatoes and peppers (*domátes/
piperiés yemistés*) might also be considered, which always ought to

be served tepid. Generally, parsley, dill, thyme and rosemary are seasonings to look to for aromatic congruence with Ilios, especially with fish.

Like the *athíri*, the red *mandilariá*, the second major grape variety of Rhodes, may have arrived from the Cyclades. It is generally called *amoryianó* on Rhodes, suggesting that it came by way of Amorgos, to the north-west. In any case the *mandilariá* could be said to have had an even happier adaptation on Rhodes than the *athíri*, in that its success in giving dry red wines all on its own is very sporadic. On Rhodes, however, the late-ripening *mandilariá* is able to ripen fully at the relatively lower altitudes, so that dry wines produced from it there do not necessarily lack in alcoholic degree, which is often a problem with dry *mandilariá* wines grown elsewhere. The vineyards for *mandilariá* are mostly situated between 50 and 300 metres above sea level, and owing to the northern exposure and breezes, Rhodian reds can have quite sufficiently lively acidity as well. With those considerations in mind, the villages of Fanes, Soroni, Kalavarda, Damatria, Tholos, Embonas, Kritinia, Siana, Monolithos, Apollona, Ayios Isidoros, Maritsa and Salakos are included in the appellation zone for Rhodian red wine. Soroni and Embonas are generally regarded as the best of them. CAIR uses *mandilariá* grapes primarily from the first five mentioned villages to produce its appellation red wine, an 11.7° alcohol wine fermented on skins only, and bottled after one year in oak, which is the minimum maturation requirement specified in the appellative rules. It is marketed under the Chevalier de Rhodes label, with vintage date. Nearly 20,000 hectolitres are produced annually.

Even before the advent of the modern cellar on Rhodes, the island had a good reputation for its red wine. The English traveller William Turner, writing in 1820, 'thought it very good; it is a sharp-tasted red wine, with a little sweetness'. The sweetness, it would seem, is a feature of the past now, assuming that Turner meant it literally. Dry red wine is all one finds today, and that is very true of Chevalier de Rhodes. Unusual among southern Aegean reds for its scant fleshiness of texture, Chevalier manages all the same to register vividly on the mouth surfaces, in its way recalling Turner's phrase, 'sharp-tasted'. Especially when young, the always orange-seeking, garnet Chevalier spreads its sensations across the entire upper surface of the tongue. Given three to six years of bottle age – how unfortunate that it is rarely given the chance – Chevalier mellows to achieve a balance with aromatic flavour. At the same time, the earlier 'sweet-spicy' bouquet gives way, to a greater or lesser extent, to a fragrance sometimes reminiscent of tulips, but usually at least floral in a general way, no matter what the vintage or bottle. The result is a wine with a most unusual and harmonious juxtaposition of a delicate freshness of aromatic flavour and stalwart tactile sensations. I would not care, though, to challenge the verdict of a Gallic gastronomic duo who assess Chevalier – on the basis of how many vintages, I do not know – as being on a par with a *petit* St-Émilion. Certainly anyone who can sit on Rhodes and think of St-Émilion while looking at, sniffing or tasting Chevalier has a very great tolerance for sun, and should be given due respect and credence.

The turnabout in the character of Chevalier de Rhodes as it ages is notable among Greek reds worthy of cellaring, so much so that it is all too easy for an attendant of it to become peevishly finicky about the bottle's age when it comes to putting together a meal. I have succumbed my share of times, and would recommend a young Chevalier for certain spreadables, like some of the commonly available herbed cheeses – but do not neglect *tapenade*, the Mediterranean crushed-olive spread. For the older wine, have a mild cheese like havarti with dill. Greek beef specialities flavoured with cinnamon or cloves, like *stifádo*, seem ideal for a young bottle, while pot roasts of many descriptions will do as well with the older wine. Young meats such as veal are appropriate for an older Chevalier, and can be flavoured somewhat robustly, as in paprika schnitzel. Chevalier always seems to please with lamb, but forethought moves me to prefer an older bottle with barbecued marinated lamb. As for vegetables, try somewhat abrasive and bitterish ones, such as spinach or zucchini with the skin on, perhaps flavoured with a little tomato sauce and nutmeg: I have fond memories of an earlyish Chevalier drunk with artichokes in a dilute, well-herbed tomato sauce.

Among its top-of-the-range wines, CAIR saves its very best for last in the course of a meal, offering its muscat wine as a finish. It would be placed, no doubt, far higher *vis-à-vis* others in its category than would either Chevalier de Rhodes or Ilios. Given the warm climate of Rhodes, sweet wine has been produced there since antiquity, and the *moskháto áspro* of Greece and the *trani* muscat introduced by the Italians are cultivated for sweet wine today. Both muscat varieties must be used for the wine to qualify for a Rhodian muscat appellation of origin. Within the appellation zone, they are grown on fewer than

47

10 hectares at present, all lying between 50 and 100 metres above sea level. The villages within the zone are situated both on the east-central coast and in the west: going anti-clockwise from the north-west, they are Fanes, Apollona, Embonas, Monolithos, Lardos, Arkhangelos, Afandou and Psinthos. The latter place is especially intriguing from the point of view of whether the ancient *psíthios* wine might have been a muscat [see p. 19], since Psinthos, which is presumed to be named for the profusion of *apsínthion* (wormwood) found there, could have lent its name to the vine of that name. Alas, even if it had, that would not prove that *psíthios* was a muscat.

CAIR produces about 500 hectolitres of appellation Rhodes muscat annually, and markets it under the Muscat de Rhodes label. The grapes come from around the villages of Arkhangelos and Lardos on the east-central coast, the sunnier side of the island where the breezes are that much more crucial to quality, and Fanes on the north-western coast. The wine is of an orange-gold colour, with an aroma of floral and sweet-spicy smells, the typical coriander tendency of muscat seeming to me to be quite distinct in it, though not in isolation. It is similar to Samos Glyko in sweetness and texture, but usually firmer and possessed of somewhat more vinous force. It has a place beside the popular Greek *glyká tou tapsioú* (pan sweets, that is, oriental pastries), but I think it at least as good with carrot cake. At any event, one should not miss Muscat de Rhodes while on the island. Drinking it, one can understand just what Savary was talking about 200 years ago.

CAIR also produces lesser-quality red and white appellation wines, on the Rodos label. A rosé (*mandilariá*) called Moulin has also appeared and, inevitably, a Retsina, from *athíri*, although the Rhodians traditionally do not resinate their wines. Additionally, there is a fortified wine called Amandia, which is meant to resemble a wine of port type. It is made from *mandilariá* (60 per cent) and the red *diminítis* (40 per cent), the latter variety probably being a local variant of the *liátiko* of eastern Crete, which has a long history of use for sweet wines. CAIR takes a special pride in its *brut* and *demi-sec* sparkling *athíri* wines under the CAIR label, which are the only sparkling wines of Greece made by the *méthode champenoise*, and more than decently underscore both CAIR's technical capability and its skill in using the environment of Rhodes to advantage.

Besides CAIR, the small private firm of Emery, belonging to the Triantafyllos family, has operated a winery at Embonas since 1968.

Emery has no vineyards of its own and buys all its grapes in Embonas. The firm makes both red and white appellation wines, and has two labels in both cases. The higher-quality and higher-alcohol wines are the 12° red Lacosta and white Grand Maître de Rhodes, of which about 2,000 and 10,000 hectolitres respectively are produced each year. They are vintage-dated. A lesser red and white, both at 11°, are released under the Rodos label. Additionally, a reserve red wine of 12.5° is produced in a quantity of about 900 hectolitres annually, and aged for three years, including one to one and a half in barrel. It is marketed under the Kava Emery label. There is also a *brut* sparkling wine under the Emery label.

THE DODECANESE

Apart from Rhodes, the islands of the south-eastern Aegean are mostly very small and unproductive, the exception being sizeable and very fertile Kos, the garden of the Aegean, and the original home of Cos or romaine lettuce. During antiquity, the island had a considerable reputation for wine, both red and white, apparently dry in the former case and sweet in the latter, but in that era its economy was thriving and its population numbered over 150,000. Hardly more than 20,000 people inhabit Kos now, and a semblance of prosperity has only recently returned after a dismal period of several hundred years. Kos evidently suffered a great deal during Ottoman times, to such an extent that in the early nineteenth century Turner, who found only white wine when visiting Kos, mentioned it as being 'in the most wretched condition of any of the Greek islands I have seen'. The relative fecundity of Kos drew to it many Turkish inhabitants, who comprised fully five-eighths of the population when Turner was there, and stayed on well beyond his day. Kos was still about half-Turkish until nearly midway through the twentieth century. The Moslem presence, which extended into the countryside, had a negative impact on viticulture on the island as a whole, and Kos was also visited by phylloxera. But a good initial recovery from its recent past has been made, and Kos is now producing bottled wines in an amount of about 5,000 hectolitres annually, all by the Vinicultural Cooperative of Kos (Vinko).

The winery of the Cooperative is located near the north-eastern coast by Kos town, but all the grapes it vinifies are produced at

Asfendiou, located in the east-central part of the interior of the island. The vineyards thereabouts are on the northern foothills of Mount Dikaios, and lie mostly between 100 and 300 metres above sea level, on a shallow layer of silty clay. The varieties grown are the wine grapes *mandilariá*, which is called *amouryianó* on Kos, and *athíri*, and the dessert grapes *rozakí áspro* and *soultanína*, all of which are used for the Cooperative's wines: Apellis, a dry red made from *mandilariá*; Glafkos, a dry white from *athíri, rozakí*, and *soultanína*; Retsina, made from a similar mixture, and comprising half of the output; and Vereniki, a semi-sweet, fortified red made from the three white varieties in addition to *mandilariá*. Apellis, produced in a quantity of about 1,200 hectolitres annually, is a 12.5° red that is usually aged in barrel for two years before bottling, although it is not bottled with a vintage date. It presents a smooth bouquet, if one less amenable to bottle age than its counterpart *mandilariá* wines from Rhodes. Could the Cooperative lure the villagers of Asfendiou away from the attraction of tourist-catering and increase plantings of *mandilariá* in the most suitable area, Apellis might perhaps be worked up into a wine that would draw attention to Kos once more.

Neither in ancient times nor in recent centuries were the other islands of the Dodecanese significant traders in wine, if they ever had much to export at all. Furthermore, most were visited by phylloxera, and emigration has been scarcely less crushing. Only very small areas of vines remain: on Patmos, in the north at Kambos, and in the south-east at Grikos and Diakofti; at Katsadia on the south-eastern coast of Lipsi; in the upland village of Emborios on Nisyros; by Livadia on the south-eastern part of the western sac of Astypalaia; around Mikro Khorio on Tilos; and to the south-west of Fri on Kasos. The varieties grown throughout the islands are primarily the *mandilariá* and *fokianó* for reddish wines, and the *athíri* and *rozakí* for whites. Retsina has been making inroads in the Dodecanese in recent years, notably on Symi. At the end of the eighteenth century, Savary called the island's wine 'good' and made no mention of resination, which would have been an exotic feature of the sort he was inclined to note, but Symi for the most part makes retsina these days. However, the Symiotes have special praise for unresinated wines grown on their satellite island of Teftlousa, to the south, which belongs to the Monastery of Panormitis on the Symiote coast opposite. It would seem a good reason to pay the monks a visit.

Among the lesser wine producers of the Dodecanese, one especially worth a wine buff's exploration is Karpathos, to the south-west of Rhodes. It was spared phylloxera, and its grape varieties predictably represent a transition between Rhodes and Crete: the red *mandilariá* and *fokianó*, and the white *athíri, thrápsa* (the *thrapsathíri* of eastern Crete), *kolokitháta, rozakí*, and *moskháto áspro*. Sweetish wines of the mountain villages of Volada, Othos, and Menetes should be sought. Although neither resinated, nor piny in flavour, they are produced with pieces of pine bark added to the must during fermentation in clay jars. For the thoroughly modern enophile engulfed by the technological hubris of the late twentieth century they can be absolutely devastating in the deliciousness they sometimes show.

CLASSICAL REFLECTIONS

In choosing Ilios, sun, as the name of a wine, CAIR of Rhodes has evoked the island's one-time association with the Sun-god, much as was done anciently by Rhodian wine traders, who used a depiction of the sun as an emblem to identify their amphorae. But the name also seems to be something of a cultural Freudian slip, in that it reveals a Greek slant on wine that is bound up in the eternal Aegean scene. It is a perspective older than the ancients' notion of an alliance of sun, fire and wine, yet fresher than the words of a recent Greek popular song, 'I want you to be an eagle, that the light of the sun be your wine.'

One kind of light has never gone out in the Greek space: that diaphanous Aegean sunlight.

> The mountains, the valley, the sea play a secondary role. The light is the resplendent Sober Dionysus who is dismembered and suffers, then rejoins his parts and triumphs. The entire scene of Greece seems to have come to be just that he might perform.
>
> (Nikos Kazantzakis, *Journey to the Morea*)

That performance caused the ancients to be fascinated by vision in a way that may seem strange to us because of the immediacy and intensity of their experience of it:

> In all probability the most active stream of [bodily] emanations [that produce sensation] is that which passes out through the eye. For vision, being of an enormous swiftness and carried by an

51

essence that gives off a flame-like brilliance, diffuses a wondrous influence. In consequence, man both experiences and produces many effects through his eyes. He is possessed and governed by either pleasure or displeasure exactly in proportion to what he sees.

(Plutarch, *Moralia*, 'Table-talk')

Thus did sight go to the heart of wine appreciation, and perhaps influence wine-growing itself.

The ancients saw that light, or rather its source, the sun, was of crucial significance to wine. Sunlight imparted to wine a fire to which was attributed both appearance and physiological effects. The Sun-god's 'tears amber-beaming' become 'the Wine-god's fire', and then 'the wine's flame', to borrow Euripides' metaphors. Wine's intimate, direct link with the sun's fire caused brilliance to become associated with wine as an essential quality, much in the sense meant by Sappho when she said that 'brightness and honour [the "natural properties of virtue"] belong to my yearning for the sun' (Athenaeus, *The Deipnosophists*). By way of alluding to its sparkling aspect, wine gained the description *éthopa* (*aithopa*), since, as Euripides related, one of the Sun-god's horses was called Aithopa (Fiery). It may have been to bring the vine closer to the sun, thereby shortening Aithopa's haul, that early Aegean vine-tenders originally moved its cultivation up mountainsides.

Colour, which Plato (*Timaeus*) defined as 'a flame which streams off from every sort of body', was also cause for wonderment under Aegean skies. Athenaeus distinguished four cardinal wine colours: *lefkós* (white), *kirrós* (tawny), *erythrós* (red) and *melénas* (black). He mostly referred to Clearclus to explain these colours. The commonality of the two extremes was the absence of reddishness, Clearclus having remarked that both water and milk are called *lefkós*, while identifying *melénas*, which literally means 'inky', with mulberry juice. In between those two was a range of more ambiguous hues in which orange or red was apparent, *kirrós* by its very name indicating the brownish yellow of bee's wax, while *erythrós* described red proper ('the radiance of [a certain sort of] fire through the moisture with which it is mingled gives blood-colour, which we call "red" ' – Plato, (*Timaeus*). To *erythrós* belonged the distinction of being specifically identified with wine, Clearclus having used wine as his example of that colour, the way he did other potable liquids for *lefkós* and *melénas*. But in wine of any colour the ancients would have expected chromatic nuances that amounted to visual analogues, and foretellers, of a *goût de terroir* ('taste of the locale'), much as when Theophrastus (*Enquiry into Plants*) observed that the colour as well as the scent of flowers varies with locality. It is what comes of a melding of grape varieties with environments, but a melding judged and directed by people who look at wine in the light of their place.

GASTRONOMIC NOTES

Surely Rhodes's gardens, which are second only to those of Kos in Dodecanese lore, must be mentioned as a primary source of raw material for the native kitchen. And it ought to be noted as well that Rhodian olive oil is generally thought the best of the Dodecanese. As concerns cooking as such, however, I would be remiss not to take into account Rhodes's special history, which brought to it long-lingering people from both west and east: Franks, Sephardic Jews, Turks, Armenians, Italians. A richly cosmopolitan streak consequently winds its way through Rhodian cuisine, although usually in subtle ways, since the foreigners' proclivities have largely been adapted to the local environment and customs, rather than preserved in isolation in alien dishes.

While not generally sharing in Rhodes's reputation for culinary skill, most of the smaller of the Dodecanese are known for certain specialities. Several islands are appreciated by Greek seafood lovers: Kos, Astypalaia, Leros, Kasos and Kastelorizo. By reason of gastronomic history, first mention in that category should perhaps go to Kasos, since fishermen there still pull in the *skáros*, which was the alpha and omega of fish as far as the classical gourmet was concerned. But Kastelorizo has staunch fans of its oysters (*strídia*) and other bivalves. Astypalaia and Leros are also known for small game: hare, partridge, doves. Spit-roasted wild goat of Teftlousa is prized on Symi. At Easter, the villagers on Nisyros prepare a local version of *kapamás*, which consists of goat meat baked in a deep, open clay pot. Generally in the Dodecanese, and on most other southern Aegean islands as well, Easter lamb is also baked in the traditional ovens, rather than spit-roasted as on the mainland. But on 1 May (*Protomayiá*), the Nisyriotes celebrate by roasting a suckling pig on the spit (*vrouláki tis soúvlas*). Several of the Dodecanese, especially Kalymnos, Kasos and Symi, are known for their honey – Kalymnos at least since Strabo's time. A confection made with honey and sesame, *sisamómeli*, is typical of several of the lesser Dodecanese, but that of Kasos is particularly well thought of. On Karpathos, *sisamómeli* is embellished with a filling of sugar-coated chickpeas.

As demonstrated by its wine-making, Karpathos has preserved some very archaic habits, and that holds true in the kitchen as well. The best-known Karpathian speciality is *psilokoúlouro*, which is a ring (*kouloúra*) of sesame-studded, rather thin (*psilós*), braided strips of dough baked in the characteristic island ovens. *Psilokoúlouro* is appreciated for its peculiarly chewy texture, and is reported to have great keeping powers, a veritable *pain de garde*. The most traditional of all Karpathian villages is Olymbo, high up in the north. It is there that a visitor is most likely to come upon the dish called *khóndros*, whose mere mention might stir readers of Athenaeus who recall his numerous references to 'gruel', which was called *khóndros*. The Karpathian dish of that name consists of meat cooked with milled wheat, and one must conclude that it was food like this that nurtured Homeric heroes. Weddings at Olymbo are celebrated by roasting oxen over charcoal, which has become a rare practice in Greece in modern times since their scarcity has made oxen too valuable as draught animals to slaughter just for the table. The custom at Olymbo could be a relic of ancient tradition, perhaps even linked to the slaughter of oxen that was part of some early rituals honouring 'ox-horn Dionysus' and 'bull-shaped Dionysus' (Nonnos, *Dionysiaca*). The connection of Dionysus with oxen may have arisen from his identification in mytholgy as the pioneer of plowing and sowing (Plutarch, *Moralia*, 'The Roman Questions'), which had probably grown out of his earlier role as the god of vegetative growth. But I suppose the Olymbians are not too concerned with all that when they sit down to a wedding feast.

3
Crete

———

The wines of Candia are excellent, reds, whites, and clarets . . . the wines of this clime have quite enough tartness to offset their lusciousness; this lusciousness, far from being flat, is accompanied by a delicious balm that makes those who have really tasted through the wines of Candia scorn all other wine.

(Joseph Tournefort, French traveller, *Relation d'un Voyage du Levant*, 1717)

The bounds of the Aegean world have ever been fixed to the south by the island of Crete, long known in the West by its Venetian name, Candia. Although an integral member of the Archipelago, and one that typifies it in many ways, Crete can hardly be considered just another Aegean island. It lies off from the rest, actually in a sea named after it, the Sea of Crete, which rivals the Aegean proper in extent. It is by far the largest island as well, and because most of its terrain other than the more mountainous interior is conducive to planting vines, Crete's wine output is commensurate with its physical size. Nearly one-fifth of Greek wine is Cretan, and it is from Crete that many of Greece's finest dry red wines – wines that will compete with the best anywhere – could issue in coming decades.

Against all the odds, given its latitudinal position, Crete is ideal for the vine. While having extensive insolation, this most southerly of the Aegean isles enjoys a climate so mild and free of extremes that the eighteenth-century French visitor Savary was prompted to say he could not think of its climatic equal among the places where he had sojourned. The only recurrent environmental hazard facing Cretan wine-growers is the possibility of severe winds blowing off the Aegean in spring, during budding or fruit-setting. During the growing season, Crete, which is long from east to west, narrow from north to south, is cooled by sea breezes along its broader northern side, while the

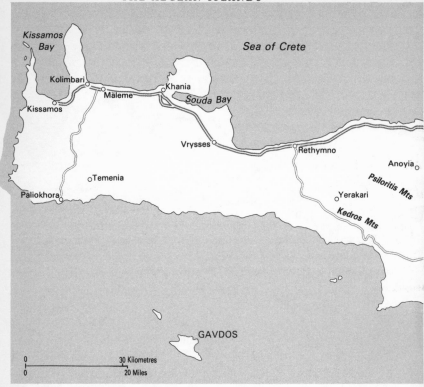

lateral extensions of Psiloritis, the Mount Ida of the ancients, provide shelter from the hot winds of North Africa. The mountains also supply plenty of water for agricultural purposes, all the way into summer too, as the snows of Psiloritis melt. The water seeps down through calcareous rock to the vineyards, and then onward again through unseen potholes, to the sea.

Crete's particularly outstanding environmental attributes have led to the development of a wine tradition second to none in all respects, including a selection of vines all its own, and more ancient than virtually any other regional tradition. Indeed, to explore the sources of the Cretan tradition is to trace the essentials of wine-growing back four millennia. Crete was certainly not among the very first places to cultivate the vine, nor even to make wine; but the remains of grapes

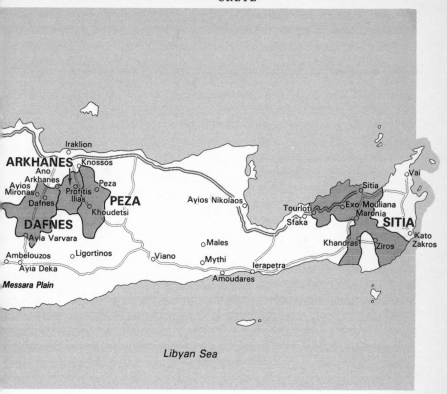

Crete

found at Kato Zakros, a site on the eastern part of the island and dating to the early second millennium BC, are the earliest conclusive evidence of systematic cultivation of grape types destined specifically for wine production. Moreover, the facilities found there for crushing the grapes indicate that Cretan, or more properly, Minoan, wine-making was technically far in advance of practice elsewhere at the time.

Following its own era of singular renown, Crete apparently was able to hold its own while progressing largely in step with innovations such as the shift to barrels. The island remained a most respected source of wine well into the modern era, even into the period of Venetian control, from the early twelfth through to the mid-seventeenth century, when Crete entered the malvasia trade (see

57

pages 74–8). Production of that sort of wine may in no small measure account for the continuity in the island's commercial wine activity during the Ottoman centuries that followed. However, Crete's trade in wine was subsequently threatened by attempts to produce wine of malvasia type in the western Mediterranean in order to take advantage of the market Crete had created, and to be in a position to fill the gap between supply and demand, should Cretan exports dry up as a result of internal problems on the island. In fact Crete became the greatest perennial trouble spot for the Porte, thereby putting the island's reliability as a supplier in jeopardy. And although wine-making at artisan level survived intact – scenes drawn by Crete's native son Nikos Kazantzakis in *Zorba the Greek* and *Freedom or Death* give the lie to any assumption that Cretan wine tradition was obliterated by Ottoman rule – Crete's repeated insurrectionary activity held back progress in wine-making at a crucial period. The insurrection of 1896, in particular, resulted in extensive destruction of Cretan vineyards.

Crete was ceded to Greece by the Turks relatively late, in 1913. A renaissance of wine-growing on the island was prompted only in the 1930s, following a large influx of refugees from Asia Minor after the Greek–Turkish exchange of minorities agreed to in 1923. The refugees settled mostly in east-central Crete, where their initial role was largely in the spread of raisin (*soultanína*) and table grape (*rozakí*) cultivation. Nevertheless, their propensity for cooperative agricultural activities was the spur needed to revamp island wine-making. The influence of the refugees was in that way so pervasive that Cretan commercial wine-making even now remains very largely the province of cooperatives, notwithstanding the entry of several privately owned wineries. The cooperatives are likely to remain predominant far into the future as well, a prospect by no means prejudicial to the future of Cretan wine. Cretan cooperatives bring to their work a mix of enthusiasm, acumen, competence and pride, of a kind that one might be tempted to identify as specifically Cretan.

The cooperatives are seeing to the rapid extension of vineyard land, especially in the appellation of origin zones (all of which have thus far been unscathed by phylloxera), and are continuously striving to update their facilities and techniques as finances permit. Grapes are carefully separated so as to be able to offer high-quality wines, and in a couple of instances wines have been produced that, when given the time due to them in bottle, and then perhaps a 'blind tasting' as well, can make Tournefort's otherwise perhaps dumbfounding early eighteenth-century assessment far more comprehensible than might seem possible to those unacquainted with the wines of Candia. It is mostly the lack of incentive as yet to take the last step and process separately the choicest fruit of only the very best vineyards, that still keeps Crete off the topmost rung of quality in bottled dry red wine.

ARKHANES AND PEZA

Most visitors to Crete arrive at its chief town of Iraklion on the north-central coast. The scattered vineyards seen along the road south from there to Knossos might be particularly evocative of the oft-repeated aphorism that the spread of Western civilization is to be traced along the tendrils of the vine. Beyond Knossos the vines become profuse, especially after the fork in the road where one must choose between making the gradual ascent into either of two hilly, upland valleys, both of which produce exceptional wine. The westerly valley, which runs up the eastern foothills of Mount Youkhtas, within sight of Psiloritis, is that of Temenos. The villages of Ano Arkhanes, Kato Arkhanes and Skalani, as well as those of Vasilies, Ayios Silas, Profitis Ilias, and Kiparisos on the western side of Youkhtas, produce dry red wine eligible for the Arkhanes appellation of origin. Nearly 500 hectares qualify at present. The valley to the east of Temenos is that of Pedias, whose vineyards comprise the core of the Peza appellation zone for dry red and white wine. A dozen and a half villages are included in the zone: Peza, Kounavi, Mirtia, Astraki, Katalagari, Ayies Paraskies, Kalloni, Ayios Vasilios, Khoudetsi, Meleses, Astritsi and Alagni, along with Sambas further east, and Patsideros, Panorama, Damania, Metaxokhori and Kharaki further south. More than 800 hectares of vineyards in this area currently qualify for the appellation.

The gravelly, white and tan ground of the twin valleys is covered over during the growing season by a most luxurious growth of vines, some for wine, some for dessert grapes, and some for raisins, the plots for each type being laid out like a patchwork quilt. The dominant red grape of the area is the very highly regarded regional peculiarity *kotsifáli*, a variety which does well on somewhat deep clayey soils of calcareous nature. Greek wine professionals tend to liken *kotsifáli* wine to Bordeaux, which is not to draw a comparison of the variety with *cabernet sauvignon* in any strict sense. Rather, they have in mind the make-up in alcohol, acidity and extract by which *kotsifáli* wine can benefit from years of maturation in bottle, especially to the advantage of bouquet development – which will indeed occur if the wine is well made from exceptional grapes of a good year, although at the end of that time the texture and the overall feel of the best *kotsifáli* wines may be reminiscent of *nebbiolo* and *brunello*. In specifics of bouquet, however, they are quite unique.

In speaking of the *kotsifáli* in connection with Bordeaux, it also ought to be emphasized that the variety is not without tendencies that beg correction. Consequently, red wines of Arkhanes and Peza, like those of Bordeaux, have typically been made from a blend of varieties, in this case two: the dominant *kotsifáli* together with the popular southern Aegean *mandilariá* – the latter generally in a proportion of not less than 20 per cent, but not more than 40 per cent. In addition to augmenting tannin content, lowering acidity, and tempering alcoholic degree in *kotsifáli* – all to the real advantage of the wine – the *mandilariá* also deepens colour and makes it more stable, which can be a problem with varietal *kotsifáli* wine generally. Fortunately for this ideal marriage of varieties, both the *kotsifáli* and the *mandilariá* ripen in central Crete around early September.

Three commercial wineries are presently at work in the Arkhanes and Peza areas. The Archanes Wine, Olive Oil and Credit Cooperative produces about 30,000 hectolitres annually of an appellation wine called Archanes, produced from a 3:1 mix of *kotsifáli* and *mandilariá*. At Peza, about 20,000 hectolitres of red wine entitled to the appellation are produced by the Union of Producer Cooperatives of Peza, and bottled under the Mantiko label. The Union is hopeful of increasing production by half over the next ten years. Their blend of *kotsifáli* and *mandilariá* is in a ratio of about 4:1. A second local producer of appellation Peza wine is Miliarakis Brothers, who turn out about 8,000 hectolitres of it annually, produced from an undisclosed proportion of the two varieties, and marketed under the Sant'Antonio label. Qualitative comparison of the three wines is made difficult by the divergence in their barrel maturation. One would have to follow bottlings of them for some years, and none of the three is vintage-dated at present. The minimum barrel-ageing time under appellation regulations for both Arkhanes and Peza red wines is one year. But Sant'Antonio receives five to six years, compared to two to three for Mantiko and rather more than one year for Archanes.

Owing to their large production, the two cooperatives have to be in the business of selling far and wide, and being thus particularly interested in export sales have abjured the longer maturation in wood given to the wines traditionally most esteemed by the Cretans. Especially at Arkhanes, the Cooperative would like their wine to impress as 'fresh and fruity', even while they also aim for rather full body. If their Archanes succeeds in that way – and I have not thought it does – it nevertheless needs two to three years in bottle to display its character, and up to six to eight years to overcome a certain toughness to its hide. Only then will it exhibit the quality the locals boast of when asserting that Arkhanes's wine is naturally superior to that of Peza because the vineyards of Temenos reach to 600–700 metres above sea level, compared to Peza's lowly 500–600 metres. But Mantiko, too, can be quite impressive at eight to ten years of age, if one has acquired it soon after bottling and stored it oneself. Perhaps these ages do not impress Bordeaux enthusiasts, but I am speaking of aged wines that show *no* untoward manifestations whatsoever. One could expect even more from limited production Arkhanes and Peza wines, and in that regard I might usefully mention an outstanding Peza wine produced and bottled by a hobbyist wine-grower, and tasted to full satisfaction in New York just under twenty-five years later.

Although a wine of deep ruby colour, Archanes does not wear its violet on its sleeve, and actually has a latent orange cast to it even while new to the bottle. Mantiko is a shade lighter. Archanes has seemed to me the longer in finish, when aged, but Mantiko more intensely bouqueted at any age. I suppose one may weigh those respective advantages as one wishes. When bottled, Mantiko offers ample features of all that can be conjured up by the Greek term *moskhovolistó* (sweet-smelling, literally 'musk-casting'), in so far as it can be applied to dry red wines. In addition to smells of spices, this wine has an almost tropical-fruity aroma, sometimes including the smell of nearly ripe banana, which seems to me to be a *kotsifáli* trait. Also floral aromas seem to accumulate with bottle age in the case of both wines, though only to the advantage of the overall impression I have characterized as *moskhovolistó*; which tempts me to say that, at peak development, Mantiko and Archanes make what is praised in the best Burgundian noses as oriental look positively occidental instead.

However, there is more to central Crete than the casting of musk, and those who hate to see not so much the dying away of tradition, as the narrowing of the range of accepted vinous flavour, will be pleased to find that Miliarakis Brothers capture that something extra in their appellation Peza wine, Sant'Antonio. Following traditional regional practice for reserve red wine, Sant'Antonio is kept long enough for it to acquire rather distinctive flavour features which are spoken of collectively as *i yéfsi tis doúgas* (the taste of the stave). The expression implies 'over'-maturation in wood, and while it is usually used pejoratively, or at least jocularly, it can be complimentary when a certain conjunction of feel and bouquet are indicated.

The condition of *i yéfsi tis doúgas* is brought about in the first place by the phenomenon of intense insolation, common in the southern Aegean, whereby acidity in fruit that stays on the vine until fully ripe is altered in a way analogous to the malolactic, or secondary, fermentation of wines, by which malic acid is converted to the softer, less acidic tasting, lactic acid. Red wines produced from such fruit consequently do not need to undergo the malo-lactic fermentation achieved in the cellar, and desirable in northerly European wine regions to bring acidity down to levels generally felt to be more palatable. On the contrary, they need protection from it if the loss of enlivening acidity, or at least that of a kind preferred today, is to be prevented. While that has been possible in good Cretan cellars – for example, those belonging to Cretan monasteries, such as the erstwhile one of Arkadi, mentioned so favourably in some early Western travelogues – and achieved consistently in modern facilities guided by contemporary enological science, such was generally not the case under village conditions. It was therefore necessary to find a way of making a vice out of a virtue, so to speak. Hence the quest for a sound manifestation of *i yéfsi tis doúgas*. For success, a full-bodied wine of relatively high alcoholic degree is needed, in other words one that will hold up in all its essentials over the years.

At 13° alcohol, Sant'Antonio is more in keeping with traditional Cretan preferences in this respect than are the 12.5° wines of the cooperatives. While hardly lacking in acidity, it is rounded to the point that it makes overtures to flatness, and yet without compromising its health or character at all. In bouquet, Sant'Antonio exhibits something of a 180° swing away from a Peza wine like

Mantiko, as though having moved away from fresh fruit towards the essence as achieved through sun-drying. It is a kind of aromatic decay, but short of that point at which so many aromas of advanced age have crept in that it would be hard to distinguish it as Peza wine among so many other over-the-hill red wines; it all has much to do with pushing the limits of 'distinctiveness of bouquet', which perhaps occurs more often in the case of cheese, as when lovers of 'ripe' blue-veined cheeses experience difficulty in identifying advanced specimens of, say, Roquefort and Gorgonzola. That aspect of Sant'Antonio is supported and enhanced by its full body and liquorous texture. Also characteristic of Sant'Antonio is its unusual colour. Staying in barrel for as long as it does, it shows clear orange highlights, although it is none the less very dark red, darker even than newly bottled Archanes.

The red wines of east-central Crete offer an excellent opportunity to serve quality red wine at meals featuring highly flavoured pork dishes. With Archanes, try roast pork with spiced apples, or red cabbage cooked with apples; with Mantiko, hickory-smoked, slightly tangy barbecued pork can be a delight. Roast duck with raspberry sauce could also be an occasional choice, but a well-aged bottle from an outstanding bottling would go perfectly with a really well-made *mousaka*. As for Sant'Antonio, the Cretans rather appreciate it with gamy meats.

Because the valleys of Temenos and Pedias have far more vineyard land than that which yields appellation of origin red wines, other wines are also produced and bottled. Two of these, Regalo, from the Union of Peza, and Vilana from Miliarakis, are dry white wines which bear an appellation and come from the demarcated Peza area, Peza being the only one of the Cretan appellation districts that has an entitlement for white wine. The only variety authorized for appellation Peza white wine is the *vilána*, an old local type whose name dates to Venetian times and is reminiscent of the French *vilain*, going back to feudal times: *vilána* was a name given to a Cretan 'manor' of sorts. The attraction of Regalo, a soft, non-crisp wine of lightish body, is primarily in its aromatic savour when caught fresh, and not served chilled as though it were a *sauvignon blanc*. It is produced from choice *vilána* grapes and bottled without spending any time in wood; *vilána* is known to yield easily oxidized wines.

The Union of Peza's second-line red and white are 12.5° wines under the Cava 33 label (the number refers to 1933, the year the

Union was established). The red and white Cava are produced, respectively, from *kotsifáli* and a mixture of *vilána* and *rozakí*. Both are bottled at about one and a half years of age, after spending one year in oak. Red Cava 33, a rare all-*kotsifáli* wine, has an advantage for the short-term visitor in the very good quality it achieves by the time it is bottled. The Union also produces good ordinary red (*kotsifáli* and *mandilariá*), rosé (*kotsifáli*) and white (*vilána*) wines under the Logado label. In addition there is a retsina, made from *vilána* and *soultanína*, and called Ekavi after an ancient name for Crete. For its part, the Archanes Cooperative offers red (*kotsifáli* and *mandilariá*), rosé (*kotsifáli*), and white (*vilána*) wines under the Armanti label, all at 12°. As a threesome, they stand out in Greece as a second-line group of wines, and are notable for their marked regional character, particularly in their fleshy texture. Perhaps the fact that a second-line group can be so good is a true indication of the vaunted superiority of Arkhanes over Peza. Miliarakis Brothers also have a 13.3° red called Castello, made from *kotsifáli* and *mandilariá* and aged three years in barrel. Its 12.5° white counterpart, Minos Kava, is also aged in wood for three years. It is a fullish, firm and somewhat woody white made from *vilána, athíri* and *thrapsathíri*, a very old varietal combination, linked to Crete's former participation in the malvasia trade.

CLASSICAL REFLECTIONS

Inasmuch as it so obviously postdates the introduction of wooden barrels, the expression *i yéfsi tis doúgas* belongs to the modern era. Yet it may well reflect a particular outlook on the ageing of wines which the ancients shared, and which also has come down to the West at large through the term *rancio* – considered as a sensory concept, a notion of flavour, rather than as a particular wine-making process – whose epicentre is in the north-western Mediterranean basin, where Greek influence was pervasive in ancient times. *Rancio* literally means rancid, and it may be for that reason that English and French connoisseurs prefer to hear the notion alluded to in other than their native tongue. In employing the term *i yéfsi tis doúgas*, the Cretans too could be avoiding the suggestion of rancidness, but the Greeks once had exactly that word for it.

Perhaps the ancient Greeks did not want to attract bad luck by appearing to the gods as complaining of any surpluses that they might have enjoyed, but they nevertheless did not overlook qualitative changes undergone by the comestibles they were able to store:

> food prepared from new or freshly slaughtered produce – not only barley-cakes, legumes, bread, and wheat, but also flesh of animals fattened on this year's fodder, does differ in flavour from the old and is more inviting to those who experience and partake of it
>
> (Plutarch, Moralia, 'Table-talk')

They became keenly aware of the process of decay in particular, whose aromatic effects they referred to as saprós (putrid/rotten):

> Putridity [saprótis] however is a general term, applied, one must say, to anything which is subject to decay: for anything which is decomposing has an evil odour – unless indeed the name be extended to sourishness [oxýtiti] in wine because the change in wine is analogous to decomposition.
>
> (Theophrastus, Concerning Odours)

Indeed they had extended the word to wine, and by Theophrastus's time had built up around their notion of 'putridity' a technology for successfully ageing wines: 'there will be as much [wine] as we desire, and it shall be very [sweet-drinking], too, with no teeth in it, already grown mellow [saprós], marvellously aged' (Alexis, The Dancing-Girl, as quoted by Athenaeus in The Deipnosophists). 'Decay' in wine, as in all else, was attributed to the action of air – today we would say 'oxygen' – and wine, according to Plutarch, was thought 'of all things whose quality air alters . . . the most susceptible' (Moralia, 'Table-talk'). However, preventing wine's contact with air was not thought possible, or even desirable. The ancients' experience with olive oil, which they saw as a highly dense liquid practically impervious to air, convinced them that oil did not age well, precisely because its relative incapacity to interact with air caused its qualities to turn in on themselves, so to speak; thus oil, in Plutarch's words, gets 'stale', and not 'better', by long storage. On the other hand, some aeration might have favourable results on wine, since, as Theophrastus indicated, not all odours which occur in conjunction with 'decay' are necessarily noxious in and of themselves, or disagreeable to the human organism.

Ageing wine for beneficial change was seen in terms of guiding the 'decay' by controlling the wine's contact with air. The chief difficulty was presented by the porosity of the earthen jars in which wine was customarily kept:

> When our peasants are bringing corn from the country into the cities in wagons, and wish to filch some away without being detected, they fill earthen jars with water and stand them among the corn; the corn then draws the moisture into itself through the jar and acquires additional bulk and weight.
>
> (Galen, *On the Natural Faculties*)

To slow down the effects of oxygen on wine, the jars could be buried in the ground and then covered over with earth, 'so that', noted Plutarch, 'as little air [the destructive element] as possible may come into contact with them' (*Moralia*, 'Table-talk'). The ancients thus appear to have anticipated the much later corked wine bottle, and to have enjoyed a certain jar bouquet in place of our bottle bouquet. Yet even in cases where extraordinary means of slowing oxidation were used, the resultant wine was understood to have been undergoing 'decay', however slow and however slight the direct role of air, since the seeds of decay were seen as having been sown by that element in any case.

A particular kind of wine produced by calculated oxidation of some sort was that called *saprías*, whose name can be translated somewhat freely as 'rotter', although classicists usually prefer to give it as 'the mellow'. The specifics of its production are not known, but it is likely that it was aged for between ten and twenty years, since in *The Deipnosophists* ten and sixteen years are suggested as being sufficient for a 'well-aged' wine, while Pliny (*Natural History*) stated that wines meant for drinking, as opposed to cooking, appreciate in value only up to twenty years – depreciating sharply thereafter – and made no exceptions, either among Greek or Italian wines. At any rate, the fifth-century BC poet Hermippus, quoted by Athenaeus, praised *saprías* highly for such qualities of smell as we value in bouqueted older wines: 'from the mouth of its jar as it is opened, there comes a fragrance of violets, a fragrance of roses, a fragrance of hyacinth.' He may have been waxing poetic, not to say flowery, but *saprías* was clearly no 'rot-gut'.

SITIA AND DAFNES

Among its unique grape varieties Crete has one which apparently is of most considerable antiquity. Called *liátiko*, it is a red variety whose lineage goes so far back that Greek ampelographers regard one variant of it as the ancestor of the Corinthian grape used in Greece since ancient times to make currants. Its age also seems to be attested by the fact that it is planted primarily in eastern Crete, which is one of Greece's very oldest wine-making areas. The name is a shortened form of *iouliátiko*, which refers to the month of July. The term has been used generally on Crete to designate early-ripening fruit of various kinds, but the *liátiko* does in fact ripen in early July, which perhaps explains, at least in part, its popularity in eastern Crete. Dryness of atmosphere increases from west to east on the island, and consequently a very early ripening variety is appreciated in the east.

The district where the *liátiko* is predominant in vineyards is that known as Sitia, which takes its name from the harbour town of that name at the eastern end of the north coast. It is an extensive area that begins a little to the east of the point where the coastal road from Iraklion is met by the inland road coming from Ierapetra on the southern coast. The topography in the Sitia area is varied, and vineyards are found on differing types of terrain, at a range of altitude from near sea level to about 650 metres above. The hillside vineyards of the semi-mountainous country from Tourloti in the west, eastward to behind Sitia town, and then south through Maronia to Ziros, make up a zone whose wines can qualify for the Sitia appellation of origin for varietal *liátiko* red wine, dry or sweet. Presently, about 600–700 hectares of *liátiko* are cultivated at the sites belonging to the appellation, which in addition to the aforementioned ones are: Mirsini, Mesa Mouliana, Exo Mouliana, Khamezi, Katsidoni, Skopi, Akhladia, Piskokefalo, Papayiannades, Ayios Spiridonas, Khandras, Armeni, Apidi and Stavromenos. The character and quality of wine is fairly uniform in the appellation zone, with the notable exception of the mountain plateau of Agrilos, not far from the village of Exo Mouliana and above those of Mesa Mouliana and Mirsini, in the north-western strip of the appellation area. Apparently named for the clayey (*agrillódes*) earth that predominates on it, Agrilos is mentioned, in tones reserved for Le Montrachet and such, as the site of Sitian wine at its best. Presumably it was the source of that for which, as the locals tell it, Lucullus himself was a devoted customer so many centuries ago.

> The pine has been dedicated to Dionysus because it is thought to sweeten wine . . . Theophrastus attributes this effect to the heat in the soil, saying that in general the pine grows in clayey soil, and clay, being hot, matures the wine, even as it also yields the lightest and sweetest spring-water.

(Plutarch, *Moralia*, 'Table-talk')

Dry red Sitian wine entitled to the appellation of origin is being produced and bottled, primarily by the Union of Agricultural Cooperatives of Sitia, which turns out about 8,000 hectolitres of it annually, maturing the wine in oak for at least two, but usually three, years before bottling. Appellation regulations call for a minimum of one year. Some grapes from Agrilos go into the Union's appellation wine, but there is no economic stimulus as yet to produce a wine only from them. Inexplicably, the label Agrilos is being used to designate the Union's second-line red and white wines of very modest quality. The only other producer who bottles is Ioannis Kokolakis, who makes about 1,200 hectolitres of appellation wine annually, marketing it after one and a half to two years in barrel. Kokolakis owns his own vineyards, but only about one-tenth of the raw material for his wine comes from them. Mostly he buys grapes from other growers having vineyards on the mountain plateaux around Khandras, Ziros and Apidi, in the southernmost part of the appellation zone. Both the Union's and Kokolakis's appellation wines, respectively at 12.5° and 12°, are marketed under a Sitia label. Neither is vintage-dated.

Sitia has no exclusive claim to the *liátiko*. The variety apparently made its way westward on the island early during the centuries of the malvasia trade, when the *liátiko* became a variety used for that sort of wine. Another area where the *liátiko* is planted widely is south-west of Iraklion, in the Dafnes region, on the northern foothills leading toward Psiloritis. The vineyards there range around 300–400 metres in elevation, and are planted mostly with white varieties, owing to the area's one-time involvement with the malvasia trade. Nevertheless, there is a good deal of *liátiko* as well. The clones of *liátiko* are different from those at Sitia, however, and tend to produce somewhat higher yields. Also, because of lower sugar content in the grapes, the red wines of Dafnes are rather lower in alcoholic degree under traditional production conditions. Only varietal red *liátiko* wine, dry or sweet, is entitled to the appellation of origin for qualifying areas of twenty villages: Dafnes, Petrokefalo, Pentamodi, Ayios Mironas, Pirgou, Siva, Kerasia, Venerato, Avyeniki, Kato Asites and Ano Asites, as well as Prinias, Ayios Thomas, Douli, Megali Vrisi, Ayia Varvara, Panasos, Yeryeri, Ano Moulia and Larani further south. At present, nearly 400 hectares of *liátiko* are planted in the appellation Dafnes zone, but no appellation wine is being produced.

The only producer-bottler in the Dafnes region is the Union of Agricultural Cooperatives of Iraklion, or Agrunion, which makes about 7,000 hectolitres annually of regional red wine that it markets under the Malvicino label. A non-vintage-dated wine of 12.5°, Malvicino is matured in cement and stainless-steel vats for at least two years before bottling. Agrunion has not had the funds to procure enough barrels to enable a worthwhile quantity of wine to qualify for appellation status by giving it the requisite one year in oak. Without the possibility of making an appellation wine, Agrunion at present also takes the liberty of mixing into Malvicino some red wine grapes other than *liátiko*, especially *mandilariá*, which gives the wine a more reddish hue than it would have otherwise. Agrunion also produces a refreshing rosé and white pair, respectively called Rodolino (*liátiko* mixed with white varieties) and Domenico (*vilána* and *rozakí*). Both take very well to chilling. A retsina (*vilána* and *rozakí*) also appears under the Domenico label.It may be questioned whether El Greco – otherwise known as Domenikos Theotokopoulos, from the vicinity of the Dafnes region – would approve of this use of his name.

The *liátiko* is a dark red variety, but gives red wine of a colour likely to astound those who behold it for the first time. It is, in a word, orange – or at least as much so as other wines are 'red', 'white' or 'rosé': 'The Superior had exquisite wines brought for us, red, white, and orange ones, cultivated on the slopes about the Monastery [of Ayios Yeoryios, near the seaside town of Ayios Nikolaos], they merited our compliments by turns' (Savary, 1788). Home-made *liátiko* wines can actually be a quite bright orange because the skins are sometimes removed early during fermentation so as to improve the quality of the brandy made from the marc. Among the bottled *liátiko* red wines, the appellation wines of Sitia are dark orange, even brownish in some of the darker-coloured bottlings, though always with just enough red to keep one from calling them tawny. Not only is no violet exhibited as such, but a quite opposite tendency towards yellow can be discernible instead. Malvicino, although not without the orange inclination, is more of a light cranberry in colour. Considering the antiquity of the *liátiko*, as well as the ancients' fascination with the relationship between fire, sun and wine, I have wondered whether *liátiko* wine is such as might have been called *pyrrós*, or 'flame-coloured'.

It can be counted an extra blessing that the utter enchantment offered the eyes by the Sitian and Dafnian wines continues into the bouquet as well. The Sitia wines of the Union and Kokolakis, which I am in favour of drinking within two to three years of their bottling, present unusual fruity aromas, sometimes including a banana-like aspect, which differs from that possibly found in *kotsifáli* wines in being reminiscent of the fully ripe fruit. Sweet-spicy smells are evident, and with a touch of piquancy, rather like mace and nutmeg compared to cinnamon. When newly bottled, the wine has sometimes reminded me of banana or walnut bread. Malvicino, a usually less bouqueted wine, seems distinguishable in smell primarily by the absence of nuances of fruit evoking equatorial images. I have on several occasions found it developing a mixed smell of nutmeg and rose with a couple years of keeping. Ample acidity and tannic astringency keep all three of the *liátiko* wines lively from initial flavour onwards. On account of their aromatic flavour and usually somewhat fleshy texture, they lean more toward lusciousness than austerity, surely befitting Lucullus's image.

The bottled *liátiko* wines are very good with plain roast pork or fresh ham, and it is worth while looking for other pork stew to go with them: for example, Hungarian-style pork goulash with Malvicino. The Sitian wines might be reserved especially for pan-fried pork chops with spiced apples, or barbecued spare ribs with tangy sauce, although with such robust dishes I would particularly recommend very new bottlings. The *liátiko* wines do not go very well with tomato, but their texture, particularly at an early age, seems to absorb the astringency of lemon easily, making them good wines for grilled pork chops or veal escalopes served with lemon wedges. They are also suited to rich Greek dishes, including *mousaká* and the most succulent versions of *pastítsio*.

KISSAMOS

In addressing Crete, wine writers of the nineteenth century did not mention dry red wines from the areas of the island that contain today's appellation of origin regions. Instead, the Cretan area whose name is particularly connected with dry reds is that of Kissamos, an area in the far west, along the northern coast. Ironically, Kissamos today seems destined to produce its typical wines ignominiously – anonymously, so to speak – for no appellation of origin is in prospect. The predicament of Kissamos wine has been brought about by certain questions pertaining to the grape variety from which it is made.

The typical wine of Kissamos, and the one identified with the name, is a dry red vinified from the *roméïko* variety, which is thought to have been brought to western Crete by the Venetians, though from elsewhere in Greece rather than from Italy. *Roméïko*, which means 'Romaic', refers to the name by which the Greeks came to call themselves after they were incorporated into the Roman Empire; the nineteenth-century traveller Pouqueville noted that the Greeks no longer called themselves 'Hellenes', but 'Romans'. Some parts of southern Greece became associated with the geographic term *Romanía*, derived from the same source. There were even Greek wines that were traded under the latter name in modern times, such as a red from the island of Zakynthos, in the Ionian Sea. Those wines, however, may have had no particular connection with the *roméïko* variety. However it reached Crete, the *roméïko* eventually spread over virtually all the western part of the island, to the point where today it covers about four-fifths of vineyard area there, or more than 2,000 hectares.

The *roméïko* is especially predominant on the low, undulating land, mostly only 100–200 metres above sea level, in the vicinity of Khania (Canea) and Souda Bay westward to the town of Kissamos (or Kastelli) at the head of Kissamos Bay, where it is planted to the near exclusion of other varieties. A major reason for the *roméïko*'s absolute supremacy is its remunerative yields, especially on low-lying areas of relatively deep soil. Also, it is a rather late-ripening variety, usually mid-September to mid-October, which offers the attraction of high sugar content in the grapes, thus assuring a high alcoholic degree in the wine. In the past, high alcohol content was considered desirable for preserving the wholesomeness of the wine as it matured in barrel prior to commercial sale. And Kissamos was most definitely a traded wine, notwithstanding the early nineteenth-century wine writer Jullien's statement, apparently based on the word of a Western visitor, that it was 'not an object of commerce' because the cost of shipping it to the port of Khania for further dispatch was prohibitive.

Greek enologists have two objections to the *roméïko* which for the time being preclude the granting of an appellation of origin entitlement, or even 'country wine' (*topikós ínos*) status, to the traditional red wine of Kissamos. One objection concerns the tendency towards relatively high yields. Although that tendency is strongly influenced by the site where the *roméïko* is planted, attempts at restriction could face difficulties. Notably, were plantings to be proscribed in the higher-yielding areas, the political wrath of winegrowers adversely affected by it would likely be incurred, inasmuch as western Crete is less developed than other parts of the island and has relatively few alternative sources of farm income. Indeed Kissamos growers have indicated a willingness to try a variety that might yield 'better' wine, but only on condition that the substitute offers yields as satisfactory as the *roméïko*.

The other objection to the *roméïko* pertains to the colour of its grapes, and that of the red wine made from them. Generally, *roméïko* grapes are of a bluish-red colour, for which reason the variety is also known as *mávro* (black) *roméïko*. However, the grapes are often considerably lighter, even pale. Bunches of them sometimes display greenish yet fully developed berries mixed among the darker, a tendency which accounts for the variety's colloquial name *loïsima*, which can be roughly translated as 'mottler'. As a result, *roméïko* grapes processed for red wine have measurably, and frequently visually, relatively little of the anthocyanin content that gives the colour usually desired for red wine. The question is not without its subjective side, however, and one might sense that the real concern of Greek enologists as regards the colour of *roméïko* wine is its saleability on the world market.

Objections to the *roméïko* notwithstanding, another voice is quietly speaking out in favour of the variety. Perhaps inspired by the good name of Kissamos wine, Greek ampelographers are out to do something about what Professor Ulysses Davides, their doyen, sarcastically refers to as 'the colour defects, so-called, of the *roméïko*'. Having worked in the Kissamos region for several years, Professor Davides is among the most knowledgeable of Greek wine professionals on the subject of the *roméïko* – far more so than any of the Greek enologists who would cast it into the Sea of Crete. He emphasizes that the variety has a great many clones, even compared with other Greek varieties notorious for their number. The clonal population exhibits significant differences in a variety of traits, ranging from yield tendency to anthocyanin content. Identifying those *roméïko* clones showing less productivity and a higher level of anthocyanins is the first step in overcoming the existing 'problems' with red *roméïko* wine, but the clonal selection programme did not get under way until after 1980. Once the preferable clones are isolated, it will be possible to spread plantings of them, and then make wine only from them, or possibly in combination with some small proportion of other varieties yielding darker red wine. Professor Davides stresses that 'modern enology can work miracles', but miracles can sometimes require financial wherewithal, and a question mark remains over this in the Kissamos region. In any case the ampelographers will have to hurry because the enologists are already mentioning such figures as a maximum of 60 per cent *roméïko* in wines eligible just for country wine status, with the rest coming from *carignan, grenache* and possibly *mandilariá*, or else solely from *carignan* and *grenache*.

It certainly must have been the variegated aspect of the *roméïko* that suggested to growers the making of variously coloured sorts of wine from it. In the Kissamos region one can virtually run the gamut of vinous colours, and all in wines made exclusively from *roméïko*. To begin with, let us note emphatically that there are reds with a perceptible violet tendency that would explain descriptions of Kissamos wine as 'claret' in nineteenth-century wine literature. If made in the rustic way, by fermenting on stalks, they can be very tannic. Rosé wines are also made from *roméïko*, but inasmuch as they are made by the same method as for red wine, though from more lightly coloured grapes, they can be quite tannic relative to what we are accustomed to in rosé. The most unusual of the coloured wines of Kissamos is a type known as *marouvás* which is an oxidized and somewhat more potent sort of *roméïko* wine that deposits much of its red colour as it ages. *Marouvás* has some similarities with sherry-type wines, and can serve well as an aperitif. Finally, dry white wines are made from the *roméïko*, probably originally to make expedient use of poorly coloured *roméïko* bunches. They tend to be rough in feel as white wines go, even when made according to contemporary white wine technique. Greek enologists report that this is due to the characteristically very high phenolic content compared with wines made from other Greek and foreign white varieties, and rather wryly note that the *roméïko* for that reason, if for no other, cannot be a candidate for sparkling wine production.

The commercial wine output of Kissamos is handled largely by the Central Union of Khania, under which four cooperative wineries operate: at Khania, Maleme, Kolimbari, and Kissamos. Additionally, the privately owned firm of Koutsourelis has been active. Both work exclusively with the *roméïko*, and produce both red and whites from it. I shall mention the whites only in passing: Clos de Creta from the Union and Kissamos from Koutsourelis. The coloured wine most likely to arouse the curiosity of visitors is the limited production Marouvas of the Union, made in a quantity of about 50 hectolitres annually, and matured in oak for four to five years before bottling. It could possibly be mistaken for Sitian wine by any but the most regionally versed eye, at least if no Sitian wine were standing next to it. However, Marouvas is yet more lightly red, and more yellow as well, than Sitian. At 14°, it is an apotheosis of gliding texture in heady, full-bodied dry wine. Some might even think of it as 'sweet' on that account, I suppose. The Union's 12° Roméïko is distinctly redder and lighter in body, and feels drier. Considerably darker than Roméïko is red Kissamos from Koutsourelis, a 13° wine aged up to five years in barrel. Even Sitian wine, entitled as it is to an appellation, is not so red – there is real violet in Kissamos – even if it is perhaps as dark in its particular way. None of the Kissamos wines are vintage-dated at this time.

MALVASIA

The renown of Cretan wine may be said to have reached its zenith in modern times, for it was while the island was under Venetian control that its name spread farthest among wine-drinking countries. The vehicle for Crete's reputation then was the wine known as malvasia, or malmsey, a type of sweet wine that became a major export from the southern Aegean to Western Europe in the thirteenth century, and which remained important until the nineteenth. Although Crete was not the original source of wine called by that name, it later became the most significant producer and shipper – so significant in fact that some Western visitors to the Aegean came away with the mistaken impression that Crete was the only source of it.

Greek malvasia wines have been disparate as regards both their place of origin and their preparation. With reference to geographic origin, it is to be noted particularly that although the 'malvasia' name itself refers to a specific place, not all wine called by that name was actually grown there. The name comes from the town called Monemvasia, founded in the late sixth century by the Byzantines, and situated on an islet appended to the coast of the south-eastern Peloponnesos, due west of the Cycladic island of Milos. Vines were cultivated on the shore of the mainland opposite, and documents of the thirteenth century show that the wines produced there were traded under the name 'Monemvasios'. On Venetian tongues the town's name was transformed into 'Malvasia' and applied to the wines as well. Because of its key position between East and West, Monemvasia became something of an *entrepôt*, and shipped westward wine similar to its own that had originated elsewhere in the Aegean. Consequently all wine of that type exported from there was called 'malvasia' by Western traders, and their 'appellation' made its way back to the various places producing it. Prominent among those were Crete, Santorini, Paros, Tinos, Rhodes, and even northerly Khios. Some early travellers mistakenly considered the malvasia name to be derived from Ariousia, via 'Arvisia' and similar corruptions of the name of that famous Khiote wine area.

The commercial importance of Monemvasia began to decline around the end of the fourteenth century, when the West converted to types of ship that could not be safely accommodated in the harbour. Local wine production fell off as a result, and was sharply curtailed following the occupation of the Peloponnesian shore by the Ottomans in the late fifteenth century, which occasioned the departure of many inhabitants; by the time Thomas Wyse paid a visit in the mid-nineteenth century, the local folk knew nothing of malmsey. Crete, still under Venetian control, took over as the trade centre for malvasia, and also became by far the largest producer-supplier. The malvasia name continued to be used in spite of the geographic shift, and was actually reinforced by the circumstance that the area to the south-west of Iraklion producing the most, and by some reports the best, Cretan malvasia had become known as Malevizi, a name which may have related either to the area's past involvement with malvasia production or to the nearby fortified position that the Venetians dubbed *mal vicino*.

From the point of view of viti-viniculture, too, malvasia wines have historically shown some considerable variation. As with geographical provenance, however, parameters can be specified. Malvasia has usually been sweet or semi-sweet wine, but produced by varying methods. The super-maturation of grapes on the vine was probably the typical means of augmenting sugar content in the must. However, no concrete evidence rules out the possibility that harvested grapes were also dried in the sun. The must may occasionally have been cooked as well. Certainly that technique was known in ancient times, and at some places on Crete malvasia was cooked a little prior to being shipped, with the intention of temporarily stabilizing it, as Greek malvasia was *not* a fortified wine, at least not during the heyday of the trade. Not all malvasia was sweet, however. Venetian documents relating to Crete indicate that a dry kind of malvasia, *malvasia garba*, was known, if perhaps only on Crete; in 1553 the traveller Pierre Belon related that usage of the term *garba*, which he gallicized as *garbe*, equated to the French terms *rude* (astringent) and *verd* (tart).

The grape varieties used for malvasia have also been various. The diversity is particularly apparent in the fact that while malvasia wines have generally been white, a red kind is also known. Yet it is in the matter of varietal composition that the unifying theme of Greek malvasia wines manifests itself. For the fact is that the varieties upon which the wines have been based all have distinct varietal aroma, though not of the 'aromatic' muscat family; old Greek and Venetian sources differentiate malvasia from muscat wines, although the two types were confused by some early Western visitors. Instead, the varieties for malvasia are of 'semi-aromatic' type: the white *monemvasiá, aïdáni áspro, athíri, thrapsathíri, vilána, takhtás* and *triferá*; and the red *liátiko, ladikinó* and *mávro aïdáni*. The multiplicity of non-muscat varieties used for malvasia accounts for, and is verified by, the disparity among non-muscat vines now cultivated in Western Europe, but originally brought from Greece, that bear names mentioning malvasia.

Typically, Greek malvasia wines have been based on a mixture of two or three of the named semi-aromatic varieties, possibly with still others, including both non-aromatic and aromatic (muscat) sorts, used to a minor extent. Etymological evidence substantiating the mixing of varieties is manifest in two old colloquial terms from the southern Aegean areas connected with malvasia, *logádo* and *xenólogo*; their root is in the ancient verb *légo*, meaning to gather, which has given rise to a number of words suggesting variousness of kind, in the sense of a collection or assortment, much as in the case of the *loïsima* synonym of the *roméïko* grape variety. On Crete, the term *logádo*, connoting 'of assorted kind', was used to describe wine of diverse varietal origin, and also a vineyard planted with several grape varieties other than the primary ones of a site, such vineyards usually being the source of *logádo* wines. On Santorini, the term *xenóloga*, connoting 'odd kinds', is used to distinguish the diverse varieties – 'odds and ends', as it were – other than the two grape varieties mostly used for wine-making on the island, while the very closely related term *xenólogo* was formerly used as an alternative name for malvasia, since the *xenóloga* varieties were the source of that wine.

Vineyards were usually planted with the intended mix for malvasia in mind. Thus, although the varietal mixture for malvasia has ever been a movable feast, it has followed a pattern from place to place. That circumstance accounts for the otherwise seemingly haphazard varietal composition found in some vineyards of the southern Aegean today, above all in the Cyclades. In central Crete, malvasia has usually been produced from a mix of *athíri*, *thrapsathíri* and *vilána* (one might in this context compare the contemporary Cretan wine Minos Kava to the *malvasia garba* of old); in eastern Crete, a mix of *thrapsathíri* and *takhtás* was typical; in the Cyclades, it was usually some proportion of *monemvasiá*, *aïdáni áspro* and *athíri*. A notable exception to the habit of varietal mixture has been red malvasia produced from the *liátiko* variety, which must necessarily be vinified as a fully varietal wine, since the *liátiko* ripens too early to have companions in the vat.

The varietal composition of the malvasia wines, being founded mostly on very old Aegean types, admits the possibility that the same kinds of wine as some of the non-Monemvasiote wines which came to be traded as 'malvasia' may actually have been in production since long before their acquisition of that name. However, that is less likely in the case of those made in the Cyclades largely from *monemvasiá*, the 'malvasia' grape proper, a variety that almost certainly spread from the south-eastern Peloponnesos just because of intentions to imitate the wine first called 'malvasia'.

In this century malvasia has so receded in importance in Greece that it is now of no commercial significance. Since the Second World War and the subsequent population exodus from the southern Aegean area, malvasia wine has also lost ground in the living folk tradition. Indeed, even the tradition of the wine's name, which is *malvazía* in Greek, has been fading from popular memory along with the wine itself. Yet there is no compelling reason for the absence of bottled Greek malvasia on the world wine market. The southern Aegean still has a capacity to produce it commercially, especially red malvasia from Crete, which may have been the only place where much of the red kind was formerly made. For that matter, both the region of Sitia and that of Dafnes are entitled to produce appellation of origin sweet red wine, unfortified or fortified, exclusively from the *liátiko*. But where are the Luculluses today to demand it?

GASTRONOMIC NOTES

Kazantzakis's scenes of Crete can undermine stereotypical images of Aegean agriculture and cuisine: for example, the pig seems to be in constant evidence. There are those unforgettable scenes from *Freedom or Death* in which those attending Captain Michalis's several-day wine orgy are plied with *loukániko* (pork sausage), or that from *Zorba the Greek* in which the freshly neutered pig seems to have a bestial comprehension of the nature of the delicacy being enjoyed in the farmyard by his owner and the guests. Crete has in fact appreciated pork since remote antiquity – and has always managed to enjoy a good supply of it, thanks to an abundance of foodstuffs such as acorns with which to feed the creatures. Some unusual preparations of pork are to be found, such as baking it and returning it to the oven with a yogurt sauce.

The spices used in Cretan cooking can be unusual compared to the rest of the Aegean. On the one hand Crete has held on to some traditional Greek flavourings for meat dishes, like coriander and the more unusual caraway ('hare stewed with fresh onions and caraway seeds', *Freedom or Death*). On the other hand it has a particular penchant for exotic spices, and perhaps black pepper most of all. Crete was introduced to Eastern spices earlier than most of the rest of Greece, and millennia before the Ottomans arrived with their wrongly supposed all-pervasive influence on Greek cookery. Moreover, the spices are used in combinations that mark the island dishes as different even when they are otherwise of generic Greek type. Indeed some Cretan preparations could, if encountered blindly, be identified as dishes from further east than Crete.

Crete grows many fruits and vegetables, and is well known for a number of them both in Greece and abroad, but perhaps most of all for its *rozakí* table grapes, especially those from the eparchy of Iraklion, and citrus fruits, particularly the mandarins of the Khania plain. As in other parts of Greece, the natives also have special praise for certain local fruits, some of which are available only in relatively small quantity. Particular mention might be made of the chestnuts of Kissamos, the cherries of Yerakari, in the eparchy of Rethymno, and the muscat grapes of Temenia, in the Sfakia district of south-western Crete. Temenia is also known for its muscat wine. The island claims the quince as its very own: its Greek name is *kydóni*, and the ancient name of Khania, where it mostly grows, was Kydonia. The ancients used quince in their cooking, even with meat dishes, and perhaps especially with game, a habit which has not been entirely forgotten by Cretans of the present day. Another curiosity of Cretan horticulture is the island's banana trees, which grow mostly along the south-eastern coast, and produce a dwarf banana (greatly disparaged by the Athenians).

The olive tree is grown nearly all over Crete, but the island oils and table olives are generally not counted amongst the foremost of the Aegean. Nevertheless, some locales of central Crete (Vasilies, Viano) and eastern Crete (Sfakia, Ayios Stefanos) are very well regarded for their oil, while Apokorono, as the area around Khania is called, is known for a speciality oil, *agourólado*, produced from unripened olives. The eparchies of Iraklion and Lasithi also have good eating olives, especially at Vasilies in the first instance and Males in the second. The mountain plateau of Nida, by Psiloritis, provides an unusual small black olive.

The cheeses of Crete earn marks as first-rate, and fortunately some types are widely available commercially. Cow's-milk cheeses from Ambelouzos and Ayia Deka, above the plain of Messara in south-western Iraklion, are well known. Among ewe's-milk cheeses, those of Ligortinos in south-eastern Iraklion, Zenia in north-western Lasithi, Males and Mythi in south-western Lasithi, and Ziros in south-eastern Lasithi, are especially sought. The semi-hard ewe's-milk *kefalotýri* and soft *myzíthra* cheeses of Yerakari, produced in caves in the Kedros Mountains, as well as Anoyia's goat's-milk *anthótyro* ('blossom-cheese'), have special reputations. Both places are in the east of Rethymno. Cretan yogurt is also generally praised, but particularly that of Vrysses, in the eparchy of Khania.

Game is plentiful in the numerous mountainous areas of Crete, and the same is true of fish in the lesser populated parts of coastal areas. However, the Kedros Mountains are especially abundant in hare, partridge and wild pigeons, while the areas of Paliokhora and Vaï, respectively in the far south-west and far north-east of the island, yield plentiful fish, especially mullet (*lethrínia*) and sea bream (*fangriá*) at Vaï.

The islet of Gavdos, Greece's southernmost possession, lying south of the Sfakia district of Crete, affords greatly prized sheep, fed on cedar fruit and briny vegetation. The Gavdian barley bread called *pakhoúda*, made of only partially ripened barley, is very much appreciated for its special flavour, and may conceivably be a Minoan recipe.

4

Santorini

─────

Barren, waterless, and windswept is the earth of Santorini. Because of that, even its production per hectare is small. However, all of its products without exception (perhaps because they are dry-farmed or 'on account of the volcanic nature of its earth') are remarkable and famous. But first and best is its wine: Santorinió krasí *by name.*
  Filipos Katsipis, 'From the Chronicle of Our Plain' (in *Santoríni*, ed. M. Danezis),
1971.

Situated along the northern rim of the Sea of Crete, about 70 miles north of Iraklion, is a crumb of land which is arguably the most remarkable vineyard in all the Dionysian realm – Santorini, or Thira.

A visitor might well expect Santorini to produce extraordinary wine, for nothing at all about the place partakes of the ordinary. A crescent of cliffs, which looks as though it had been hacked out with one fell swoop of an Olympian axe, walls in the island's bay on the north, east and south, while the islet of Thirassia is a barrier along the north-west. The bay itself is unusual, being a caldera and harbouring a dormant volcano. Santorini's appearance and nature owe their origin to the cumulative effects of the catastrophic volcanic activity that has overwhelmed it several times since the ancient era. While some consider that Santorini may be the legendary Atlantis, there is no question but that an eruption of a former volcano on the island around 1500 BC, which is thought to have been the largest volcanic eruption in recorded history, precipitated the decline of the Minoan civilization by force of the destruction it wrought on Crete. Other major volcanic eruptions and earthquakes have struck since. Notably, in 1649 and 1650 a great frequency of strong seismic activity culminated in the appearance of a volcano out of the sea about 3–4 miles to the north-east of Santorini. Sending forth exhalations of igneous material and sulphurous smoke, the volcano coloured the sea a bright green with the dust of the spewed debris, and clouded even far-off Constantinople. The various eruptions have added to Santorini layers of volcanic material with which the island's fruits may be infused, and in effect dictated to the inhabitants that the very essence of Santorini should be their wines. The result is emphatically, as one travelled Santoriniote wine-grower says without the least exaggeration: 'Santorini's wines cannot be compared to any others in Greece or in Europe. They are entirely "of their own kind".'

The vineyards of Santorini do not file down from an Etna-like volcanic summit. The one-time peak was blown off in the eruption of 1500 BC that left the caldera. Instead, the island's cultivated area, including its vineyards, sprawls out across a plateau that slopes from about 300 metres above sea level on the west, where the multicoloured, nearly perpendicular cliffs ring the caldera, to sea level on the east, where Santorini's black stone beaches are found. The ground itself is perhaps the most bizarre to be seen at any wine site, and can be likened to the mock-up of the moon's surface on display at the National Air and Space Museum in Washington, DC. The generally unseen base of chalk and shale has been covered over by ash, lava and smashed pumice stone, so that one might imagine, in looking at the ashen greyness of the vineyards, that the vine could be made to yield fruit on the surface of the moon, if only there were sunlight, oxygen and a drop of water. Owing to the special needs for nutriment arising from these environmental circumstances, the spacing of vines, at 2–2.5 metres apart, is more or less double that found in most of Greece. And yet the plant is nevertheless stressed to the limit.

Winds have blown so forcefully over Santorini since 1500 BC – the olive tree, which thrived until then, has ever after been able to grow only in a few sheltered places – that the inhabitants developed a practice of training the low-lying vines into the form of a basket, actually called a *stefáni* (crown), to assure survival in the winds during the fifteen to twenty years of growth the vines require before they can support themselves. After that period, the practice can be discontinued in the depressions the Santoriniotes call 'amphitheatres', but in raised areas, which are particularly threatened by wind, the 'crown' is maintained throughout the life of the plant. The winds also tend to dry up what moisture might otherwise be taken up from the insular atmosphere. The only water the plants have is that released at night by the island's layer of china clay, which manages to absorb some moisture from the air. Equally important during the very warm ripening period is the preclusion by the winds of condensation on the grapes themselves. In this way acidity in the fruit, far from being lost, on the contrary fully keeps up with the mounting sugar content, rarely surpassed elsewhere in the Aegean.

The leading grape variety of Santorini is the white *asýrtiko,* which accounts for about 70 per cent of vineyard area. It is traditional only on Santorini, which is a rather unusual occurrence in Greek viticulture and would seem to lend credence to suppositions that it arrived from abroad in recent centuries, although its exact derivation is not known. One old Santoriniote explanation is that the *asýrtiko* arrived from the Jerez region of Spain, but this has not been the subject of systematic ampelographic research. The lore on this point presupposes that the variety's name was derived from the Greek version of the name 'sherry' or *sérri: asýrtiko* would signify 'sherrian' in that case. Yet it is also possible that the Jerez/'sherry' region may have been referred to by those who gave the *asýrtiko* its name because the relatively tannin-rich white wines oxidize easily. When *asýrtiko* grapes are high in sugar content their always high content of aromatic substances soars, and they can then be elaborated to produce unfortified wine analogous to sherry. The *asýrtiko* ripens on Santorini in mid-September and is remarkable for its cooperation with a native 'super-strain' of yeast in producing wines of as high as 18° natural alcohol.

Another 20 per cent of Santorini's vineyards are planted with the black *mandilariá*, which can succeed unusually well under the local conditions. The remaining 10 per cent is taken up by some forty other sorts of grapes, all of which are used more or less frequently in wine-making, but most of all the whites *athíri* and *aïdáni áspro* (the latter surely must be the *edáni* grape mentioned by the lexicographer Hesychius around the fifth century AD) which are often significant in a varietal mixture. The island's varietal make-up heavily favours the making of white wine, which in fact comprises nearly 80 per cent of Santorini's production. Largely in consideration of that, Santorini, including Thirassia, is an authorized appellation of origin zone for qualifying dry or sweet white wines produced from the varieties *asýrtiko, athíri* or *aïdáni áspro*, in any combination, or individually, although fully varietal *athíri* or *aïdáni áspro* wine is most unlikely to be made.

'The Santoriniotes', wrote the eighteenth-century resident French priest Abbé Pègues, 'well understand how to fabricate their wine.'

Their cellars must have afforded them the chance to observe and consider the matter. Traditionally, Santorini's wines have been made in small cellars hewn out of the pumice stone known locally as *áspa*. Structures almost identical to the cellars were used for animal quarters as recently as the nineteenth century, and were very likely once indistinguishable from human dwellings. The overlap of purpose can be understood from the very sound resistance such structures have to earthquakes, and from the stability of temperature they provide. *Áspa* structures are cool in the warm weather, while requiring no heating in the cold months, and so are quite capable of providing a very healthy environment for the long maturation of wines to which nature guarantees abundant alcohol, acidity and extract. The traditional cellars are now going out of use in favour of more modern facilities, however.

The most usual type of traditional Santoriniote wine is that which goes by the generic name *broúsko*, a name acquired during the time of Venetian rule on the island, from the thirteenth to the mid-sixteenth century. *Broúsko* may be white, red or rosé. *Asýrtiko* supplies by far the greater part of the must for white *broúsko*, which is expected to have an incipient brownishness that the native writer Katsipis describes as 'cinnamony'. However, other white varieties are included as well, especially the *aïdáni áspro* because of the esteem in which its aromatic qualities are held. For red *broúsko*, the *mandilariá* is most important, but other black and red varieties are also used, and often some *asýrtiko* is added; not all Santoriniote reds conform to Greek conceptions of 'black' wine. Rosé wine, of which there is only a small quantity, is made from a mix of white with black and red grapes, mostly *asýrtiko* and *mandilariá*, but in a proportion much to the detriment of red colour in the wine. In the traditional Greek eye the rosé may none the less qualify as 'reddish'; *erythróxantho*, literally 'red-blonde', is the term usually heard on Santorini.

Under traditional conditions, it has been customary to collect the bulk of the grapes for *broúsko* wines in the crushing basins of the cellars for two to four days before wine-making gets under way. Traditionally crushed by foot – today's major commercial producers generally use mechanical equipment – these grapes go into the vats to ferment with the skins and stems for an extended period. The musts typically ferment out to about 16°, but 17° is not uncommon. Because of the long contact of the juice with the skins after harvesting, the wines thus produced are somewhat astringent – even the white wines, since the *asýrtiko* is relatively tannic. The high level of overall non-sugar extract content, in combination with high acidity, also makes them slightly coarse, and all the more so if they happen to be made from later pressings of the grapes. This is how these wines acquired the *broúsko* name, which signifies 'rough'. Some Santoriniotes maintain that maturation in barrel over several years is traditionally considered indispensable for *broúsko* of any colour, but they are indicating an exceptional one. In practice, traditional *broúsko* wine accorded a lengthy barrel maturation is usually made from free-run must and destined for family consumption and preferred customers. However, whether matured this way or not, *broúsko* wines can be of resounding excellence, if even then unlikely to attract every favourable descriptive wine term currently in vogue. Santorini is that special.

Another type of Santoriniote dry wine is the one traditionally called *nyktéri*, a name which may be best translated as 'the night one'. The late nineteenth-century Cycladic explorer James Bent related that it takes its name from the expression *tis nyktós* or 'of the night', the grapes for it being picked before sunrise, so as to enhance flavour. The thinking behind such a practice would seem to be a relic of ancient times, when apparently considerable attention was paid to the time of day at which edibles were to be gathered or hunted, the object being to enjoy peak flavour. The tendency was so widespread then that it moved Horace to wryness: 'After this he informed me that the honey-apples were red because picked in the light of the waning moon. What difference that makes you would learn better from himself.' Lucian quotes Eucrates telling of a vintage season, when 'passing through the farm at midday, I left the labourers gathering the grapes' (*The Lover of Lies*), from which we might assume that daytime collection was the norm and anything else extraordinary. Greek enologists today know for a fact that dawn harvesting of grapes in the Aegean generally is desirable if fresher-tasting, less oxidation-prone dry white wines are to be produced. Still, Bent's explanation of *nyktéri*'s name is refuted by present-day Santoriniotes. Their explanation is that the choice grapes used are processed on the same day they are picked – a practice also recommended by the enologists – which entails working into the night in the cellars. Indeed the Aegean idiom 'to do *nyktéri*' means 'to work late'.

Nyktéri is always white. Its typical varietal make-up is *asýrtiko* with admixture of *aïdáni áspro* and *athíri*. As with white *broúsko*, fermentation is on stems and skins, but in this case same-day processing of the select grapes results in a colour which Katsipis has described as 'whiter even than retsina'. Or as another old-timer has expressed it, *nyktéri* 'shouldn't have colour'. These descriptions are meant to indicate yellow colour devoid of any brownish nuance, and that seems to be the essential visual expectation for *nyktéri*, in spite of the five years or more of barrel maturation regarded as necessary if the wine is to have been worth the extra effort in harvesting and vinifying. Generally, *nyktéri* is somewhat lower in alcohol than a white *broúsko* would be under traditional production conditions, because of the speedy processing of the grapes, but 15° is usual.

Santorini's uniqueness is vivid in its ultra-sweet *visánto*, a wine that has carried its Italian name only since Venetian times. Its tradition is doubtlessly far older. In age-old fashion, the well-ripened grapes are spread in the sun for one to two weeks, according to seasonal conditions, which is probably what caused the Venetians to think of *vin santo*. After the grapes have darkened to a state called 'half-baked' (*misopsiména*), the grapes are crushed by foot. Fermentation is on skins and stems. Owing to the exceptionally high sugar content, the must undergoes a very slow initial fermentation, lasting about fifty days. A decade in barrel is quite usual for maturation, but even then a *visánto* reaches only 8–9° alcohol. *Visánto* can be white, red or rosé, but Santoriniotes solidly grounded in their wine-making tradition are agreed in specifying that the basic island varieties, *asýrtiko* and *mandilariá*, are the foundation for true *visánto* wine, and this is confirmed by Pègues's eighteenth-century report. Depending on the colour of the intended *visánto*, white (*áspro*) or black (*mávro*) *aïdáni* usually has a role as well. Sometimes *athíri* grapes, again white or black, the latter sort being called *mavrathíri*, are also included.

Perhaps because neither all Santoriniotes nor all of their customers ordinarily cared to have a wine as sweet as *visánto*, a less sweet offshoot also developed in island tradition. Colloquially called *médzo*, from the Italian term *mezzo* (medium), but more formally referred to as *imíglyko* (semi-sweet), for the sake of other Greeks, that wine is produced in either of two ways. Must of fresh grapes and 'half-baked' ones may be mixed half-and-half, or all of the grapes may be 'baked' half as long as for *visánto*. Alcohol is usually at 15–16°.

Another traditional sweet wine is *malvazía*, or *malavazías* as it is called on Santorini. It differs from *visánto* with respect both to varietal make-up and treatment of the grapes. Unlike *visánto*, a true *malvazía* is based on varieties other than *asýrtiko* and *mandilariá*, and always several of them. Indeed, *malvazía* was once also known on the island as *xenólogo*, a term connoting 'from various kinds', much as *xenóloga* is the term by which the island's many minor varieties are collectively called. Another divergence from *visánto* is that the formation of high sugar content in the grapes is achieved mostly or entirely by super-maturation on the vine. If sun-drying is used, it is only for a minority of the grapes, and usually for *aïdáni áspro* in particular, the must from which is subsequently added to the wine of the other grapes. The wine obtained in either case is a fully sweet one, but always less sweet and of higher alcohol degree, 15–16°, than *visánto*. However, almost nothing is heard of *malvazía* on Santorini now. A very few wines which are substantially just that are still produced, but post-Second World War reports on *visánto* by non-Santoriniote wine professionals suggest a tendency towards fusion of the *visánto* and *malvazía* concepts in the mind of some Santoriniote wine-growers in recent decades. It is notable particularly in the use of the island's less usual varieties as the basis for wines produced more like a *visánto* than a *malvazía*, and therefore called *visánto*. Also, true *malvazía* is occasionally called *visánto* if some of the harvested grapes have been sun-dried.

At present, Santorini's commercial bottlers are also facing pressure to accommodate the singular nature of true Santoriniote wine to more conventional tastes. The dilemma in this 'internationalization' of Santorini wine, which lies in making the accommodation without forfeiting the remarkable character of the best traditional wines, is especially acute with respect to dry wines. On account of the high alcohol degree of the traditional wines – *broúsko* and *nyktéri* – Santorini's bottlers found it difficult to persuade outsiders to try them as mealtime beverages more than once. Visitors would sample them, but found them 'deliciously treacherous', to quote one comment, since their vibrant acidity and unmatched aromatics effectively throw a deceptive mask over the wines' potency, as the unsuspecting newcomers subsequently discovered. Consequently, the dry wines now produced for bottling are mostly what might be thought of as modified *broúsko*: wine made along the general lines for *broúsko*, but with earlier harvesting of the grapes so as to produce wine of restrained alcoholic degree. In dry white wines in particular, the traditional distinction between *broúsko* and *nyktéri* seems to be eroding as well. Needless to say, perhaps, the bottlers, who in any case generally evince little interest in appellations of origin, do not all share the viewpoint of those professionals at the Greek Wine Institute who argue that appellation regulations for Santorini should be revised to require a minimum of 15° alcohol for dry white wine.

The bottling of wine on Santorini is something of an innovation, and does not go back much before the 1970s, although sporadic attempts were made in earlier decades. The perseverance of the bottlers at this time, however, is of special importance because it offers the chief hope of bringing a halt to the ongoing abandonment of the Santorini vineyard. In the mid-nineteenth century, when Russian demand for Santorini's wine was at fever-pitch, around 4,000 hectares were producing. After Russian demand subsided early in this century, an alternative to wine-growing on Santorini appeared in the form of a dwarf tomato plant that gives a paste of extraordinary flavour, so that without the aid of phylloxera, vineyard area had fallen back to about 3,400 hectares by 1950. More recently the tomato-processing industry has sharply retrenched, and yet wine-growing, far from taking up the slack in the island's economy, has continued on an increasingly rapid downward spiral, owing to emigration, the lure of the tourist industry and rising labour costs. Currently, only about 1,500 hectares of vines are producing. Some Santoriniotes direly predict the eventual disappearance of vines altogether if labour costs continue to gain on wine prices, a sad prospect indeed for the island that has yielded the earliest pictures of clusters of wine grapes of modern type, on an earthen vessel dating to about 1500 BC.

Competition between bottling wineries could possibly reverse the deteriorating profitability of vine cultivation. Six wineries are currently producing and bottling. The largest is that of the Union of Agricultural Cooperatives of Santorini Products ('Santo'), which until very recently had confined itself to wine expressly made for blending purposes. In the mid-1980s it undertook the production of wines for bottled sales, beginning with a threesome of red, white and rosé wines of 13°, all on the Vedema label; '*vedéma*', another term left over from Venetian times, is the island word for 'vintage'. A better white, three years old and of 14°, was marketed on the Irini label. A dry white appellation white of 14° was put out in 1987.

Called Santorini, it is made from *asýrtiko* (80 per cent), *aïdáni áspro* (10 per cent), and *athíri* (10 per cent). It was initially produced in a quantity of less than 100 hectolitres. Altogether, the Union produces about 40,000–50,000 hectolitres of wine annually, of which only about 20 per cent is being bottled. Future plans envisage a complete refurbishing of the winery, and a considerable expansion of bottling activity, with budgetary aid from the EEC. At present, the Union has no barrels, and matures its wines in cement tanks.

The Koutsouyanopoulos Brothers own the largest of the privately run bottling wineries on Santorini. It is a family wine business dating back to 1886, though only to 1974 in bottling. Grapes are bought in from numerous island wine-growers, but about 10 per cent comes from the family's vineyards. The winery produces 4,500–5,000 hectolitres of wine annually, of which three-quarters is white. That bottled as Volcan is three-year-old white *broúsko* of the new sort, while that called Lava has only one year in barrel. These are excellent white wines of fullish body, even if it is 'too much to say that there is an eruption in every bottle', as one traveller said of some other Santorini wines a few years back. Koutsouyanopoulos produce no *visánto* or other sweet wine, in line with their stated intent to be geared to tourists' tastes, which they have divined to be for the dry as well as the tamely alcoholic. All of the Koutsouyanopoulos wines are in the range of 12° alcohol.

The Markezinis winery, located in Messaria, has been bottling since 1971 – the family has been in wine since 1827 – and produces about 1,500 hectolitres annually. About 80 per cent of the wine is white, the best of it thus far having been Santinos white, a somewhat amber, nascently pinkish *broúsko* in the new fashion (12.2°), with fullish body. Despite the winery's emphasis on white wine, its outstanding products have been dry red and rosé wines from the *mandilariá*: Santinos red (12.2°) and Cava Atlantis rosé (13°), both produced from free-run must. The latter wine was to be the fore-runner of a series of reserve white, rosé and red wines that should be very well worth the small premium that will be asked, if one judges by the rosé, which takes rosé wine to previously undreamt-of heights, though at the expense of the 'lightness' some seek in this type of wine. The plain Atlantis series has been the winery's line of lesser-quality and lower-alcohol wines. Considering Markezinis's knack for spotting excellent *mandilariá* grapes, it is to be regretted that no red *visánto* is produced at his winery, but he personally does not relish *visánto* of any colour.

Canava Roussos is another old family operation, dating back to 1836; *kánava* is the Santoriniote term for 'cellar'. Based in the seaside village of Kamari, Roussos has been bottling since 1974, producing 500–600 hectolitres annually of various wines, none of which is in quantities of more than a few hundred litres each in the year of production. About 60–70 per cent of the raw material comes from the family's vineyards. Roussos is for the most part a stickler for tradition, right down to having the grapes crushed by foot, at least in so far as traditional wine types are concerned. The top products of his winery, Nykteri and Visanto, attest to the value of this practice, though I would not necessarily attribute their quality to the use of feet in particular! Roussos's flights of fancy also tend to be inspired by tradition, as in the case of a sweet red Mavrathiro, a 15° wine produced from sun-exposed *mavrathíri* and *mandilariá* in about equal proportions, and matured in barrel for more than a decade before bottling. Canava Roussos wines were the first of the island to appear with vintage dates.

The smallest of Santorini's bottling wineries is that of the Venetsanos Brothers, located in the village of Megalo Khorio. They have been bottling since 1970, but the family has been involved in the wine trade since the 1840s. About 500 hectolitres of wine are bottled annually under the Ven-San label. Nearly 400 hectolitres of it is white *broúsko* (loose definition) and *nyktéri*. White *imíglyko* wines are also produced. Even the white *broúsko* stays in barrel ʿ-- almost a decade, emerging with exceptional flavours typical of the style, with the exception that, again, at around 12°, the sensations are not the most traditional for *broúsko*. The view of the elderly Venetsanos brothers, however, is that what is central to the Santoriniote tradition of *broúsko* is not a specific degree of alcohol, but rather the method of collecting the grapes, a fermentation on skins and stems, and an appropriate maturation of the wine. These, they say, are what gives the wine its requisite and inimitable aromatic character.

Most recently, a winery has been erected on the island by the Boutari firm of Macedonia. Its production in the future is likely to be second only to that of the Union in quantity, although its first bottling, in 1988, from the 1987 vintage, was of a minor quantity of white appellation wine produced on a trial basis. It was made entirely from *asýrtiko*, and marketed under a Santorini label.

As can be gleaned from this survey of Santorini's bottled wine output, the great majority is dry white wine. Just about any individual wine could be highlighted to the advantage of the island's name, but, in view of tradition as well as quality, I am inclined to single out Nykteri from Canava Roussos. One of the most fully yellow dry wines around, Nykteri's richness of colour is reflected most of all in the deep yellowishness it holds even at the outermost rim of the glass, with no tendency to brownishness. Only its lustre hinders perception of that richness. Matured for six to seven years in barrel, the 13° Nykteri has both a bouquet of honeyed fruit and a characteristic earthiness of smell, unique to Santorini, that seems to lie where garlickiness links up with smokiness. In the mouth, Nykteri is full-bodied, with ample fleshiness of texture to balance a kind of tactile edge not encountered in other dry white wines at its lofty level of quality. Many would mistake it for a red in closed-eyes tasting; it is not alone among Santorini's whites in that respect. Nykteri should be considered especially as an accompaniment to smoked fowl, roast kid and *cassoulet*, and goes well with garlicky dishes generally. Nor do ripe Fontina, Brie and blue-veined cheeses overwhelm Nykteri.

Something must also be said of the disinherited Santorini wines, the reds, which are not entitled to an appellation of origin. When the appellation regulations for Santorini were drawn up in 1971, Greek enological authorities regarded incentives for increased planting of the black *mandilariá* as undesirable, because it might occur at the expense of the *asýrtiko*, which is considered more typical of Santorini, and generally more crucial to wine quality there. Also, some Greek wine professionals sought to keep red wine out of the island's entitlement because of a negative bias rooted in the circumstance that during most of this century island red wines have mostly been *broúsko*s literally made to order for blending. Based on that commercial necessity, it became an almost axiomatic belief among some non-Santoriniote Greek wine specialists that nothing of high quality could be expected of Santorini in the way of dry *mandilariá* wine. Yet back in the days before Santorini was reduced to a source of blending-wine, Western travellers in the Aegean knew the island to have the capability of yielding excellent dry red. For instance James Denman, who seems to have been the only nineteenth-century wine writer ever to visit Santorini, testified to it in one of the more puzzling wine descriptions on record: 'The best red growth is called Santorin, and being dry, spirituous, and agreeable to the palate, a rich Claret in character with a genuine Port-wine flavour, well sustains the high reputation it has acquired' (*The Vine and its Fruit*, 1864). But anyone who tries to describe Santorini's wines tersely can sympathize with Denman's predicament.

Markezinis and Roussos have been experimenting with dry red wine with a view to producing outstanding products at a level of alcohol content below the traditional range. Markezinis's Santinos red is a *mandilariá* wine of 12.2° alcohol, matured for four to five years in oak, while the Cava Atlantis red that he plans will have more age at bottling, and more alcohol. Roussos has concentrated his efforts on Caldera, a 13.5° *mandilariá* wine aged for six to seven years in barrel. Santinos and Caldera are dark ruby in colour, certainly among the darkest wines bottled in the Aegean. The medium-bodied Santinos is the easier to drink at the time of bottling, although it has repaid several years' keeping. Caldera is full-bodied, with a notable astringency which some will find distracting until the wine has at least several years of bottle-age. At any age, however, to serve Caldera at all chilled is liable to prove a disappointing experience. On Santorini, try Santinos red or Caldera with a plate of the island's fava beans, to enjoy the flavours of Santorini in all their glory, or else with the stuffed eggplant dish *papoutsákia* (slippers).

Canava Roussos is the only island winery to have bottled *visánto* wines recently. A rosé version has particularly impressed me. It is obtained from *mandilariá* with admixture of *asýrtiko* and *aïdáni áspro*. Fermentation takes place with stalks and stems, and bottling comes about a decade later. Like all *visánto*, Canava Roussos's rosé is so sweet that most people can only take it in small doses, and even then only by intermittent sipping. It tries the patience and thirsty gullet of some ('some people feel most impelled towards wine when the drink they most want is water', Plutarch, *Moralia*, 'Table-talk'). A few perhaps will find it impossible to take to the sweetness at all. The Englishman Bent called *visánto* 'abominably luscious', and even the Santoriniote Markezinis disparagingly calls it 'a syrup'. One should, however, try the wine at various ages before making such inflexible judgments.

Canava Roussos Visanto rosé at first baffles the taster who expects familiar rosy shades, and never so much as when newly bottled, for then it presents a brownish-orange hue approaching reddishness, while also working towards a golden-green at the rim. It is a most finely structured progression of tints. Aromas associated with those of dried stone fruits like apricots and prunes are plainly in evidence; in suggesting a comparability between *visánto* and Commandaria, Edmond About described the latter as becoming brown with age, and resembling prune juice in flavour as well as colour ('amateurs often pay very dear for putting into their cellars, that which they might have for nothing from their kitchens'). But there is much more to Visanto's bouquet than the browning of fruit sugars. Like so many Santorini wines, it displays distinctive 'earthy' smells which have no remote approximation in the wines of other places. In due course, a bitterish tone also appears, together with the aftermath of acidity fostering a sensation reminiscent of limes.

Perhaps the most amazing thing about Visanto is that it has an alcohol content of only 8.5°. It is nevertheless unassailably, consummately, vinous. Elsewhere in the wine world, the particular phenomenon of low alcohol and imposing vinosity has been recorded only at Tokaj, and there only in the case of genuine *essencia*, a wine (or syrup?) which would only be sold for a king's ransom. Yet Canava Roussos Visanto can be purchased for next to nothing, or scarcely more drachmas than one would pay for a bowlful of limes, prunes and dried apricots. It goes on in bottle indefinitely, too, albeit mellowing as it goes, which will not, I suspect, be preferred by everyone. A considerable sediment is thrown even if Visanto is kept only several years, so that it usually needs decanting, and preferably two or three days ahead of time if older than fifteen years or so altogether. Enjoy a glass with an unpeeled peach, or a slice of that rather liquid American confection from pecans, which tenuously slips by under the rubric 'pie'.

CLASSICAL REFLECTIONS

Among the written works remaining from antiquity there is none corresponding to a modern popular book on wine, and the information about wine that is available to us in the ancient record usually is not presented in a way that relates the nature of specific wines to particular wine-making techniques. The result is that it is most difficult to compare a specific wine of modern Greece to one of the ancient era without over-indulging in speculation about ancient wine and falling into the trap of self-delusion. However, there is an exception, and it pertains to *visánto*.

Drying grapes in the sun has been employed virtually throughout the Aegean since antiquity. The drying takes place on a specially suitable surface called a *liástra*, or 'sunner', which is the *iliastírion* of antiquity; the wines which result from the vinification of those grapes are then called *liastó* (sunned). Usually the *liástra* is a particularly suitable spot among the vineyards and fields. On Santorini, however, although the latter sort of *liástra* is not unknown, the typical kind used in making *visánto* has been the flat rooftops of the traditional cellars. Moreover, the rooftop position of the grapes is protected by a low wall built all around the perimeter of the roof. Alternatively, the grapes for *visánto* are 'baked' in enclosed courtyards by the cellars. In view of all this, but especially of the placing of grapes in a raised position, it is nearly impossible not to recall the ancient Greek wine called *diákhyton*, mentioned by the Roman Pliny:

> a wine called in Greek 'strained wine' ['diachyton' (*sic*)], to make which the grapes are dried in the sun for seven days raised seven feet from the ground on hurdles, in an enclosed place where at night they are protected from the damp; on the eighth day they are trodden out, and this process produces a wine of extremely good bouquet and flavour.
>
> (*Natural History*)

Yet what is most relevant to *visánto* in Pliny's mention of *diákhyton* is that he identified that wine as belonging to the class of wines falling 'between the sirops and real wines'. Also included in that class were *aigleucos*, or 'Ever-must', *prótropon*, or 'First-urged' (the wine produced from the juice expressed by the weight of the grapes themselves), and wine produced from honey and must. The wines concerned would have been distinguished not only by their relatively high sugar content, but also by their relatively low alcohol content, which would have been occasioned by the very great concentration of sugar in the indicated musts, and a consequent greatly burdened fermentation. And then, too, 'real wines' for Pliny were those of relatively high alcohol content, an exemplar being Maronean, which he noted was drunk with twenty parts water in Homer's time, in order to temper the alcohol. In this regard it must be noted as well that Aegean *liastó* wines, including ones so called on Santorini, are of 15–16° alcohol, rather than the 8–9° of *visánto*.

Visánto is probably the sort of Greek wine most likely to engender musing about ancient wines on account of its own features, rather than just one's own propensity to do so. For as it ages, *visánto*'s tremendous vigour subsides, so that the taster becomes most conscious of its viscosity, and in that way is reminded of wines the ancient writers mentioned as 'sweet' and 'thick'. Indeed, a twenty-year-old bottle of Canava Roussos Visanto might be decanted, with a bit of it then being left in the decanter for two weeks or so, at which point it bears an equal volume of water in such a way as pleasurably to recall Aristotle's statement that 'well-mixed wine obscures all perception of water, and only gives a sensation of soft wine' (*Problems*).

One school of thought has it that the ancients doted on wines so thick as to demand mixture with water if they were to be drunk, rather than ingested as an early form of Greek 'spoon sweets'. Pliny is often cited in that regard, since he mentioned 200-year-old wines which had been 'reduced to the consistency of honey' (*Natural History*). But it is just as frequently overlooked that he also went on to say that those wines were unpleasant to drink even if well watered, and instead were reserved 'as a seasoning for improving other wines'. It is Aristotle, however, who really sets the record straight, by mentioning wine among the 'watery liquids' which are 'affected by drying [evaporation]' (*Meteorologica*). Elsewhere he even cast aspersions on the winehood of sweet wines, so that it must be doubted whether they were of such great popularity as has often been assumed by historians of wine:

> Why do not men become drunk under the influence of sweet wine, which is more pleasant? Is it because sweet wine has a flavour which does not belong to wine, but to something else? The man who is under its influence [that is, has become drunk on it] is therefore rather fond of the sweet than fond of wine.
>
> (*Problems*)

Aristotle may have identified that 'something else' as excessive 'oiliness', since in *Meteorologica* he notes that oil 'gives off fumes but does not evaporate'.

In considering the ancients' attitude towards the sweetest wines, it is useful to refer to Hippocrates. He explained that what is uncompounded in taste is 'strong', since it is undiluted and unopposed, and by definition necessarily 'painful', because it works on the palate rather in the way of a primal force:

The strongest part of the sweet is the sweetest, of the bitter the most bitter, of the acid the most acid, and each of all the component parts of man has its extremes . . . for there is in man salt and bitter, sweet and acid, astringent and insipid, and a vast number of other things, possessing properties of all sorts, both in number and in strength. These, when mixed and compounded with one another are neither apparent nor do they hurt a man; but when one of them is separated off, and stands alone, then it is apparent and hurts a man.

(*Ancient Medicine*)

To avoid the pain of unmitigated sweetness in wine, resort was often made to the use of flavouring substances; Theophrastus noted that sweet wine, 'because it has no "relish" of its own', is especially in need of the savouriness of a well-chosen additive (*Concerning Odours*), much as we might 'spike' stewed plums with mace. Hence the appreciation that would have been felt for any sweet wine with sufficient 'relish' of its own:

the mixed [savour] is pleasanter than the unmixed, if one can achieve perception of both elements at the same time. For wine is pleasanter than oxymel because things mixed by nature are more completely blended than when mixed by us. For wine is a mixture of bitter and sweet flavour. The so-called wine-pomegranates prove this.

(Aristotle, *Problems*)

But even more to the point, so does Santorini's *visánto*.

5
Paros and the Cyclades

There can be no doubt whatsoever that Paroikia is built on the ruins of the ancient Pariote capital . . . there is a church dedicated to the Drunken St George. Here, I thought, must be a true descendant of Bacchus; an instance of how the Greeks still love to deify their coarser passions; and on enquiry I was told that on November 3, the day of the anniversary of St George's death, the Pariotes usually tap their new-made wine and get drunk . . .
(James Bent, British traveller, The Cyclades, 1885)

Sometimes it may seem as though no stretch of Winedom has been left uncharted, and that no true adventures are left for the wine traveller. All the more reason to approach the Cyclades and happily prove oneself wrong: these islands are almost always left off wine maps today. Named for the circle (*kýklos*) they seemed to form around the holy island of Delos during antiquity, they comprise around twenty significant islands that spread south-eastward in rather angularly arranged clusters from off the seaward tip of Attica, which is Sounion, into the mid-southern Aegean, beginning with Tzia (Kea) and ending with Amorgos.

There is no little irony in the obscurity of the Cyclades at this late date, since it was an area to which Dionysus formed a particular attachment at a very early time. Cycladic wine exports were so considerable during antiquity that the first-century BC Roman agriculturist Columella, in his *De Re Rustica*, indicated them as a reason for Latium's preference to import wine rather than cultivate the vine in his day. The productivity of the Cyclades continued through Byzantine times, and into recent centuries as well. Cycladic wines also went westward in modern times, although few Westerners who drank them were aware of their origin, since the Cyclades were an important source of malvasia, a wine usually sold only under its

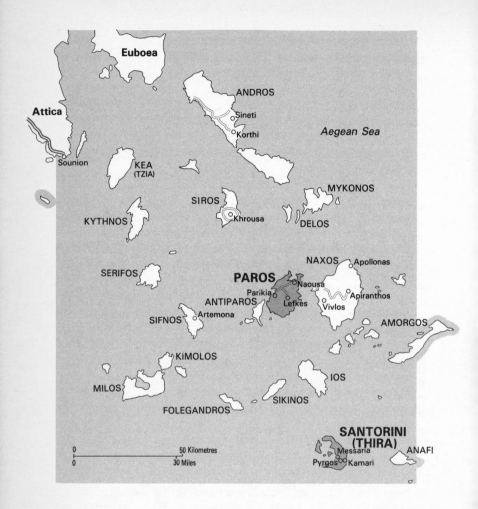

The Cyclades

generic name. In the nineteenth century, however, the Cyclades
drifted ever further towards the periphery of the European economy,
becoming increasingly dependent on the West and constrained to
export what was asked of them. After phylloxera struck France,
what was asked of the Cyclades was blending-wine. In the twentieth
century, distantly headquartered Greek wine companies, no more
concerned than their Western counterparts about encouraging the
best efforts, joined in patronizing the Cyclades.

PAROS

While the legacy of blending-wine production still hangs over the traditions and name of the Cyclades, a breach has been made in its formidable walls. This has been achieved at Paros, a largish member of the group that lies far closer to its geographical centre than does Delos. Paros was a prestigious producer of malvasia, but none the less, or perhaps all the more, targeted by the blending-wine buyers. In recent decades, sales of blending-wine for the making of generic Greek rosé wines for export westward have been the mainstay of Pariote viticulture. The island could hardly have looked forward to any other role in wine, until improved Greek economic conditions in the 1970s, and perhaps most of all the influence of tourism, opened up other possibilities. The bottling of wine was undertaken, and in 1981, contrary to what anyone expected of Paros a decade earlier when Greece had provided for the granting of appellations of origin, the island was elevated to appellation of origin status on the basis of a type of dry red wine which combines the best of island traditions with technologically sound, contemporary enological practice. It is indeed cause for Bacchic revelry in the Cyclades.

Weather conditions on Paros more or less typify those which influence Cycladic wine-growing generally. Although characterized by an absence of rain during the growing season, the Pariote climate is somewhat humid, but variably so from year to year, so that annual conditions for grape maturation vary as well. Air currents do not have the profound impact that they have on Santorini, but breezes can be stiff, and have influenced traditional vine cultivation techniques. Apparently in order to protect young shoots from the breezes, the stocks of the vines are typically encouraged to grow at a sharp incline, so that the tendrils will creep along the ground. Such tendrils, called *aplotariés* (spreaders, but perhaps more accurately described as runners), can reach up to 5 metres or so in length. Consequently grape clusters, too, grow by the ground in such instances ('All the vines about Lesbos, being neither high-grown nor propped with trees, incline themselves and protend their palmits towards the ground, and creep like the ivy; so that indeed a very infant, if that his hands be loose from his swathes, may easily reach and pull a bunch,' Longus, *Daphnis and Chloe*, second to third century AD).

Varietal make-up on Paros is also very typical of the Cyclades, all of the varieties grown being usual ones for this part of the Aegean.

The blending-wine trade appears to have had a serious negative impact on Paros's varietal profile, however, in that it favoured the unbridled spread of the tannin-rich black *mandilariá*, a variety not entirely well suited to the island. Judging by the *mandilariá*'s predominance even in old vineyards in the upland interior of Paros, it may be supposed that it has long been the major variety. Still, without a crucial commercial role it is unlikely that the *mandilariá* would have achieved the 85 per cent hold on island vineyard area that it had in the years prior to the Second World War. Because it is a relatively late-ripening variety, in this case planted in an environment where a humid summer can delay ripening and cause rotting, the *mandilariá*'s performance is markedly variable from one year to the next at all island sites, irrespective of their exposure, elevation and soil composition. It was perhaps in empirical recognition of the idiosyncratic behaviour of the *mandilariá* on their island that tra-ditional Pariote wine-makers attentive to quality have taken care to limit its role in their wines, especially dry red ones. Its usefulness for blending enabled the *mandilariá* to gain ground none the less, and also stimulated planting of it on low-lying, poorly drained soils, unsuitable for the production of quality dry red wine in any year.

While the *mandilariá* was extending its territory, Paros's chief white variety, the *monemvasiá* (usually called *monovasiá* by grow-ers), was in decline. The variety's name, which is that of the place on the Peloponnesian coast to the west where malvasia was once made, suggests an arrival on the island in the late Middle Ages, when the malvasia trade began to grow in importance. For malvasia production, grapes high in sugar content were needed, and the *monemvasiá* suited the purpose ideally, being an early-ripening sort that continues to increase in sugar content for virtually as long into the Pariote growing season as it is allowed to remain on the vine. When grown at relatively higher elevations on the island, and cultivated well, the *monemvasiá* is capable of yielding high-quality wine of a sweet and alcoholic nature, yet not lacking in acidity. The loss of the malvasia trade and the later uptake in the blending-wine trade, however, caused both a loss in plantings and less careful tending of the *monemvasiá*. Finally, without a real economic role the variety lost still more ground in the post-war period, when the higher yielding *savatianó* was brought from the mainland.

The historical circumstances of island viticulture encouraged an assortment of habits among island wine-makers. Some of the most popular are unacceptable from the standpoint of contemporary, world-standard wine-making. Notably, the practice of letting the *monemvasiá* gain as much sugar as possible during maturation, in order to increase alcohol content in the wines, and thus disease-resistance as well, results in wines both overly alcoholic and deficient in acidity for cosmopolitan tastes today. Also, to obtain drier-tasting white wines from those grapes, some Pariotes started adding water to the must, which has the effect of reducing acidity along with sugar content. Some islanders, however, have made wines from a mix of red and white grapes, a practice also encountered elsewhere in the Cyclades. When the wines are made skilfully from properly ripe grapes, the results can be very admirable. The Greek Wine Institute, in considering the awarding of an appellation of origin to Paros, therefore chose that strain of Cycladic tradition. Consequently the appellation regulations for Paros call for a dry red wine produced from a must that is two-thirds *monemvasiá* and one-third *mandilariá*, with the proportion having to be measured in terms of grape weight, since *mandilariá* grapes and *monemvasiá* must are combined in the vat for vinification. Until 1989, however, a proportion of half and half was permitted in order to allow time to extend plantings of the *monemvasiá*.

The Wine Institute's main partner in developing the appellation requirements was the Union of Agricultural Cooperatives of Paros, with its headquarters at the chief island town and port of Parikia. The Union produces 25,000–30,000 hectolitres of wine annually, from various parts of the island. Nearly two-fifths of the must comes from the western coast, in the vicinity of Parikia, while another fifth comes from the Naousa area on the north-eastern coast. Both areas are predominantly low-lying, at less than 20 metres above sea level. By common consent of the Pariotes, the best wine grapes come from the mid-island village of Lefkes, whose steeply inclined, north-east-facing vineyards are the highest on Paros, at 300–400 metres. But Lefkes is a relatively small producer, and the Union purchases only about 5 per cent of its grapes there. Additionally, about one-tenth of the Union's must originates on Antiparos, Paros's sister island just off its south-western coast; Antiparos is not included in the appellation Paros zone. Growing only red wine varieties, Antiparos produces some of the best *mandilariá* grapes, which probably explains the nineteenth-century visitor Bent's having tasted an 'excellent wine' there, but also the variety called *váftra* (or *vápsa* (tinter) for its coloured pulp. The *váftra* gained ground in the late nineteenth century, when Bent noted Antipariote wine being 'sent to France to make claret with', an instance of the sort of 'incentive' that has particularly contributed towards keeping the Cyclades 'down on the farm' in the twentieth-century world of wine.

The Union has mostly produced, and continues to depend on, wine for blending. Furthermore, in so far as it has bottled, it has been constrained by financial considerations to concentrate on sound wines of average quality, especially the trio of its Trovatore series: a white (*monemvasiá*), a rosé (*mandilariá*) and a red (*mandilariá* with a little *váftra*), all at 12° alcohol. Only the medium-bodied Trovatore white would be likely to attract a second look from abroad. More recently a red called Madon has appeared, intended as a step up from Trovatore red. A Retsina from *savatianó* is also produced, as well as a dry white called Nisiotissa, which is made from lesser *monemvasiá* grapes from some of the better vineyards of the semi-mountainous area. Nisiotissa is the Union's vain attempt at crispness, for which a price I deem too high is extracted from the wine: the absence of the discernibly Pariote character that requires no self-justification.

The wines produced and bottled by Manolis Moraïtis, who operates his winery at Naousa, bottling nearly 4,000 hectolitres annually, have generally been more attractive than the Union's wines. Over two-thirds of Moraïtis's wine is the product of his own vineyards and those of a number of other growers around Paros from whom he buys grapes. The rest is must bought from the Union. Moraïtis's better red and white wines are under the Kavarnis label, at 12° alcohol. Lagari is the label for his second-line pair, at 11.5°. Kavarnis white is made in about equal proportion from *monemvasiá* and *savatianó*, a very usual mix for home-made whites on Paros these days. Like Trovatore white, Kavarnis white has the acidity and aromatic flavour to place it among the 'fresh and fruity' white wines of Greece, although unfortunately it is not crisp. In favour of Moraïtis's medium-bodied Kavarnis red, I would say it is very good red wine by any standard, and was the best bottled red of Paros . . . until the Union came out with its appellation wine.

The Union made the island's first appellation wine, Paros, from the 1981 vintage, in accordance with the dispensation pertaining to the proportion of *mandilariá* and *monemvasiá*. The wine was marketed by the Botrys firm of Attica, with due attribution to the Union on the label. Paros is a 12° wine that is bottled after spending about fifteen months in barrel. The Union expects to turn out about 5,000 hectolitres of appellation wine annually in coming years, after adding the storage space needed to give that much wine its required year of maturation in oak. The addition is currently being implemented, in part with funds channelled from the European Community. Production of 8,000–10,000 hectolitres is hoped for in the more distant future, but that could well prove over optimistic. For one thing, the Union is liable to have competition in producing appellation wines. Moraïtis says that he will produce an appellation wine, and the Macedonian firm of Boutari has already produced and marketed a small amount of appellation Paros wine, a 12.5° wine under their Paros label, on a trial basis.

A more basic constraint on the production of appellation wine on Paros is the need for a very extensive replanting with *monemvasiá*. At present, the ratio of output between *mandilariá* and *monemvasiá* is approximately 3:1, which is rather the reverse of what the appellation requirement calls for. It is hoped that an increase in price offered for *monemvasiá* grapes will stimulate plantings, and certainly the competition of three major bottlers should help in that direction. The administrative step of halting plantings of *savatianó* has also been taken so as to benefit the *monemvasiá*. At present, over 800 hectares of vineyards are cultivated, but there is most definitely room for more, notably on the 200-metre-high ridge to the rear of Parikia. The island has not suffered phylloxera's ravages, but the ridge's extensive vineyards were devastated by a fire a couple decades back, and tourism, which tends always to be a double-edged knife for Greek wine, has in the meantime assumed such significance in the Pariote economy that viticulture must take a back seat to the service industry. However, another factor hindering optimal output of the appellation wine is the difficulty in finding suitably ripened grapes of both the *mandilariá* and *monemvasiá* varieties to be harvested the same day, a practice found to produce the best wine for the contemporary world market.

One might not expect a wine with the varietal make-up of appellation Paros red to be *really* red. Nevertheless, the Union's Paros is indeed a most dark red, despite the removal of the *mandilariá* skins after only two days of fermentation. It ought to be emphasized, however, that it is a definitive *red*ness, just short of that truly violet cast which generally qualifies Pariote red wines as 'black' in the islanders' eyes, although it could be said that Paros offers a colour quite like the darkest flesh of 'black' cherries exposed by a bite. Aromatically, the newly bottled wine displays several facets: berry fruits, sweet spices and balsamic smells, all in their sweetest manifestation. Perhaps the strongest tug is in the direction of sweet spices, which seems to be the case with Pariote red wine generally. Several years of bottle age weave the several aromatic threads more closely, but the wine is eminently drinkable right at bottling, even by people without much taste for tannic red wine, and that is perhaps the best time at which to experience and enjoy the very characteristic feel of Pariote wine. Paros is soft initially, because of texture, and remains unobtrusive on the sides of the tongue throughout the duration of a mouthful. Yet, it is not at all flabby. Does it have anything to do with island morphology? Bent wrote that Paros, which enjoyed singular fame for its marble during antiquity, 'is nothing but one huge block of marble covered with a thin coating of soil' – a not entirely accurate depiction – and Pliny mentioned that the ancient Greeks sometimes added marble dust to wine to make it softer. But at rock bottom, the influence of the Pariote bedrock on the island wines is a mystery to me.

If the elegance of marble does not rub off on Pariote wine, Paros none the less is quality dry red wine that would not disgrace tables with more elegant veneers than formica. Some people might find in it the advantage of a chameleon-like quality as an accompaniment to food: its property of varied flavour sensations, so evenly arranged within the whole, that the wine remains recognizably itself even as one detects the equilibrium of sensations shifting this way or that under influence of the food. I have therefore been unable to persuade myself that some intrinsic quality might cause beef, lamb, pork, or even chicken to be the preferred meat with Paros, although, perhaps overlooking that even marble can be ground to a fine dust, my reckoning is that newcomers to the wine will spot its merits the better with certain ground meat dishes, such as *soudzoukákia*, which are minced meat rolls flavoured with cumin and served with a special tomato sauce. I will cautiously mention meatloaf too, hoping not to disparage Paros by doing so. I might really sabotage its prospects for respect by recommending, with a view to side dishes for meatloaf and such, that here at last is a red wine suited to everything about the essence of beets. Less controversially, I would suggest a variety of cheeses, especially semi-soft ones. Havarti, Edam, Gouda and Munster perhaps have an advantage when flavoured with caraway, cumin or cloves. Mild varieties of the Cheddar family nevertheless seem as good, and one need not carry home bottles to check on it. I have no idea what cows are doing in the Cyclades, but at Prodromos, on the eastern side of Paros, the cooperative dairy uses local cows' milk to produce a very good, semi-hard cheese distinctly reminiscent of Cheddar types. The differences of kind can be attributed to the influence of marble on the cow's forage.

In the future the Pariotes would like to see an extension of their appellation entitlement. It is believed that Pariote dry white wine can be deserving, but given the present shortage of *monemvasiá*, a move in this direction would spell decreased production of the more typical red. Furthermore, in order to meet contemporary tastes a new method of vine cultivation, most likely entailing a system of high-trained vines, might have to be inaugurated at least in some areas of the island. On another front, the Union is hopeful of gaining Paros an appellation for semi-sweet red wine from sun-dried grapes, a type of wine in which Paros is deemed to have advantages. In Lefkes, where it is averred that the best is produced, up to fifteen or sixteen varieties of grape, most of which are planted to only a very minor extent, are used for it, but always with *mandilariá* dominant. After spending about one week in the sun, the grapes are crushed and the must fermented with the stems as well as the skins. The wine is sometimes made and kept in chestnut, in order, it is said, to obtain the preferred darker colour. The 16° semi-sweet wine is popular in part because of the feeling of warmth it engenders in the cold weather, when most of it is drunk, beginning in November as Bent mentioned back in 1885.

THE CYCLADES

The wine explorer setting out to tramp the Cycladic donkey lanes and goat paths leading to such vinous treasures as remain could benefit from some advice, since it is all too easy to miss what one should be looking for, or else to mistake what one has found. Most of the Cyclades have not been touched by phylloxera, and the vineyards that have survived emigration, which has been an implacable foe of viticulture in this century, still reflect the complex varietal history of the islands. As a gross generalization about the Cyclades, it may be said that the varieties *mandilariá, monemvasiá, athíri* and *aïdáni áspro*, the last three of which reflect past involvement with malvasia production, are widespread, and tend to be more or less significant where they are found. However, Greek ampelographers have identified over sixty-five varieties in the Cyclades to date, and others besides the aforementioned ones can be quite important locally. The varietal confusion is not helped by the fact that the vineyards are planted with a multiplicity of varieties, but substantial conformity to a pattern is discernible at individual sites.

Two circumstances can throw wine buffs off the scent of local tradition. First of all, it is possible to run across anomalous wines, that is, ones whose occurrence is exceptional and the result of special circumstances. This would have happened to me at Lefkes on Paros had I not known beforehand that I was looking for semi-sweet red wines. I met a fellow who was producing a superb semi-sweet white wine in the malvasia tradition, the explanation for which turned out to be that he was a native of Naxos who had married into Lefkes and planted the vineyard his wife brought as part of her dowry with white varieties, so as to produce the sort of wine he had known on his native island. It is also possible to encounter one kind of wine virtually everywhere on an island and assume that it is *the* island wine, when in fact another kind from a particular village is traditionally the most esteemed wine, though so little is now made that nothing is heard of it by visitors. This can happen notably with retsina. Although resinated white wine is found virtually everywhere in the Cyclades today, possibly even to the exclusion of other wines in some places, it is not truly traditional. Bent came upon retsina only on Kythnos among the Cyclades in the late nineteenth century, and an elderly wine-grower on Paros told me that production there does not go back more than forty years or so. Retsina seems to have spread along with the *savatianó*, the usual mainland variety for this wine, since the Second World War.

A selection of Cycladic ports of call could usefully begin with Mykonos, which is as much the hub of the Cyclades for hedonists today as Delos was anciently for the religious. The stories tourists usually swap about the place are of interest to a wine traveller in so far as they reveal bareness as being as characteristic of Mykonos now as in antiquity, when Strabo noted the great frequency of baldness among the inhabitants. The islanders perhaps were already guilty anciently of crimes against Dionysus for which divine retribution was brought down on their heads. Anyhow, Tournefort alleged that what was sold as wine on Mykonos was 'mostly coloured water', while a century later Galt wrote that although there was a celebrated dry red resembling Bordeaux to be had, its producers 'will rather cheat you than give it genuine'. It might be unfair to consider such practices peculiar to Mykonos, and indeed Tournefort used his experience there to support his contention that the Greeks at large 'cannot forbear playing their tricks'. More recently, Philip Sherrard has considered that alleged Greek trait:

> Talented, versatile, indefatigably active, subtle, and insinuating, they prefer obtaining their object by intrigue and stratagem to gaining it honestly by industry and perseverance, in neither of which qualities, however, are they at all deficient.
>
> (*The Pursuit of Greece*, 1964)

We shall leave the Greeks to a perhaps uncharacteristic soul-searching, pondering the rewards of industry and perseverance in the new era that seems to be opening for them, but visitors to Mykonos are in the meantime advised to steer clear of bald wine-makers when looking for dry red wines based on the island's typical *ayianiótiko* variety!

Other islands of the northern Cyclades are Tinos, Andros and Syros. Tinos in the past was known for a variety of wines, including a malvasia made from *monemvasiá*, for which the island was famous. Today Tiniote wines are mostly dry, with semi-sweet ones made largely from the old variety *potamísia*, which takes both a black and a white form. Grapes intended for semi-sweet wine are dried in the sun for about a week and mixed with a little water during crushing. Andros, the northernmost and one of the largest of the Cyclades, did not have the reputation of its neighbours, but the early visitor Paul Lucas (1714) was not apprised of that and thought the island's wines 'exquisite'. He was particularly impressed to find them being matured in barrel for six years or so, which was unusual in Western Europe in those times, before bottles came into vogue and when such ageing as a wine received occurred in barrel. Ravaged by phylloxera, Andros has now been substantially replanted, and some of the red wines of the villages of Korthi and Sineti in the south are once again showing that Lucas was not exaggerating much on quality, bearing in mind that in those times tastes might have been more amenable to rather heady wine. Significant on Andros are the grape varieties *armeletoúsa*, *koumári* and *potamíssi* (*potamísia*), all black. To the south, Syros grows mainly black and white variants of the *xylomakheroúda* variety. Khrousa, south of the island port and capital of Ermoupolis, is the best-known wine area of Syros.

Among the southern Cyclades, large Naxos, which lies just east of Paros, stands out by reason of history. The island was considered sacred to Dionysus, and produced one of the earliest of the renowned Aegean vintages, Bibline: 'But at times let me have a shady rock and wine of Biblis . . .' (Hesiod, *Works and Days*, seventh century BC). Although there is a village called Vivlos in the central western part of the island, the name of the ancient wine is thought to have been taken from that of an island stream, probably in order to suggest free-flowing abundance. Naxos kept its repute for millennia, and was a producer of malvasia. The wine held in most special esteem even today is a sweet white one produced mostly from *aïdáni áspro* and *athíri*, at the high east-central village of Apiranthos. However, only a little of that wine is made now. Most Naxiote wine is red and from Apollonas, at the northernmost tip of the island, where a number of typical Cycladic red varieties are grown, such as *mandilariá, váftra, rodítis* and *mavrostáfylo*. The vineyards of Apollonas sit above marble that is second only to Pariote.

Off to the south-west from Naxos is sizeable Milos, which has certainly had its up and downs. In 1717, Tournefort called its wines 'exquisite' and said they were the equal of the best of Crete, for which his praise was unstinting. In 1788, however, Savary reported finding no native wine at all, owing to a loss of inhabitants to plague some years earlier. By the time Leake visited in the first half of the nineteenth century, some recovery had occurred, but wine quality was spotty. In the twentieth century, emigration has reduced availability. The *mandilariá* and the Cretan *liátiko* are the leading varieties grown for dry red wine on Milos. To the east of Milos, tiny Sikinos was known for its excellent sweet white wine produced from the *monemvasiá*, a little of which is still produced, despite the island's decimation by an emigration it could scarcely afford.

As with Mykonos in the north, I must single out Amorgos in the south and note a dubious distinction that was recorded in one of the old travelogues. The reporter in this case was none other than the Cycladist Bent, and his plaint was in having drunk wine from a goatskin that nearly made him become sick to his stomach. Bent's experience can be better imagined by considering Hobhouse's report from western Greece, in which he stated that 'the unpleasant strong savour of the goat in the new wine' was caused by the hairy side being turned inwards; furthermore, Theophrastus remarked that 'goat-skins are sympathetically affected when the breeding season comes round' (*Concerning Odours*). I am afraid that all of this puts Amorgos in a very bad light, and, as with Mykonos, not quite fairly. The facts are that wine-making practices representing various levels of technology manage to coexist happily in the Cyclades, and that the 'wine-skins' (*kraserá askiá*) have not entirely disappeared from any of the Cyclades, not even from recently upgraded Paros. On Amorgos, the wines to look for are red ones based on the old *voudómato* or *voïdomátis* (cow-eye) variety, and preferably in skin, to enable one to enjoy that archaic predecessor of today's prized and heady vinous perfume known as 'sweaty saddle'.

On my shoulder in place of the wonted kirtle, bind, I pray, tight over my breast a dapple-back fawn-skin, full of the perfume of Maronian nectar, and let Homer and deep-sea Eidothea keep the rank skin of the seal for Menelaos. Give me the jocund tambours and the goatskins!

(Nonnos, *Dionysiaca*)

CLASSICAL REFLECTIONS

The explorer Bent concentrated his life's work in the Cyclades because he anticipated a bountiful hunting ground on which to spot vestiges of ancient Greek life. With bacchanalia in mind, he was particularly struck by the uninhibited Pariote celebrations that marked their tapping of the new wine on 3 November, the day of 'Drunken St George' (*Áyios Yeóryios Methistí*). Besides the carousal on Paros, Bent noted that on Serifos local aficionados made the rounds of the island's cellars on St Minas's Day, 11 November. Activities like that on Serifos take place on Santorini and Crete, respectively on the days of St Abercius (22 October) and Drunken St George, with the purpose of trying the newly made wines to see if they 'are drinking'.

With the exception of the one at Serifos, these respective events come about six weeks after the local vintages, which suggests that they were fitted into the Christian liturgical calendar according to long-standing experience as to the suitability of the new wines for drinking:

> the particular district makes a considerable difference even as between places which are not far apart; thus the crops of Salamis are far earlier than those of the rest of Attica, and so in general are those places by the sea.
>
> (Theophrastus, *Enquiry into Plants*)

Also, the concentration of the events in late October and early November may well have grown out of the age-old Aegean cycle of agriculture, wherein the clearing of the new wines generally coincides with a lull in field-work; on Crete, the October–November period in between the sowing of winter crops and the harvesting of olives is colloquially known as *katharomoústia*, or 'must-clearing', that is, 'clearing of the new wines', and is regarded a convenient and appropriate time for weddings. Consequently, on Serifos, where Bent reported that the vintage began on 6 August and the new wine was considered 'fit to drink' after a month's fermentation, the festivities were put off until the slack days of November.

The classicist E. R. Dodds (1960) has expressed his opinion that spring was the exclusive 'right time for holy drunkenness', because in ancient Athens the 'Feast of Cups' was included in the rites called 'Anthesteria', which celebrated blossoming, as the name indicates, and was held in the period from late February to early March, which comprised the month of Anthesterion and which, in the Aegean, could bring out the first blossoms. Surely early worshippers, who identified Dionysus with the mysteries of regeneration that they saw in the yearly budding of vines, must have derived a kindred feeling of self-renewal in a wine-fuelled revel at springtime. However, in further support of his view, Dodds states that the wine of the previous vintage was only then drinkable, which must be an idea that he took from Plutarch: 'those who drink the new wine at the very earliest, do so in the month of Anthesterion, after the winter is gone' (*Moralia*, 'Table-talk').

Yet it must be remembered that virtually all the information that remains to us concerning bacchanalia relates only to Athenian and Attic customs. Furthermore, there is too little information concerning the Little, or Rural, Dionysia of the Attic peasants, which was held in autumn, for us to be able to say categorically that new wine was not sampled until spring. Some customs, particularly in the countryside, might have harked back to times long before thought was given to 'wine maturation', when wine supplies were routinely finished off between one vintage and the next ('Chloe . . . served [the vintagers] with drink of the old wine', Longus, *Daphnis and Chloe*). In those days wine might have been drunk fairly soon after fermentation ended, or perhaps even sooner:

> The wine spurted up in the grape-filled hollow, the rivulets were empurpled; pressed by the alternating tread the fruit bubbled out red juice with white foam. They scooped it up with oxhorns . . .
>
> (Nonnos, *Dionysiaca*)

It ought to be noted too, lest one should get the wrong idea about the Pariotes because of their annual wine bash, that Dodds has explained the origin of ritualized bacchanalia as a probable reaction to 'spontaneous attacks of mass hysteria', instances of which he cites in recent Western European history, that 'kept it within bounds, and gave it a relatively harmless outlet'. They were also a successful resolution of what Dodds calls our 'ambivalence' towards wine: 'To resist Dionysus is to repress the elemental in one's own nature; the punishment is the sudden collapse of the inward dykes when the elemental breaks through perforce and civilization vanishes.' Anyhow, the Pariotes have the reputation of being the most even-tempered and fair-minded of all Aegean inhabitants, so much so that Tournefort noted they were usually called in to arbitrate disputes among other Cycladic islands.

GASTRONOMIC NOTES

If Cycladic gastronomy can be said to have a centre, it must be Sifnos, to the west of Paros. It is somewhat curious that the distinction should fall on Sifnos, for it is among the smaller islands of the group, has no product peculiar to it, and none of its products are thought of as 'best'. Even the island's onions, which are so plentiful that in Bent's time the expression 'give a Sifniote an onion' was equivalent to 'taking coals to Newcastle', were deemed by Tournefort to be inferior to those of Serifos. What has gained Sifnos its reputation is its cooks. Georges Moussa, a Frenchman who resided on Paros for several years and wrote a book each on Paros and Sifnos, gave me his theory that the Sifniotes probably developed their culinary skills as mess cooks on ships. From there, apparently, they graduated to Constantinople, where Bent observed that most cooks were in fact Sifniotes. Yet perhaps they were preordained for that role before signing aboard Aegean vessels, since the Sifniotes have long been master potters, a trade which must have developed in tandem with cookery.

The most highly regarded native Sifniote dish, really not reproduceable elsewhere because of the utter Sifnioteness of every ingredient in the pot – and the pot too for that matter – and of course said to cook to perfection in the traditional native ovens on Sifnos, is baked fava beans. But the Sifniote talent is amply demonstrated in a variety of *plats du jour* available in the island's modest eateries; Georges could hardly stop praising a hole-in-the-wall *rôtisserie* in the village of Artemona. The Sifniote wine to expect with them nowadays – one must make do with it even in Artemona – is retsina, a fact which perhaps need not be too much lamented if it is native wine that is sought; Sifniote retsina can be quite good, and in my experience about the most characteristic to be had outside Central Greece and Euboea.

The Cyclades are brimming with little-known local specialities which the tourist generally will not encounter. Rudimentary local marketing habits often make them invisible to the casual visitor, and sometimes seasonal or overall availability is an obstacle to the outsider's acquaintance. Prominent among the happy exceptions, which is not to say that the visitor will never need to make inquiries, are the *louzés*, or air-cured pork sausages, of Mykonos, the partridges (*pérdika*) of Kythnos, the 'baby beef' (*moskhári*) of Tinos, the octopus (*khtapódi*) of Paros and Milos, the oysters (*strídia*) of Milos, the tomato paste and fava beans of Santorini, the Turkish delight (*loukoúmi*) of Syros, the honey-and-sesame *pastéli* of Ios and Kythnos, and the sugar-coated almonds (*kouféta*) of Anafi. Country cheeses abound on most of the Cyclades. Soft *myzíthra*, made from sheep's or goat's milk, is especially good, popular and widespread. Various local versions have their adherents, the islanders being well attuned and very partial to native flavours, but certainly a special mention could go to that produced from goat's milk at Pyrgos on Santorini. The excellent Santoriniote Easter cookie called *melitíni* requires soft *myzíthra*. A hard version of the cheese, called *xiromyzíthra*, is also available.

Naxos is a special case: 'Everywhere huge piles of melons, peaches, and figs . . . drowsy Naxiot [*sic*] well-being' (Kazantzakis, *Report to Greco*). The ancients thought it was the most favoured of the Cyclades on account of the abundance and quality of its fruit, which perhaps is why they especially associated Dionysus with that island. Naxos is also said to yield the best olive oil of the Cyclades, and its large, green *throúmbes* table olives are well known. There is also outstanding *kefalotýri* cheese and Apiranthos ham (*zambón Apirán-thou*). The finishing touches to the soporific Naxiote table come with the island figs, whose quality caused the visiting Lord Charlemont (1749) to remark that 'Those of Marseilles, so greatly esteemed by us, are insipid when compared to them,' and the spirit called *kitrórako*, which the Naxiotes make from their citrons.

PART II
MAINLAND GREECE

———

6

Macedonia

====

The red wines of Macedonia of the areas of Naousa, Amyntaion, Ayios
Panteleimonas, Goumenissa, Kozani, Grevena, Arnea, and others, present
an excellent harmony of composition, analogous to certain choice red wines
internationally recognized.
    G. Georgakopoulos, Greek enologist, *The Composition and Quality of the Wines*
                                                       of Macedonia, 1957

Greece is not wholly an olive grove. That most characteristic Mediterranean fruit will not grow at all in some places. On the circuitous
train ride to south-western Bulgaria from Thessaloniki, the chief
city and port of the northern Greek region of Macedonia, the
disappearance of olive trees is a readily observable change in scenery
as the train heads inland, and they are soon replaced by a variety of
deciduous fruit trees and generally rather northern vegetation. The
shift is as indicative as anything might be of entering a part of Greece
having an agricultural and gastronomic tradition divergent from
Aegean patterns and particulars, a tradition which is apparent as
well in wine.

    In its inland and upland parts, Macedonia virtually duplicates the
natural environment found across the borders, in the Pirin section of
south-westernmost Bulgaria and below Skoplje in southernmost
Yugoslavia. A sure sign of the similarity in traditional tastes is the
graduated esteem in which *raki* is held going northward from
Thessaloniki. A potent distilled beverage, *raki* can be found made
from any of a number of fruits in northern Macedonia, and is much
appreciated there during the rigorous winters. Indeed, ever since
Greece acquired the region in 1913, agricultural experts concerned
with reducing surplus national wine production, which is concentrated in the south, have regarded *raki* as a local competitor tending

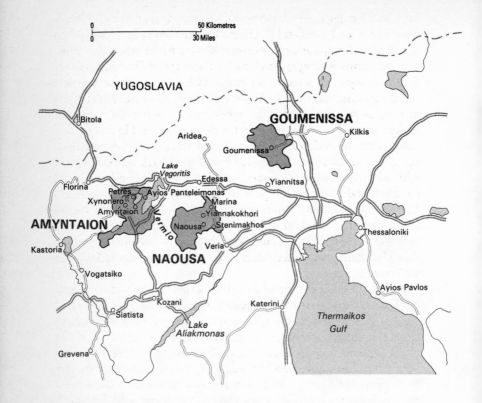

Western and Central Macedonia

to hold back wine consumption in rural Macedonia. Relatively low wine consumption in Macedonia has not, however, been a circumstance attributable only to a taste for *rakí*. Historical factors have also been at play.

Numerous areas of Macedonia had vines during the centuries of Ottoman rule. The seventeenth-century Turkish traveller Evlia Chelebi ticked off a string of places across Macedonia having abundant vineyards: (moving from west to east) Kastoria, Skopia, Florina, Edessa, Naousa, Veria, Zikhni, Serres, Doxato. In the early nineteenth century, the French traveller Ami Boué also found flourishing vineyards. As the nineteenth century progressed, however, Macedonia became inhospitable to peaceful pursuits like wine-growing. The region spent most of the century eating up its energies in political struggles fomented by the new secular religion of nationalism, which had predictable effects on an ethnically hotch-potch population (I suppose most gourmets know why the term *macédoine* came to signify *mélange*) which had had enough of Ottoman rule yet could not agree on what to replace it with. It was not the moment for the grafting there of the Western scientific advances being made in various practical fields, like agriculture. The twentieth century looked scarcely kinder until after the midway point. Phylloxera and emigration, in addition to wars fought largely on this territory, conspired to uproot most vineyards and hold back replanting. But with all factions now minimally satisfied, and sufficiently sickened by the bloodletting of the past to see some good in the present, Macedonia is rapidly confirming itself as the cornucopia nature clearly intended much of it to be. The region is making up for lost time in wine-growing too, and some bottled wines already suggest that Macedonia is poised to scale peaks of quality in dry red wine as we know it.

Making possible the recent Macedonian success in bottled wine is a traditional grape variety of the region, the *xynómavro* (sour/acid black). Well suited to the semi-continental and even continental climatic conditions under which it is grown, the *xynómavro* enjoys near hegemony over a larger continuous area than does any other red wine grape in Greece. Its domain extends from the eastern rim of the mountains of central Macedonia, westward to the Pindos Mountains at the far end of the region, south to Thessaly, and north to around the Yugoslav border. Within that area are a dozen or so locales known in the past for their excellent wine. While some of those places still support vineyards, few have really recovered from phylloxera. Among the notable sites awaiting rejuvenation are Siatista, Vogatsiko, Kozani and Grevena. Until now, only three places have been substantially restored to their former regional importance: Naousa, Goumenissa and Amyntaion. They are showing the *xynómavro* to considerable advantage, and it is to be hoped that wider acquaintance with these wines will redound to the benefit of Macedonian wine places that are still languishing.

NAOUSA

The dominant constellation of mountains in Macedonia is that known as Mount Vermio. On a bluff of its south-eastern edge, facing a distant and unseen Aegean, the town of Naousa looks out over extensive vineyards, as well as neat orchards of fruit trees. Naousa's name apparently derives from Niaousta, and in turn from Nea Avgousta, which was how the Romans' name for the place, Nova Augusta, came out in Greek. The place has been inhabited since antiquity, a fact which the early nineteenth-century French visitor Cousinéry, taken by 'its beautiful vineyards', attributed to its great suitability for the vine. After the Ottomans arrived, the townsmen managed to wrest a few privileges, including a relatively bearable tax burden and the absence of a Turkish garrison, so that Naousa was able to maintain its vineyards and actually increase its commerce in wine.

It paid the Naousans to bring ingenuity to bear. Since the town did not have convenient conditions for underground cellars, the Naousans set about putting the underground waters of Vermio to work for them. The houses of wine merchants were constructed above the underground currents to allow the ground-level cellars to benefit from the cooling effects of the water below. The choice sites were adjacent to the stream Arapitsa, which runs through what naturally became the most valuable real estate in town, where the most substantial of Naousa's old homes are to be seen today. Thanks to their cellars, the Naousans could confidently give a long maturation in barrel to their very tannic wine, then produced by a long fermentation on stalks as well as skins. The French traveller Pouqueville, writing in 1826, noted that Naousa's wine was rarely drunk before four to five years of age. It was, however, a worthwhile wait for Naousa's wine merchants:

> The wine of Naousa is in Macedonia what the wine of Burgundy is in France; it sells at double the other wines, even those of the most nearby countryside. It is transported to Salonika and Serres, where it is much consumed.
>
> (Cousinéry, *Voyage dans la Macédoine*, 1831)

The premium paid for Naousan wine in Cousinéry's day must have been in part a reflection of greatly reduced availability, since the early nineteenth century had been most disruptive for Naousan wine-growing. In 1804, the political rivalry of two Naousan leaders came to a head, resulting in much destruction to the environs, and subsequent heavy tribute paid from town resources by the winning side for outside military forces that had been brought in to ensure victory. Only a year later, the British traveller Leake visited, and noted that all considerable merchants had vacated Naousa, leaving it a much diminished place. Hardly was a recovery in progress when an even greater disaster took its toll. As news of Greek rebellion against the Ottomans began to pour in during 1821, the Naousans, spurred by a temerity fostered by their centuries of privileges, armed themselves and declared independence. An Ottoman army was dispatched to quell the Naousan uprising with the result that about 2,000 inhabitants perished, while at least as many more fled permanently. In addition, extensive damage was done to the town, its cellars and its lands. When Cousinéry was there in the latter part of the decade he found that what had been a little town before the insurrection was only a village in the years following it. Those years were not favourable for wine production, making it all the more curious that Cousinéry, who well knew the town's recent past, made no qualifying remarks when he assessed Naousan wine, apparently in the rating framework of André Jullien, in a rather modest way: 'considered as *vin d'ordinaire* . . . really the best of all Turkey'. It was rather as though Michelin had awarded a restaurant one-star status in perpetuity based upon its troubled performance around the time of D-Day.

It is easy to get the wrong idea from Cousinéry, and too few contemporary wine-lovers make the sort of intimate acquaintance with Naousa that would encourage challenging the old rating. Yet now is the time to be doing just that. An appellation of origin has been authorized since 1971 for dry red Naousan wine made exclusively from *xynómavro* grapes grown in designated vineyard areas of Naousa town, as well as the villages of Stenimakhos, Yiannakokhori, Marina, Lefkadia, Kopanos and Trilofos. Nearly 700 hectares of vines are planted in the appellation zone alone, mostly on clay-pyrite soils lying between 150 and 300 metres above sea level. Several private wineries and a cooperative one are producing Naousan red wines, and they follow the same general wine-making procedure. Following the vintage in late September, the must is fermented on skins alone – no stems as in olden times – for about fifteen days, then for one to two weeks more with the skins removed.

The wines range from about 12–13° in alcohol, with *káva*, or 'reserve', wines usually towards the upper end. Appellation wines must have a minimum of one year in barrel, but in practice they are given one and a half to two years. The *káva* wines spend two to three years longer in oak. All of the appellation wines have been vintage-dated, while some of the reserve wines have not. Because producers of reserve wines chose to name those wines in ways which convey extra quality, they were not allowed to market them as appellation Naousa wines until legislation in 1989 made it possible.

Pride of historic place at Naousa belongs to the large Boutari wine firm, which is the oldest bottler of Naousan wine, dating back to 1879; it is not, however, an uninterrupted history. Although based in Thessaloniki, Boutari's main winery is at Stenimakhos, below Naousa. Visitors to Macedonia desirous of appreciating something of the background of contemporary Macedonian wine could hardly do better than to look around Stenimakhos. The village is inhabited by Greek refugee families from near Plovdiv (Philippopolis) in south-central Bulgaria, where most were expert viticulturalists at the renowned wine town of Asenovgrad, formerly called Stenimakhos and Stanimaka. They have been a significant factor in Naousa's recovery. Especially to Boutari's credit is its having led in the replanting of vineyards at Naousa after a long lapse in interest following the arrival of phylloxera several years before the First World War. The firm has about 50 hectares of its own in Yiannako-khori, most of which were planted between 1970 and 1975. When planting there, Boutari abandoned the old method of unsupported vines, instead adopting the training of vines along cordons, which has become the exclusive practice in the Naousan vineyards. Boutari produces about 15,000 hectolitres of appellation Naousa wine annually, for which about one-quarter of the grapes is their own fruit, while the rest is bought in from numerous small wine-growers. The firm's *káva* wine is Grande Réserve Boutari, a vintage-dated wine of 12.5°, which since 1983 has been produced solely from Boutari's Yiannakokhori estate. Earlier, the grapes were not all from within the appellation zone, and the wine was at 12°.

In terms of quantity, Boutari has only two major competitors on the Greek market for Naousan wine. By far the largest and indeed now the largest producer of Naousan wines, is the GAOS 'Naousa' Cooperative, whose members cultivate 350–400 hectares of vines within the appellation zone, as well as other vineyards outside the zone. The Cooperative, which boasts the most up-to-date cooperative winery in Greece at the present time, is turning out from 15,000 to 17,000 hectolitres of appellation wine annually. Their first vintage was in 1984, from which the appellation wine was bottled in 1986. A 13° reserve wine from that vintage was kept in barrel for four years and marketed in 1988 under the Cava Vaeni label. The reserve would have been ineligible for the Naousa appellation whatever its name, because nearly one-fifth of it was from *cabernet sauvignon*, a variety not authorized under the appellation regulations but now being grown in the region to a minor extent. The Cooperative offers lesser red and rosé *xynómavro* wines under the Vaeni label; its white wine in that series is a blend of 60 per cent Rhodian wine with *xynómavro* vinified for white wine.

The other major producer of Naousan wine is the Tsantalis firm. Although headquartered at Ayios Pavlos on the Khalkidiki peninsula south-east of Thessaloniki, Tsantalis maintains a winery just below the town of Naousa, again underscoring the old interest in Naousan wine throughout Macedonia. Tsantalis has about 20 hectares of vineyards, dating back to 1972, planted in the low-lying, rolling Strandza area of Naousa, but buys in about four-fifths of the grapes used to produce nearly 10,000 hectolitres of appellation wine annually – or at least that is the amount it was producing before the Cooperative appeared on the scene. Tsantalis produces no reserve wine from the Naousan vintage.

Several family wineries operated by locals are also producing and bottling Naousan wines. The largest of them is that of the Kastaniotis family, who have about 15 hectares by Marina, in the northern part of the appellation zone, where they planted in the late 1970s. From those vineyards exclusively, they produce about 1,600 hectolitres of wine in each vintage. A reserve wine of 12.6° was bottled and marketed under the Kava Kastaniotis label in 1988, after seven years in cask. Another firm is that of the Khrisokhoou brothers. They produce about 1,000 hectolitres each year, mostly from the 10 hectares of their own vines in the gently sloping Rodakino area adjacent to Naousa town. A supplementary 20–30 per cent of the grapes used come from two or three other excellent vineyard properties nearby. The Khrisokhoou vineyards were planted from 1976 onwards, and their first vintage was 1979, which yielded an appellation wine. They have since added a reserve wine, Kava Khrisokhoou, produced from selected grapes of the same vineyards.

Still smaller producers are Markovitis and Melitzanis. Markovitis makes about 450 hectolitres in a vintage, all the grapes for which come from his 6 hectares of vines planted up in Pola Nera, north-west of Marina, an upland area of the appellation zone where ripening can be slightly retarded in some years. Although Markovitis's vines were planted in 1970, he did not process any of the fruit himself until over a decade later. His first bottling was in 1983, when the 1981 vintage appeared under the Pigasos label, with appellation of origin. Subsequently he has occasionally also used a Château Pigasos label, and when he did his wine was disqualified for the appellation, on the Ministry of Agriculture's principle that unverifiable superior quality is suggested. A reserve wine is in the offing, and Markovitis is also considering expanding production by buying in some carefully selected grapes. A fourth small-scale winery is that of the Melitzanis brothers, who produce about 150 hectolitres annually, very largely from their own 3.5 hectares of vineyards, planted in 1973 in the Gastra area of Naousa. The first bottling was in 1978. Their reserve wine is Kava Melitzanis, which is of 13° alcohol and aged five years in cask.

The marketing of the Naousan wines varies with the size of the wineries. The Boutari, Cooperative and Tsantalis wines are distributed widely in Greece, particularly the first two, which benefit from highly developed marketing networks. All of those have been exported as well. The smaller wineries mostly market regionally, especially Melitzanis, a large part of whose wines are sold from their own shop in Naousa, at Dimarkhias 8–1. Nearby is the shop of the Khrisokhoou brothers, at Dimarkhias 41, but much of their wine is also sold in Thessaloniki and the towns of central Macedonia. Kastaniotis sells mostly in Athens, Thessaloniki and Kavala, but has exported as well, especially to West Germany. Markovitis's wine goes to various retailers in Macedonia and Athens, but he limits the quantity sold to any one of them, with the exception of the Kava Zakharopoulos shops of Athens, with whom he has a special arrangement.

GOUMENISSA

Way up in *raki* country, about 30 miles to the north-east of Naousa near the Yugoslav border, the town of Goumenissa acquired an appellation of origin for its red wine in 1981. Though it is no Naousa by reputation, Goumenissa's name in wine might have travelled further than it did were it not for a disadvantageous trading location. The town was in the unenviable position of being caught between the marketing spheres of two most outstanding wine towns of Ottoman Europe, Naousa to the south-west, and Melnik, a once largely Greek town now in the corner of Bulgaria, to the north-east. Goumenissa could hardly get due recognition from where it sat. The new marketing spheres created as a result of the redrawing of borders after the Balkan Wars of 1912–13 would perhaps have helped to acquaint more Greeks with Goumenissa's wine, but the ravages of phylloxera prevented taking advantage of the new marketing possibilities until after the Second World War.

From a viticultural point of view, nothing about Goumenissa's location has ever been particularly unfortunate. Its vineyards, presently occupying about 150 hectares in the appellation zone, are set out on the eastern inclines of the Païko Mountains, in the range of about 250 metres above sea level. The slopes are situated where the southern Macedonian upland descends to meet the valley of the Axios, which is the Vardar of southern Yugoslavia, a river that empties into the Aegean not far west of Thessaloniki. The influence of the Aegean is felt more strongly than at Naousa, although the vintage nevertheless takes place in late September. The greater warmth together with the lower calcium content in the soil constitute the environmental situation generally averred to make Goumenissa's wine somewhat softer than Naousan, and relatively more early-maturing as well. Also, however, the varietal composition of the vineyards at Goumenissa makes a contribution, since the *xynómavro* is not alone there. A variety called *negóska*, from the Slavic name for Naousa, which is Negush, is also cultivated; and although it may be closely related to the *xynómavro*, it has a tendency to develop more sugar during ripening. Appellation regulations call for a must of *xynómavro* and *negóska* in a ratio of 4:1. Traditionally, a small amount of another dark variety, *séfka*, which is the *shefka* of southern Bulgaria, was also part of the blend for many Goumenissan wines. The *séfka* is still found sporadically, and finds its way into some home-made wines, but is likely to disappear as a consequence of appellation regulations.

Currently, two appellation Goumenissa wines are produced, one by the Boutari firm, and the other by a local individual, Yeoryios

Aïdarinis. Using purchased grapes, Boutari turns out about 2,000–2,500 hectolitres annually, while Aïdarinis produces only about 200 hectolitres, for which about half of the grapes come from his own 3 hectares of vines. Aïdarinis's first bottling was in 1983. A major point of divergence in the production of the two wines is that the Boutari version is initially fermented for about fifteen days on skins alone, while the Aïdarinis wine spends about ten to twelve days on stalks as well as skins, which is the traditional method at Goumenissa. Both wines are at about 12° alcohol and spend about fifteen months in oak before bottling under their respective Goumenissa labels; appellation regulations specify a one-year minimum in oak. They are vintage-dated wines. Boutari's is available almost as widely as its Naousan wines, but it is necessary as yet to go to central Macedonia to find Aïdarinis's.

AMYNTAION

In heading westward from Goumenissa, vineyards are seen only occasionally. Formerly the area was settled overwhelmingly by a Turkish Moslem population whose presence effectively excluded wine-growing. Newer residents, mostly Greek refugee families from Turkey, who have replaced the Turks, have for the most part adopted the farming of crops and orchards as being more lucrative than grapes. Only around the large village of Amyntaion in the vicinity of Lake Vegoritis, on the far side of Mount Vermio from Naousa, do vineyards once again come into their own as a significant feature of the landscape. The area had been badly hit by phylloxera around the time of the Balkan Wars of 1912–13, and initially was slow in recovering, in part because the main market for its wine was traditionally northward, especially around Bitola (Monastiri), in land ceded to Yugoslavia as a result of the war. However, the area's old reputation for wine – the local folk claim the place has traded wine since antiquity – brought viticulture to the attention of refugee families settling in that area in the late 1920s and 1930s. Vineyards consequently grew in number and size until the development was set back by the Second World War and the Greek Civil War, the latter being particularly severe because of the proximity of Communist Yugoslavia.

Nearly 550 hectares of vines are planted at present in the area entitled, since 1971, to the Amyntaion appellation. According to the legal demarcation, fifteen villages besides the name-giving one belong to the appellation zone: Ayios Panteleimonas, Vegoras, Petres, Xynonero, Lakkia, Kleidi, Antigonos, Maniaki, Rodona, Aetos, Pedino, Fanos, Agrapidia, Anargyri and Variko. However, only the first four of these and Amyntaion are of significance at present, and Ayios Panteleimonas and Xynonero alone supply the great majority of the grapes, including about four-fifths of those processed by the region's only producer of appellation wines, the Union of Agricultural Cooperatives of Amyntaion. The only grape variety authorized for those wines is the *xynómavro*, which is generally called *popólka* in this area where Slavophone Greeks are still found. (Amyntaion itself was known as Sorovits/Surovichevo until the conclusion of the Balkan Wars, when it was renamed after Amyntas, the father of Philip of Macedon, who in turn sired Alexander the Great.)

Although Amyntaion is only 20 miles distant from Naousa as the crow flies, it lies on the far side of Vermio, blocked off from the influence of the Aegean. As one penetrates the region by car from Naousa, the elevation changes almost imperceptibly, and it comes as rather a surprise to learn that Amyntaion is around 650 metres above sea level, or about twice the altitude of the vineyards in the upper part of the appellation Naousa zone. These features of Amyntaion's setting cause the local climate to be entirely continental, though moderated somewhat by the influence of Lake Vegoritis, and set the vintage back to mid-October. Annual fluctuations in grape quantity and quality are as wide as those known at northerly European red wine sites, and the climatic situation is further compounded by significant divergences in vineyard position and soil, especially between Ayios Panteleimonas and Xynonero. The former village is on the plains area just west of little Lake Petron, while the latter is on the slopes west of Amyntaion proper. Soil tends to be a sandy clay around Xynonero, and a sandy loam around Ayios Panteleimonas, with considerable variation in calcium content from vineyard to vineyard at both places. It is exactly the sort of environmental situation that led to the emphasis on vintage dates and individual vineyard properties which became characteristic of parts of Western Europe once economic conditions were ripe for it.

In surveying the varied conditions and wines of the region, viti-vinicultural researchers working at Amyntaion found a steady relationship in annual grape maturation tendency among the individual vineyards, and in alcohol, acid, tannin and anthocyanin content in the wines produced from them. Consequently, it has been possible to categorize vineyards according to tendency, and know which ones to look to for the raw material for the Union's several wines. Indeed the Union produces a wide range of wines relative to its total output, in order to make the best it can of three sorts of wine. Its total output usually ranges between 2,000 and 5,000 hectolitres yearly, although occasionally it reaches 7,000–8,000 hectolitres. Only 500–1,000 hectolitres become their appellation Amyntaion red wine. The Union would like to make a wine of still more limited production, but has no incentive for it at present. Usually, at least half of their output consists of dry and semi-dry rosé wines under the Astron label, which are also entitled to the appellation, as well as another red under that label which is not entitled, and an ordinary red and rosé under the Zephyr label. The remainder of their wine comprises sparkling wines produced by the closed-cuve method. The dry one labelled Amyntaion carries the appellation, while the dry and semi-dry ones under the Doukissa label do not. Neither the rosé nor the sparkling wines have any tradition in the region, but the better ones are entitled to the appellation in order to justify favourable prices to growers in unfavourable years, or on some less favourable plots, thereby keeping viticulture perennially attractive.

The red wine of Amyntaion was traditionally produced by a fermentation of the must on both stalks and skins for more than a month, which is still the method of peasant wine-makers, who prefer the more puckery sensation thus induced, a sensation which in any case tends to be pronounced in young red wines in this region because of the high acidity level the climate generally encourages; it is said that the *xynómavro* really justifies its name, 'sour/acid black', at Amyntaion. The Union, however, ferments the must on the skins alone for somewhat more than a week, the full fermentation lasting about three weeks. The result is a wine of 12° alcohol that matures more quickly than the traditional wine would. Nevertheless, Amyntaion red is only bottled after three years of maturation in oak; appellation rules require only one year. It is bottled with vintage indication, and marketed mostly in Macedonia and Athens.

THREE OF A KIND

The early nineteenth-century French traveller Boué called Naousa 'a red wine somewhat resembling Bordeaux with its acidity'. Well over a century later, the Greek enologist Georgakopoulos confirmed with laboratory data that there exists a most striking similarity between the detailed acid content of the Macedonian *xynómavro* wines and those of Bordeaux. That is not to say, however, that everyone tasting *xynómavro* wines will always think that Bordeaux is the correct association to make, not even if restricting the comparison to the feel of the wines. Some people find that the acidity in certain young Naousan wines today reminds them of one or another of the *grand crus* of Beaujolais. Other tasters think of certain Chiantis when they push Goumenissa wines about the mouth. But there was a reporter of the inter-war period who was reminded of Chianti by a Naousan wine. When tasting Amyntaion wines, some people make mention of the northernmost Italian reds, like Carema, perhaps in order to suggest an austerity of feel. As to the aromatics of *xynómavro* wines, thoughts turn in other directions. Greek enologists, among others, speak of *pinot noir*, an association that I am afraid will come to mind all the quicker after tasting the sparkling wines of Amyntaion. I have thought of certain Hungarian *kadarka* wines, such as Szekszárdi, in smelling some bottle-ready Naousan wines. Then there is the matter of colour, in which case none of the above associations will do. Rioja, perhaps, would make a pertinent comparison in that respect. One could almost think there is hardly any reason to have *xynómavro*, yet the fact is that when one gets down to a glass of these Macedonian wines, they defy comparison, which is saying quite a lot.

The appellation wines of Naousa hover over the dark cranberry range of redness, while the *káva* wines tend to be darker, though still fitting the Rioja association. But there are exceptions: Cava Vaeni, with its *cabernet* component, is noticeably darker than the others; Kava Melitzanis, with its five years in wood, seems to drop a lot of colour and is a light brick-red tinged with yellow; and Tsantalis's appellation wine Naousa has been unusually dark for an all-*xynómavro* wine since at least the 1984 vintage. Overall, Goumenissa wines are less deeply coloured than Naousan wines, and tend towards an orange tint at the rim at an earlier age. Amyntaion wine is the lightest of the group, being what the Greeks call 'red-black', with a slight orange tendency by bottling time in the case of the Union's Amyntaion red.

The relatively light colour of the *xynómavro* wines should not mislead about their feel, however. The *xynómavro* happens to yield quite tannic wine, but with a content of anthocyanins relatively low in relation to the tannin. Naousan wine in particular, while varying somewhat in body among samples, harbours a bold astringency that tends to look better in the rounder, fuller wines, especially Pigasos and Kava Khrisokhoou. Naousa is always firm wine, sometimes even bracing if given no bottle-age, and exerts quite a grip on the tongue, fitting its sensations over that organ like a glove. Goumenissa's wine is of relatively lighter body, and both softer in texture and less forceful. Amyntaion wine offers a particularly zesty quality that makes it seem as close to 'crisp' as we may legitimately speak of in relation to dry red wines suitable for bottle-ageing. The common aromatic aspect of the *xynómavro* wines seems to be an uncharted area between raspberry and strawberry jams and sweet potato. Allspice seems to be present too, at least in Kava Khrisokhoou, Pigasos and Grande Réserve Boutari, and floral smells come on with age in most cases. The best Naousan wines can be laid down advantageously for four to eight years, but perhaps longer as the vines gain some age, while those of Goumenissa and Amyntaion do not, in my experience, benefit by more than three to five years at best.

Having mistaken one of the *xynómavro* wines for another more than once – it can happen easily enough across vintages – perhaps I am not entitled to be very choosy on the matter of their matching to foods. Venturing where gourmet angels would fear to tread, I will nevertheless suggest that, in the pan-Hellenic kitchen, the Naousan wines should be tried with lamb *giouvétsi* or *kapamá*, a recent Kava Khrisokhoou or Pigasos with *mousaká*, Tsantalis's Naousa with *soudzoukákia*, Boutari's Goumenissa with *youvarlákia*, and Amyntaion with meat-stuffed vine leaves with *avgolémono* sauce. If familiarity of sensation is desired, Amyntaion ought to be taken with char-grilled steak, the Cooperative's Naousa with baked ham or roast pork, and Naousan wines generally with *coq au vin* and *bœuf bourgignon*, using the wine as confidently in the pot as on the table if one has a mind to. On the other hand there is something to be said for jettisoning all semblance of familiarity of sensation and going Cantonese instead: Amyntaion for beef with bok choy, Boutari's Goumenissa with beef chow foon, and Cava Vaeni with spare ribs in blackbean sauce. I shall close the list of possibilities by noting that Cousinéry, whom we know to have been as much given to qualitative distinctions as we are, complained not at all about having had to drink Naousan wine with trout at the lakeside in nearby Edessa.

SIATISTA

Situated about midway between Kozani and Grevena, on the southwestern rim of the Vermio range, the town of Siatista lies hidden in a cleft in the south-facing slopes leading up to Mount Siniatsiko. Only the vineyards stretching out from that opening eastward towards Kozani alert the passing motorist for signs of settlement. The gravelly, limestone-dappled slopes might suggest that the vine has been cultivated at Siatista since time immemorial, although the town apparently grew into a wine centre only after the coming of the Ottomans. Earlier, Siatista, positioned at an altitude of about 970 metres, was no more than a small settlement of Vlakhs, a pastoral people of Latin speech. The late fifteenth-century influx of Greek-speaking refugees from more onerously governed places eventually resulted in the complete hellenization of Siatista, and with that a switch from animal husbandry to viticulture as the primary agricultural pursuit.

During the centuries of Ottoman rule, Siatista sold its wines in Macedonia and Thessaly, and was in the forefront of Ottoman wine-growing in the early nineteenth century: 'Each considerable owner has a wine-press, and there are cellars under all the larger houses, exhibiting the agreeable spectacle of butts, arranged in order , as in civilized Europe' (Leake, *Travels in Northern Greece*, 1835). Even today the visitor may visit Siatistan wine cellars and marvel nostalgically at their equipment. Perhaps no place in all of Greece has home cellars that announce so emphatically that the occupants have long meant business about wine. But the scene is one of a past plateau of technological excellence, rather as if it were frozen in time.

Since the late nineteenth century, Siatista has had practically no incentive to keep pace with wine-making advances. After phylloxera struck France, French merchants dusted off and cracked open the old travelogues and wine books, where they found mention of the town (Chatista or Schatista) in glowing terms; in a later edition of Jullien's book, Siatista's wines were called 'the best of Macedonia', just as they had been by Pouqueville. The merchants found their way there too, but of course had no interest in seeing the Siatistans bottle wine, or indeed that anything much should become of the place. They only wanted casks of the town's dry red wine with which to forge 'Bordeaux' back in France. The loss of that market after the French vineyards recovered was followed by phylloxera's attack on the town's own vineyards in 1926–8, and then by emigration, which has lasted down to the present time. Consequently, Siatista's wine-making facilities have never been substantially updated. Its enological development has seemingly atrophied irreversibly, and Siatista, once in the vanguard of wine-making, has become a backwater, dependent on furs for its continued survival. None the less it is possible to leave the town convinced that technological level is not always and everywhere an adequate indicator of wine quality.

Incredible as it may seem today, nearly 1,700 hectares of vines had spread across the clay-gravel inclines near Siatista in the early years of this century. They were planted mostly on the middle of the slopes, up to about 550 metres above sea level, hail being a very troublesome problem on the upper slopes. How sadly barren that tract looks now! Only around 100 hectares remain in production, and that very largely on the more easily worked lower slopes. The extra effort in planting and tending higher up is generally not deemed worth while, especially by the elderly people who do most of the vineyard work while those of their offspring who have remained behind prepare and peddle furs. Besides, the hazards for the Siatistan vintage are quite serious even on the lower slopes. Hail can thrash the fruit any time from late spring into early summer, and the climate, being wholly continental, can delay grape maturity menacingly. In any year the grapes are harvested late for Greece, not earlier than mid-October.

The English traveller Leake (1835) mentioned four Siatistan wines: a dry red, a dry white, a sweet white, and a wine flavoured with wormwood called *apsithinón*. All except the last are still made. Red wine is dominant, as it always has been, and made largely from *xynómavro*, which the Siatistans usually call *xynostáfylo*, or 'sour/acid grape'. Two other dark varieties grown to a small extent are *stavrotó* and *valándovo*. However, the variety of most special interest at Siatista is yet another one that is known as *moskhómavro*. Its name means 'musky black', yet it is not the 'black muscat' variety known in the West. The *moskhómavro* owes its significance to being the basis for Siatista's most highly regarded wine, the sweet *liastó*:

'The good reputation of the mutton and hare of Siatista is surpassed only by that of the wines, which, made in every house in its own way, reach their ultimate generosity in the *krasí iliastó*' (Leonhard Schultze, *Makedonien*, 1927). Early in this century, *liastó* was selling at ten times the price of the town's highly esteemed dry red.

In making *liastó*, *moskhómavro* is traditionally mixed with the other varieties, including *xynómavro*, but the proportion varies somewhat from cellar to cellar. Apart from this, the method of producing *liastó* is very much the same among all the Siatistan producers. The specially selected, well-ripened grapes are spread in the sun for about a week (hence the name *liastó*, and also that by which Leake called it, *liouménon*, both meaning 'sunned'), or else in airy rooms for about six weeks, depending on the weather and the availability of facilities. After losing approximately half their weight by dehydration, the grapes are crushed, and the mass of liquids and solids is passed through pouches of clean goat's wool. This process may have ancient origins: 'Question 7: Whether it is right to strain wine: "... those who draw off the impurities and unpalatable elements are simply tending and cleaning it" ' (Aristion, in Plutarch, *Moralia*, 'Table-talk'). The must is then put to ferment in small casks, sometimes of chestnut and sometimes of *róbolo*, a local pine-wood – sometimes it is actually called 'Roumeliote pine' or 'Macedonian pine' – although it does not give a piny flavour to *liastó*. After ten to fifteen days, the casks are closed and fermentation goes on for a further twenty-five to thirty days, at which time cold weather intervenes to impede the progress of the yeasts until about May the following year. Fermentation then recommences, and is allowed to come to a halt naturally, when the wine has reached 15–16° alcohol.

Two or three decades ago, six to seven years in cask was considered necessary for *liastó*. But nowadays producers who have some to sell find an ample profit in selling it at two to three years of age to the small coterie of Greeks who know about *liastó* and come looking for it. First of all, there is the colour to enthuse over. Leake described it as a white wine, as do the Siatistans, but its hue is a rare light amber shot with a variety of colours, including a certain budding pinkishness. *Liastó*'s colour is matched by the clarity of its bouquet which can justly be called phenomenal, although the facets of this aromatic gem are very difficult to identify individually. I might mention a certain nuance that is like ripe strawberries, but this seems too trite to do justice to such an uncommon wine. On the other hand

I might risk overdoing images of the exotic by mentioning guava paste. Better that I just describe the bouquet as an inextricable blend of unique fruity, nutty and floral aromas, and leave it at that ('the aim and object is not to make the mixture smell of one particular thing, but to produce a general scent derived from them all,' Theophrastus, *Concerning Odours*). Equally remarkable is the aromatic savour, *liastó* being as sheer on the mouth surfaces as any dessert wine might be and in no way distracting.

Far more stimulus than exists today is going to be required to replant the vineyards of Siatista and get *liastó* into bottle for common enjoyment. What hope there is seems at this time to rest with the Association of Viticulturalists of Siatista (*Sýllogos Ambelourgón Siátistas*), an organization which could in time become the nucleus of a cooperative association that would lead to a general rejuvenation of wine-growing at this most undeservedly obscure Macedonian town. In the meantime, visitors may contact the Association, possibly via the town hall (*dimarkhíon*), to gain entrée to the remaining Siatistan cellars.

KHALKIDIKI (CHALCIDICE)

Macedonia also has an Aegean front, most notably the three-pronged Khalkidiki peninsula projecting south and deep into the Aegean from east of Thessaloniki. The written record of the ancient Greeks, which perhaps is deficient on inland Macedonia, indicates that the most esteemed Macedonian vintages in antiquity were grown on Khalkidiki, especially at Mendi (Mende) and Skioni (Scione) on the south-western part of the western prong called Kassandra, and at Akanthos (Acanthus) at the head of the eastern prong called Akti. In recent centuries, the best wine of Khalkidiki was considered to be that of Arnea, located in the east-central part of the peninsula's main sac. At present not of real commercial significance, the wine of Arnea is a dry red made from the ancient *limnió* variety, which has been the major grape variety of Khalkidiki in modern times, if not for some time earlier as well. Lately the *limnió*, with some outside help, is enjoying a revival on the peninsula generally, and has drawn Western attention to Khalkidiki, if sometimes for questionable reasons.

The locale that has been in the limelight is a 450-hectare vineyard estate near the community of Nea Marmaras, along the western rim of the middle prong of Khalkidiki, Sithonia, on which numerous vineyards were planted during ancient times. The estate belongs to the wealthy Carras family, who own the Porto Carras resort complex hard by it. Extending from 190–350 metres above sea level on hilly, sloping land of finely broken schist, the warm and dry Carras vineyard benefits from the proximity of the sea, as well as from an arc of pines enclosing it, which combine to moderate both warmth and dryness. The estate, which could be expanded by 100 hectares or so in coming years, was planted as from 1966 with both Greek and French grape varieties, selected to suit the environment, and actually planted in separate parcels, according to micro-environment, with the avowed intention of producing 'wines of European type'.

The rockier and drier southern part of the Carras estate was planted primarily with the Greek white varieties *savatianó* and *rodítis*, both brought from Attica, with the former growing on the poorer soils. The main exception in that area was the red *cinsault*. Red varieties were generally planted on the relatively richer soils of the more humid northern part of the estate, which is also its higher area, towards the pines. The *limnió* dominated in plantings there, followed by *cabernet sauvignon* and *cabernet franc*, as well as several other French varieties, mainly *merlot*, *petit syrah* and *grenache*. The Macedonian *xynómavro* was also planted, but proved to be outside the environmental zone in which it really succeeds. In addition, the Greek white varieties *athíri* and *asýrtiko*, respectively brought from Rhodes and Santorini, were planted in the north, and so were smaller areas of *sauvignon blanc* and *ugni blanc*. On the basis of a decade of experience in growing and vinifying the several varieties, an appellation of origin was authorized for the Carras estate in 1981, under the unlikely Greek name 'Playies Melitona', which translates as the distinctly French 'Côtes de Meliton'. 'Meliton' refers to the mount on whose slopes the estate is planted. The regulation specifies red wines composed of 70 per cent *limnió* and 15 per cent each of the two *cabernets*, and white wines of 50 per cent *athíri*, 35 per cent *rodítis*, and 15 per cent *asýrtiko*. The percentages only became compulsory in 1989.

About 900 hectolitres of wine are produced annually at the Carras estate, of which about half is appellation white wine on the Domaine Carras label, which up until now has been made from *asýrtiko* (30 per cent), *athíri* (30 per cent), *rodítis* (20 per cent), *sauvignon blanc* (10 per cent), and *ugni blanc* (10 per cent). A white Carras Reserve, now also bearing the appellation, has been composed of *asýrtiko* and *sauvignon blanc* in a ratio of 7:3, and produced in a quantity of about 100 hectolitres annually. Three reds have borne the appellation: Domaine Carras, which is from a mix of *cabernet sauvignon* and *limnió*; Cava Carras, an all-*cabernet sauvignon* entry; and Château Carras, made from 30 per cent each of the two *cabernets* and *limnió*, plus *merlot*. They are produced in quantities of, respectively, about 150, 120 and 40 hectolitres annually. Cava Carras and Château Carras spend two to four years in bottle before being marketed, in addition to eighteen to twenty months in barrel, and are *vins de garde*, especially Château Carras. But the quicker-maturing Domaine Carras has its own charms, even at six to seven years of age, with a special character all its own. A Carras Rosé Special is also made mostly from *limnió, cinsault* and *merlot*. It will be noticed that both the red and the white Domaine Carras wines are closest in make-up to what the appellation regulations call for. Presumably, the composition will have to change if the appellation is to be retained after 1989, in order not to give the impression of a cosy relationship between the Carras family and the Ministry of Agriculture.

The general resemblance of the Carras wines to Western European prototypes has won the Carras project the plaudits of Western wine commentators, some of whom are quite lavish in their praise, suggesting the wines as the best of Greece, and the project as the most interesting in Greek wine. However that may be, the sensibilities of at least a few Greek wine professionals are offended by the Carras philosophy. They cannot conceive of Greek wine that does not spring directly from a local populace and its habits, and worry that Greece is all too prone to relinquish its own heritage in wine for the sake of catering to the taste of a Western clientele, becoming rather like what one detractor of the Carras project calls 'a water-carrier to Europe'. Maybe it is not too late to hope, however, that a real local tradition will evolve as fruitfully as happened when the French landed in Rioja, but I think that would require greater recognition of the remarkable *limnió*.

East of Sithonia, the Akti arm of Khalkidiki has become the source of wines related to those from the Carras estate, though perhaps with some greater claim to indigenous tradition. Akti is for all practical purposes synonymous with Mount Athos, or Ayion Oros (Holy Mountain), the pan-Orthodox community of all-male monasteries. Vineyards proliferated on Athos after the Ottomans came to power and the monasteries there lost the lands that they had held elsewhere. The vines planted were primarily *limnió*, but also included varieties brought by monks from the Black Sea coast of Georgia. The Georgian varieties were appreciated for their resistance to disease, easy cultivation and high yields. However, they were not of *vinifera* type, and their fruit displayed the so-called 'foxy' aroma associated with *labrusca*, etc. The monks therefore typically diluted the Georgian flavour with *limnió*. The best wine of Athos, however, was considered to be varietal *limnió* from the 'Monoxylitis' vineyard belonging to the Monastery of Ayios Dionysius, directly below Ayion Oros proper.

The Tsantalis firm reached an agreement with the monks whereby several of the same varieties grown at the Carras estate were planted, in addition to more of the *limnió* already at Athos. The locale used is that called Khromitsa, belonging to the lands of the Russian Monastery of Ayios Panteleimonas. About 6,000 hectolitres of Tsantalis's red and white Ayioritiko wines are produced each year. Though not an appellation of origin, the Ayioritiko name, which indicates 'Ayion Oros', has been authorized since 1981 as a legal *vin de pays* designation for red and white wines with the same respective varietal make-up as their counterparts from Playies Melitona, except that in the case of the red, *cabernet sauvignon* and *cabernet franc* may be in any proportion as long as together they comprise 30 per cent. As with Playies Melitona, the varietal proportions for both the red and the white wine became compulsory only in 1989. A red Ayioritiko from *limnió*, *fokianó* and other red varieties grown at Monoxylitis has lately been offered by the little Protopapas winery.

THRACE

Thus far, Greece's 'pan-handle' region of Thrace, to the east of Macedonia, has not participated in the growing Greek trend towards bottling wine. Thrace is perhaps just a bit too far away from Greece's main population centres to be encouraged to develop wine-growing. Moreover, the region proved to have such outstanding conditions for oriental tobacco cultivation, that the vine has generally been unable to compete, although some land is otherwise quite suitable for it. Even prior to the vogue for smoking, however, the rural Moslem population, which is still found in many places, had kept Thrace poor in vineyards during recent centuries. Inhabitants of the

Eastern Macedonia and Western Thrace

towns of Aegean Thrace were largely supplied with quality wine by
the northerly islands of the Archipelago, especially Thasos and
Bozcaada (Tenedos), or from places now in adjacent Bulgaria, such
as Asenovgrad, and Turkey, like Kirklareli.

Despite the historical hindrances to the development of commercial
wine-growing in Thrace, a local reputation was enjoyed by wines
from the hills north-west of Xanthi, where the *mavroúdi Thrákis*, or
'blackie of Thrace', which is probably a clone of the *mavrud* variety
grown across the Rodopi Mountains at Asenovgrad, is prominent

138

for red wine, and the *zoumiátiko*, known as *dimiat* in Bulgaria, for white. In the far east of Thrace, around Orestias, Didimotikho and Soufli, the variety *pamídi* (or *pamíti*), known as *pamid* in Bulgaria, is grown for dry table wines. *Pamídi*'s name is usually associated with red wine, but the variety has white, red and black forms. Its name, believed to have been compounded from the Greek words *pan* (all) and *méthi* (inebriation), that is *'pamméthi'*, suggests an origin in the remote past when Thrace gave rise to the cult of Dionysus.

MISCELLANY

As the home base of two of the most important wine firms in Greece, Boutari and Tsantalis, the north-eastern mainland is supplying the grapes for a number of wines that have no very precise geographic origin. Some of them are nevertheless 'typical' of the north in the broadest way, usually because of the grape varieties used. In future years, several may serve as a basis for instituting respective *vin de pays* (*topikós ínos*) categories, and be improved as a result. Notable in that regard are the red and white wines sold under the Makedonikos Tsantali label, which are made, respectively, from *xynómavro* grapes of various places and *zoumiátiko* of Serres and Nea Ankhialos by Thessaloniki, as well as Roditis Tsantali, a rosé wine made from *rodítis* grapes grown at Mesemvria and the same Nea Ankhialos.

More eclectic wines are also offered by Boutari and Tsantalis. Rosé Boutari, once an all-*xynómavro* wine, first of Ayios Panteleimonas near Amyntaion, and then of west-central Macedonia at large, has become a blend of *xynómavro* with *ayioryítiko* of Nemea in the Peloponnesos. It is a very slightly off-dry rosé. The dry red Cava Boutari has always been a half-and-half mix of *xynómavro* of the Naousa area and Nemean *ayioryítiko*. It is aged in oak for at least four years and released in vintage-dated bottles. Cava Boutari is a boon to tourists in that it is easily found in half-bottles virtually throughout Greece, and sells sufficiently fast for it always to show as its producer would wish. Tsantalis offers a dry red wine that is a half-and-half mix of *xynómavro* from the Naousa area and *cabernet sauvignon* from Khalkidiki, called Cava Tsantali. Actually it is the firm's reserve red wine, produced in a quantity of about 2,000 hectolitres annually. Full in body and somewhat fleshy in texture when at its best, Cava Tsantali is remarkable for presenting decided character in spite of its mixed origin, and vivid proof that the Greeks have not entirely lost their touch as mixers:

> [A beneficial] result also follows, it is said, from the mixture of different wines – for example, if a strong fragrant wine be mixed with one that is mild and without fragrance (for instance, if the wine of Heraclea be mixed with the wine of Erythrae), since the latter contributes its mildness and the former its fragrance: for the effect is that they simultaneously destroy one another's inferior qualities through the mildness of the one and the fragrance of the other. There are many other such blends mentioned by and known to experts.
>
> (Theophrastus, *Concerning Odours*)

CLASSICAL REFLECTIONS

Some evidence from northern Greece suggests that the ancients' sophisticated debate over wine's relationship to fire and water, which in a real sense was a probing of the question of 'balance', was intricately bound up with the earliest notions pertaining to the nature of Dionysus.

Several of the Greek writers addressed the question of whether wine is 'hot' or 'cold', that is, whether it belongs to the element of fire or water. Noticing both that fermentation engenders 'heat' (or 'seething'), and that wine causes 'heating' in the body, the ancients generally attributed wine's essential nature to fire. On the other hand, however, Plato (*Timaeus*) mentioned wine as a kind of water that had passed through the plants of earth, while Aristotle (*Meteorologica*) observed that wines to a greater or lesser extent behave like watery liquids, in that they evaporate. Furthermore, the ancients also noticed that the sweat provoked by wine 'cools' the body. Plutarch concluded that 'wine is not hot in an absolute sense' (*Moralia*, 'Table-talk'), and in another context suggests that that is just as well since 'fire without moisture is unsustaining and arid', just as 'water without heat is unproductive and inactive' (*Moralia*, 'The Roman Questions'). The yang/yin relationship of the two is also discernible in the Dionysian legends: 'The ethereal flame [Zeus's 'fiery bolt'] blazed with livelier sparks through the water of the torrents which struck it; the thirsty water boiled and steamed, and the liquid essence dried up in the red-hot mass' (Nonnos, *Dionysiaca*).

In eastern Macedonia, south-west of the town of Drama, a prehistoric site called Sitagri has yielded grape seeds whose conformation positively dates grape varieties approximating to the modern cultivated type to as early as the third millennium BC. Significantly, the site is on an artificially drained plain. This strongly suggests that the earliest vine-tenders regarded ample water as a requisite for successful cultivation of the vine. Their judgement had probably originated in their having noticed that the wild vine grew near springs, streams and other relatively wet places where natural vegetation flourished, since it was apparently that same observation which suggested to them a means of propping up vines:

'Spare me, Dionysus, the river-fed from Zeus! Be gracious to my fertilizing waters! for your own goodly fruitage of grapes has grown up from water. I have sinned, Dionysus, nurseling of fire! . . . Destroy not my canes, the growth of my streams, which grow up to support the shoots and grapes of your vine! Do not the reeds tied together carry your well-watered fruit?'

(The nymph Hydapses, in Nonnos's *Dionysiaca*)

Hence too was it related that Hermes had given 'in charge of the daughters of Lamos, river nymphs – the son of Zeus, the vineplanter' Dionysus (*Dionysiaca*). Dionysus's transformation from a god of vegetative growth into a god of the vine could also be explained by the vine's early association with riparian environments.

North-east of Thessaloniki, at the village of Langadas, Greeks relocated from the vicinity of the Black Sea coast in eastern Thrace earlier in this century observe a rite known as the *anastenária*, beginning on 2 May, the Feast of SS Constantine and Helen. Thrace was the source of the Dionysian cult, and the *anastenária*, although long ago christianized, is considered linked by its particulars to true bacchanalia. Among its features are intemperate drinking and the ceremonial slaughter of animals, but the most striking part of the celebration is a barefooted romp on live coals by ecstatic dancers, who suffer no burns in consequence. The circumstance of the dance constitutes perhaps the most telling evidence of the symbolic link between fire, Dionysus and wine in the mind of the early Aegean wine drinker.

Mythology told that Dionysus's mother, Semele, was set afire by

Zeus's thunderbolt when she asked him to reveal his glory, and that while she burned Zeus took the child and sewed it into his leg until it was ready for birth. Consequently, 'the weapon of Dionysus is fire, because it is his father's and comes from the thunderbolt' (Lucian, *Dionysus*). If the myth was not something in the way of a metaphor recommending a Zeus-fearing approach to wine – and perhaps also one intimating an 'unnatural' aspect of the thirst for it – the custom of the *anastenária* dancers in any case seems to reflect a tacit belief that even if Dionysus stood with his feet in water he could be a hothead all the same. 'He set Bacchus more in a flame, since wine excites the mind for desire, and wine finds unbridled youth much more obedient to the rein when it is charmed with the prick of unreason' (Nonnos, *Dionysiaca*).

GASTRONOMIC NOTES

The inland part of northern Greece was marked not merely by certain regional specialities but also by a dietary pattern that separated it from the Aegean world. It could be called Greece's 'continental cuisine', and marked a transition from the Aegean to the central Balkans. While the Aegean area relied on olive oil for fat all year round, the northerly mainland areas used olive oil principally in warm weather and during religious fasting periods, buying the oil from coastal merchants. During the rest of the year, animal fats were customary. Sheep's-milk butter was widely used in the summer, while sheep's suet was typical of late autumn and early winter. In some parts of the far north, pork fat was predominant. Similarly, the consumption of meat by type was also highly seasonal, although in any season meat consumption was greater than in the Aegean. The traditional pattern was lamb in spring and early summer, poultry in late summer, pork in early winter, mutton in late winter, and game throughout the colder months. Beef, however, was not typical of any season, but instead was only an occasional meat, usually available when work animals had been slaughtered. Preserved meats were also very popular and commonplace, especially in the colder weather. Two favourites were *soudgioútsia*, sausages of pork or beef, and *bastourmá*, a smoked meat, usually of sheep or goat.

Traditional northern main courses tend to be meat-heavy compared to their Aegean counterparts. They are generally subsumed under one of three headings: *giouvétsi, kebáb* and *stamnáki*. *Giou-vétsi*, which is named for the open ceramic vessel in which it is baked, is most often a mix of meat and vegetables, although in warm weather possibly a phantasmagoria of fresh vegetables. In any case, northern *giouvétsi* is not to be identified with the pan-Hellenic pot of pasta and meat which goes by that name. *Kebáb* is not usually a skewered preparation, but rather a sort of ragoût stewed in a pan with onion and assorted flavourings. The meat is cut into little pieces to be picked up with a fork, hence the connection with the skewered specialities. *Stamnáki* (little jug) refers to the small-mouthed earthenware container, apparently akin to the ancient *stámnos*, in which a stew is baked under a lid sealed with a dough of flour and water. *Stamnáki* used to be known also by the Turkish-sounding term *tsoblék-kebab* (jug kebab), which again attests to bite-size chunks of meat.

Among the vast repertoire of variations on the three main-course themes, the one that seems to have survived regularly in the cuisine of the *tavérna*, is *tás-kebab*. It is made in a pan, with small chunks of beef or pork, onion, bay leaf, a touch of hot paprika, and perhaps a dash of cinnamon. Olive oil rather than suet serves as the cooking fat nowadays. Traditional northerners must be scandalized by what usually goes under the name *tás-kebab* elsewhere in Greece, good though those dishes may be. Try with *tás-kebab* a newly bottled Kava Khrisokhoou or Pigasos. More unusual, and most rare now – it is hardly to be encountered in the usual town *tavérna* even in its season – is *kavourmás-kebab*, made from pieces of *kavourmás*, which is the Macedonian version of *confit*: pieces of mutton kept in their fat in a sheep's stomach. Drink with it whatever may be available.

In the more northern reaches of Macedonia and Thrace, typically Mediterranean vegetables like aubergine, okra and artichoke were scarcely known before this century. Similarly, the tomato, which was widely adopted in Aegean cooking by the nineteenth century, remained unusual in parts of Macedonia and Thrace until the early twentieth century. Instead, the north had a particular partiality for leek, the gourd-like squashes, and cabbage. Savoury pastries, or *pítes*, filled with leek or squash mixtures were very popular, and both Naousa and Siatista were famous for them, even exporting them to distant towns. Sour cabbage was also known. The area around Kastoria in western Macedonia still makes *armiópita*, a *píta* with a sour cabbage filling; its name is a contraction of *almyrí píta*, which might be rendered in English as 'brine pie'. Choose Amyntaion red to go with it. A sweetish *píta* typical of Macedonia and Thrace is *kolokithópita*, which might be described, however roughly, as a sort of pumpkin strudel. If you can contrive to, drink a glass of Siatista's *liastó* with it.

An important native seasoning is parsley. The Greek names for it are *magdanós* and *makedonísi*, both of which attest to the popular belief that Macedonia is the original provenance of the herb. Parsley appears – or at least it used to appear – as a major flavouring in many dishes. The capsicum family of spice, although not indigenous, has long been known in northern Greece, having spread like wildfire after its introduction in areas of Turkish population. One such area was between Amyntaion and Goumenissa, which today produces virtually all Greek paprika. The centre of production is Aridea. Visitors to Macedonia in the nineteenth century noted the use of paprika in cooking, but other pungent spices were also known, though sweet ones like cinnamon and cloves were not used so often or so emphatically as in the Aegean. Cumin was especially popular in preserved meats. Saffron was also known in Macedonia, and even grown in some places. Herbs and spices were often pounded into composite mixtures, or with still other ingredients into spreads, generically called *piperítsa*, to be used mostly as condiments for bread. *Piperítsa* offers remarkable improvisational opportunities for complementing a wine's aromatic character.

7

Thessaly

In Thessaly there are some excellent growths [crus] on the slopes of Pelion and Ossa, as at Ambelakia, in the valley of Tempe, as well as at the foot of the mountain, toward Farsala, to the north of Trikala, and below the monasteries of Meteora, near Kalambaka.

(Ami Boué, French traveller, *La Turquie d'Europe*, 1840)

Set in the middle of continental Greece, the region of Thessaly sprawls out across a monotonous and fertile plain whose flatness would seem to show little promise wine-wise. In fact, Thessaly's agricultural renown has always rested on its large output of field crops, as attested by archaeological finds that go back to times long before the evidence of written records. Thessaly was Greece's granary during antiquity, and in that regard is second only to much larger Macedonia today. Yet the vine grows wild in parts of Thessaly and viticulture is an ancient branch of farming in the region. A few Thessalian wines may have been well regarded in antiquity, though perhaps mostly ones grown on the periphery of the plain. Thessaly is bounded by mountains and sea, which afford it environments altogether suited to yielding excellent wine. Those areas have been used for wine-growing in recent centuries, and several are at present being tapped for the Greek market. The results with several bottled wines are most encouraging for the future.

RAPSANI

Just before it enters the Vale of Tempe, the National Highway (*Ethnikí Odós*) leading from Thessaloniki south to Athens jags through the south-eastern foothills of Olympus, and in the area

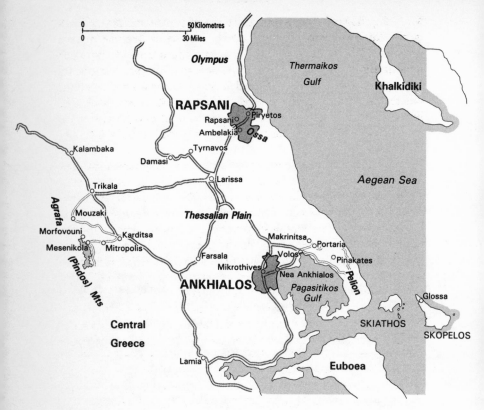

Thessaly

around Mount Kissavos, the ancient Ossa, passes near the vineyards producing Rapsani, the sole Thessalian red wine currently entitled to an appellation of origin, and traditionally one of the most touted of the mainland. Vineyards may have been planted on Kissavos in ancient times, but, if so, they were not precisely those of Rapsani. Founded in the late fifteenth century, the village is another living monument to the Ottoman occupation, when refugees fled out of sight, into the mountains. Ever since its settlement, Rapsani has been the chief wine village of the area, and today supplies 80–90 per cent of the raw material grown in the appellation zone. The only other villages of this tiny wine district are neighbouring Piryetos, Krania and Ambelakia. Excepting Piryetos, which was in the thrall of Turkish and Greek landlords until around the time of the First World

War, they have a long tradition of interdependence, dating back to the late eighteenth century, when Ambelakia became a most prominent Thessalian town, owing to its manufacture and export of high-quality yarn, which spawned a cooperative-like production unit linking the three villages. The demise of the yarn trade in the nineteenth century plunged Ambelakia into obscurity, and then into decline as a settlement. Once a substantial producer of wine, Ambelakia, whose name means 'Little Vineyards', is quite insignificant now.

Earlier in this century, before phylloxera and emigration took their toll, about 500 hectares of vines were cultivated in the Rapsani area. At present, the total is about 300 hectares. The vineyards are situated mostly in the range of 300–500 metres above sea level, and generally face south-east. The juxtaposition of the Olympus massif and the Aegean Sea creates a delicate climatic situation: while the influence of Olympus works towards lowering air temperature, exposure to the Aegean environment has a contrary influence. The result is that the Rapsani vintage is one of the most quixotic on the mainland for the wine-grower to contend with. Too much of a swing one way or the other during the growing season skews the character of the vintage, especially towards excessive malic acid and somewhat severe wine if the weather is too cool, and highly alcoholic yet thin wine if too warm. Of special concern is the *lívas*, the very warm, dry southwesterly wind that blows through the Tempe Gorge in summer, and which can rob the fruit of needed moisture. Some protection from the *lívas* is afforded by the ample autumn and winter precipitation that characterizes the Olympus area, and seeps down through Kissavos further into the year, nourishing, but not collecting in, the calcareous land on which the Rapsani vineyards are planted.

Mostly, three dark grape varieties are grown around Rapsani: *xynómavro, stavrotó* (also called *ambelakiótiko* locally) and *krasáto*. The varietal complement apparently reflects geographic location. Rapsani is the southernmost major traditional site of the Macedonian *xynómavro*, while also one of the more northerly sites of the *stavrotó*, which in spite of having the synonym 'Ambelakiote' is thought to have originated on Euboea, off the Thessalian coast to the south-east. Only the *krasáto* is considered native to the general area around Kissavos. Whatever its lineage, the *krasáto* evokes ancient associations by its name alone, which means 'wine-coloured'. The term frequently occurs in classical literature as a description of the

147

range of colour from purple to bluish-black, though in the classical Greek terms *ínops (oenops)* (wine-looking) and *inódis (oenodis)* (winy), the latter as in Homer's 'wine-dark sea'. Curiously then, if the *krasáto* looks 'wine-dark' on the vine, it is actually relatively lacking in the anthocyanins that give violet colour to deeply red wines, and needs to be vinified with other varieties in order for the colour of its wine to be darkened and intensified. However, while the appellation regulation for Rapsani wine requires the use of all three of the named varieties, no proportion is specified. Traditionally, village habits in the latter regard have varied. Indeed at Ambelakia the *stavrotó* has always been the most favoured variety, and is sometimes used to the near-exclusion of the other two varieties, or else with a fourth red sort, the *limnió* (called *limnióna* locally).

Nearly 1,000 tons of grapes are harvested from the Rapsani vintage in an average year. About 300–400 tons of that is processed by the Wine Production Cooperative of Rapsani. Although it is the major producer of Rapsani wines, the Cooperative buys a relatively small share of local grape production, owing to its stipulation that the vineyards from which it buys must be planted one-third to each of the varieties required by the appellation rules; hence Ambelakia, so heavily given over to *stavrotó*, sells less to the Cooperative than even Piryetos and Krania. The measure is intended to enhance wine quality by assuring evenness of quality in the purchased grapes of the three varieties. Also, the Cooperative hopes that by offering higher prices for qualifying grapes, they will encourage local growers to plant in a corresponding manner, thereby enabling production of a greater quantity of wine in the future. They are not fully able to stimulate and guide development of the Rapsani region as they see fit, though. Their winery, which sits alongside the National Highway near the turn-off for the village of Rapsani, belongs, not to the Cooperative, but to the Agricultural Bank of Greece, which financed its construction and has kept it under its not always very green thumb ever since. The Cooperative is not particularly pleased by the situation, feeling that the Bank, an interloper in the region, so to speak, retards the area's viticultural revival. They hope to take over control completely in the future.

The vintage at Rapsani takes place in late September. Fermentation of the must is on skins only, for about one month; home-made wines are fermented on stalks as well. Between 60 and 70 per cent of the grapes delivered to the Cooperative become appellation wine, or about 1,200–2,000 hectolitres annually, to be bottled under the Rapsani label. It is a 12.5° wine, bottled after at least three years in oak. Appellation regulations specify a minimum of only one year, which seems rather optimistic in view of the usual need – even in an ideal vintage – for an extensive malolactic, or secondary, fermentation. The Cooperative also produces two other wines: Rosso, one of the best second-line red wines in Greece; and an unusual and savoury rosé called Bella Rosa.

A second producer of Rapsani wine is Mitrakos Brothers, whose annual production has varied from 50–100 hectolitres since they began bottling in 1982. Their wine, called Kentavros (Centaur), is produced entirely from grapes bought from a select few wine-growers around Rapsani, but may not carry an appellation since it is vinified outside the Rapsani zone, at Pournari, to the south near Larisa. Mitrakos Brothers also vinify the three requisite varieties in approximately equal proportion. Kentavros usually spends at least eighteen months in barrel, but more time is given to those wines chosen to be designated further by a 'Réserve Spéciale' neck label. It is planned that in the best years the entire output will justifiably be bottled with that distinction. In lesser years, only those barrels whose contents meet rigorous objective (measurable) and sensory standards will be marketed as 'Réserve Spéciale'. For instance, only one barrel from the first vintage for which the designation was used, 1984 – a very good one – met them. In some years, too, there will be none. The 'Réserve Spéciale' is marked especially by very formidable body and 13.5–14.5° alcohol. The plain Kentavros is considerably lighter and at 12.5°, generally, it is in all respects more like the Cooperative's appellation wine, which should by no means be overlooked.

Among Greek red wines coming from appellation regions, I have found none so radically divergent, one from the other, as Rapsani and Kentavros 'Réserve Spéciale'. Bottle-ready Rapsani varies in colour from dark copper with full onion-skin tones at the rim, to a particular orange-red which only some manufacturers of children's wax crayons seem to reproduce. Kentavros, on the other hand, is a blackish-red trying to pass for mahogany. Other features of the two wines are in no less striking contrast. The bouquet of Rapsani combines something of berries with more of plums, and perhaps still more of stewed rhubarb. And yet none of that manages to submerge an aspect I have heard likened, with some reason, to the Middle Eastern eggplant-sesame-lemon creation, *baba ghanouj*. Kentavros is evocative of the aromas of leather and tobacco, but somehow, I also spot the humble celery seed in there – in the nicest way, to be sure. In the finish, Rapsani is marked by an emphatic vigour of after-taste featuring a healthy, citrus-like tang, and a rinsing of the palate which at times seems to occur quite literally 'in waves', while Kentavros trails off like the biggest and grandest kind of Barolo imaginable.

Nor have I ever so utterly despaired of finding a straight answer to the intrusive question, so disruptive of enjoyment, as to which of two wines is a more worthy representative of their region. While I would have to concede a conventional superiority to the eminently age-worthy Kentavros 'Réserve Spéciale', I have never been able to pour off the last glass from a bottle of Rapsani without feeling profoundly grateful that it is as it is. What might otherwise be disparaged as a certain 'roughness' has in Rapsani been raised to a virtue worthy of Olympus and its gambolling, vying, almost flesh-and-blood deities whom I expect would be sorely disappointed with any drink we mortals might call 'divine' or 'heavenly'. More than any other sort of red wine I have come upon, Rapsani's feel has demonstrated to me why the Greeks would have applied their word *kharaktír* to a wine: 'character' literally indicates a 'notching'. Do not make the mistake of treating this rolling stone as though it were one of our moss-gathering wines. Be sure to drink it within a couple of years of its bottling, before it has lost its splendid nerve and inimitable, arresting display of 'harmony-in-motion'.

Owing to its finish, Rapsani may please many who normally would not choose a red of more than light-medium body as a pre-dinner wine. The persistent crackling sensations of appetizers like *tyrópita* and *spanakotyrópita* triangles provide a curious counterweight to the wine's finish. Bitterish morsels, like olives, are accommodated, and so are frankly salty titbits. Well-herbed *souvláki* is a good choice for more substantial snacks, although I would not claim it superior to pastrami on rye. If bringing a bottle home from holiday, one should not neglect poultry dishes in which the crisp, browned skin of the bird figures as a prize morsel, whether Cantonese roast duck with Chinese broccoli, Peking duck, or, more mundanely, chicken glazed with honey. A grand accompaniment is minced rabbit and spinach *en croûte* with Dijon sauce. Kentavros 'Réserve Spéciale' gets my approval for the heartiest stews, casseroles, and game dishes.

ANKHIALOS

Thessaly also has an appellation of origin entitlement for a white wine, produced at Ankhialos, a seaside community of Magnisia located a few miles south of Thessaly's port city of Volos, on the Pagasitikos Gulf. Included in the boundaries of the appellation zone are vineyards of the name-giving place, which is by far the major source of grapes, as well as Mikrothives, the only other significant producer, and, nominally, Aïdinio and Krokki. The appellation entitlement specifies dry white wine of at least 85 per cent *rodítis* grapes and the remainder *savatianó*, two white varieties which respectively occupy about 75 and 10 per cent of the nearly 400 hectares of vines planted.

Several additional requirements pertain to the production of appellation Ankhialos wine. All of the grapes must be grown on unsupported vines, since those trained on cordons in this area yield four times as much fruit, and wine of palpably lesser quality. Also, none of the slightly reddish colour in the skin of *rodítis* grapes grown at Ankhialos may be picked up by the wine. Traditionally in the area, some household producers encourage a rosy tint by fermenting on the skins a few days. The stipulation for the appellation wine is motivated in part because the variety concerned is the white *rodítis*, and in part because tannins that would be imparted to the wine along with colour would detract from 'freshness'. Also with the aim of achieving freshness, the wine must not come into contact with wood. The extra expense entailed by the latter provision hinders individual growers who might otherwise care to attempt to produce and bottle an appellation wine. None is soon likely to refurbish and compete with the local Dimitra Cooperative, which is producing a very good appellation wine, under the Anchialos label. It is a 90 per cent *rodítis* wine bottled about six months after the vintage, with vintage indication. The first bottling was in 1983 (1982 vintage), in an amount of 1,000 hectolitres, compared to Dimitra's total output of 40,000 hectolitres. More Anchialos is planned for future years.

The nature of Anchialos owes a great deal to its origin in a very low-lying wine district which fronts on to the sea. Most of its vineyards are in the range of about 100 metres above sea level, and some go right down to the water's edge, though few of these qualify for appellation wine because they are mostly cordon-trained. None of the vineyards goes above the 200-metre mark – most of those are found at Mikrothives. Because of the proximity of the sea, and especially its saturation of the local soil, a notable characteristic of Anchialos is a very high level of dry extract, but particularly sodium chloride. Attributed to that is an impression of medium body that the wine's alcohol alone, at 11.5°, would be unlikely to leave. The particular make-up of extract content is also credited with a most unusual sensation: an immediate, intense and long-lasting drying feel on the forward upper surface of the tongue. Yet neither fruitiness nor freshness is lacking, or at least not while the wine is within a year or so of the vintage date and holds its silvery greenish-straw colour. The barest carbonic sensation provides a certain sprightliness as well.

For accompanying Anchialos, this most unusual white wine, I would especially recommend any kind of salted crisp served with guacamole dip, and relatively plain foods that can be served with sour cream or yogurt, such as potato pancakes or meatless stuffed grapevine leaves. Despite its seaside birthplace, Anchialos has not impressed me as having a special affinity for seafood, though one day I may smuggle a flask of it into my favourite sushi bar, where it can meet up with its element in the raw.

Other wines of the Dimitra Cooperative also convey pelagic notions of vinous harmony. Prominent among them is the dry white Nymphe, formerly their flagship wine. A lesser white is Lefkos Xiros ('White Dry'). Its red counterpart, Erythros Xiros ('Red Dry'), is produced from the *sykiótis*, a black variety occupying about 15 per cent of vineyard land around Ankhialos. As one might expect of a red wine grown in this area, Erythros Xiros is nearly parching, even though it is not remarkably tannic at all. Dimitra's Retsina, a wine with virtually no tradition in Thessaly except in some areas adjacent to Central Greece, perhaps qualifies as the really quintessential Greek wine: product of vine, pine and brine.

KARDITSA-AGRAFA

One of the larger vineyard areas of Thessaly is situated all the way inland, due west of Volos, and centred around the large country town of Karditsa. A majority of the nearly 1,600 hectares of vines is planted in proximity to the town itself, but all fall within the nomarchy of Karditsa. Consequently, the bottled wines being produced in the area, all by the Union of Agricultural Cooperatives of Karditsa, tend to be identified as 'Karditsa wine'. In a very real sense, however, two quite distinct wine regions are subsumed under that name. The one comprises the level fields of vines around Karditsa, which are surrounded by far more fields of crops. Mostly dessert or dual-purpose grapes are grown: *moskháto amvoúrgou* (muscat of Hamburg); *batíki*, which is a sort commonly found in Thessaly, but originally brought from Asia Minor; *rozakí*; and *fráoula*. Plantings of strictly wine grape varieties are quite in the minority, and a very large portion of those is *savatianó*.

The other vineyard zone of Karditsa consists of the villages of Agrafa, the latter name being that applied to the mountains in the south-east of the Pindos range. Agrafa has had a somewhat peculiar history for an area in the centre of the mainland. It escaped the reach of spreading feudalism in Byzantine times because its terrain and meagre lands for farming were not conducive to the easy imposition of land concentration that took place on the plain. Later, the Agrafa villages offered sufficient armed resistance to the Ottomans to persuade the conquerors that this particular conquest was not worth their while, so that the lands there were never collected up into fiefdoms as on the plain. The peasants were thus left free to cultivate whatever they were wont to, and most maintained vineyards.

The most important wine villages of Agrafa are Mesenikola, Moskhato, Morfovouni and Mitropoli, while a lesser role is played by Ayios Yeoryios, Xynoneri, Mouzaki, Paliouri and Dafnospilia. Their vineyards are primarily planted with wine grape varieties, including *savatianó* in post-phylloxera times, but featuring the *mávro mesenikóla* (Mesenikola black), which will probably gain Karditsa – not Agrafa – an appellation of origin entitlement within a few years' time. Despite its name, which would appear to stake a firm claim to indigenous origin, the *mávro mesenikóla* is mentioned in local lore as having been brought to Agrafa from Western Europe in Ottoman times, by a certain Monsieur Nicolas (*Mesenikóla*) who lent his name first to the village, and through that to the grape. However that may be, the *mávro mesenikóla* became the most highly regarded variety on Agrafa, and was extensively planted. Nevertheless, only about 100 hectares of the variety are cultivated today, owing to the decline in vineyard area that was caused by the arrival of phylloxera in the late 1920s, as well as the post-Second World War population exodus. The vineyards are located primarily in the range of 250–600 metres above sea level, which roughly comprises the semi-mountainous zone, but also reach Lake Tavropos, or Megdova, at 800 metres. The utilized land is mostly sloping, except at Mitropoli and Xynoneri, where level land is more usual.

The leading wine of the Union is Erato, a 12° alcohol, 100 per cent varietal *mávro mesenikóla* wine made from free-run must of carefully selected grapes, fermented on skins only, and matured for two to three years in oak before bottling. About 3,000 hectolitres are made annually, but Erato is not released as vintage-dated wine. Its bright cherry-red colour is likely to please, and its light flavour can appeal as well. If Erato has a shortcoming, it must be that it is 'clean' to a fault, not quite suggesting that it has a place it calls home, much less one as individual as Agrafa. Plans call for deepening the colour and raising extract content by deriving 10–12 per cent of the must from either *petit syrah* or *cabernet sauvignon*, while also gaining an appellation of origin entitlement based on a like varietal formula. It remains to be seen, however, whether that step alone will contribute the facet Erato seems to lack. Perhaps a better result would be produced if the Union were also to realize their hope of eventually producing a reserve (*káva*) wine from *mávro mesenikóla* grapes grown only in the best vineyards of the semi-mountainous zone of Agrafa.

At this time, perhaps the more convincing proof of the quality inherent in the *mávro mesenikóla* is the Union's Rozé. Produced in an amount of nearly 2,000 hectolitres each year, it is an all-*mávro mesenikóla* rosé of free-run must. Firm and crisp, and with a characteristic fruit flavour, the orange-tinged Rozé is on a par with all but the very best rosé wines of Greece. Other wines of the Union, all of which appear under the Tavropos brand, include a pair each of red and white dry wines under the Lito and Nefeli labels, respectively the better and lesser. The reds are made in part with *mávro mesenikóla* must, but also *moskháto amvoúrgou*, as well as other red varieties grown to a small extent around Karditsa, such as *séfko (séfka/shevka)* and *senzó (cinsault)*. The whites are derived from *savatianó* and *batíki*. A retsina is produced exclusively from *savatianó*, and is among the few grown outside Central Greece that compares really well with the typical bottled retsinas of that region. The Union's wine offerings are completed by its Imiglyko, a semi-sweet red produced from *moskháto amvoúrgou*.

TYRNAVOS

The greatest concentration of Thessalian vineyards is in the north-easterly area around Tyrnavos, another country town, just to the north-west of the regional capital of Larisa. A Greek codex from 1792 indicates that the wines from this area had a good name, despite their origin on the plain. It should be noted as well, lest one think that Tyrnavos could have enjoyed its little bit of repute only among the miserable peasantry of Ottoman times, that the English traveller Leake wrote in 1835 that 'good wine' can be produced on the plain when attentive care is given. In Ottoman times, however, there was not much scope for exploiting the potential. The large Turkish agricultural estates, *chifliks*, typical of the plain, mostly produced grain. Even after the Greek state took control of Thessaly in 1881, economic conditions on the plain scarcely changed, Greek landlords merely replacing Turkish ones. Grapes could not compete with grain on their abacus either. The turning-point for viticulture, as for all other agricultural pursuits in Thessaly, was an agrarian uprising at the Kileler estate in 1910. Land distribution was begun in consequence, and only after that did conditions for wine-growing improve substantially.

The environment for viticulture is perhaps not quite so negative as one might think in taking a panoramic view of the Tyrnavos area. For one thing, elevation, at about 130 metres above sea level, is not quite so low as it might seem; also, upon closer examination, some incline is perceptible in places. The area is consequently not entirely at the mercy of blistering insolation or waterlogged soil. The soil, for that matter, is a sandy clay very suitable for the vine. The real Achilles' heel of the region seems to be, rather, its varietal complement. Of the nearly 3,000 hectares of vines now crowding Tyrnavos, the preponderant part is in the dual-purpose variety *moskháto amvoúrgou*, with a dwindling amount of *batíki* as well. The *savatianó* is the only significant wine grape. The Thessalian plain has grown mainly dessert grapes at least since Ottoman days, when the Turkish landlords had them cultivated for their table. Except for the introduction of the *savatianó* after phylloxera struck, there has been little tendency to break out of that pattern and seek suitable wine-grape varieties. On account of the use of *moskháto amvoúrgou* and *batíki* for wine, Tyrnavos is ineligible for an appellation of origin.

The bottled Tyrnavos wine deserving most attention is the dry red

61, produced by the Wine Cooperative of Tyrnavos, and named after the year in which the present winery was established. A limited-production wine, made in a quantity of about 500 hectolitres annually, 61 is the product exclusively of free-run juice of selected *moskháto amvoúrgou* grapes, a significant amount of which comes from the village of Damasi. It receives four to five years in oak before being bottled as a non-vintage wine. Alcohol is at 12.5°. A crimson rose-coloured wine of lightish body, 61 displays the marked softness typical of Tyrnavos wines, although it does linger finally to refresh with acidity. The aromatics are of an unabashedly perfumed flower-iness. Altogether, one may be reminded of that passage of *The Deipnosophists* in which it was said that the Thessalians 'emulated Persian luxury and extravagance' and were 'the most extravagant of all the Greeks in the matter both of clothing and food'. For some Westerners, 61 is not at all as red table wine ought to be.

The rosé and white companions in the Cooperative's trio of better wines are marketed respectively under the Maïstrali and Arletta labels, the first being another *moskháto amvoúrgou* wine, and the second a combination of *batíki* with the predominant *savatianó*. Lesser dry wines are whites labelled Areto and Lefkos, the rosé Kokkineli, and the red Erythros. The Cooperative also makes sweet red wines from the *moskháto amvoúrgou*, relying partially on concentrated must for sweetness, and grape spirits for alcohol. Fivos, of free-run must, and Ira, respectively the more and less fortified, are the fully sweet wines, while a lesser Imiglyko, a semi-sweet wine, is also produced. Enjoyment of them depends very greatly on their freshness in bottle, although even then their character as sweet muscat wines seems somewhat muted. A second producer of plains' wines, Vasdavanos Brothers, bottles dry white, rosé, and red wines under the Leda label, which seem to me to fall somewhere between the better and lesser wines of the respective types produced by the Cooperative. The Leda wines have not travelled securely beyond Piraeus.

PELION AND SKOPELOS

Another Thessalian area which, like Rapsani, had quite a reputation for its dry red wine in the past is Pelion, the mountainous peninsula and scenic gem of Magnisia, curving around to the south-east from

1 Samos (Eastern Sporades). Terraced vineyards of *moskháto áspro* in the north-central semi-mountainous zone.

2 Samos. A rainbow of muscat wine – from young dry wine from fresh grapes on the left, to aged sweet wine from partially raisined grapes on the right.

3 Rhodes (Dodecanese). Plantings of *athíri* on the flanks of Mt. Ataviros by Embouas.

4 Santorini (Cyclades). Vineyards on the island's inclined plateau, looking north from Fira.

5 Naousa (Macedonia). Rows of *xynómavro* at Yiannakokhori.

6 Rapsani (Thessaly). Vintage-time on the spínes of Mt. Kissavos, the Ossa of the ancients.

7 Nemea (Peloponnesos). *Ayioryítiko* ripening in 'the deep valley of Nemea' (Pindar, *The Nemean Odes*)

8 Cephalonia (Ionian Islands). View southeast towards the island capital of Argostoli, from *robóla* vineyards in the appellation zone near Dilinata.

Volos. Currently, though, Pelion is of no commercial significance in wine, having suffered a string of economic reverses in the nineteenth century, followed by phylloxera and emigration in the twentieth. The visitor mostly finds red wines that go by the generic name *Piliorítiko broúsko*. At the high villages of Makrinitsa and Portaria, they are made from a varying assortment of grapes, which may reflect post-phylloxera chaos in planting.

Pelion's only remaining wines of note are found in the village of Pinakates, somewhat further down the arm of Pelion, and a couple of hundred metres lower in altitude. Its repute long ago made wine an important part of Pinakates' livelihood, and perhaps has in some measure helped preserve the varietal profile of earlier times. The *sykiótis*, a typical Magnisian sort for red wine, is the main variety, with some *vradianó* as well, and a little bit of *limnió* supplementing those. The *vradianó* arrived on Pelion from Euboea, where it is said to have been brought by Frenchmen who had come there for wine even before the phylloxera episode. It is also known as *vordianó*, a name alluding more recognizably to the popular belief that it hailed from Bordeaux. Pinakates' wine still has a clientele on Pelion and in Volos, but that will not do much to help put it up in corked and labelled bottles in the near future.

Spreading eastward off Pelion are the Northern Sporades group of islands, which are administered as part of Thessaly. Their tradition in wine seems to be something of an amalgam of coastal and deepwater Aegean influences, woven together by a northern mainland sensibility about wine. Probably because of nearby Euboea, the pineforested Northern Sporades are not unfamiliar with resination. However, their main grape variety is the *limnió*, whose wine is not usually resinated. The largest wine producer among them is Skopelos, where the *limnió* is especially characteristic. Although resin is a product of the island, the folk who peopled Skopelos in the midsixteenth century (at the behest of a *chef des cuisines* of the Sultan, related Pouqueville) were from Thessaly and Macedonia, two mainland regions with little or no acquaintance with resination. Pouqueville considered that Skopeliote wine 'deserves to be regarded as the best of the islands of the Aegean Sea' – presumably he would not have said that of a resinated wine – and in his day it was widely traded in the Aegean, since Skopelos, unlike most of the small offshore islands near the east-central mainland, had a substantial surplus to export. In this century, however, phylloxera and the competition of plum trees, whose dried fruit has found a more remunerative market than wine, have left vineyard area on Skopelos greatly reduced in extent. The main wine village is Glossa, in the north.

CLASSICAL REFLECTIONS

Could the wine of Ankhialos reflect a recidivist Greek penchant for *thalassítis*, the ancient wine made with admixture of seawater?

Although *thalassítis* may seem to us the most bizarre and indefensible of ancient Greek wines, its fabrication was none the less carried out with reason and great care. Seawater was not thought an appropriate addition to all wines, and in those cases in which it was, the proportion of water to wine could vary. Furthermore, local lore dictated where and when to take the water, for not all seawater was thought suitable. For example, Pliny noted one rule of thumb in use in Greece:

> [the water should be] obtained a long way out to sea at the spring equinox and then kept in store, or at all events it should be taken up during the night at the time of the solstice and when a north wind is blowing, or if it is obtained about vintage time it should be boiled before being used.
>
> (*Natural History*)

Also, it may have been a technique reserved for use in conjunction with certain other procedures, since Pliny indicated that such was the case with the wine which the Greeks called 'white Koan', the most famous *thalassítis* of all.

As with other admixtures, the addition of seawater in making wine would probably have been justified in terms of the established principle for mixing things of different kind, as stated by Galen: 'it is impossible for anything to be assimilated by, and to change into anything else unless they already possess a certain community and affinity in their qualities' (*On the Natural Faculties*). Seawater's 'community and affinity' with wine stemmed from the salt it contained. Salt, having both a burning taste and a drying physiological effect, was seen as belonging to the realm of 'hot' and 'heating' things to which wine also essentially belonged. A physical property of seawater in which salt's nature was manifest was that of 'oiliness' (*liparótita*):

> Why is the sea less cold than fresh water . . . ? . . . is it because sea-water is more greasy [*liparotéra*), and so does not extinguish the heat? The same thing is true of other substances. For that which is more greasy is warmer.

> (Aristotle, *Problems*)

Indeed, seawater was mentioned as 'flammable' by Plutarch (*Moralia*, 'Table-talk').

Pliny's aforementioned instruction on boiling seawater not taken at the appropriate time, makes it apparent that it was specifically the 'oil' contained in it that was sought by wine-makers, since the watery part of the liquid would evaporate. Still, the desired flavour effect, as opposed to any preservative quality, may have varied from wine to wine. In the case of certain sweet wines, such as 'white Koan', the purpose was probably to impart some of the 'piquant' taste of salt's 'oil'. Conversely, for some other wines – primarily dry ones, we may presume – smoother feel, or texture, may have been the goal; along parallel lines, it was said that 'moderately salty foods, on account of their pleasant taste, bring out the sweetness and smoothness of any kind of wine' (Plutarch, *Moralia*, 'Table-talk'). In all cases, however, the underlying objective always would have been to render the wine more vinous by having it draw in some way on the kindred 'heat' of seawater.

But in addition to *thalassítis*, the ancients also knew wines that acquired their sea legs on the vine itself, owing to the site. Theophrastus mentioned the wine of Erythrae, near Smyrna on the littoral of Asia Minor, as having 'a taste of brine', and Pliny referred to a wine of Lesvos which 'by dint of its own nature smacks of the sea'. Growing vines by the seaside, and adding seawater during wine-making, must be different kettles of fish, however. The wines of Ankhialos, anyway, are short of 'oil' and suggest their seaworthiness only in their peculiar species of dryness.

GASTRONOMIC NOTES

Mealtimes in Thessaly could seem a mostly offal experience. The region's most characteristic eatery, at any rate, seems to be the *skembedzídiko*, or tripery, where wine is sometimes available and sometimes not. Ask for Tyrnavos's 61 if it is to hand. Although *skembés* has no exclusive connection with Thessaly, so many Greek cattle are raised and slaughtered in the region that tripe is abundant, and probably always has been ('These cattle must have been of Thessalian stock,' Pausanias, *Description of Greece*). Mutton, in the form of whole-roasted rams or barren ewes, is an old speciality of Thessaly, and used to be associated with the merchants' fairs held round about the plain. Ewe's-milk cheeses from the mountainous western part of the region are generally considered to be the best of Thessaly, but cow's-milk cheese from the plain has become far more prevalent as a commercial product in recent decades. Both the ewe's-milk and the cow's-milk cheeses are well complemented by either the green olives of Pelion or the larger, brownish and very round olives that bear the name of Volos.

At Ambelakia, the villagers make a special dish of meat cooked with quince in a tomato sauce. The best known local dish of Thessaly is, however, one from Pelion called *spétsofaï*, which is a kind of sausage made from sheep or goat meat and flavoured with cumin, red pepper and black pepper. These days *Piliorítiko loukániko* (Peliorite sausage) is made mostly down in Volos by professional butchers. Their product differs from the home-made kind more in appearance than in flavour, the prototype being shorter and of smaller diameter – actually similar to a standard cigar – but the Peliorites consider that the Volos-made sausage does not have quite the same savour as their very own, which is made only from Pelion's animals. Nothing is to be done, however, because the sheep and goat population of Pelion has been falling at a faster rate than Greek tourist demand for *spétsofaï* has been growing, on account of the declining availability of shepherds. The dish consists of sausage segments, or discs if the larger commercial kind is used, simmered in olive oil with tomatoes and green peppers. It is served at all of the *tavérnas* in Makrinitsa and Portaria, most of which also have some of the local *broúsko* wine.

Appropriately for Thessaly, its most renowned specialities are the grain-based sweets of Farsala. These are classed as halvah: *sousám-khalvás* is made from sesame, wheat starch, chick-peas and sugar; *kommát-khalvás* is a rather hard, white variety of halvah sold in small pieces; *assouté-khalvás* is a softer halvah of wheat, made for consumption within a short time after preparation; *pirínts-khalvás* is based on rice flour; and *sapouné-khalvás* is made from durum semolina, sugar and blanched almond slices. The latter, whose name means 'soapy halvah' and alludes to the opaque, greasy, brownish-yellow appearance of its interior, is considered the best of all. It is widely known in Greece under the name *khalvás Farsálon* (halvah of Farsala) as well, the town's name having become associated with it because of the exceptional quality of the area's durum wheat, and because that sort of *khalvás* became a perennial favourite at the annual fair of Farsala, which is still held in mid-August. Baked to a crusty golden-brown in large, round, shallow tins, the true version will bring words like Zorba's 'splendiferous' to mind in gazing at it. *Khalvás Farsálon* is dense and unctuous – perhaps *sapouné* should be translated as 'lathered' – but crisp as well. Toasts to the Persian extravagance of the Thessalians are in order.

8

Central Greece and Euboea

Indeed Attica is the place for retsina, and retsina is the drink for Attica, whether in the city, inland or by the sea. The resin which gives its name and its peculiar taste to the wine seems to me not only a preservative, but to infuse something of the sharpness and brilliance of the bright air around the mountain pine woods. It is not, however, to everyone's stomach. Some will tell you that it is an acquired taste and will describe how they themselves have laboriously acquired it. Others, like myself, will enjoy it from the very first sip. Some unfortunates will never enjoy it at all. Indeed they are to be pitied...

Rex Warner, English traveller, Views of Attica, 1950

Below Epirus and Thessaly, the mainland explorer enters the area Western travellers of past centuries customarily referred to as 'Lower Greece', which was to say the southern part of the mainland. The Greeks actually call the area between Epirus and Thessaly on the north, and the Gulf of Corinth on the south, 'Mainland Greece' (Sterea Ellas). Other names for it, respectively colloquial and official, are Roumeli and Central Greece (Kentriki Ellas). Central Greece stretches from the Ionian Sea on the west to the Aegean on the east, where the large island of Euboea (Evia) hugs its north-eastern coast and consequently has been attached to it administratively. As a combined region, Central Greece and Euboea have the largest wine production among the Greek regions, amounting to nearly one-third of the country's total. The great majority of the region's wine is produced in its eastern portion, comprising the nomarchies of Boeotia (Viotia) and Attica (Attiki), which occupy the part of the mainland that juts out into the Aegean, as well as Euboea. The area is really very much a part of the Aegean world in terms of environment and agriculture, as shown by the profusion of olive trees, in addition to the extensive plantings of vines.

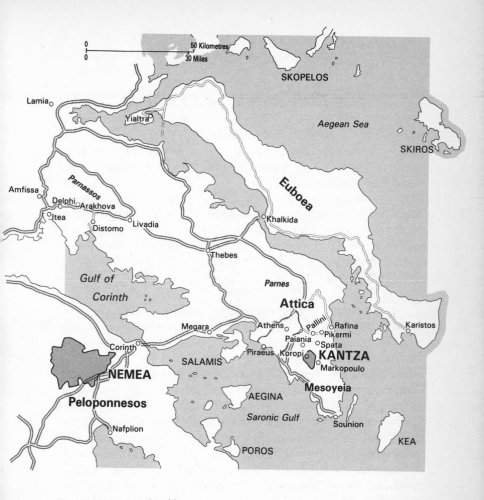

Boeotia, Attica and Euboea

The most salient characteristic of wine-growing in Central Greece and Euboea, after its concentration in the east, is the overwhelming predominance of one type of wine, the resinated dry white wine known far and wide, retsina. The predominance of retsina, which most Greeks still think of as a regional wine and associate specifically with Central Greece and Euboea, is attributable in large part to characteristic environmental factors that exerted a very strong influence on both wine production and wine consumption habits in the region's traditional rural life. Also, trade between Attica, through

163

the port of Piraeus, and the Archipelago, which has been active since antiquity, served over the centuries to reinforce these factors by carrying the domination of retsina over into the sphere of commercial wine. A rudimentary 'division of labour' evolved, whereby esteemed, and more stable, unresinated wines of the Archipelago, especially those from the nearby Cyclades, were imported into Athens and the rest of Attica, generally making it difficult for local wine-growers to compete in the town markets for unresinated wines, given the costs that would have been entailed in producing sound unresinated wines under local conditions.

Retsina's hold on Central Greece and Euboea has in turn favoured two grape varieties, the white *savatianó* and a red-dish *rodítis*, from which most retsina is made. The *savatianó*, which turns up elsewhere in Greece under a variety of names, is the more important of the two, and occupies about 90 per cent of vineyard land in Attica, 70–80 per cent in most parts of Euboea, and 50 per cent in Boeotia. It owes its dominance in part to relatively high yields and to its suitability for the very warm and dry climate in the parts of the region where it is grown, but also to the replanting that took place in Central Greece and Euboea during the inter-war years, in the aftermath of phylloxera. Government agronomists at that time advised growers to plant the remuneratively yielding *savatianó* in order to secure farm income and thus hurry along the replanting. As a consequence, the variety today is frequently found cultivated in places where it would not have been the chosen variety under less urgent circumstances. Yet, grown on appropriate land, *savatianó* vines of good clone can yield the firm, though not crisp, wines that have earned it high marks as a wine-grape variety from authorities ranging from the Greek ampelographer Krimbas (1943), to the French viticulturalist Viala (1921), and the Italian enologist Di Stefano (1968). Moreover, in coming decades, as the wine companies and cooperatives of Central Greece and Euboea give more attention to quality unresinated *savatianó* wines than they did in the past, the variety perhaps will gradually recover its reputation, damaged by association with retsina, which today plagues its image outside Greece, and even win a modicum of admiration for the not inconsiderable qualities it can display.

RETSINA

A feature distinguishing the eastern portion of Central Greece and Euboea from the Archipelago is the area's widespread pine forests, which have been exploited since antiquity for commercial purposes as well as for household needs. On account of the accessibility of that resource, it was perhaps inevitable that the resin of the trees would in one way or another make contact with the abundant wine of the region. Certainly the several stories the Greeks traditionally tell purporting to explain the origin of resination suggest an accidental discovery such as would have been likely to occur only where the pine tree was sufficiently profuse to be systematically made use of for its several products.

The oral traditions also agree in linking the initial popularity of resination to the preservation of wines. On the one hand, the application of resinous material for sealing purposes could make wine containers relatively airtight prior to their being broached. On the other hand, the disintegration of resinous material in the wine would cause an imperceptible film of turpentine oil to float on the surface, thereby hindering the wine's contact with oxygen after the container was broached, though only until the next vintage or so. The preservative effect of resinous material probably had no association with the notion of laying wine aside for beneficial ageing, that is 'improvement', for the Greeks would seem to have been doubtful about the duration of resination's possible effectiveness in that way: Plutarch regarded it as axiomatic that 'all mixtures are more likely to putrefy than what is unmixed', because mixture 'produces conflict, conflict produces change, and putrefaction is a kind of change' (*Moralia*, 'Table-talk').

Some time after it was observed that resin had a preservative effect on wine, resination also became associated with wine amelioration. The correction of inherent faults in wine was of about equal concern in ancient times with preservation, hence the use of gypsum, lime, herbs and other materials as ameliorative agents. Resin, too, was found to overcome some faults in wine, which has occasioned the mistaken belief among some observers today that a resinated wine must necessarily be a wine of poor quality, resinated to mask its defects. It seems to have been regarded as an inferior ameliorative agent, however – at any rate, Cato listed it last in a list of ameliorative measures. It might therefore have finally spelled resination's disappearance at many wine sites once the preservative effect could be dispensed with because of advances that might have occurred in wine-making technique.

One of the most striking facts in the somewhat nebulous history of resination is its geographical retreat over time. Once practised over a vast part of the ancient world, it became ever more territorially restricted in the modern era. Although the timing of resination's geographical recession cannot be traced on the basis of available information, it can be stated that between the time of Pliny, in the first century AD, when he indicated the use of resination in parts of Italy, and the twelfth century, when a provincial *Greek* bishop was surprised upon being introduced to resinated wine in Athens, the technique had become largely restricted to the several areas of Greece where it is customarily practised by villagers today. The record of Western travellers to Greece since around the sixteenth century consequently indicates the absence of resination in Macedonia, Thrace, Thessaly, Crete and the Ionian islands.

Resination's dual-purpose role – preservative/ameliorative – in wine-making enabled it to outlast various other antique techniques that had only the one or the other end, and to maintain its nearly exclusive hold into recent centuries in the very warm and low-lying parts of the mainland where conditions for storing wine generally remained very poor. At some places, moreover, resination became the sole 'extra' procedure in wine-making, where previously it had typically been used in conjunction with others. As if with some surprise after what he had encountered elsewhere, the early nineteenth-century traveller Boué found it 'curious to observe, in southern Albania [Epirus], some districts, as those of Zagora . . . where conservation is not required except with resin'. The proliferation of places where only resination was practised was of considerable significance to the further development of retsina as a wine type, since with competing wine treatments out of the way wine-growers could take the trouble to experiment with resination with an eye to particular flavour or presumed physiological effects that had long since passed into the oral traditions pertaining to resination.

The wine writer Cyrus Redding wrote in 1836 that resin was 'introduced with the notion of *flavouring* and preserving wine' (emphasis added). He had probably picked up that thought from Pliny, in whose time the notion was already 'ancient':

The object of the mixture is in the one case simply the production of a particular odour and the gratification of the corresponding sense, in the other there is a desire to produce, as it were, a pleasanter taste: this instance is the object of flavouring wine with perfumes or of putting spices into it.

(Theophrastus, *Concerning Odours*, 5th century BC)

Over the millennia, the non-technical justifications for resinating wine grew in number as they became more specific. Theophrastus remarked that in the case of all odoriferous additions to wine 'the odour . . . acts as a sort of relish to the draught', and noted also that the tendency of most of them is to add the properties of astringency and 'heat', which was to say that they influence the feel as well as the aroma of wine. In recent centuries, Westerners have reported various explanations for the desirability of resination, other than for preservative effects: it imparts 'strength' (Hobhouse, 1817); 'to imitate the pungency of old wines' (Henderson, 1824); it 'aids the digestive forces' (Pouqueville, 1826); it 'acts as a tonic and in hot weather is very refreshing' (Bent, 1888). It would have been difficult, however, to isolate and hone, as it were, the flavour and physiological effects of resination as long as various treatments were employed simultaneously and the practice of resination lacked uniformity.

Until well into the nineteenth century, methods of resinating wine varied considerably. Pitch was used instead of resin in some areas, hence the term 'pitch wine', found in old travelogues. Smashed pine cones were also a means of resinating. Usually, the resinous material was added to the liquid, either must or wine, but was sometimes applied to the interior of the container. Although the use of pine barrels was also known, barrels of any kind were hardly universal. Large earthenware jars, called *pithária*, after the ancient *píthi (pithoi)*, or more commonly *kioúpia*, after the Turkish, remained prevalent in many areas of Central Greece, even near Athens, until early in this century. The amount of resinous material used also varied from place to place, and so too, though to a much lesser extent, did the kind of pine tree from which it came. The grapes, also, were various in kind.

Effective 'standardization' of retsina as a wine type began to develop only very late in the nineteenth century, after the gradual growth of Athens and Patras in free Greece, those more southern areas relinquished by the Ottomans in 1829, had favoured some specialized commercial production of resinated wine. By the time the enologist P. Pyrlas wrote of retsina in 1911, the direction of that wine had been effectively taken out of the hands of home wine-makers: 'The preparation of these [resinated] wines is generally not by viticulturalists, but by those wine merchants who are supplied during vintage time with must which is vinified in their cellars, where they also sell that wine by retail.' With the approach of vintage time, about mid-August in most of eastern Central Greece and Euboea, the commercial producers would scout the vineyards, choosing grapes as they grew on the vine, haggling over price, and arranging the details of collection or delivery. Based on their accumulated experience of regional viticulture on the one hand and customer preference on the other, the opinion of wine merchants settled on the *savatianó* as the variety *par excellence* for retsina. Wines of properly ripe *savatianó* grapes were appreciated for their vinosity and firmness, which hold up under resination and support retsina's special 'sharpness' of flavour. Indeed *savatianó* wine has a rare capacity for aromatic compatibility with pininess, including a capacity to assert its own varietal aroma. Furthermore, *savatianó* wines are relatively quick-maturing. All in all, the various features of *savatianó* wine are most favourable to the impression of *droserótita* (cooling freshness), which the producers understood was particularly desired by retsina customers in the towns where they sold.

With respect to the actual process of resination, the commercial producers eliminated outstanding differences in technique, starting with the selection of the resin, a step whose importance was clear to the Greeks as long ago as Theophrastus:

> There is no fixed rule for the combination and mixture of spices in the sense that the same components will always produce a satisfactory and a uniform result: the result varies by reason of the varying quality of the virtues found in the spices. For this there are several reasons. One, which applies also to fruits, is the character of the season.... Another is to be found in the time of collection.... A third cause operates after the collection ... for here too it is possible to be too soon or too late.

> (*Concerning Odours*)

The prevalent type of pine tree in Central Greece and Euboea is the Aleppo, whose resin was praised for its delicacy of smell by Theophrastus. Commercial producers of retsina made the Aleppo pine their exclusive source of resin, which was feasible because the ancient task of resin collection, a seasonal endeavour, had become a quite specialized occupation in free Greece as the Greek merchant marine grew and required more pine products for naval stores.[1]

Improved resin quality, along with improvements in wine-making and changes in consumer tastes, was a factor influencing commercial retsina producers to decrease the amount of resin used. In 1795, the British naturalist John Sibthorp recorded figures indicating 7.5 per cent as a typical proportion of resin to wine, which might account for Dodwell's mention in 1819 of a resinated wine 'so impregnated with resin, that it almost took the skin from our lips'. As recently as the 1950s, 2.5–4 per cent was typical in Central Greece and Euboea. The amount used in home-made retsina has been decreasing since then, but already in Pyrlas's time (1911) commercial retsina was typically made with 1–2 per cent. More recently, with Greece's entry into the EEC in 1981, the amount to be used in commercially bottled retsina has been legally fixed at 0.15–1 kilogram of resin per hectolitre of wine, an amount, I should add, that would be insufficient to camouflage the flavour defects of a wine, were that archaic purpose still the *raison d'être* of resination, as some commentators would have it believed.

The commercial producers of retsina also favoured adding the resin to the must, rather than to the wine. Doing so lengthened overall fermentation by about ten days, to a total forty days or so, as a result of the turpentine oil inhibiting the yeasts in gaining oxygen. However, addition to the must had the practical advantage of offering the most

---

[1] A statement – chock-full of little insights into Greek provincial life – by an Attic resin collector serves as a somewhat poignant tribute to an unsung activity of great antiquity:

'I had to begin again from nothing [after the German occupation]. My father, who owns all the trees as well, let me come out and gather the resin to sell to merchants in Megara. I had never done it before, and had to teach myself what season the sap runs best and how to make the gashes in the trunk just deep enough to keep the resin flowing into their tins, yet not so deep as to kill the tree either. Then, while I was learning all this, the Superintendent of Forests came out and saw me ruining a few trees and told me to stop. He said I was destroying the national wealth. I told him to go and lose himself. He called me a blockhead and I fell upon him with my fists and dropped him up. Ever since, the *keratá* [cuckold] has been threatening to take me to court . . . I haven't the money to pay him to leave me alone, nor have I any chickens or goats now to give the judge so he'll let me off.'

(Kevin Andrews, *The Flight of Ikaros*, 1959).

control over the resin's effects on the flavour of the wine, while the final fall of the resin's solids to the bottom was a sure sign that fermentation was completed. The resin could be removed immediately after fermentation, leaving the wine without alteration of either its physical nature or chemical composition; in this latter respect, as well as in the fact that no neutralized, pre-processed 'base wine' is involved, retsina is not like vermouth or other 'derived products', as has mistakenly been thought by many Westerners, going back at least as far as Viala. Nowadays the wine is generally racked after about one week, that is, after initial fermentation, leaving the resin and lees behind. A glass of retsina consequently has no invisible layer of turpentine oil.

When Pyrlas addressed resination in 1911, hoping to clear up many misconceptions, retsina was still a wine sold almost exclusively 'on tap'. It was around that time that bottled retsina started appearing, in consequence of urbanization at Athens and Patras, which had encouraged the growth of several relatively large firms that seized the opportunity bottling offered. Being located at the epicentre of resinated wine production and consumption, those firms wanted to test the market for a bottled wine of that kind. Yet various vineyard afflictions and unstable economic conditions prevented the real success of bottling until into the 1960s. Although many sceptics or outright opponents remain – one non-Greek writer expresses their feelings in calling retsina from the barrel 'real retsina' – the trend toward bottling has been irreversible. In Athens itself these days, retsina 'on tap' is the hard-to-find exception, and is often a bottler's wine when it *is* found; peasant wine can sometimes be a disappointment.

A development of the post-Second World War period that could not have been expected following the numerous centuries of resination's steady contraction has been the geographic redissemination of the technique. Retsina is now being produced and bottled in areas where resination was either never known, as is likely in Crete and Macedonia, or known only in places adjacent to Central Greece and Euboea, as along the Thessalian border and on the offshore islands of the Aegean. The development in part reflects the taste for retsina that has grown with the spread of bottled sales within Greece as the country has become more of a single market. Hardly anyone born anywhere in Greece now grows up without having sampled retsina on many occasions, whereas less than a half-century ago Greeks in many places had not encountered it at all. Also, retsina is in demand among the millions of foreign tourists who, having spent their hard-earned money getting to Greece, want as much of 'the Greek experience' as possible no matter where in Greece they find themselves. For some wine producers, especially cooperative wineries, the tourist market, which must include visiting Athenians, is an excellent outlet for surpluses of white wine. So profitable is it, that some private producers, both larger and smaller, in various parts of the country, bring must from distant corners of Greece to produce retsina on their own premises, thereby also advantageously using capacity that might otherwise remain idle.

Greek legislation allows all producers of retsina to put the designation 'traditional appellation' on their labels, provided that the wine has been made according to the specified procedures and meets certain objective, measurable standards for content of acid (minimum total of 4.5 grams per litre expressed as tartaric acid) and alcohol (10–13.5°). Beyond that, implicit acknowledgement of Greek opinion in favour of the retsina of Central Greece and Euboea has been built into the legislation, by specifying certain place-names that may be used for resinated white and rosé (*kokkinéli*) wines produced from *savatianó* and *rodítis* (the reddish *rodítis* being indispensable to *kokkinéli*): the nomarchies of Attica, Boeotia and Euboea; the area of Mesoyeia within Attica (that is the plains area south-east of Athens, encompassing Keratea, Koropi, Markopoulo, Spata, Kalivi, Thoriko, Kouvara, Paiania, Pallini, Pikermi and Stavro); as well as the individual communities of Koropi, Markopoulo, Paiania, Pallini, Pikermi, Spata and Megara in Attica; the eparchy of Thebes in Boeotia; and Yialtra (township of Aidipsos) and the eparchies of Karistos and Khalkida on Euboea. To date, few bottlers have made use of the appellation framework. I suppose one must assume that after at least two and a half millennia of non-appellation resinated wine, a decade or two more will not matter. But several of the major bottlers do use it, so a good deal of appellation-status retsina is available.

Both the bottled and unbottled retsinas one encounters can vary considerably. Some are atypical in terms of the 'criteria' for the wine on its home ground. Resination's new lease of life has meant that grape varieties not particularly suitable for retsina are being used, and occasionally, too, the wine is of a quality a commercial producer might not consider of sufficiently high standard for an unresinated product. Also, some retsinas – at times it seems more and more of them – are so lightly resinated as to be hardly retsinas at all, though they qualify technically as 'resinated wine'. Generally, the quality of retsinas produced outside the areas where it is a habitual wine is deficient in some respect relative to 'standard'. Prominent among the reliable bottlers are Achaia-Clauss, the Association of Wine Growers of Thebes, Botrys, Cambas, Kourtakis, Marko and Pikermi. This is not to say that at their best those products will taste the same, but only that one can be fairly sure of getting a characteristic retsina; Greeks who drink bottled retsina can display a brand-loyalty equal in fervour to that of Greeks who will not touch any but that in barrel. My own experience with the lot of them is that more often than not the truer samples turn out to be from the most recently released batches, for which reason I generally buy only in Greek ethnic foodstores when at home, since the turnover in retsina is more rapid among a Greek clientele.

Greek aficionados can split hairs over various retsinas with just as much enthusiasm as other connoisseurs bring to the consideration of the merits and weaknesses of the classified Bordeaux wines of the various vintages. An inspection usually begins with colour. Pyrlas specified 'light amber-yellow' as the colour to look for, but one may perhaps be confused by cross-cultural differences in colour perception as expressed in words. Retsina is more of a light golden-yellow that suggests no more of the brownishness of amber than that seen in dilute apple juice of the standard commercial kind. None the less, the hallmark of retsina is the pungent pininess of both its smell and its aromatic flavour. Pininess in retsina, rather like the drone of a bagpipe, gears up before all else, lasts beyond all else, and decisively influences all perceptions in between. Yet while varietal aroma will become apparent only after pininess, it should not be neutralized, although the distinction is difficult to make until one is familiar with the variety in question. Unfortunately, the neutralization of varietal aroma is often occasioned by excessive chilling of retsina, which leaves pininess predominant.

Just as one might expect after reading Theophrastus on the subject of the various perfumed substances added to wine, the pininess of smell in retsina is accompanied by 'mouth-feel' features associated either directly or indirectly with the use of resin as a flavouring agent. The most characteristic and notable of these is a 'pseudo-cooling' sensation: an aspect of the aromatic savour which gives the impression of a drop in mouth cavity temperature greater than that induced by the cool serving temperature alone. Related to the effect of menthol, the sensation evokes the notion of 'balm'. A very low serving temperature co-opts the pseudo-cooling sensation. (It will be recalled, however, that heavily resinated wines can also have an opposite, caustic touch – a vinous 'dry ice', so to speak.)

Pininess of aromatic flavour also provides a lead-in to a lightly bitterish finish, which is reinforced by the slightest prickle of carbonic gas. The after-taste engendered is distinctly reminiscent of that of hoppy lager beers. Indeed, it may have been more than coincidence that caused Dodwell, in 1819, to think of beer in arguing that it is impossible to acquire a taste for retsina ('I have no hesitation in asserting, that the sour beer of England is in general preferable to the resinous beverage of Greece'), and again, in 1885, caused Bent to think of it in arguing that the taste *can* be acquired ('I do not think the flavour worse than beer must be when you first drink it'). Yet no early traveller referred to fizzy resinated wine, and such is still unusual to find in village cellars throughout Central Greece and Euboea. However, in the vicinity of Athens, some peasant wine-makers early in this century learned to close the fermentation vessels towards the end of the process, while some sugar still remained, thereby trapping considerable amounts of carbonic gas. Retsina of that kind is now preferred by some Athenians, who in the absence of fizziness add carbonated water.

Far be it from me to contend that we ought to sully the wininess of retsina or indeed any other wine by taking food with them, but I must note here that Greek aficionados can argue endlessly about the foods that pininess 'goes with'. Going over their heads to consult everyday practice, the cookery writer Khrysa Paradisis blithely relates that retsina is drunk 'chiefly with heavy foods' – for its digestive function – 'but customarily in Greece with everything'. We are thus at liberty to indulge to our heart's content with pairing of retsina with *mousaká*, a combination which apparently, judging by its popularity, can conjure visions of Greece like almost nothing else at the table. The cost of habitually making the combination, however, is to miss some outstanding possibilities for other partnerships. At the very least, the retsina/*mousaká* fixation, which perhaps is just as 'touristy' as *sangria/paella*, should not be construed as what is often called these days 'a classic combination'. The classically minded will simply want to get down to the nitty-gritty and grate *kefalotýri* cheese and barley biscuit into their retsina. To the extent that we might speak at all of traditional wine–food partners, retsina's 'classic' accompaniment – and how horrific it must sound to the Burgundy lover – is spit-roasted lamb, the familiar Roumeliote centrepiece of the Easter meal, which occurs in the period when retsina casks were traditionally first tapped, that is, in the spring after supplies of unresinated wines had given out. The seasonal nature of retsina consumption was probably a major influence on its development towards a style that emphasized the refreshing quality of pininess.

Going by my own observations, I am inclined to think that in Greece most retsina is not drunk with meals properly speaking, but instead with the substantial snacks so popular throughout the Levant. A Greek lady long resident abroad in an official capacity once gave me a rather dramatic statement of the Greek view of retsina on such occasions. She was voicing understanding for the novelty retsina must present to the uninitiated, but then leaped to the defence, saying, 'But with *mezédes* [Greek hors d'oeuvres] . . .' Her words dropped off as she tilted her head slightly up and to the side, with lips pursed as if on the brink of a smile, brows raised, and cupped palm making a tight circular motion at abdomen level – all of which constitutes the habitual Greek description of anything implicitly understood to be incomparably good, but for which even the Greeks have no words. She must have been overcome by visions of *féta*, Nafplion olives enhanced with garlic, *dolmadákia, spanakotyrópita, taramosaláta, tzatzíki*, and who knows how many other delicacies. Generally, garlic and lemon are flavours the Greeks especially prefer with retsina.

Chunks of cold roast meats served with the garlicky *skordaliá* sauce also go well, although the *coup de grâce* is more ingratiatingly delivered by a presentation of *rôtisserie*-grilled *kokorétsi* sausages.

UNRESINATED WHITE WINES OF ATTICA

Not being insensible to the plaints of those whose palates rebel against retsina, a number of wine firms and cooperatives in recent years have taken an interest in producing unresinated white wines from Central Greece and Euboea. The wines are, and will continue to be, of *savatianó*. Also, all have come from Mesoyeia, but in future years greater effort is likely to be made to make a higher proportion of unresinated whites from *savatianó* grown at the higher elevations,

300–550 metres above sea level, in northern Attica, as around Mount Parnes, whose wines are endowed with the particularly fresh taste of malic acid not found in the heavier wines of Mesoyeia.

Prominent among the better Mesoyeian *savatianó* wines that have been offered are Château Marko of Marko, Château Matsa of Boutari, Paleokitsi-Matsa of Nomikos, Semeli of Kokotos and Villitsa of Papakharalambos, all of which are dry wines that should be drunk when recently bottled, and preferably at cool room temperature. A wine that is aged in the bottle for several years is Cava Cambas. Another Cambas wine, Kantza, might be mentioned separately, because it has the distinction of possessing appellation of origin status. The Kantza appellation belongs to an area of poor limestone soils in Mesoyeia, near Koropi, lying about 170 metres above the Aegean. One might suspect that the appellation was presented to Cambas as a token of appreciation for its efforts in Greek wine, since its headquarters, complete with vineyard estate, has been ensconced at Kantza for nearly a century. Anyway, Cambas is the only producer of an appellation wine. Château Matsa and Paleokitsi-Matsa, however, are also wines of Kantza, but their producers have preferred to carry the name of the Matsas family estate where the wines are grown. Altogether, about 50 hectares of vines are cultivated in the appellation area of Kantza.

ARAKHOVA

The only place in all Central Greece and Euboea that has enjoyed real fame for wine of the unresinated kind is the Boeotian village of Arakhova, situated below Mount Parnassos, about twenty minutes by car east of Delphi. Arakhova is virtually on the same site as a settlement called Anemoria, or Anemolia, during antiquity. The ancient name means 'windswept', and was given, wrote Strabo, because 'squalls of wind sweep down upon it'. His explanation is quite readily understood while taking in the panorama from Arakhova's lofty position at nearly 1,000 metres. Arakhova's dry red wine acquired great renown after the Turkish occupation set in, when the settlement burgeoned to accommodate refugees from the lowlands. Dwellings and vineyards multiplied on the slopes, and for most of the village's history thereafter wine was the major source of cash income. The inhabitants worked at it with commensurate diligence, as commented on by the early nineteenth-century visitor Thomas Raikes:

> The declivity was cultivated with an industry worthy of Switzerland. Every spot of vegetable soil was covered with low vines; and I remarked one attention to the value of productive ground which occurred no where else in Greece . . . Aracova is famous for the quality of its wines.
> (In *Travels in Various Countries of the East*, ed. Robert Walpole, 1820).

Shortly before the Greek War of Independence that began in 1821, 'Arracoba' was described by William Gell as 'a large place, abounding in wine'. It did not emerge from the war in as good shape. In a crucial battle of 1826 that tied down an Ottoman army, Arakhova sacrificed many of its inhabitants and much of its wealth. For the rest of the century it remained a lesser settlement than it had been. Migration to Athens in the early twentieth century reduced the population, leaving Arakhova in a weakened position from which to tackle the unrelenting troubles that it has faced since. An attempt at forming a wine cooperative in the late 1930s was thwarted by the repercussions of a world wine glut, and was laid to rest by the onset of the Second World War; some of the defunct co-op's wine tanks still sit as a melancholy reminder at the edge of the village. In its vulnerable position, wine-growing at Arakhova entered a serious decline during the war years, when financial returns for olive oil, produced from fruit harvested down towards the Gulf of Corinth, far outpaced those for less needed wine. Arakhova began to rely on oil for its livelihood, and that reliance grew through the Greek Civil War of 1947–9. The decade of the 1950s saw a flood of migration to urban centres and overseas, and phylloxera topped it all by beginning its devastation in 1960. Covering as much as 500 hectares even in the early twentieth century – their traces may still be seen all about the surrounding slopes – the vineyards of Arakhova now occupy only about 30 hectares.

In an effort to combat phylloxera, old vines are gradually being removed and replaced with vines grafted on to American root-stocks. Some Arakhovites are optimistic about the slow re-extension of vineyard land, especially because of improving profitability for wine relative to olive oil in recent years. They nevertheless acknowledge that it will be some time before production covers much more than household and local *tavérna* needs. With the exception of the rudely stoppered bottles of lesser wine on sale in some village shops, it is unlikely that Arakhovite wine will be seen in bottle in this century; in the village and elsewhere, a commercially bottled wine called Arakhova can be found, but it has no origin in Arakhova's vineyards – and its producer, the Loukas Tsotras firm of Piraeus, would give no information as to just where it does come from – nor can it be mistaken for Arakhovite wine in its characteristics. Whatever good reputation remains to an old wine village in Arakhova's current predicament is consequently largely left to Fate, visitors' opinions depending on the wines they have chanced to encounter on a quick stopover on the way to Delphi.

No matter the small production, a number of factors influence qualitative differences in the wines of Arakhova. Most vineyards are shielded to the north and west, while open to the south-west leading down the Pleistos Gorge to the Gulf of Corinth, but they differ greatly in exposure. Elevation is equally various, the range being from 600–1,050 metres above sea level; Arakhova's highest vineyards are the highest in Greece. The remaining vineyards consist mostly of pre-phylloxera vines, some of which are reported to be producing satisfactorily at ages of as much as 120 years old, although half that age is more usual. But there are other vines, grafted ones, which have been planted only during the past two decades. Varietal composition can also vary somewhat. The local grape assortment includes several black-skinned varieties: *korífi, ravdístra, moukhtoúri, skylopníkhtis* (dog-choker), and *kastelióti* (which may be just a clone of *skylopníkhtis*). There is also the red-skinned *rodítis*, which is called *kokkinári* locally. However, the *korífi*, or *mávro Arakhóvis* (black of Arakhova), is dominant, comprising about 80 per cent of the vines: for all producers, this is the variety that gives character to their wines. Wine quality can differ also according to the mixture, if any, of free-run must (*prórrogo*) and press (*stypsátiko*) juices. Furthermore, some producers feel compelled to stretch their must by buying some grapes or must from the not very distant lowland village of Distomo, to the south-east towards Levadia, where yields are as much as five times greater than at Arakhova.

The small Arakhovite production is spread thinly over four kinds of wine, whose availability varies during the course of the year. The principal one, and that to which the village owes its reputation, is the red wine locals call *broúsko*, or just *mávro* (black). After the vintage in the second half of October, which is very late for Central Greece, the must ferments for forty to fifty days on stalks and skins. Nowadays the villagers begin drinking the *broúsko* soon after fermentation ends, and go on consuming it during the cold weather, usually until it is all gone. Occasionally it is kept in barrel for two or three years, and some producers will cork a few bottles of it to put away for a special family occasion. Old-timers tell of how not so very long ago fifteen-year-old *broúsko* could be found in barrel, and claim that in a secure and well-stored bottle the best of it is none the worse for several decades' ageing.

While most young red wines veer strongly towards violet, the colour of Arakhova's *broúsko* does not soon merge with others one can remember, for it is one of the most decidedly purple shades to be seen in wine. The darkest of it positively suggests blue, and perhaps explains the synonym *galanó* (blue) for the *korífi*. A wine of very full body, true *Arakhovítiko broúsko* is robust, and *corsé*, too, when drunk so very young as it is these days, but it has the attraction even then of a most individual aromatic character, in which may be found smells like berries, cloves, black pepper, thyme, and others, but all playing second fiddle to myrrh. Actually, in smelling Arakhova's *broúsko*, but even more so in taking in its aromatic flavour, one can have the impression of incense. And the smell of Arakhova's best *broúsko*s can in fact be approximated by adding a scant drop of tincture of myrrh to a glass of certain red wines.

Using the identical process as for the *broúsko*, but adding pine resin during fermentation, some Arakhovite producers also make a resinated version of the same. 'Red retsina', as non-Greeks are apt to call it, must be Greece's best-kept vinous secret – 'best-kept indeed,' some will say – its skeleton in the cupboard, so to speak, since it is rare to find even Greeks who have heard of it. It must have been otherwise during antiquity, when just about any wine might have turned up resinated, so as to benefit from the preservative effect. That tradition, however, has died out in all but a very few places, notwithstanding the fact that resination has persisted over a wide area. The Attic enthusiast Rex Warner called Arakhova's 'red retsina' a *kokkinéli*, and compared it unfavourably to that of Attica, writing that the Arakhovite, compared with the Attic, is 'heavier and thicker and somewhat lustreless'. I would call its appearance less translucent, rather than 'lustreless', and consider that Warner's comparison is evidence mostly of a different set of vinous characteristics, and therefore another sort of resinated wine. Arakhovites who make it actually balk when their resinated red is called after the rose-coloured variety known as *kokkinéli* in Central Greece. Looking beyond its resinated nature, they often simply call it, too, '*mávro*'. When they feel like being more precise, they call it '*mávro retsináto*' (black resinated).

Despite its resinated nature, *mávro retsináto* has precious little in common with retsina, or even with *kokkinéli*, and the difference extends beyond colour and astringency. Especially, it provides none of the pseudo-cooling effect. On the contrary, pininess in this case actually seems to assimilate to the balsamic, myrrh-like smell, although more resin is typically used than in making retsina, so that in some samples it is difficult to identify by name just what is different from an unresinated *broúsko*. I am speaking of resinated reds from musts that would produce a characterful *broúsko*, however. Producers of lighter and relatively weakly scented wines can succeed in covering over the original aroma, and do really get something like 'red retsina'. The tendency of pininess to refresh usually works only sufficiently to divert attention somewhat from tannic astringency, much as the use of mint in the North African salad *tabbouleh* distracts from the chafing of the parsley. The *broúsko* is thereby rendered more quaffable, and at an earlier point in its life. Given the circumstance that the production of wine in Arakhova today yields only enough for a year's consumption, that aspect of *mávro retsináto* probably accounts for its having become more typical of the village's wine output than it was in the past.

Two other wines are also made at Arakhova. One is retsina, made largely from *savatianó*, which is called *stamatianó* in the Parnassos area. The best of it is excellent, though fuller in body and generally of more impact than the typical retsina of Central Greece. If possible it should not be missed by visitors, but the retsina casks are rarely opened before late spring. Some Arakhovite wine-makers also offer a dry aperitif wine made from the same sort of must as the village's dark wines, but with the juice staying on the skins only long enough to pick up a dark pink or light reddish colouring. That sort of wine, for which I have heard no specific name mentioned, is usually matured for four to eight years in barrel, turning from its original colour to light onion-skin or light amberish-pink, and growing in alcoholic degree, apparently through a differential evaporation of water and alcohol, to the advantage of the alcohol. Before the indicated age, this wine can be disappointing, since oxidation plays an important role and takes some years to bring out the potential inherent in the better samples.

CLASSICAL REFLECTIONS

The earliest indication of the mingling of wine and pine is a fourth-millennium BC Egyptian depiction of pitch being applied to a wine vessel. It has not been possible to ascertain, however, whether or not the Greeks acquired the habit of resination from Egypt. It is curious in that regard that although the Egyptians influenced Aegean wine-making by way of Crete, resination seems not to have been practised on Crete in ancient times. It is possible, instead, that resination came into use spontaneously in different places, at different times and in different ways, although in each instance it was spread, within a certain area, by imitation.

Three oral traditions as to the origin of resination are in circulation among the latter-day Greeks. The most usual story holds that resination developed from the practice of sealing wine amphoras with a mixture containing pitch, or of mending amphoras with a resinous mixture. Although it has been argued that the Greeks were masters at making amphoras, so that sealing mixtures would not have been needed, and that mending would in any case have been superfluous because of the abundant supply of the vessels, those objections may not be valid for all times and places of antiquity. A third version has it that must or wine was, on the occasion of a superabundant vintage, placed in makeshift pine vessels to supplement other vessels. The explanation seems improbable on the face of it, since the ancient Greeks did not use wooden barrels. The story may have become garbled through time, however. Pine may have been used in lieu of other wood for various implements and lesser containers used during the vintage. Wooden wine-making equipment is readily identifiable in ancient Greek artwork depicting the vintage, and it is relevant to note that the contemporary enologist Émile Peynaud has told of a piny Graves that was being inadvertently 'resinated' just by coming into contact with pine fittings in the winery's equipment (*Le Goût du Vin*, 1980). Therefore, all three explanations of the origin of resination could have some validity, and underscore the possibility of a non-uniform origin.

The wine writer and historian H. Warner Allen (*A History of Wine*, 1961), who neither liked retsina ('a taste difficult to acquire and not worth acquiring if other wine is available') nor could imagine that ancients of his calibre might have indulged a taste he could not abide ('As for the taste of retsina, it revolted the connoisseur of the Roman Empire'), thought the combination of pine with wine an 'unholy wedlock'. It is highly unlikely that the ancient Greeks saw the union that way.

Plutarch made reference to resination in the context of telling how the ancients (relative to his own generation of the first century AD) had dedicated the pine to Dionysus the Tree-god as well as to Poseidon the Life-giver, both of whom were revered as 'sovereign over the domains of the moist and generative' (*Moralia*, 'Table-talk'). The sappy pine was a choice tree to be associated with them, and all the more so in the case of Dionysus because of the popular belief that land very suitable for the pine was also most favourable for the vine. Plutarch himself further gave his opinion that the presence of pines beside or among vineyards was of benefit to the vines and their wine, and alone could enhance the longevity of wine. Plato, in the *Timaeus*, had actually linked resins and wine, in classing both as 'saps' ('forms of water . . . filtered through the plants of earth'), and saying, moreover, that both have 'a fiery nature', in that wine 'heats the soul and body together', while resin 'appears bright and shining to view and glistening' and so participates in other, visual properties of the element of fire.

With both cultic and early scientific thought behind it, the concept of resination could have been accommodated by the advancing culture of the ancient Greeks, including those most enlightened ones of the Golden Age. Allen therefore seems to have missed the forest for the trees in his anxiety to pin the responsibility for the pine's splash in wine on anyone but those most revered Greeks of the fifth century BC.

GASTRONOMIC NOTES

The food most generally associated with Central Greece is *kokorétsi*, which consists of chopped, seasoned sheep's offal and fat compactly held together in several-inch-diameter, metre-long sausages, in a wrapping of intestines. Traditionally, this is a spit-roasted Easter treat, but in Athens, large towns, and just about anywhere with a clutch of *tavérna*s, *kokorétsi* can be found at any time of the year. In Athens, *tavérna*s in the Marousi quarter have long been frequented for *kokorétsi*. Two meat specialities of the northern Athenian suburbs are suckling pig at Varybobi, and Easter spit-roasted goat at Akharnes. Deeper in Central Greece, at the large country town of Levadia, on the road to Arakhova and Delphi, the speciality is *souvláki*, the widely known little skewers of lamb, or now, more frequently, pork. Athenian lore has it that the commercial *souvláki* stand originated at Levadia, which, if one considers how it has spread world-wide, must make the town something of a gastronomic shrine. Certainly Athenian tourists bound for Delphi feel cheated if their tour-bus does not make a stop at Levadia and let them sample the *souvláki*.

At Arakhova, fine flavour is by no means restricted to the village wines. The Arakhovites rely on the superb lamb, mutton, goat and kid meat from animals grazed on Parnassos, and cook with Parnassos greens and aromatics, the latter reminding one that the ancients knew the area as an important source of medicinal plants. The culinary results emphatically feature 'local flavour' in its most profound sense: an inimitable savour that is derived from a very special location. This is what Greeks through the millennia have for the most part prized over anything that can be produced by kitchen artifice. Seasonal availability is of course telling at Arakhova, and a special mention in that regard must go to a particular sheep's-milk cheese, *formaélla*, which the inhabitants of Parnassos alone make. It takes its name from a cylindrical mould used to shape it, the *fórma*, whose name comes from the ancient Greek term *fórmos*, which yielded the familiar Western terms *formaggio* and *fromage*. The *fórma* gives the cheese the look of a waxed, yellowish-white roll of cord about 5 inches in length and 2½ inches in diameter. A semi-hard cheese, *formaélla* is eaten either plain, or Arakhovite-style, cut into half-inch discs and fried slowly in olive oil to a crispy golden brown and served with a squeeze of lemon. It is usually available only from March to the end of June, occasionally into July. Arakhovite *féta* cheese, which is usually superlative, is plentiful most of the year, as is the outstanding yogurt (*yiaoúrti*) of Parnassos. When in the neighbourhood, one should also ask for the excellent, largish, dark Amfissa olives from the sea of olive trees down towards the coastal settlement of Itea.

Central Greece has an extensive coastline, and a number of areas are known for their fruits of the sea. They are mostly concentrated at the western and eastern ends of the region. One area with a particular reputation for fish is that between Nafpaktos and Etoliko, towards the western extremity of Central Greece, along the Gulf of Patras. Further west, along the coast of the Ionian Sea, one might ask for light, unresinated local white wines to go with the fish. They are usually made from grape varieties more typical of the Ionian islands than Central Greece. At Mesolongi, the lagoon village south-east of Etoliko where Lord Byron met his untimely death, several seafood specialities are offered. The most prosaic of them is *petália*, or salted and sun-dried fish, and the most unusual, for Greece, is turtle (*khéli*), of which there are three kinds: *pritspáta*, which is cut in half and roasted; *katharókhela*, a type available in winter and roasted whole; and *souvlomoutára*, available in spring and roasted on a spit (*soúvla*). Finally, the best-known, and most expensive, of the Mesolongi specialities is *avgotárakho*, or botargo. It is made from grey mullet roe that is pressed into a flat shape in its membrane, then smoked and dipped in melted wax. Mesolongi exports its *avgotárakho* far and wide in Greece, and in Athens it can be found at specialist food shops.

At the eastern end of Central Greece, Euboea attracts many Athenians for whom summer holidays are inconceivable without plenty of fresh fish and local retsina. The area around Rafina, on the Aegean coast, east of Athens and the retsina country of Mesoyeia, is known for its seafood *tavérna*s, some of which can provide a good home-made retsina. One might also take a hint from Denton Snider, an American in Greece in the 1880s. In Mesoyeia once, Snider, who needed some time to fall into retsina's Romaic embrace ('only after much preliminary training and chastising does the rebellious palate suffer this fluid to pass its portal'), was greatly pleased when drinking it with 'the supreme delicacy of the meal . . . a species of clam . . . which was roasted in the hot ashes of the earth and flavoured with a drop of lemon juice'. While thus indulging, those who would challenge the winehood of retsina might ponder whether the morsel is still a clam.

9

Peloponnesos

━━━━━━

Through the plain is the direction of the road from the village of Agios Georgios to Corinth: the former of these places is distant an hour's journey from Nemea: it produces the best wine in the Morea, great quantities of which passed us on the backs of asses and mules, while we were examining the ruins; and our servants did not neglect this opportunity of filling the spherical wood barrels which they wore slung round their shoulders.
(Peter Laurent, British traveller, *Recollections of a Classical Tour*, 1821)

The southernmost region of the Greek mainland is practically an island, to which even its age-old name attests – Peloponnesos, or the 'Island of Pelops', the Pelopses having been a ruling clan of very early times. Its colloquial name is 'Morea', which was attached in much more recent centuries, most likely because mulberry (*moréa*) trees covered parts of its north-western area. All but surrounded by water, the Peloponnesos's physical connection to Central Greece is as tenuous as could be, and consists only of the Isthmus of Corinth in the north-east, which leads in from Megara and Athens. Even that point of contact has been artificially severed by the 4–mile-long Corinth Canal, cut through during 1882–93.

Crossing southward over the Canal, a visitor can easily experience the feeling of leaving the mainland behind. But as far as wine-growing is concerned, a break may not be so readily apparent, since local retsina continues to be offered all about, no matter the direction in which one proceeds. It is nevertheless illusory to conceive of the Peloponnesos as trailing along in the wake of Central Greece. Rarely is retsina the only sort of wine made at individual places, and even where it might qualify as a typical wine it is usually but one of a number of them. In fact, Peloponnesian wine is characterized by a diversity considerable enough for the region to stake a claim as the

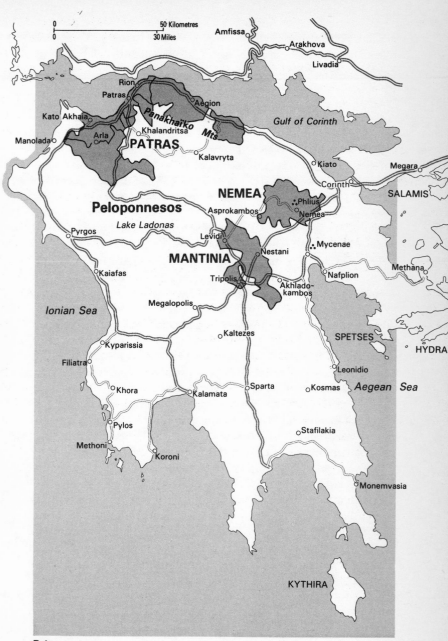

Peloponnesos

most versatile wine-grower of the mainland, for which it perhaps has its insular qualities to thank.

Incursions of Slavs from the north into the middle uplands of the Morea in the late Middle Ages drove many of the earlier inhabitants towards the coast, resulting in a concentration of population there. The consequent growth of port towns, particularly Nafplion in the north-east, Monemvasia in the south-east, Methoni in the south-west, and Patras in the north-west, led to increased maritime activity, which occasioned a great deal of procurement and dispatch of vines between the Peloponnesos and other parts of Greece. Some non-native varieties were adopted in the hinterland of the port towns, so that, while native varieties are planted in the Morea and are sometimes preponderant, as in the interior, the varietal complement along the periphery, where most vineyards are located, usually bears some greater or lesser resemblance to that found at the nearest land-point across the respective areas of water the region faces on its several sides. For example, the varietal influence of the Ionian islands is discernible in the western and north-western Morea, while the varieties of Crete and the Cyclades are met with in the south.

Large volume and highly uneven geographic distribution are also features of Peloponnesian wine production. The region accounts for just over one-quarter of Greek wine, and is barely second to Central Greece on that score. Production is very heavily concentrated in the northern half, and most of all around the perimeter, although not usually right along the coast, where currants and table grapes dominate, but instead further inland, mostly from 5–20 miles, on the higher and often steeply sloping terrain. The concentration in the north is attributable in part to the growth of the town and port of Patras after the Greek War of Independence, and also to proximity to the Athenian market, which burgeoned in the twentieth century. But the influence of currant production must be reckoned as well. Its profitability in the northern Morea in recent centuries generally served to maintain interest in viticulture, but in some areas was actually a threat to wine production at times, since growers were tempted to replant virtually all of their vineyards with currant vines. National legislation early in this century put an end to the currant's encroachment, while the inception of growers' cooperatives, as well as increased activity by large private wine firms, brought more attention to wine-grape cultivation.

NEMEA

The most storied of Peloponnesian wine-growing areas is in the north-east, hardly half-an-hour's drive from the Corinth Canal. It lies just west of the road to Mycenae (Mykines), where there are plenty of geographic reminders that this area must have supplied the 'palace wine' of Agamemnon. The vineyards in question produce wine that has been called 'Nemean' (*Nemeátiko*) for at least the past 500 years or so, that is, since the time of the Ottoman takeover of the area. The name comes from that of the wide upland plain of Nemea ('Nemea' meant pastures), where Hercules strangled the fearsome local lion and the biennial Nemean olympiad was held, yet does not quite suggest the full antiquity of tradition to which the wine region so called is heir. Included also is the Phlius valley just beyond the Trikaranon Mountains to the west ('the shady primeval mountains of Phlius', Pindar, *The Nemean Odes*). In much earlier times, it was the city-state of Phlius that gave its name to the region's wine.

If we judge by the fourth-century BC poet Antiphanes' mention of 'wine of Phlius', when he named cities and the special products with which their names were commonly associated, we should have to conclude that Phliasian wine was the earliest on the mainland to have enjoyed a reputation at Athens. Phliasian wine goes back long before Antiphanes' time, however. It is apparent from Pausanias' description of the city of Phlius that viticulture had become the lifeblood of the area at a very early date:

> On the market-place is a votive offering, a bronze she-goat for the most part covered with gold. The following is the reason why it has received honours among the Phliasians. The constellation which they call the Goat on its rising causes continual damage to the vines. In order that they may suffer nothing unpleasant from it, the Phliasians pay honour to the bronze goat.
>
> (Pausanias, *Description of Greece*)

Phlius and Phliasia were named after a son of Dionysus, Phlius, who lived by the headwaters of the Asopos (Asopus), the river that runs through Phliasia and bears the name of a river-god said by some of the ancients to have been a son of Poseidon; it is instructive to recall that the earliest vineplanters preferred river environments, since Phlius and Asopos can be seen as surrogates for the two gods 'sovereign over the domain of the moist and generative' (Plutarch, *Moralia*, 'Table-talk'). Phlius was in fact founded by Dorians from neighbouring Argos, to the south-east, a part of which was once ruled by Melampus, a heralded seer who was said by Herodotus to have taught the Greeks the worship of Dionysus. The connection with Argos in any case explains the presence of the old shrine to Dionysus at Phlius, which was mentioned by Pausanias, and perhaps also the attachment of the early inhabitants to the goddess Hebe, whom they also called Ganymede, the cup-bearer to the gods.

It was no mean feat that the vineyards of Phlius survived the Ottoman occupation. What remained of the former city of Phlius was destroyed in 1460, when the inhabitants, making the most they could of their position on the side of Trikaranon, attempted to resist Ottoman forces. By that time, however, the village of Ayios Yeoryios, or 'St George', had become the main wine producer of the area. Ayios Yeoryios is located about 4 miles east of where Phlius was, on the Nemean side of Trikaranon, but where it meets the Phliasian side, and all within the territory of the one-time city-state of Phlius. Writing of Ayios Yeoryios in 1820, the visitor Dodwell told of a populous place, and assumed that no Turks lived in the area, since it was 'swarming with pigs'. Nevertheless, had Dodwell looked further, he might have learned that the Turks knew how to get to Ayios Yeoryios blindfolded at tax time, which came at ever more frequent intervals, with taxes assessed at ever more arbitrary rates, in the years leading up to the Greek War of Independence, which freed the area and saved its vineyards not a moment too soon. Pouqueville, who thought 'the excellent wines of the slopes' as much a proof of the 'Doric extraction' of the peasants as the local dialect, noted that the Ottoman potentates came out to fill their purses five times in the year 1815 alone, leaving wine-growers at Ayios Yeoryios pondering whether to continue.

Having outlasted the Turks, the 'Dorians' of Ayios Yeoryios and its neighbourhood managed to overcome their far less protracted struggle with a newer but equally ferocious 'Nemean lion', phylloxera – the north-eastern quadrant of the Morea being the only part of the region to have been struck – and did so by turning to modern viticultural science, rather than reverting to their tradition of adorning bronze she-goats. Ayios Yeoryios remains very much the centre of Nemean wine production today, but under the name 'Nemea', with which the village was rechristened earlier in this century. An appellation of origin was authorized in 1971, and in addition to the large village of Nemea includes 15 smaller settlements; Arkhaia ['Ancient'] Nemea, Arkhaïï Kleones, Koutsi, Bozika, Titani, Kastraki, Asprokambos, Dafni, Psari, Petri, Aidonia, Galatas, Leondio, Gymno and Malandreni. About 1,900 of the more than 3,000 hectares of vineyards there qualify. Those are planted with the black *ayioryítiko* ('St George's') variety, which is grown almost exclusively in the Nemea area, and indeed is so well adapted to its little domain that attempts to grow it elsewhere in Greece have virtually all proved dismal, which is a reason for thinking that the *ayioryítiko* has had an extraordinarily long time to become wedded to its environment. Both dry and sweet red wines may qualify for the Nemea appellation. Besides *ayioryítiko*, the white *savatianó* is also grown, and used primarily to make the local retsina. The appellation entitlement does not extend to *savatianó* wines.

Research conducted by the Greek Wine Institute has demonstrated that three zones of production can be delineated in the present Nemea appellation district, a fact which is being viewed as reason to make some further distinction in the appellation. The three areas are the slopes of the semi-mountainous zone, which lie at 450–650 metres above sea level, the lower slopes and plains, which go down to 250 metres, and the mountain plain of Asprokambos, which is at 750–800 metres. The first area gives the traditionally most esteemed wines, dark, extract-rich and full-bodied, which earned the Nemean wine the sobriquets of 'blood of Hercules' and 'blood of the lion'. They tend to reach around 13° in alcohol, and are excellent for barrel-ageing and bouquet development. At the lower altitudes, the grapes ripen much more swiftly, and reach an alcohol potential of 14–15°. It was because of that potential for high sugar content that the Nemea appellation was expanded from the original conception, which confined it to dry wines, to include sweet wines as well. At the higher altitudes, on the other hand, lightly coloured wines of much lower alcoholic degree – around 11.5° – are grown. Their higher malic acid content, fresher taste and characteristic *ayioryítiko* fruit aroma could lead to a separate appellation – perhaps to be called 'Nemea Mountains' – which would serve a certain section of the wine market. However, actual use of the additional appellation would require a commercial winery in the zone to be delineated. None now exists in the upper part of the present appellation Nemea territory.

Nemean wine production is almost entirely in the hands of the

Cooperative of Wine Producers of Nemea. Their tight hold on local wine-growing is derived from a policy of maintaining the *ayioryítiko* as the most highly priced variety for red wine in all of Greece – such, at least, is the claim of the Cooperative – which is intended to discourage emigration and vineyard abandonment. As a consequence, outside wine firms are rarely willing to set up wineries and compete for the raw material. If they want Nemean wine, they usually just buy it from the Cooperative, which has plenty to sell: about 30,000–35,000 hectolitres of appellation-qualifying wine alone are produced annually. Not a few Greek firms choose to do that, with the consequence that a good many appellation and non-appellation Nemean red wines are on the market.

The Cooperative is occupied with the vintage from the first part of September until mid-October, the later harvesting being for grapes grown at the higher altitudes. The *ayioryítiko* musts are fermented for about three weeks, including an initial fermentation of five to six days on skins only. Most of the best wine is sold as appellation wine under the Cooperative's own label, Nemea. It is 12–12.5° wine that has usually been matured in oak for at least three years, and possibly longer for the better vintages; one year is the minimum under appellation regulations. Nemea is always marketed in vintage-dated bottles, usually of slender Rhine-type, but in squat bottles for the very best vintages, which are marked additionally by a Kava Nemea neck band. Kava Nemea in particular can be an excellent example of the recurrent, individual features of Nemean wine, although variation is to be expected among the vintages of it that appear.

Conforming to the traditional image of Nemean wine, Kava Nemea has a discernibly violet overlay to its rather dark ruby hue: I wonder if the fifth-century BC poet Bacchylides was alluding to wine when he wrote, 'the inspired prophet of the violet-eyed Muses is ready to sing of Phlius . . .' Much of that colour can hold for eight to ten years beyond the vintage date, while Kava Nemea develops its other qualities. The characteristic bouquet might be broadly pigeon-holed as sweet-spicy, but I would contrast it with some other similarly described Greek reds by mentioning a certain piquancy of smell emanating from a fusion of ginger, nutmeg and cloves. Cedar is also apparent sometimes, and does come as a great relief after all the pine in Greek wine. A fullish wine when drunk in good time, Kava Nemea starts off supple, while ending with a tenacious tingling sensation. A well-matured Kava Nemea is among Greece's fine reds to accompany roast beef and lamb, even with mint sauce or red-currant jelly. It also takes well to lamb or kid stewed with vegetables in the Greek *avgolémono* style, or Greek-style pork stewed with oil or butter, white wine, garlic and Nafplion olives. Vine leaves stuffed with highly seasoned aubergine is a more unusual accompaniment, which can be served either as a side dish or a vegetarian entrée.

Kava Nemea has had a most formidable competitor in Grand Palais, a limited-production appellation wine from the large Oinotrans company; the grand name was apparently allowed because it refers to Agamemnon's palace. Grand Palais has been the most imposing of Nemean wines: firmest, roundest, longest. Also darker, it is just about the darkest Greek red in bottle, particularly among ones bearing an appellation of origin, and is actually rather blackish. The bouquet has been redolent of an aroma akin to rosemary, and a cedary-piny balsamic scent. Usually not released until four to five years after the vintage, Grand Palais can go on for some years in bottle; the 1976 vintage was just coming into its best years a decade later. Unfortunately, Oinotrans has recently sharply cut back its participation in the bottled-wine market, and the fate of Grand Palais is in doubt. If a bottle comes your way from a caring keeper, drink to good fortune with it over *chèvre* cheese, crusty whole-grain bread, and lamb casseroled with lentils, herbs and tomato.

CENTRAL AND SOUTHERN AREAS

To head south from Nemea, into the east-central Morea and the territory of Arcadia, is to move into wine country notorious even among resin-addicted Greeks for its liberally pine-laced retsina. What a surprise, then, to find that the area is also home to one of the most delicate of Greek vintages, Mantinia. The wine has been called after the deep-soiled plateau where it is grown, which takes its name from an ancient religious site. An appellation of origin is authorized for about 550 hectares of vines, extending from north-east to south-east of Tripolis, and including vineyards belonging to that town, as well as to the villages of Levidi, Artemisio, Simades, Pikerni, Kapsas, Nestani, Louka, Sangka, Zevgolatio and Partheni. The qualifying grape varieties are the semi-aromatic *moskhofílero* and *asproúdes*. The former predominates in plantings, and is a variety having more or less reddish skin, although the entitled wine produced from it must be white.

At Mantinia, grapes mature relatively late for southern continental Greece, usually in the second half of September, because the region, at about 650 metres altitude, is subject to frequent storms and rain in the summer, and to temperatures lower than at most places on the mainland. Even at maturation, sugar content is relatively low and acid content high for an area so far south. The wine usually produced is a lightish dry white of slight 'aromatic' character. However, the Mantinia appellation authorization also permits a semi-sweet wine, which is typically produced by giving only a weak pressing to the best-ripened grapes. But none of that kind of Mantinian wine is being marketed. Sparkling wines of Mantinia, although not entitled to the appellation, are highly thought of among Greek wine professionals, whose praise for them could lead one to think sparkling Mantinian wine the Peloponnesian equivalent of *mousseux* from the Loire. But none of that type is available commercially either.

Although Mantinian wines have been bottled by various firms over the years, at present the only one proclaiming itself a product of that area is a dry still one of the Cambas firm of Attica, which makes its appellation wine Mantinia in a quantity of about 500 hectolitres annually, entirely from their own 70 hectares of vines in the region. It is vintage-dated wine of 11.5°. Mantinia should not be subjected to the deep chill before serving, lest the best part of its nose is lost. I have had a hard time finding foods I think it shows well against, and therefore am inclined to mention it as Greek 'sipping wine'. But at a pinch, do this: spread boiled cabbage leaves in a shallow casserole, cover them with a cooked mixture of minced veal, butter, white wine, parsley and thyme, then add another layer of leaves, and finally cover it all with a yogurt-egg mixture before placing it in a medium oven to bake until golden. I cannot imagine anything in a Balkan vein much better suited to Mantinia, although the natives around Tripolis would certainly think such an outlook oddly limiting.

South of Arcadia, the Peloponnesos as yet affords only some very localized wine surpluses of any size. Moreover, those are exploited by bottlers from elsewhere in Greece, who use them to produce brand-name wines of no particular origin. A truly native, contemporary wine industry is only just now emerging. None of that should be mistaken as evidence of a lack of qualitative potential, however. In fact certain southern locales have a reputation for above-average or excellent wines, although mostly confined to the Peloponnesos until now, because the area is off the beaten path even for most Greeks. Some of these places are quite small, such as Stafilakia, formerly known as Grammousa, a mountainside village deep in the south-east, in Laconia. It is the sort of place Peloponnesians from south of Arcadia do not bother telling anyone about, but visit as need be to fill up demi-johns. The villagers of Stafilakia boast of growing over twenty grape varieties, and of having nearly as many sorts of wine. The village's taming would seem to be several decades away. In contrast, Filiatra, located along the south-western coast, is a much more extensive vineyard area, and its dry white wines based wholly or largely on the *filéri* enjoy a very good reputation at least as far north as Athens. The work of the local 'Nestor' cooperative could result in 'country wine' status for varietal *filéri* whites of Filiatra in coming years.

Perhaps indicative of stirrings in the south is the seemingly unlikely planting of *cabernet sauvignon* vines in the hilly vicinity of Khora, south-east of Filiatra, which Nestor hopes to make commercial use of at some point in the future. The light red *cabernet* wine of Khora that I tasted will not pass for a Médoc, but it none the less serves notice that the Peloponnesos, and most definitely the south, has by no means exhausted its possibilities.

PATRAS AND AKHAÏA (ACHAIA)

The most widely known of Peloponnesian wines, and one of the very best known of Greece, is the sweet red 'mavrodaphne of Patras', whose history is not so very old as Greek wine traditions go. Produced in the hilly north-western area called Akhaïa to the south and west of the port of Patras, the wine is based on, and takes its name from, the *mavrodáfni* variety, which arrived there from the Ionian islands in recent centuries, most likely through the numerous Ionian merchants and nobles who came to reside at the once cosmopolitan metropolis of the Morea. However, the currant grape, which is the *mávri korinthiakí* ('black Corinthian'), also came to be used together with the *mavrodáfni* to make the wine. In Akhaïa, the *mavrodáfni* does not develop as much sugar as it does on its home islands, and so when Patras was the world centre for trade in the more sugar-rich currant in the latter part of the nineteenth century, and gluts were occurring, it was found useful to use fresh currant grapes along with *mavrodáfni*. Both varieties ripen in early September in Akhaïa. However, wine entitled to the Mavrodaphne of Patras appellation must be composed of at least 50 per cent *mavrodáfni*.

The appellation zone encompasses vineyards within an area that extends from several miles east of the port, south-east towards Khalandritsa to about 15 miles inland, west to several miles beyond Kato Akhaïa, and south-west to Arla. Vineyard land within that territory varies considerably in most respects, but the suitable land for the *mavrodáfni* in particular is almost entirely calcareous in nature. At present, 300 hectares of vineyards qualify for production of appellation wine. Two long-established Akhaïan wineries, those of the Achaia-Clauss firm and the Union of Agricultural Cooperatives of Patras, or 'Patraïki', enjoy very close connections with growers in the region, and have garnered virtually the entire output of *mavrodáfni* in the appellation-qualifying vineyards. Because of its low yields, the *mavrodáfni* is an expensive grape to grow, and consequently non-Akhaïan firms have stayed away. Instead they accept a role akin to that of an *éleveur*, purchasing wines from Achaia-Clauss or Patraïki after the wines have spent their requisite year in oak in Akhaïa, and then maturing them further, and possibly blending them as well, in their own cellars outside Akhaïa. Thus it is that numerous Greek wine firms market a Mavrodaphne of Patras under their own label, sometimes indicating themselves thereon as the 'producer'. However, every so often a small Akhaïan winery ventures into bottling a minor amount all its own.

Mavrodaphne of Patras wine as it is generally known is attributable to the winery of Achaia-Clauss. The Bavarian Gustav Clauss came to Patras in the mid-nineteenth century, and after a period of making excursions into the surrounding Akhaïan countryside bought some land, established a vineyard, and in 1861 founded Achaia-Clauss. That was also the year in which he made his first *mavrodáfni* wine. An apocryphal story promoted by Achaia-Clauss claims that Gustav named his wine after a sweetheart named Daphne, but in fact the *mavrodáfni* was already being used to make naturally sweetish red wines. Clauss, apparently having some familiarity with port, modified the wine by cutting short fermentation through the introduction of grape spirits, thus making the wine higher in both sugar and alcohol content. He also brought the wine past full maturity in barrel, carefully controlling and monitoring its development towards an advanced age as the wine absorbed oxygen. By reason of the slow, extensive oxidation that takes place during its ageing – it's 'curing in air' – Mavrodaphne of Patras made after the Clauss fashion becomes relatively immune to the deleterious effects on flavour that rapid oxygenation otherwise has after a bottle is opened. An opened bottle of Mavrodaphne of Patras of this type can consequently be corked up and sit essentially unharmed for some days. On the other hand, because it is aged to a peak of bouquet such as oxidation might induce, the wine really has nothing to gain from the oxygen-excluding environment that produces 'bottle bouquet'. However, the appellation regulation does not require that wine called Mavrodaphne of Patras should be made according to the Clauss procedure.

The great majority of the Mavrodaphne of Patras wine released under Achaia-Clauss's own labels is that for its Imperial brand. Until around the end of the Second World War, the 16° Imperial was aged for six years in oak, including a year in large casks placed outdoors. The firm maintains that the same bouquet and flavour are now achieved by the less complicated technique of ageing the wine indoors for eight years. Clauss's Imperial is recognized by its dark amberish-garnet colour, which progresses towards yellowish rings at the rim. The bouquet incorporates signs of oak: both cherry and vanilla can occur. The browning of fruit sugars is also in evidence: aromas of dried fruit, especially raisins, manifest themselves. The aromatic flavour usually exhibits more of that sort of browning than does the nose, and sometimes it goes so far as to have a slightly chocolate-like aspect, an impression to which the abiding feel of tannin contributes. I consider these features to account for Imperial's frequently cited overlap with Italian *recioto* wines, a comparison which sometimes has the unfortunate effect of putting the onus on Mavrodaphne of Patras wines to conform to *recioto* wines in all other respects as well.

The premium commercial wine of Achaia-Clauss is its Mavrodaphne of Patras under the Old Reserve label (or that at least is the label used on the Greek market). It is specially selected wine, aged for twenty years in barrel. Its colour is a very brownish-mahogany with a slightly yellow cast to it throughout; reddishness has regressed, so to speak, to the point of nascency. Old Reserve has more features of browning in its bouquet than has Imperial, including a warm toastiness akin to that in macaroon biscuits permeated with a cocoa flavour; the aromatic features of Imperial attributable to oak actually seem fully absorbed by these. The wine's vinosity is also very considerable, as if that were heightened by the full incorporation of tannin; nothing bitterish is sensible in the finish of Old Reserve, which displays sweetness that seems as much the work of alcohol and glycerin as of sugar. To my utter bafflement, I once found all those characteristics in a bottling sold as Imperial in the United States.

The grand Achaia-Clauss 'mavrodaphne of Patras' wine is, in the firm's estimation, that from its two mammoth casks of '1882 Mavrodaphne', although the wine is not precisely from the 1882 vintage, to be sure. As wine was drawn off, ever so slowly, it had to be replaced with younger wine. As in the case of a sherry *solera* system, the casks of '1882 Mavrodaphne' at some point reached a stable equilibrium of bouquet and flavour, which is maintained today by the most stringent limitations on bottling. Only ten to twenty bottles are drawn annually, and these are reserved exclusively for VIP entertainment of the very highest order. Enophiles must turn to Socrates for consolation:

> 'Antiphon, you seem to have a notion that my life is so miserable, that I feel sure you would choose death in preference to a life like mine. . . . Do you not know that the greater the enjoyment of eating the less the need of the sauce; the greater the enjoyment of drinking, the less the desire for drinks that are not available?
>
> (Xenophon, *Memorabilia*)

Because of its old and special association with Mavrodaphne of Patras, Achaia-Clauss can easily cause prospective customers to overlook other purveyors for that wine. Yet, the wine of Patraïki, a 14° one matured for two to four years in oak, and perhaps more like Akhaïan *mavrodáfni* wine was before Clauss arrived on the scene, certainly ought not to be ignored. Nor should the wines of Boutari, Cambas and Nicolaou be passed up out of an erroneous notion that they are somehow not the real thing. Furthermore, when sipping virtually any Mavrodaphne of Patras in between bites of an almond-or chocolate-flavoured sweet, no one is likely to grumble about just whose wine is being poured. As regards accompaniment, I might note also, for the sake of the more adventurous, that Greeks can be observed sipping Mavrodaphne of Patras during meals. I had better not recommend taking that tack, though, except for the Patraïki version with Cantonese sweet-and-sour dishes and such.

Two other dessert wines also bear the Patras name commercially: Muscat of Patras and Muscat of Rion of Patras. Both are produced entirely from the *moskháto áspro* variety, which also arrived from the Ionian islands, and is called *moskhoúdi* colloquially in Akhaïa. These wines may be either fortified or unfortified. The Muscat of Patras appellation covers a wide area of hills to the east of Patras, from the coast south to the foothills of the Panakhaïko Mountains, as well as to the south-west, including much of the same area in that direction as does the Mavrodaphne of Patras appellation. The territorial bounds for the Muscat of Rion of Patras appellation enclose only the northernmost strip of the eastern portion of the Muscat of Patras zone, wherein the gravelly coastal plain areas east of the Rion car ferry for Central Greece yield the qualifying wines. Presently, about 70 and 80 hectares respectively qualify for the Muscat of Patras and Muscat of Rion of Patras appellations. Scarcely three decades ago twice that area was planted.

Achaia-Clauss, Nicolaou and Patraïki have produced Patran muscat wines entitled to an appellation designation. Achaia-Clauss's orangeish-gold Muscat of Patras is distinguished by its finesse, which is especially notable in its clarity of aroma. The Nicolaou version on their label of that name can claim considerable idiosyncrasy, as might be supposed just in looking at its complex shading of colours, comprising brownish-orange with a leaning towards greenish-yellow. The wine has been that way in bottling after bottling, and I have never found reason to suspect its health because of it. Patraïki's Muscat of Rion is of golden-yellow colour, with a highly perfumed sort of floral scent, although a tendency towards the 'hot' sweet spices, like nutmeg, can be sensed as well. Perhaps for reasons of name recognition, Patraïki has exported its wine under a Muscat of Patras label, although the Greek initials MP on the appellation banderole certainly identify it as a Muscat of Rion of Patras. Patras also offers dry wines that meet the deceptive demands of a burning thirst, including ones entitled to an appellation of origin. The appellation applies to unresinated white wines from *rodítis* grapes coming from a vast area of Akhaïan countryside stretching south and east from the rear of the town. I shall dispense with the endless list of unfamiliar village names, and note only that 1,350 hectares within the area at present qualify.

Despite the size of the appellation zone, I had despaired of seeing a worthy representative, until Achaia-Clauss and Patraïki came out with their Patras wines, which agreeably smell as though bitterish herbs had been strewn in the fruit. Kourtakis of Attica market a

lighter-bodied   s label. Two other
versions are a   oussis, respectively
under Patras a   ight, and 'crisp' as
well, though la   . All the appellation
Patras dry win   taking the trouble
to seek out a b   of the vintage.

In the far eas   ïa, just to the north
of Arcadia, the   Kalavryta has had a
good reputation for both red and white wines. Indeed Kalavryta,
situated by the Voureïkos Gorge at over 700 metres high, below
Mount Velia, is the successor to the ancient Kynaithes (Cynaethae),
which was a settlement of an apparently unruly tribe of Dionysus-
devoted Arcadians:

> The most notable things [among the Cynaetheans] include a
> sanctuary of Dionysus, to whom they hold a feast in winter, at
> which men smeared with grease take up from a herd of cattle a
> bull, whichever one the god suggests to them, and carry it to the
> sanctuary. This is the manner of their sacrifice.
>
> (Pausanias, *Description of Greece*)

However, in recent decades, Kalavryta has suffered setbacks, beginning with an execution of over 1,400 of the town's male population
on 13 December 1943, during the wartime occupation. Emigration
has been a more or less steady problem since then. The loss of
population has had a negative effect on agriculture in the area.

Several dark grape varieties are grown at Kalavryta, mostly *liano-
mávroudo* ('little blackie') and *khondromávroudo* ('big blackie').
Patraïki uses those as well as some *mavrodáfni* grown outside the
Mavrodaphne of Patras zone to make its red Santa Laura; the nearby
monastery of Ayia Lavra (Santa Laura) is known to all Greeks as the
place where Germanos, Bishop of Patras, raised the banner of
insurrection against the Ottomans on 21 March 1821. Red Santa
Laura is a vintage-dated, 12° wine aged for at least one year in oak
before bottling, and has usually been worth cellaring for three to five
years beyond the vintage date, at which time I have thought I might
mistake it for a Dão wine in a blind tasting, and perhaps with eyes
open as well, for the colour of Santa Laura red is also in the range of
Dão.

A white variety that used to be important around Kalavryta is the
lagórthi. I have wondered whether it was the source of the wine

offered to the traveller Thomas Wyse at the Monastery of Mega Spilion, which is also nearby, in the mid-nineteenth century. At dinner, the monks brought out 'a specimen of the best', which Wyse did not like because it ' "foamed", unmetaphorically, and tasted hard and strong'; those were times when many Europeans had yet to be won over to an appreciation of sparkling wines. Perhaps the question can only be answered at the Monastery, because the home wine-makers around Kalavryta do not seem to be making any sparkling wine today. In any case, the *lagórthi* is very well regarded by Greek enologists. But there is so little of it around Kalavryta today, that no legal recognition can be considered at this time.

CLASSICAL REFLECTIONS

Greeks frequently serve Mavrodaphne of Patras as an aperitif. The habit, which is hardly without its parallels elsewhere along the northern Mediterranean, invites consideration of certain notions and practices of the ancients in ordering the serving of wine and food.

Although one can hardly survey the ancient record and presume an absolute conformity of habits among places and periods during early times, it may be said that for some time before Plutarch in the first century AD, wine was customarily not drunk until a main course was being eaten. Among some of the ancients, depending perhaps on their personal disposition as well as their times and social class, even that was thought too early: '*after the food* [emphasis added] only so much unmixed wine should be taken by all as should be a taste and ensample of the good god's power, but after that all other wine must be drunk mixed' (Theophrastus, *On Drunkenness*, fourth century BC, quoted by Athenaeus, *The Deipnosophists*). For food was thought an antidote to intoxication, and intoxication was considered permissible only during bacchanalia, even if it was common at wineshops.

However, around Plutarch's time a change was introduced through a shuffling in the ordering of courses: 'The "cold-course" as it used to be called, with oysters, sea-urchins, and raw vegetables, has like a body of light-armed troops been shifted from the rear to the front, and holds first place instead of last' (*Moralia*, 'Table -talk'). That shift, which Plutarch attributed to decadence, and which perhaps occurred mostly among the affluent, ushered in an expansion of the 'cold-course', such that it became the forerunner of what would at a much later date be dubbed 'the cocktail hour':

> The serving of the so-called aperitives [*propomáton*] is a great change too. The ancients did not even drink water before the dessert course, but nowadays people get themselves intoxicated before eating a thing, and take food after their bodies are soaked and feverish with wine, serving hors-d'œuvres of light and sharp-flavoured and sour foods as a stimulant to the appetite and then, in this condition, eating heartily of the rest of the meal.
>
> (Moralia, 'Table-talk')

To take Plutarch's viewpoint, the likely culprit was salt: 'it is conventional before a main course to take appetizers that are sharp or briny, and in general anything that has a highly salty character' ('Table-talk'). For salt provokes a thirst that some would try to quench with wine. Indeed Plutarch remarked that priests 'use no salt with their food during their periods of holy living . . . because salt, by sharpening the appetite makes them more inclined to drinking [wine] and eating' (*Moralia*, 'Isis and Osiris').

During pre-prandial nibbling, sweet wines probably would have been deemed to have the advantage over dry ones, since sweet wines were understood to forestall intoxication; Hagias said that sweetness is filling, so that one ordinarily cannot drink enough to get drunk (Plutarch, *Moralia*, 'Table-talk'). Furthermore, sweet red wine might have been seen as allaying the drying property of salt on account of its 'moistness': 'sweet dark wines are moister and weaker' than other kinds (Hippocrates, *Ancient Medicine*).

GASTRONOMIC NOTES

As concerns food, the name of the Peloponnesos seems destined to remain inextricably bound up with currants and olives. The region is the world's centre of currant production; they grow primarily along the northern rim, but also down the west coast. The black currants of Aegion (Vostitsa) have a particular repute, while those of Kiato usually gain first mention among the less characteristic amber kind. However, olive trees are far more widespread than currant vines in the Morea. The region's oil is plentiful and almost universally very good. Exceptional ones include the best of Kyparissia on the south-western coast, Leonidio on the south-eastern coast, and the valley of Sparta in the south-central area. Two sorts of table olive have taken the region's name far among olive enthusiasts the world over: Kalamata and Nafplion. The Kalamata is grown in the vicinity of the town of that name along the south-central coast, and is readily distinguishable by its blackish-purple colour, almond shape, and lengthwise slit. Unlike most Greek black olives, it is harvested before complete ripeness, and cured quickly, in about two weeks, compared to six months for most, so as to preserve the colour and enhance the tang appropriate to the particular state of ripeness. Poles apart from the Kalamata, the Nafplion olive comes from the area of the town of that name in the north-eastern Peloponnesos, and is smallish, green and cracked across its width. In Greek grocery stores, olives called *tsakistés*, the 'cracked ones', are usually Nafplion olives, and are often flavoured with garlic or herbs.

Outstanding fresh seafood can be had virtually all around the coast of the Morea, but particular mention must be made of the areas of Methoni and Koroni, situated on opposite sides of the far south-western peninsula of the region. Along the central western coast, the lake by Kaiafas provides excellent fish, and some turtles as well. Far inland, about midway between Pyrgos and Mantinia, the artificially created Lake Ladonas is visited for its trout (*péstrofa*). Small game such as hare and partridge abound, notably at Kaltezes, midway between Tripolis and Sparta, and in the vicinity of Leonidio. Wild goat is a prized meat in mountainous areas. Around Akhladokambos, midway between Tripolis and Nafplion, roasted old she-goat (*ghiósa*) is the speciality, while Kosmas, by Mount Parnonas in the south-east, prides itself on kid cooked in and served with a special broth. Dairy products made from ewe's milk have won popular recognition for several locales: yogurt of Manolada in the north-west and Megalopolis in the central south; cheeses from Kosmas and other lofty areas around Parnonas, where the animals graze exclusively on wild savory; and Parnonas is especially appreciated for its rare goat's-milk *myzíthra*, a soft cheese. In some villages in the mountainous south-east, *korkofíngi* may also be encountered. It is made by frying, omelette-fashion, the rich, thick milk of a ewe or she-goat that has given birth, and served cut in pieces with sugar sprinkled over it.

PART III
WESTERN GREECE

The Ionian Islands and Epirus

IO

The Ionian Islands

The best wines of the Ionian Islands are those of Ithaca and Cephalonia, and the hilly and mountainous parts of Zante. They are all sufficiently strong, and would bear exportation; and, were they allowed to have age, I believe would be approved in [England], especially the red wine of Ithaca, the best white wine of Cephalonia, and the verdea of Zante.
(John Davy, British officer, *Notes and Observations on the Ionian Islands and Malta*, 1842)

So strong is the tendency to view Greece from the Aegean perspective that the country's westernmost hem, the Ionian islands, is frequently overlooked, almost irrespective of the topic, although it is in all respects among the most fascinating parts of the country. Lying off the west coast of the mainland, on the eastern rim of the Ionian Sea separating Greece from the heel of Italy, they comprise, from south to north, Zakynthos, Cephalonia, Ithaca, Lefkas, Antipaxi, Paxi and Corfu, as well as some lesser islets, and are generally called the Eftanisa by the Greeks, which is an old colloquial name meaning 'Seven Isles' (historically, the seventh was not little Antipaxi, but considerable Kythira, far to the south and around behind the Peloponnesos, an island now administratively attached to Central Greece). Strung out over a sizeable stretch of sea, and mostly large enough to fend for themselves economically, the Eftanisa have been bound together primarily by a shared history that diverges from the rest of Greece in their having spent but a token period under the Ottomans. They were instead controlled by Western powers most of the time, with the consequence that they are not only Greece's most westerly region geographically, but also its most Western in orientation.

The Ionian islands were under Western rule of one kind or another for nearly seven centuries, beginning in the thirteenth century with various so-called Frankish overlords, most of whom represented certain powerful Italian families that in turn answered to Venice. The Venetians controlled the Eftanisa directly from the late fifteenth century until the end of the eighteenth century, though not all of the islands at all times. The era of Western rule closed with a brief occupation by France, and finally status as a British protectorate from 1815 until 1864, when the Ionians were ceded to the Greek state.

However, while the Ionians might count themselves lucky for having slipped away from the Ottomans' grasp, the impact of Western control was not always positive as far as wine-growing was concerned. Most notably, the Venetians propagated the currant vine, whose cultivation skewed the evolution of viticulture at many villages, often to the detriment of wine-growing. Also, the prod-uction, consumption and trade in wine were taxed at rates which in some periods discouraged wine-growing or encouraged unfortunate wine-making practices. In view of that past, it is little wonder that travellers reported quite variously on both the quantity and quality of wine in the Eftanisa. Some of the circumstances of earlier times are still reflected in Ionian wine-growing, which has never been attacked by phylloxera and forced to alter the patterns of bygone times on the pest's account, and inhibit the release of the full potential these islands still hold.

ZAKYNTHOS

The southernmost of today's Eftanisa is Zakynthos, which was known to generations of Europeans by its French name, Zante. Largely low-lying and verdant, the island was dubbed 'the flower of the Levant' by the Venetians, who seem to have had a special liking for the place. Zakynthos was their favourite island in which to reside, and their influence on life there was commensurate. Not the least significant impact was the rejuvenation of a degenerate Byzantine feudal society. The remnants of the Byzantine nobility eventually died out virtually everywhere else in Greece, but the Venetians propped them up at Zakynthos by offering an array of enticements that drew down-and-out members of the Italian aristocracy to settle on the island. Among other consequences of the perpetuation of a landed nobility was the preservation of certain island wine traditions, long after the island economy underwent a fundamental change that made preservation generally impracticable.

Vineyards for wine production have been significant on Zante since very early times. The islanders apparently discarded few if any of the numerous grape varieties that came their way during their history. Indeed, on this account Zakynthos holds a special place in the annals of Greek ampelography, the earliest modern record of Greek grape varieties dating to a poem of 1601 that mentions the names of thirty-four varieties cultivated on the island:

Grapes on Zakynthos are the *kozanítis*,
Mygdáli, fléri, razakiá, khlóra, and *moronítis*,
Lardéra and *skylóklima, voíthamos, fterougátis*,
Tragána, petrokóritho, pávlos, and *khoukhouliátis*,
Others are the most beautiful *robóla* and *aïtonýkhi*,
Moskháto, ambelokóritho, ftákilos, and *ksyríkhi*,
Katzakoúlias, kondokládi, kakotrýgi, voïdomátis,
Glykeríthra, lianorróïdi, goustoulídi, and *agoustiátis*,
Glykopáti . . ., *vósos*, and the *koutzoumbéli*,
And the *nýkhi tou kokórou* which adorns the *ambéli* [vineyard],
After all those comes the *skylopníkhtis*,
But the most famous of all is the red *roïdítis*.

Three centuries later, in 1904, Ludwig Salvator listed more than eighty varieties in his monumental work on Zakynthos, since a good many of the grape varieties grown have more than one colour variant.

The Venetians fomented a profound change in island viticulture in 1516, when they saw to the transplantation of the currant vine from the Peloponnesos, in the hope of profiting from the lucrative trade with Western Europe. In fact they succeeded resoundingly, because of the very high quality of the product obtained. The currant became Zante's so-called 'black gold', and its characteristic product. European demand was so strong (one thinks of the many Elizabethan recipes calling for currants) that in 1673 the Venetians undertook the draining of the east-central part of the plain in order to enable a further expansion of currant vines. Even today, about two-thirds of the approximately 3,300 hectares of vineyard land on Zakynthos are planted with the currant vine. Islanders, however, do not enumerate the currant with other grape varieties, but instead refer on the one hand to their 'vineyards' (*ambélia*) when speaking of their plantings of wine and dessert grapes, and on the other hand to 'raisins' (*stafídes*) when speaking of their plantings of currants.

The currant relegated other island products to a supplementary role in the local economy, and wine was foremost among these. However, it would appear from available reports that wine's decline in importance was gradual, even somewhat erratic, and marked more by changes in tradition than by a major, lasting fall-off in the quantity produced. For example, while in 1541 a Venetian administrator of the Ionians noted that island wine production served mostly to cover local needs and was not worth taxing as an export article, in 1579 the visitor Carlier de Pinon noted considerable exports, to as far off as Constantinople. Over time, however, island tradition as concerned wine types shifted and deteriorated. A development of especially forceful impact was the periodic surpluses of dried fruit that occurred as currant cultivation spread in the Ionians and the Peloponnesos. Zakynthiote merchants began making wine from the fresh fruit, so that by the late nineteenth century 'currant wine', or *stafidítis*, as it is properly called in Greek, became the characteristic commercial island wine. Thus, while in 1579 Carlier de Pinon mentioned exports of red wine called 'Romania', whose varietal origin is not known, and a white wine called 'Ribola', which was made from the variety of that name mentioned in the poem of 1601, Richard Farrer mentioned in 1882 that currant wine was 'the Zante wine usually sold in Greece or exported to England'. Also, the number of available wine types diminished. According to the report of Thomas Hughes in 1820, at least 'forty different sorts' of wine were being made at that time, as though the various wine grapes were being used to make varietal wines. More detailed notes of 1795 by John Sibthorp, who addressed individual grape varieties, suggest that half that number of wine types could not have been an over-estimate, even if few were readily available commercially. Whatever their number may have been, some Zakynthiote wine types were eventually lost to the island's preoccupation with the currant.

Of most special note among the wines which did not survive the impact of the currant was the one most likely to have earned Zakynthos an enviable reputation: *lianorróïdi*, or *lianorrógi*. It was a sweet white wine produced, as its names indicate, from 'small berries'. The grape varieties used to make it were, alternatively, the native *goustoulídi*, a semi-aromatic sort whose qualities were highly praised by the French ampelographer Guillon, and the *robóla*, which was brought by the Venetians in the thirteenth century. Availability determined whether the one variety or the other was used. The Italian visitor Saverio Scrofani, writing in 1801, likened *jenorrodi* [*sic*] to both Italian Piccolit and Hungarian Tokay, and further lauded it as 'preferable to all other liqueurs of the Levant'. Around that time, however, currant wine, or at least that of the very best quality – for currant wine generally was not deemed a first-rank wine – also became associated with the *lianorróïdi* name, in all likelihood because the currant too, on account of its small berries, was known colloquially as *lianorrógi*.

Although some wine of genuine *lianorróïdi* type apparently was made for a time into the 1800s, it eventually ceased to be called by that name; even before the middle of the century, the wine writer Cyrus Redding, apparently unfamiliar with travellers' notes, had no idea that the name might belong to any *but* currant wine. The genuine sort finally became extinct altogether, probably in the late nineteenth century. The burgher class, which had grown in numbers and political strength thanks in part to the currant trade, forced the democratization of Zakynthiote society in the early nineteenth century, with the result that most of the nobility, the class most able to afford a luxury wine, gradually became impoverished. When the island lost its special trading privileges with Britain, the largest customer for currants, after Britain relinquished the Ionians in 1864, a general economic decline ensued. No true *lianorróïdi* has been made in the lifetime of the oldest living Zakynthiotes.

A far more enduring sort of wine proved to be that called *verdéa*, which not only survived the currant but apparently grew in popularity, to the point that it remains the island's major wine today. Historical information about *verdéa* does not allow its rise to dominance to be tracked precisely, but it may be noted that in the 1830s Davy found *verdéa* produced in such a quantity that he could suggest exporting it, whereas several decades earlier, at the turn of the nineteenth century, neither Sibthorp nor Scrofani referred to a wine by that name. *Verdéa*'s resilience may be due primarily to a certain fluidity in concept over the centuries. It has had a rather general association with white wine, since its name comes from the Italian for 'green', but its tradition otherwise has been somewhat chequered, and plagues it still.

Verdéa may have originated as a varietal wine, although, if so, the basis for it is not clear. Its name is the same as that carried by a one-time Tuscan wine, widely known in the Middle Ages and later, which was produced from the *verdea d'arcetri* variety, mentioned as *vardea* by Alexandre Odart in his *Ampelographie* of 1845. Around that same time, a variety called *verdéa* and described as 'greenish' in a Greek account was cultivated on Corfu; *vardéa* is still found on Lefkas. But such a varietal name, if it ever was known on Zakynthos, has not been known there for a very long time. It was not mentioned in the poem of 1601, for instance. However, that poem does mention a variety called *khlóra*, as in 'chlorophyll', which Sibthorp noted gave a greenish wine. In favour of a varietal explanation, too, it might be reiterated that varietal or largely varietal wines were once usual on Zakynthos.

On the other hand, *verdéa* may have originated as a mixed-varietal wine, which it is today. The Venetians could have applied that name to it on account of its colour alone, independently of a varietal name, because they were reminded in that way of Tuscan verdea. The nineteenth-century wine writer Alexander Henderson noted that the Tuscan wine was 'so called from its colour inclining to green', and a greenish tinge is still usually expected of Zakynthiote *verdéa*, at least while it is young: 'Every spring the Zakynthiotes set out [on a picnic] with . . . flasks of *verdéa*, the peppery gold-green local wine' (Dionysios Romas, 1957). The greenish colour of the original Zakynthiote *verdéa* may have resulted from a mix of ripe and unripe grapes, ones likely to have been various in kind and in ripening time. Were that habit indeed the origin of *verdéa*, wine of its type could long antedate the Venetians and the name they gave it, since the Greeks anciently made a sort of wine, called *omfakítis*, meaning 'sour-grape [*ómfax*] wine', for which unripe grapes were purposely vinified with over-ripe ones, perhaps with the intent of achieving both the strength of a high alcoholic degree and a fresh savour. Even if that were so, *verdéa*'s rather recent growth as a typical wine, of mixed-varietal nature, would seem to reflect a phasing out of the practice of separately collecting and vinifying most of the white varieties grown.

At the present time, *verdéa* is associated *only* with mixed-varietal white wine. It is made by harvesting and vinifying several white varieties together, in mid-September. Perhaps its harvesting was earlier at one time, since the most characteristic variety used in making it is the *goustoulídi*, whose name comes from the Greek for 'August', *Ávgoustos*. If it in fact used to be harvested in August on Zakynthos, the *goustoulídi* could account for *verdéa*'s name, since its mixture with other varieties which had not ripened as fully so early could have resulted in lightening, and even swaying towards green, its own yellowish wine. Later on, the *goustoulídi*'s harvesting may have been pushed back to gain more sugar in the grapes and more alcohol in the wine. Or else maybe the harvest for mixed-varietal *verdéa* has always been in September and the variety was given its name back in the time of the Julian calendar. Whatever was done in the past, today the *goustoulídi*, which is generally regarded as a variety especially important to the quality of *verdéa*, is not considered fit for picking and vinifying until mid-September. The other varieties most often used in making *verdéa* are *robóla*, *pávlos* and *skiadópoulo*, all of which ripen in September. The varietal mix is quite variable, however. Indeed *verdéa* remains something of a *bouillabaisse* of wine, complete with firm views as to which 'fish' may go in it, for which reason an appellation of origin eludes it for the time being. The Greek Wine Institute is monitoring the *verdéa* puzzle from a distance, but their work is hampered when producers of a mixed-varietal wine have not settled on a typical mix.

Verdéa has been represented on the bottled wine market for over three decades by the product of Count Comoutos, but his version is a somewhat unusual one. The noble Comoutos family, the *crème de la crème* of the old Zakynthiote aristocracy, has been making wine since 1638 at their agricultural estate 'Agria', which is situated in the vicinity of Makhairado and Lagopodo, two villages on the south-western rim of the main plain where it meets the island's major line of low mountains to the west. Although Agria is well inland, its nearly 12 hectares of vineyards are at an elevation of but 10 metres above sea level; vineyards on the plain do not rise much above the 50-metre mark. Porous soil and a base of limestone, like that observable on the mountains, keep vineyards on the fringes of the plain well drained. For his *verdéa*, Count Comoutos uses *robóla*, *goustoulídi*, *pinot gris* (which he calls '*tokay*'), *skiadópoulo*, *pávlos*, *aretí* and Zakynthiote *asproúdi* (other white varieties in Greece also go by this name, 'whitey'). *Robóla* provides a major part of his mix, but the Count regards *goustoulídi* and *pinot gris* as crucial for the wine's character. The grapes are crushed immediately after harvesting, the skins are removed, and the must is left to ferment vigorously for seven to ten days, followed by another thirty to forty days of slow fermentation. The wine is then matured in oak barrels for at least five years prior to bottling as Comouto Verdea, with vintage indication. About 500 hectolitres are made in each vintage.

Its lengthy time in barrel, and not the varietal mix, takes Comouto Verdea forever beyond greenishness. What meets the eye is a golden-orange colour overlaid by a sort of rosiness, rather where amber might run into pink. Barrel maturation has an equally strong influence on bouquet, a dominant aroma being one that straddles the cherry and vanilla effects oak can induce. Sometimes it leans one way, and sometimes the other. Also characteristic is a hard-to-describe ethereal smell attributed to certain bluebloods among vinous odours, which, whether or not one has hobnobbed much with their ilk, make one feel quite at home when they turn up in Comouto Verdea in the classy guise of all that is noble in rotten apples and such. This *rancio* aspect might recall wines like sherry and tokay dry *szamorodni*, but unlike those wines Comouto Verdea is always kept topped up in bunged barrels, and so is not influenced by the development of a *flor*. If not typical of *verdéa*, since few producers could have afforded the long maturation, apparently some *verdéa* in the past, too, was left a relatively long time in barrel; the good Zakynthiote white wine Farrer mentioned in 1882 as 'resembling old natural sherry' was probably an older *verdéa*. In the mouth, the sweetness of alcohol noticeable in texture serves as a counterpoint to a certain astringency, but if a bottle is laid away care should be taken not to leave it for so long that the wine 'dries out'. Depending on the quality of the vintage, more than fifteen to twenty years beyond the posted date might be risky.

Count Comoutos considers his *verdéa* both an aperitif and a dinner wine, and says that most Zakynthiote customers drink it with meals. I am tempted to think that its proper accompaniment must be game birds: it happens that Zakynthos sits beneath the north–south path of various migratory birds: mid-April to mid-May and late August to early October are the seasons for dove (*trigónia*) and quail (*ortíkia*), while November and December are the months for woodcock (*bekátses*). They can be found served with the Venetians' favourite starch, *polenta*, which is occasionally studded with local currants. Roast turkey or chicken stuffed with chestnut dressing is as good with a souvenir bottle. As concerns seafood, 'rotten apples' might not generally be thought of as a complementary flavour, but Comouto Verdea can none the less be recommended for the popular Greek

Lenten dish of squid or octopus *krasáto*, for which the wine sauce is dark and slightly sweet.

Verdéa had long been a wine of 15–16° alcohol until Comoutos introduced his 14.2° version. His fellow Zakynthiotes once considered it too light, while most other Greeks found even that too strong for their ordinary usage. Having since won a place for his *verdéa* both on and off the island, the Count has been able to stand by his concept. Comoutos's market-place victory over the Zakynthiote old guard made way for *verdéa* of still lower alcohol content. Theodoros Voultsos, a commoner, is now producing both a dry and a semi-dry *verdéa* of 12.5°, under the Callinico Verdea label. He vinifies *goustoulídi, pávlos, skiadópoulo* and *robóla* grapes grown in his own vineyards at Kalipado, as well as selected fruit bought from wine-growers scattered about the plain. Nearly 1,250 hectolitres are made annually, and bottled after one year in oak, but without vintage indication. A winery expansion is planned. The Union of Agricultural Cooperatives of Zakynthos, whose major wine previously was the mixed-varietal white Delizia, has recently added a limited production Verdea of 12–12.5°. The Union's version is made from *pávlos* and *skiadópoulo*, harvested from the villages of Pantokrator, Makhairado, Langadakia, Vouyiato, Galaro and Katastari.

Excellent fruit for wine-making can be grown even on the plain proper, where it is drained by sink-holes. However, the Voultsos and Union white wines are somewhat disappointing to those who know Zakynthiote wine thoroughly, and suggest that the right 'formula' for low-alcohol *verdéa* of the fresh kind has yet to be hit upon. The foreigner may be disappointed that none looks greenish, but on the other hand we ought to be grateful not to be sold a bottle whose contents have begun to look like Comouto Verdea: they are wines for early enjoyment. The touring enophile desirous of finding high-quality *verdéa* in the old style is advised that Salvator mentioned the villages of Lagana and Layou as the island's best places for white wine. Some Zakynthiotes further specify the sandy soil areas of Lagana.

Fussing over *verdéa*, it is all too easy to overlook another patch of Zakynthiote wine tradition. White wine has been dominant on the island, but red wine has always had its place, perhaps because the locals, as Salvator reported, like dark wines in winter. The main variety used is the roguish though upstanding *avgoustiátis*, another

variety named for August which these days is said to be unfit for
the vat until well into September. Sibthorp thought it the *mavrodáfni*,
but if it ever had that synonym Greek ampelographers do not know
it, and treat the *avgoustiátis* quite apart from the grape of Patras
fame. As in the case of a number of other varieties on the island, both
red and black variants of the *avgoustiátis* are known, and traditionally
have been vinified separately, although usually with others of their
colour tendency, so as to make wines respectively called 'red' and
'black'. Salvator indicated that most Zakynthiote red wine was black,
very little red being produced. He also mentioned Lithakia and Fayas
as the best villages for black wine, and Makhairado for red.

Most Zakynthiote bottled wines of violet persuasion have recently
been red, in island terms, but their producers would rather capitalize
on current fashion by calling them 'rosé'. To Westerners, they might
appear neither really red nor really rosé. They are made by giving a
long fermentation on the skins to a must obtained from grapes of a
colour too light to yield black wine. Count Comoutos's representative
is Comouto Rosé, a 12.6° wine made in an amount of about 250
hectolitres annually from a mixture of *avgoustiátis, katsakoúlia,
ayiomavrítiko, fléri*, (elsewhere called *filéri), mandilariá* and *xynómavro* (the latter two are new to Zakynthos). Comouto Rosé is
matured in oak for three years. The counterpart from Voultsos is the
12.5° Callinico Rosé, made from the varieties *rodítis, violedó* and
katsakoúlia. About 500 hectolitres are produced annually. The
Union's entry is Delizia Rosé, at 12.5° wine from a similar varietal
mix. In addition, Voultsos has a darker wine, Callinico Erythros, an
all-*avgoustiátis* wine. None of the reddish Zakynthiote wines carries
a vintage date, or even an indication of when they were bottled,
which is too bad because they will sometimes bear age.

CLASSICAL REFLECTIONS

The *lianorróïdi*, or *lianorrógi*, of Zakynthos may have been a wine
of quite ancient lineage in type, as regards both the grapes used to
make it and their elaboration after harvesting.

The ampelographer Krimbas (1947) explained the name of *lianorróïdi* wine as indicating 'coming from small berries', much as the
related term *lianorrógi* literally means 'small berries'. Both terms
suggest the persistence of an archaic distinction, for Pliny mentioned

Greek vines called *leptóragas*, meaning 'fine berry', because of small grapes growing among large ones and rivalling those in sweetness. In modern times, the successor terms to *leptóragas* have been applied to several Greek grape varieties, but usually as an alternative name for small-berried clones of them, or for manifestations of small berries characteristic of them under particular conditions. Thus, although the Zakynthiote poem of 1601 mentions a *lianorróïdi*, while Scrofani in 1801 stated that wine of that name was made from grapes so called, the name actually may not have been a varietal name as such, but rather a name for a specific manifestation within a variety, to be recognized visually and made practical use of. For that matter, Greek ampelographies mention no separate variety known primarily as *lianorróïdi* or *lianorrógi*.

On Zakynthos, both the *goustoulídi* and the *robóla* have been associated with the *lianorróïdi/lianorrógi* terminology, as pertains to grapes as well as to wines. The native lexicographer Zoïs stated that the *lianorróïdo* [*sic*] and *lianorrógi* names were used to refer to small-berried, pipless grapes of *goustoulídi* type. Since the *goustoulídi* proper is known on Zakynthos as a variety having pips, the pipless kind may have taken on an identity of its own: it is perhaps significant in that regard that in the poem of 1601 the *lianorróïdi* and *goustoulídi* names appeared side by side. In his report of 1795, however, Sibthorp attributed the name of *lianorógi* [*sic*] wine to the name by which the Zakynthiotes called the tiny grapes typical of the *robóla* vine when it had attained a great age. Because he had no inkling of a connection of the name with *goustoulídi*, Sibthorp considered *lianorógi* wine produced from that variety something of an imitation ('wine which is sold for the Lianorogi') resorted to because of an insufficiency of the requisite old *robóla* vines. Yet, considering the antiquity of the 'small berry' idea, and that the *goustoulídi* is a native variety, while the *robóla* is not, the likelihood is that the *goustoulídi* was the earlier source.

The actual preparation of *lianorróïdi* wine also entailed a special procedure. Sibthorp noted that when either *goustoulídi* or *robóla* grapes were used they were first dried in the sun a little; the use of sun-drying may have contributed to the transferral of the *lianorróïdi* name to currant wine, if the currants were occasionally dried partially before vinification. Notes by Davy suggest, however, that an alternative means may also have been used: '[a wine] made from choice white grapes, not subjected to the pressure of the feet or of the press;

the must is obtained merely by the pressure of the grapes on each other heaped together.' Or it is possible that that procedure was used in conjunction with the shrivelling of grapes mentioned by Sibthorp. It is just that combination of techniques which yields Tokay Essence, a wine which, interestingly, is not known to antedate the presence of a substantial expatriate Greek wine merchant community at Tokaj.

The technique Davy described is essentially that for the ancient Greek wine called *prótropon*, which was a sweet wine of low alcoholic degree. Although Davy associated the technique with wine he understood to be called *verdéa*, it was probably, more precisely, wine of the type earlier known only as *lianorróïdi*. In fact, the Zakynthiotes know of no tradition of sweet *verdéa* – *verdéa* proper – nor of any technique for wine of that name more expensive than the use of free-run must. Moreover, Davy's suggestion that *verdéa* could be exported contradicted his estimation of the available quantity of the sort of wine produced by the *prótropon* technique: 'made only in small quantities, and with great care; it is chiefly given in presents by the rich proprietors'. An elite wine would have been just the role of genuine *lianorróïdi*, and not that of *verdéa*, a wine which, on the contrary, was so plentiful that ham cured in *verdéa* became an island country speciality. The explanation for the confusion is that, probably because both the *goustoulídi* and the *robóla* varieties were associated with those two wines, genuine *lianorróïdi/lianorrógi* also came under the *verdéa* rubric as the nineteenth century progressed and a term was needed to differentiate it from currant wine called *lianorrógi*.

CEPHALONIA (KEFALLINIA)

For the time being, and for the foreseeable future as well, the only appellation of origin entitlements in the Eftanisa will belong to Cephalonia, which possesses three of them, all granted immediately upon implementation of the Greek appellative legislation in 1971, in recognition of the island's long-standing reputation for the kinds of wine concerned: Robola, Muscat and Mavrodaphne. It is tempting to attribute Cephalonia's vinous preeminence entirely to environmental advantage, especially if arriving by way of the steamer from Patras, for the trip impresses upon the traveller the imposing heights of Mount Ainos (or Mavrovouni) and the rocky, limestone nature of the island, both of those features auguring some of the best conditions for Mediterranean wine-growing. However, it took the combination of a variety of historical factors for advantage to be taken of natural conditions and Cephalonia to be put in a position to gain its appellation rights.

For many centuries it could not have been predicted with any certainty that Cephalonia would take the lead in Ionian wine-growing distinction. The island declined greatly during late antiquity, when it was left off major trade routes and population plummeted. The inhabitants who remained mostly abandoned the land for the sea, either as merchant mariners or pirates. The turn away from agriculture was reinforced when the Cephalonians were drawn to service as mercenaries in the civil wars of the Romans. In early Christian times, island wine production barely sufficed for local consumption, and a codex of 1264 indicates that vineyards were very limited in extent even much later. With the control of the island by Franks in those years came some commercial interest in wine, and even a minor export trade, but both quantity and quality remained far below their potential. Grain production in the lower parts of Cephalonia was for the most part a better-paid enterprise than viticulture, while the period of Frankish rule lacked the stability that could have encouraged construction of the upland terraces generally needed on Cephalonia to produce the best wine.

It was precisely stability that Venice brought to the island in 1500, when it ousted the Turks, who had held Cephalonia for scarcely two decades after they wrested control from the Franks. But a variety of more specific measures also came to the aid of viticulture during Venetian times, the most important of which was the imposition of fines for leaving land uncultivated. Consequently, the previously barren uplands were covered with vines, olive trees, and cotton plantations by 1621. Also, taxes on imported wines were raised to the advantage of local wines in 1691. Yet negative developments also occurred in Venetian days. Viticulture fell back in importance relative to olive cultivation after the fall of Crete to the Ottomans in 1669, because until then Crete was also in Venetian hands and had been supplying much of Cephalonia's oil needs. To that period may date an old Cephalonian saying, 'the olive drinks the wine'. Also, Venice became a jealous customer for Cephalonian muscat wine, and eventually prohibited its export to any other destination, with the result that the price for muscat tumbled. Wine-growers sought to recoup their losses by whatever means they could, and started using less expensively produced grapes, in whatever proportion possible, in preparing 'muscat'. Wine-growing also suffered from interest in currants at times. The Venetians had brought the currant vine to Cephalonia too, and, although it did not have the lasting, extensive success there that it had on Zakynthos, it was adopted as a mainstay of agriculture in some areas of the island. Gluts and low prices led to production of currant wine, and to its admixture in 'muscat'.

British rule in the Ionians followed upon a French occupation that had been disastrous for Cephalonian wine-growers because of a lowering of wine import tariffs, which made native wines uncompetitive with imports from Provence and Bordeaux, and from elsewhere as well. Under Britain, agriculture, and therefore viticulture too, benefited by the cutting of a road through the mostly rugged terrain from the east coast port of Sami to the westerly port and capital of Argostoli, which greatly facilitated the marketing of farm products, and went a long way towards making a single market out of an island whose three rather divergent sections had previously resisted that development. Even British rule, though, was marked by adverse developments for Cephalonian wine, especially a resurgence of currant cultivation that took place because Europe's chief customer for currants – Britain – had taken over the stewardship of the only source – the Ionians – capable of replacing the Peloponnesos when the latter's currant export trade was interrupted by the Greek War of Independence that broke out in 1821. Also, in 1848, the European year of popular revolutions, a spate of peasant rebellions occurred in the Ionians with the object of achieving union with Greece, and was particularly destructive on Cephalonia.

Signs that Cephalonia would move ahead of the other Ionian islands in wine came in the second half of the nineteenth century, beginning around 1850, when a French firm set up operations to make and bottle local wines. Although it is a matter of speculation, it is just possible that the firm was drawn to the island by a book written by Charles Napier, an early nineteenth-century British governor of the Ionians. Napier had resided at Cephalonia, and in his book he pointedly tried to interest Western entrepreneurs in developing the possibilities he felt the island had in wine, but which the natives might not be able to develop fully for lack of capital.

The Cefalonians are poor, will be poorer, and ought to be rich. . . .
It is to be regretted that some speculator, versed in the mode of
making wine in Madeira, or in France, does not settle in Cefalonia.
There can be no doubt that he would succeed.

The French venture soon failed, however, reportedly because its
bottled wines were more expensive than the country wines, and yet
neither better nor as resistant to the Ionian climate. Nevertheless, the
episode apparently provided the Cephalonians with a window on
the future that afforded them a headstart in modernizing the island
wine industry.

From the time of the French attempt, on into the twentieth century,
even islanders endeavoured to found upgraded wine companies,
though by fits and starts because of setbacks caused by vineyard
diseases and economic downturns, and without attempting bottling,
presumably because of the extra expense of importing bottles.
However, in 1872 the British entrepreneur Ernest Toole, perhaps
also under Napier's influence, took over, expanded and thoroughly
refurbished a Cephalonian winery, and enjoyed great success, such
that the firm opened a second winery in 1898, where bottling
was once again undertaken. The Cephalonian wine industry was
sufficiently robust to rebound from the devastating pernospora
epidemic of 1900, and was strengthened further by the return of a
native who had earned a degree in wine-growing in France and put
his knowledge to use back home in 1911. But the First World War
caused the Toole wines to lose their all-important German market,
and with that Cephalonian wine-growing went into a tailspin.
Subsequent efforts at recovery were cut short by a world wine
glut, a six-year occupation during the Second World War, and the
calamitous mid-Ionian earthquake of 1953 which drove away nearly
half of the island's population and brought down the vineyard area
by almost as much. Still, as a result of its experiences since the mid-
nineteenth century, Cephalonia had relatively the most progressive
wine industry in the Ionians in the mid-twentieth century.

Some of Cephalonia's predominance in the Ionians must be
attributed to its having had the chance to specialize in and stick to
producing grape varieties that had come upon ideal environments
there. By far the most significant of those varieties at the present
time is the *robóla*, whose Italian origin has been forgotten now.
Cephalonian explanations of the varietal name usually proceed from

the mistaken assumption that it must be a Greek word, but the variety was once known also as 'malvasia of Venice', and its earliest spelling in the Ionians, *ribóla*, also betrays its Italian origin, for Italian *ribolla* is the old Venetian dialectical word for the 'tiller' of a rudder. The earliest written mention of the *robóla* on Cephalonia comes from a document of 1520, but the variety could have appeared as early as the thirteenth century, the date of its appearance on Zakynthos. Certainly the divergences found in the *robóla* vine cultivated on the two islands could be explained by an adaptation of the variety to the respective environments beginning before the sixteenth century. The *robóla* grew in importance on Cephalonia during the sixteenth and seventeenth centuries, when cultivation of the uplands was being extended, especially on the western side of Mount Ainos. The latter area proved largely unsuitable for the currant vine, and the *robóla*'s tendency to ripen there in early September fitted nicely into the farming pattern, since its ripening came after the currant harvest and before the collection of olives, so that labour for the vintage was plentifully available. However, *robóla* was also planted in lowland areas, where quality did not come up to that achieved on the mountainsides. Consequently, lowland *robóla* was often vinified with *tsaoúsi*, a possibly related but lesser-quality variety. Even the latter mixture was sold as 'Robola' wine, though at a lower price. Cephalonians still distinguish *oriní robóla*, or 'mountain Robola', from *kambísia robóla*, or 'plains Robola', wine.

Writing in 1946, the ampelographer Krimbas noted that the *robóla* is 'valued, despite its small yield, for the exceptional quality of its wine', and specified 'mountainous places almost lacking in soil', which exactly describes the wine-growing areas by Mount Ainos. Vineyards there are embedded in broken limestone, the vines being planted in pockets laboriously created among the stones and then filled in with earth brought from elsewhere. Surely it must have been the wine of this area that Napier had in mind when he mentioned the island's 'strong dry wine, called "vino di sasso", or wine of stone, from the love of stony ground evinced by the plant'. Cephalonia's current appellation of origin entitlement for Robola wine applies mostly to vines cultivated on the flats and inclines of Omalai, the barren upland plateau to the east and north-east of Argostoli, heading towards the peaks of Ainos. The villages specified are Davgata, Dilinata, Frangata, Valsamata, Troianata, Metaxata and Epanokhori, whose vineyards extend from 250 to 800 metres above the Ionian Sea. Currently, about 320 hectares are in production in the appellation zone, out of a total island wine grape area of about 1,400 hectares.

About 10,000 hectolitres of appellation of origin Robola of Cephalonia wine are bottled annually, primarily by the private firm of Inoexagoyiki, which is more commonly called by the family name Calligas, and the Agro-Industrial Cooperative of Producers of Robola of Cephalonia. Both buy in grapes from around the appellation area, but Calligas relies initially on its own 40 hectares of vines by the little village of Razata, which lies due south of Dilinata and east of Argostoli, and within the appellation zone. A second private firm, Komitopoulos, was also producing an appellation wine, but has sharply curtailed production in the wake of internal difficulties that now threaten to eliminate their participation in the market.

In most respects, the bottled Robola wines from Calligas and the Cooperative have been a lot like country wines of Omalai. Most important, I think, is that they share with those wines a sort of 'mineralic' savour that serves to distinguish Cephalonian Robola from *ribolla/rebula* wines grown in the northern Adriatic area. However, the bottled Robola wines are lighter in alcohol, at 11.5–12°, and without as much textural glide. Excellent country wine of Omalai, beaming medium-yellow, usually reaches 13–13.5° alcohol and is remarkably firm, in its way comparing altogether favourably with white Burgundy of no mean stature. The bottled wines, which are produced without spending any time in barrel and bottled within about six months of the vintage, have tended to reach the market with a slight spritziness considered anathema by peasant producers of Omalai, although some producers of 'plains Robola' offer wines like that nowadays. However, the spritz is marginal and usually dissipates after a year or so in bottle, or else after some aeration before serving. When calmed down, the bottled wines of some vintages can, in my view, stand qualitative comparison with the country wines, stylistic differences notwithstanding. But some Cephalonians would never agree with me, and think the bottlers have got it all wrong. I have had some sympathy for their sensibilities on the occasions when I have drunk the Komitopoulos wine, which in my experience has never come up even to respectable 'plains Robola'.

Were I to suppose that food in some measure encouraged the Cephalonians to grow Robola wine, fish would have to be mentioned first, since the wine consumption tax imposed on the Ionians by the

Venetians was at one time administered on Cephalonia through the government fishing monopoly, which took the opportunity to tie wine retail licences to the serving of fish. Consequently, the 'fish-tavern' (*psarotavérna*) was a long-time fixture of Cephalonian social life, especially at Argostoli near Robola country. Grilled tuna, swordfish or salmon sprinkled with lemon juice are especially good with Robola, and capers are a good flavouring to work into more elaborate fish dishes. Raw oysters seem just as acceptable with Robola as with Chablis: only the sensations differ. Visitors to Cephalonia may want to search for the island's famous sea urchins (*ekhíni*), which are enjoyed raw with a squirt of lemon: it may have been these that secured Robola's place in the islanders' affections.

Or it could be deduced from reading Napier that a vegetarian diet must have been instrumental in making a place for Robola: 'The Greek peasant [of Cephalonia] trusts to nature for vegetables, and makes a dish of weeds . . . the chief ingredient being dandylions; the poorest live upon this, and eat with it, as much bread, and oil, as they can afford.' I have thought Robola just the thing for green salads dressed with olive oil and lemon, or even vinaigrette, with radishes and olives of one's choice. Among cooked vegetables, collard greens and turnips, fried green tomatoes, and okra merit special recommendation, and the more so if cornbread is also on the table. I should not be surprised if ham hocks are accommodated as well, and Robola also goes well with sauerkraut.

The two other wines entitled to the Cephalonia appellation, Muscat and Mavrodaphne, are presently in a sorry state. Muscat, once the Cephalonian standard-bearer in the wine trade, and likened by Napier to that of Constantia, has never recovered from the setbacks to wine-growing in this century, especially the 1953 earthquake. Only about 5 hectares are planted with the *moskháto áspro* variety in the specified appellation zone, which comprises the areas of Lixouri, Soulara, Katoyi, Skinea, Khavdata and Zola, all on or by the island's western sac, as well as Poros, far off by the south-eastern coast beyond Mount Ainos. No sweet Muscat is being bottled. Cephalonia's Mavrodaphne wine, which Napier thought the equal of Madeira, is in nearly as unfortunate a situation. The dark *mavrodáfni* variety from which it is made is likewise grown on only about 5 hectares in its appellation zone, in which are included twenty-two villages, mostly in the far south-eastern corner of Cephalonia. Additionally, the village of Perakhorio in the south of neighbouring

Ithaca is included in the Mavrodaphne of Cephalonia zone; but Ithaca is generally best known for dry red wine made from the dark variant of the *robóla*. Unlike muscat, however, Mavrodaphne has made it into bottles recently. A very minor quantity of it was released, with the appellation, by the Calligas firm, which used only grapes grown in its own vineyards to make it. Calligas hopes to better the situation for both muscat and Mavrodaphne of Cephalonia in the future.

As the figures concerning vineyard land indicate, only around one-quarter of the area for wine grapes on Cephalonia is eligible to produce appellation wine. The rest is mostly planted with other varieties that have long been cultivated in certain areas, but whose wines never earned the reputation of those produced from *robóla, moskháto aspro*, and *mavrodáfni*. Notable among white sorts is the *goustoulídi*, which is colloquially called *vostilídi* on Cephalonia. Although it is the variety of that name found on Zakynthos, the *goustoulídi* of Cephalonia, like most of the island's vines which are also found on Zakynthos, differs from the Zakynthiote one, and is not regarded nearly so favourably as that grown on Zakynthos. On Cephalonia it is mostly grown in the vicinity of Sami. Komitopoulos was marketing a good wine of that type – I thought it markedly better than their Robola – on the Manzavino Gustolidi label. Other white varieties that are found are *kozanítes (kozanítis), zakynthinó, thiakó*, and *perakhorítiko*, which are occasionally mixed with a little *mavrodáfni* planted here and there, to produce rosé wines. The old *tsaoúsi* variety still flourishes too, and an important attempt to upgrade its wine is being made by Nikolaos Cosmetatos, who since 1984 has been applying contemporary vinification methods to *tsaoúsi* grapes purchased from growers around Minies, on the low hills south of Argostoli. About 250 hectolitres are produced from each vintage, and appear under the Gentilini and Fumé labels, the latter being the same wine as the former, but matured lightly in new French oak. Cosmetatos plans to move further afield in the future with varietal *sauvignon blanc* and *chardonnay* wines from the vines he has planted recently on his own 2-hectare vineyard.

Dry red wines are particularly associated with the western sac of Cephalonia. The *papadikó* and *araklinós* are two red-wine types commonly found there. However, a more important variety, and one of some commercial significance just now, is the *thiniátiko*. The Calligas firm uses it to produce a light dry red called Calliga Ruby, a vintage-dated wine worth cellaring for several years. Another of their wines based on *thiniátiko* is Calliga Rosé Demi-Sec, in which *tsaoúsi* and *moskháto áspro* also play a part; Calliga Rosé Sec, however, is not a Cephalonian wine, but rather a *filéri* wine of unspecified geographic origin. The *thiniátiko* is an old native sort similar to *mavrodáfni*, but unique to Cephalonia. Its name is bound up with island tradition, and originally signified 'Cephalonian'. According to an ancient myth, when Kefalos, son of the god Hermes and the mortal Herses, was driven from Athens, he went to settle on Cephalonia, calling it *'Athinaía yí'*, or 'Athenian earth', because it was an Athenian colony at that time. The expression eventually became *'Thinaía yí'*, and finally *'Thiniá'*. Of course Kefalos had the presence of mind to take a vine with him when he was expelled, and he duly planted it upon landing on Cephalonia. But it might be advisable to reserve judgement on whether or not the *thiniátiko* is that vine, since in more recent times the geographic term 'Thinia' has been used by the islanders to refer to the north-western part of the island, from around Zola south to Argostoli Bay, where the *thiniátiko* is mostly grown.

LEFKAS

During the tourist season, a ferry runs between Cephalonia and the next island north, Lefkas, whose main products since antiquity have been olive oil and wine, which were traded for staples, especially grain, needed from across the way on the mainland around Vonitsa and Preveza. Venice became a major market for Lefkadite wine when the island, thereafter widely known as Santa Maura, came under its suzerainty. The Venetians apparently attempted to spread the currant on to Lefkas too, but its finicky vine generally did not succeed there, or certainly not to a degree sufficiently remunerative for currant cultivation to become competitive with the island's wine trade. None the less the Venetians had a significant influence on viticultural developments on Lefkas, for it was through them that the island received the wine grape variety that would eventually displace most others, the *vertzamí*, whose varietal name is a corruption of *martzaví*, the more usual Ionian corruption of the Italian name *marzemino*.

The *vertzamí* came to the Ionians from the Trentino area to the west of Venice. High yields of grapes for good, exportable red wine gave it an advantage on Lefkas from the time of its introduction, but it was only in the latter part of the nineteenth century that the variety received its great boost. After phylloxera destroyed the French vineyards, French traders discovered Lefkas as a source of blending-wine made from the highly coloured *vertzamí*. Vineyard plantings expanded by leaps and bounds, even on to land previously occupied by crops. The inhabitants of certain villages in the semi-mountainous zone – Englouvi, Karia, Exanthia, Sfakiotes, Kalamitsi – became entirely engaged in wine-growing. In 1892, Lefkas was producing over three-and-a-half times the amount of wine it did in 1800, and that wine was overwhelmingly *vertzamí*, which had secured a 90 per cent share of the island vineyard area. After France recovered, demand for the island's wine shrank. Many vineyards were abandoned, forcing many Lefkadites to emigrate abroad. Nevertheless, only Corfu among the Ionian islands has more area under wine grapes today than Lefkas's 1,700 hectares, and the *vertzamí* has remained Lefkas's dominant variety, its wine being valued particularly by Greek firms blending it with white wine to produce generic *kokkinéli* wines.

Lefkas will not gain an appellation of origin entitlement for *vertzamí* wine, since the variety is generally regarded as a plebeian sort. Although exceptional 'black *marzemino*' wines are reported from north-eastern Italy, the occurrence has apparently been too rare to gain the sort of acclaim for the variety that would qualify it for the varietal peerage. Also, on Lefkas, during the period when the *vertzamí* spread all over, it reached areas where it is out of place. In the zone from 200 – 500 metres above sea level, the *vertzamí* produces 13–14° wine of high dry extract content, and among the highest recorded levels of red-colour-yielding anthocyanin content. Sound vinification of grapes from carefully tended and harvested vines in that zone can give remarkably good wines. In the zone above 500 metres, on the other hand, the *vertzamí*, which ripens in late September, cannot ripen properly because of early cold winds blowing in from off the Pindos Mountains on the mainland. At the 800-metre level, it yields wine of uncharacteristically rose colour, low dry extract content, and only 8–9° alcohol. Consequently, the upper zone of vineyards on Lefkas is to be replanted with early-maturing Greek white varieties.

The emphasis on the blending-wine trade, and perhaps the general poverty of the island as well, has made Lefkas an exception among the Ionians, in that its wine-growers long ago chose to be confined within the bounds of a cooperative organization, the Union of Agricultural Cooperatives of Lefkas, also known popularly by its old acronym, TAOL. Although necessarily sustained by sales of bulk wine, the Union bottles a dry and a semi-dry *vertzamí* wine, both under the Madonna label. One must admire the Union's pride in skirting the matter of an appellation of origin, which it will not have, by prominently featuring the 'Santa Maura' name as well. The Madonna wines have been mentioned as wholesome, a word hardly to be objected to if one has Plutarch in mind:

> In regard to food and drink it is expedient to note what kinds are wholesome rather than what are pleasant, and to be better acquainted with those that are good in the stomach rather than in the mouth, and those that do not disturb the digestion rather than those that greatly tickle the palate.
>
> (*Moralia*, 'Advice on Keeping Well')

CORFU (KERKYRA)

Hardly any Greek island today displays as much village-to-village variation in wine types as Corfu. I have grown to suspect that there was more to it than irony when Lawrence Durrell, in *Prospero's Cell*, told of his friend Ivan Zarian 'making an exhaustive study of the island wines' while both were sojourning there in 1937. Corfu's diversity in wines may be attributable primarily to its having two very distinct regions, discernible as soon as the island comes into view from the deck of the ferry from Igoumenitsa on the coast of Epirus opposite. The long, narrow, low and rolling southern stretch reaches over 100 metres above the sea in only a few areas, while the short, wide, mostly raised northern part averages about 300–400 metres, but peaking at more than 900. Furthermore, soil tends to be deep and relatively coarse-grained in the south, while shallow and fine-grained in the north. However, Corfu's many-layered history of settlement would also seem to have had an impact on the kinds of grapes grown at one place or another, with new types entering the island's varietal pool from time to time through the conduits of non-Corfiote settlers and trade contacts.

In speaking of Corfu's varietal diversity, a superficial incongruity surfaces right away. White varieties are in the overwhelming majority in the south, while red and black sorts are characteristic of the north. Moreover, the island's 1,800 hectares of vineyards taken as a whole are dominated by the white *kakotríyis* and the red *petrokóritho*. The *kakotríyis*, whose name 'hard-to-harvest' refers to the difficulty of detaching the pedicle, is the leading variety on the island, in the south covering about 90 per cent of the vineyard area. But the plot thickens. There are red and black variants of the *kakotríyis*, and also a white *petrokóritho*, which, although basically a table grape, is occasionally vinified as part of a varietally mixed white wine. The *robóla* is also present, the white variety being found at various places on the island, while the black recurs in the north. Both the black *skopelítiko* and white *kozanítis* also turn up in the north. In the south, the white *fidiá* is encountered sporadically, and there is no dearth of others. In fact most Ionian grape varieties are represented, save the currant , which never gained a place, partly because of environmental unsuitability, and partly because of Venetian intentions to secure the currant trade to Zakynthos and Cephalonia.

The non-typical varieties of Corfu tend to have a more or less crucial influence where they are grown. For example, at Spartilas, on the south-eastern part of the upland, the *mavrodáfni*, a real rarity on Corfu, is grown along with *petrokóritho*, the two being used in a ratio of about 1:9 to produce a sometimes very tasty semi-dry red that finishes dry, and even like a *broúsko*, in spite of the initial sweet streak. The outcropper varieties are also used to make fully varietal wines in some places. Just north of Spartilas, at Strinilas, where the vineyards rise to about 700 metres, sweet muscat wine is grown, and has been in all likelihood since antiquity; early French ampelographers recorded the name *muscat de Corfou* for the *moskháto áspro* that later French ampelographers would prefer to call *muscat de Frontignan*. At Lakones, on the south-western part of the upland above the resort area of Paleokastritsa, the 'volcano's blood' described by Durrell ('a wine that bubbles ever so slightly; an undertone of sulphur and rock') is a very dry red wine made from the *martzaví*, the *vertzamí* of Lefkas, brought to Corfu in Venetian times. Even in the far south around Lefkimi, where the vineyards are virtually a sea of white *kakotríyis*, crimson wines of the black *kakotríyis* can be found. So it goes on Corfu.

There is every reason to think that Corfiotes appreciate their variety in wines. Durrell found they had 'so delicate a palate as to be

connoisseurs of cold water', while about the same time the French
visitor Jacques Boulenger observed that 'the peasants, who are
connoisseurs, distinguish those [waters] of various fountains as we
do the wines of our vineyards, or little less'. For what it is worth then
– perhaps it will at least counteract any damaging impression left by
a foreign commentator's ignorance – I must mention here a ranking
of Corfu's wine areas given by a native, Ioannis Bounias, in his
comprehensive island primer of 1954. Bounias, a lawyer and codifier,
put Petalia and Strinilas at the top, followed by Spartilas and
Sgourades, and then Payi, Prinilas and Kratsalo, all of which are on
the northern upland. All other areas of the island, including the
remaining northern ones, comprise the bottom rung, although Bounias states that 'excellent' (áristo) wines are produced at those places
as well. Does his ranking reflect local lore, judicious personal
consideration, or arbitrary subjective bias? Had Bounias not overcome a hang-up about southern wine the way Durrell's northern
friend Father Nicolas had 'finally conquered his prejudice against
southern women'? Perhaps it is unfortunate that Ivan Zarian never
issued the findings of his 'exhaustive study', against which to check
Bounias. But on the other hand there will never be a substitute for
making our own survey of the island wines.

Corfu's variety in wines is usually missed by the short-term visitor.
The random wine sampling to which we are prone while on holiday
can easily yield an impression of vinous monotony, in the form of
semi-dry wines that can be otherwise characterized as 'sweet-sour'.
Samples of them are ubiquitous. White, rosé and red ones are offered
in stoppered bottles at villagers' makeshift roadside stands, where
the tourist is sometimes persuaded to buy some almonds as well.
Even commercial firms have marketed wines of that kind. It might
be presumed that a sweet-sour notion of flavour harmony has as
much validity in wine as in food, yet it is apparently not a first-choice
native inclination on Corfu, and seems to succeed there rarely. Its
origin on the island is due to the attempt of household wine producers
to retain enough residual sugar to counteract coarseness in wines
produced by a fermentation on the skins in unsulphured barrels,
under conditions of relatively high temperature, using a must derived
from the several pressings of the grape material.

The Agricultural Committee of Corfu published an article in
1911 chiding the many producers who resorted to the retention of
sweetness, and advising other means 'to rid our wines of excessive

acridity'. The wine-making practices of peasant producers have improved since that time, particularly in the production of dry, so-called *broúsko* whites, which were singled out for criticism in the article, which still has some contemporary relevance. They are now usually harmonious even though, contrary to the advice of 1911, they are still fermented on the skins; and the skin of the white *kakotríyis* in particular is relatively high in tannin for a white variety. *Broúsko* whites made only of free-run juice can be excellent, leaving no doubt as to Corfu's potential in dry white wine. Their wines of that type have already convinced some peasant producers to move further in that direction, so that the sweet-sour type of wine is receding, and is popular in only a few places, like Spartilas, where environmental factors and varietal complement favour a worthwhile product. Elsewhere, types of wine antedating the sweet-sour wines are making a come-back. While still making the latter for sale at their stands, village producers generally do not much drink them, preferring their dry wines instead. But they see the sweet-sour wines, so often reviled in retrospect by Greek and non-Greek visitors alike, as being to the taste of the passing tourist. Well, the tourists do in fact buy them. Maybe it is the almonds.

The legacy of the sweet-sour wines is not the only matter plaguing Corfu's image. In particular, the shortcomings of the local wine-bottling industry have been legion. Conspicuously absent is a co-operative winery that might set the pace. The cooperative movement on the island has stayed out of wine-growing, concentrating on olive oil instead. An all-island cooperative winery would probably be able to harness the southern stretch of Corfu within a few years, even gaining an appellation of origin entitlement for white *kakotríyis* wine. It would probably be some more years, however, before wine-making activities could be diversified sufficiently to be able to handle the diversity in traditional local wines in a way, perhaps with an eye to Bounias's ranking, that would do the island justice. Yet if a plethora of small producer-bottlers is theoretically the ideal arrangement for Corfu, that framework has not proved very effective in practice. Thus far in the island's short history of commercial wine-bottling, little effort has been made to do more than slake the considerable thirst of the tourists, a task apparently accomplished quite handily by just about anything served cool enough, including the sweet-sour wines.

The small size of Corfu's individual commercial wineries is not in itself a drawback, but their under-capitalization is a formidable obstacle to be overcome. Investing minimally in plant, most wine producers who have bottled have apparently had no particular reason to stay on the market, and in fact they have tended to enter and leave it with quixotic rapidity, so much so that next year's visitor to Corfu may not find the wines mentioned in last year's guidebook to the island. The frame of mind bent on milking the market for what it is worth, either on a one-shot basis or by sporadic incursions, has bred a lack of concern for just what goes into bottle. Exceptions have of course turned up, such as Paloumbi, a 13.5° black *kakotríyis* wine produced by Alexandros Vasilakis of Synarades in west-central Corfu, which I mention in case it appears again. Typically, however, Corfiote bottlers blend various wines or musts from different parts of the island, or even add wine or must from elsewhere in Greece, in spite of Corfu's abundance of wine. Amidst these circumstances, an appellation of origin is out of the question, and unstable market participation in any case prejudices the prospect by impeding the establishment of specific commercial wine types, which the Greek Wine Institute requires as part of the appellation qualifying process.

Convenient as it is to blame Corfiote character for the prevailing attitude, it is still easier to overlook the pervasive role of tourism and its attendant effects on commercial behaviour. The general Corfiote attitude is probably no different from that which small-scale producers of modest means anywhere else would adopt if gaining the means to bottle mostly on account of tourism. So many Greek and non-Greek tourists become willing captive customers on Corfu each year that the typical island bottler finds his small allocation of wine disappearing quickly, no matter what its quality. Having no need to sell elsewhere in Greece, and with no thought to sales abroad, he has no great interest in anyone's opinion of the wine he puts up for sale, which might well not be what he drinks himself, much less in investment in plant to produce anything better for preoccupied sun-worshippers and honeymooners. Furthermore, with sales confined to the island, the Corfiote bottlers will probably be the last in Greece to clamour for appellations of origin, that boon to the exporter which usually provides a firm basis for quality in bottled wine.

In view of the continuing temptations fostered by tourism, it is remarkable and heartening that a few Corfiote wine producers, mostly at first no exception to the pattern outlined, are breaking out of the typical mould. Their acquisition of a modicum of marketing skills is persuading them that the apparent permanence of tourism is good cause to increase investment in their wineries, and with that to upgrade wine quality. For example, the little firm of Karpo, centred in Corfu Town, has been bottling dry white and red wines using grapes respectively from Lefkimi in the south and Sokraki in the north, with about two-fifths non-Kerkyran wine added in both cases. After a recent expansion of facilities, however, Karpo is considering using those wines as a financial net over which to produce all-Corfiote wines that would tie up some capital during their maturation. Down in Ano Lefkimi, the Koulouris family came on the market with the full intention of being a stable participant, and are producing about 500 hectolitres annually of dry white (white *kakotríyis*) and red (black *kakotríyis*) wines from the flat and low land around Lefkimi, including the family's own 3 hectares of vineyards there. The wines, which are light 11.5° ones under the Santa Domenica label, do not yet represent the very best of which Lefkimi is capable, but they faithfully and favourably portray the intensely floral aroma which the late-ripening *kakotríyis* achieves in a warm corner of Corfu peculiar for its very deep soil; the *kakotríyis* does not ripen earlier than mid-September. What is more, says one of the Koulouris brothers resolutely, 'Our plans for the future are the updating of our plant with the latest means of production, and an ongoing effort to offer consumers the best we can from the *kakotríyis* variety.'

The most notable example of what a wine lover might hope for in the way of a gathering new wave in the northern Ionian is the winery of Theodoros Vasilakis, at Ayios Ioannis on the low central plain called Roppa. After several years of turning out wines made in part from Cephalonian wine, and bottling wines bought from the Patraïki cooperative of Patras, Vasilakis decided in the mid-1970s to test Corfiote waters for limited-production, quality red and white wines entirely of local origin. The first were made in 1976. Then and in every year since, 60–70 hectolitres of white and 30–40 hectolitres of red have been produced, respectively from white and black *kakotríyis* grapes, mostly purchased from other wine-growers in the vicinity, but including the fruit of Vasilakis's own 1.5 hectares of vineyards as well. Both wines are of 12° alcohol and matured for five to six years in barrel. They are bottled under the Grovino label, but without vintage indication. After a week or so of the sweet-sour wines, the lightish, garnet-red Grovino may seem a wine of real excellence. However it impresses then, it really does approach that sort of quality after three to six years in bottle, and makes Edward Dodwell's comment of 1819 quite plausible: 'The wines of Corfu are much esteemed; particularly those which are made with care.'

The long-standing exception among Corfiote bottlers is Count Theotokis, the latest in the line of Corfu's most illustrious family. The first bottler of wine on the island, having begun forty or more years ago, the Count has never faltered. The Theotokis family's vineyard estate is situated on a slight eastward incline along Roppa, a few miles to the north of the Vasilakis winery. The estate consists of 8.5 hectares (soon to be 10), planted with white and black *kakotríyis*, white *robóla* and red *petrokóritho*, with some *sauvignon blanc* planned for the future. About 30 hectolitres of white wine and 20 hectolitres of rosé, both at 12° alcohol, are produced annually, and released with vintage date under the Theotoki Roppa label, a proprietary name which, because of its geographic indication, explains the Count's utter indifference to appellations of origin. Almost 20 hectolitres from each vintage are given away as gifts, which helps to sustain the aura of exclusivity that has long attached to the Theotoki Roppa name. Most of the rest is sold to a few prestigious establishments, like the Grande Bretagne Hotel in Athens, and to a handful of retailers, like the Kava Zakharopoulos shops of Athens.

The Theotoki Roppa wines are world-class, and certainly bear out Bounias's confidence in lowland Corfu. The rosé, up with the best of its kind anywhere, has a pleasing, rather tart flavour peculiar to it, and should be drunk young; but beware the powdery pink sediment that seems so very typical of wines produced from black *kakotríyis*. The white, however, may come as an even greater surprise, at least to those who do not expect refreshment from Greek whites. Its colour varies from light straw to pale gold, depending on the vintage and time in barrel. Usually some carbonic gas is readily perceptible, although bottling takes place two to three years after the vintage in the case of the white. Sprightly yet firm, crisp but of fullish medium body, Theotoki Roppa white of a good vintage can sustain its character for half a dozen or so years after bottling if given good cellaring conditions. The long finish of this very dry wine has something reminiscent of quinine water, which is perhaps in part the work of an aromatic facet. I have qualms about specifying any aromatic tendencies, however, because in a couple of vintages I have been reminded too much of both the ginger root used to produce ginger beer (that popular bequest to the Corfiotes by the British), and the paprika the islanders love to cook with. They seem all too obvious associations, and not quite accurate, no matter how conscientious the reporting.

Matching Corfiote wines to foods could turn into a more exhaustive study than a foray through the wines alone. Having already found an island combination that seems to me about the equal of any, little Santa Domenica white from the south and a mixed salad dressed only with the aromatically unsurpassed olive oil of upland Corfu, I have no particular desire to take up that Herculean gastronomic task. To ease the workload of the unrelenting gourmet, I might suggest herbed goat cheese and the more bitter kinds of olive as savouries for the Theotoki Roppa wines, and *avgolémono*-style meat-and-vegetable dishes as main courses, especially when the vegetable is artichoke; never heeding the wine commentators who, unfamiliar with the Theotokis wines, rail against artichoke. Other good main courses are lamb baked with herbs in paper for the rosé, and lamb baked with olives and *féta* cheese for the white, although a switch of partners would probably not be regretted. I find that the white wine has a special rapport with spiced shrimp, perhaps especially when there is a touch of ginger in the spicing. Grovino red is complemented by cheeses like *kefalograviéra* and Caerphilly. Meat dishes to keep in mind are *saltimbocca alla romana*, steak-and-kidney pie, and braised sweetbreads. Yet it is hardly a second-best to choose plain grilled lamb chops, especially with an older bottle. Asparagus with *beurre noisette*, broccoli with cheese sauce, and Brussels sprouts with fried breadcrumbs are vegetable side dishes to consider.

GASTRONOMIC NOTES

A cautionary remark or two are in order on the subject of Ionian cuisine. As with so many aspects of the regional culture, Venetian influence will be apparent at many turns, especially on Zakynthos and Corfu, and most of all at their eponymous chief towns. For example, one can scarcely avoid thoughts of the Venetians if presented with Zakynthos's old version of *kolokithópita* (marrow pie), which is filled with 'Venetian pumpkin', better known to us as courgettes, and pine nuts. However, it must be borne in mind that in reckoning the real Venetian gustatory impact in the islands, it would be necessary first to subtract those elements of the pre-existing, pan-Adriatic-Ionian kitchen upon which Venice elaborated. And sometimes, for that matter, the Venetians influenced names more than substance, as in the case of Zakynthiote *porpétes*, which are only the fried meatballs otherwise known universally in Greece as *keftédes*, using Near Eastern terminology of course, but called after Italian *polpetti* on Zakynthos, much as the Zakynthiotes call the vintage *vedéma*, after a Venetian dialectical word, rather than by the Greek *triyitó*.

The foundation for excellent cooking in the Ionians is superlative olive oil, which can be found on all of the islands. The best of Paxi, upland Corfu and Zakynthos are championed, especially the first. However, the oils of Lefkas and Cephalonia are also much appreciated in Greece. Table olives, too, are exceptional throughout the Ionians, although some would award the palm to Cephalonia, or else to Zakynthos. Were one to build around the olives and prepare a platter of Ionian *mezédes* (appetizers), cheese to be sought would be the ewe's-milk *féta* of Cephalonia, the goat's-milk cheeses of Ithaca, some of which are fresh, and the cured-in-oil, ewe's-milk *ladotýri* ('oil-cheese') of Lefkas. The latter island is also known for a particularly porky-tasting dry sausage, *Lefkadítiko loukániko* ('Lefkadite sausage'), whose pinkish colour and little chunks of fat sprinkled through make it readily recognizable in delicatessen display cases as something of a pygmy *mortadella*; the sausage is exported from Lefkas, and can be found in Athens. Some excellent hams and fresh *loukániko* are produced on Corfu from the local breeds of hogs, and a whole new perspective on Corfu's lamented sweet-sour wines can be gained by trying them with those specialities.

Corfu's cooks were praised by the resident George Fitzmaurice in 1864, and their descendants seemingly turn up in a few of the commercial kitchens of the island today. Corfu has its own way of cooking, too, and some dishes it calls its own, though the names by which they are called sound as Italian as some scenes in Corfu Town look. The premier island dish is *pastitsáda*, which has only a loose relationship to its Venetian namesake. Small pieces of 'baby beef' (*moskhári*) are simmered with wine, oil, and seasonings, under cover in the oven. That mixture is later poured over macaroni mixed with butter and grated *kefalotýri* cheese. For Corfiotes, *pastitsáda* is a speciality for festive occasions, but these days it is standard restaurant fare, and not at its best in every establishment. Even more difficult to find done expertly in tourist-oriented kitchens is the garlicky beef steak dish known as *sofríto*, which is largely a speciality of Corfu Town, although nowadays it is offered at restaurants round about the island. For *pastitsáda*, the Theotoki Roppa wines, if available, make good choices for accompaniment, while the rather fullish and sturdy Grovino white is fine for *sofríto*, even if most diners might be more comfortable with the red in the company of beef and garlic.

Corfu also has a seafood dish that betrays its long association with the Adriatic, *bourdéto*. A pan-Adriatic menu feature, *bourdéto* on Corfu is always a stove-top dish using only one kind of fish – but never shellfish – that starts out with onions simmering in oil and a thin tomato sauce. If made with dried cod, potatoes are added. Indispensable to Corfiote *bourdéto* is a touch of hot paprika, a spice the Corfiotes probably became acquainted with more than two centuries ago, when the Dalmatian city of Dubrovnik was in close commercial contact with both the Ionians and the deep interior of the Balkans where paprika became popular early. *Bourdéto* is the most typical dish of Corfu, in that it is a workaday dish throughout the island. Excellent dry white wine should not necessarily be eschewed as accompaniment for *bourdéto* on account of the slightly caustic flavour. My advice would be to seek a generous one in barrel from Lefkimi.

To finish off Ionian meals, there is *mandoláto*, the characteristic Zakynthiote almond nougat, which many an islander would agree with the native author Romas in calling 'the most Zakynthiote' product, even if it is a Venetian hold-over. If one visits Corfu in autumn, there is a good chance of finding *sykópita* (fig-pie), which is made with fresh figs. A post-prandial drink that some might enjoy in any season is a kumquat liqueur offered by the Vasilakis winery. The kumquat, which is planted only on Corfu in Greece, was introduced, not by the Venetians, but by an avid British gardener resident there in the nineteenth century.

II

EPIRUS

Zitza is a [head village] *of 110 houses; its heights seem admirably adapted by soil and aspect to the vine; and accordingly, the chief production is wine, which has the reputation of being the best in Epirus . . .*
(William Leake, British traveller, *Travels in Northern Greece*, 1835)

Westward beyond Macedonia and the northern part of the Pindos mountains lies the mostly rugged north-western corner of mainland Greece – Epirus. Because of its position on the far side of Pindos, the region is treated as part of western Greece in Greek geography, although neither from an environmental nor a historical-cultural perspective does it have much in common with the Ionians. Epirus abuts Albania, and in fact was also known as 'southern Albania' to Western Europeans of the nineteenth century, because of the historical figure Ali Pasha, an Epirote Albanian who governed Epirus and much of Albania virtually independently of his Ottoman overlords from 1788 to 1822.

The origins of wine-growing in Epirus are obscure. Nothing specific is known about it from the ancient record. Nevertheless, if we consider the areas around the town of Konitsa, near the Albanian border, where vines are still sometimes trained up trees, it is difficult not to think of wine-growing as an activity of some considerable tradition ('The twining growth of the fruit crowned the opposite pine, shading its own sheltered growth by its mass of twigs, and delighted the heart of Pan; the pine swayed by Boreas brought her branches near the bunches of grapes and shook her fragrant leafage soaked in the blood,' Nonnos, *Dionysiaca*). Indeed, it could be said that the rewards of combing Epirus go mostly to the student of wine acting as cultural anthropologist, in which capacity we could head up to the declining villages of Grava, Lia, Drimades and Stavroskiadi,

236

all near the Albanian border, whose inhabitants formerly were known far and wide in Greece as itinerant coopers skilled in fashioning wine barrels.

Epirus today is not ideal wine lover's country. The region has been perhaps the one hardest hit in all Greece by emigration in recent decades, with whole sections of the countryside now left virtually deserted. Regional wine production is small – smaller even than on some of the individual Greek islands – and for the most part widely scattered, on a tiny scale at many places. However, this is far from saying that Epirus has no wines worth looking in on. It has its very own wine traditions, too, since its contacts with both Corfu to the west and Macedonia to the east were limited in modern times, in the former case by poorly developed sea communications, political separation and apparently just plain mutual indifference, and in the latter by the formidable barrier of Pindos, which has only recently been breached by the construction of a major roadway directly linking Epirus to Macedonia. Except for some Ionian grape varieties grown along its coast, in wine terms the region has held largely to its own separate course.

ZITSA

Although right in the middle of what was considered by many Westerners a wild European province of the Ottoman Empire – an image created by accounts of fierce Greek and Albanian clans, and the activities of Ali Pasha – the town of Ioannina was a notable centre of commerce, culture and scholasticism, even under Ali. Its population of Greek Orthodox Christians, Greek Jews and Albanian Moslems was large and prosperous, and their requirements in wine were commensurate, bearing in mind that even the Albanian Moslems, who apparently were sceptical converts to Islam, shamelessly indulged in drinking it. Vines were cultivated on hilly tracts within the town limits, especially St George's Hill, and in nearby villages to the west, particularly around Grammeno. However, after the founding of Zitsa, a village just 15 miles north-west, the inhabitants of Ioannina began looking primarily to that area as a source for wine of special quality. This was also where the Jews of the town went to make their kosher wine, as has been done in recent years by the small Jewish community of Athens.

Zitsa was established around the turn of the fifteenth century by people who hoped to minimize Ottoman interference in their daily life. The village stands out of the way, a few hundred metres up the side of a large protuberance rising out of already raised land, so that altogether elevation is about 600 metres above sea level. The early villagers planted vines on the rocky, calcareous, sloping terrain round about, down to approximately 500 metres. Several grape varieties were planted, of which the predominant one was the white *debína*, whose origin is probably very old, although this remains unclarified because of confusion over its name. Some think that *debína* might be a corruption of Italian *del vino* and suppose that the variety must have arrived from the Italian peninsula long ago. Others see in that resemblance of sounds a geographic connection: further north in Epirus there is a village called Delvinaki. But for that matter, across the border in Albania, in the area the Greeks call 'northern Epirus', there is a Delvinë, or Delvino in Greek; certainly the *debína*, under the names *debin* and *debinë* is widely cultivated in southernmost Albania, and could even be regarded as more characteristic of vineyards there than in Epirus generally. A geographic explanation has otherwise been supposed by those who think that *debína* may derive from the more distant village of Dembeni, to the north-east, on the western rim of Greek Macedonia on the way from Kastoria to the Albanian town of Korçë. To complicate matters further, the variety is also called *dibína* in the Greek marches, where local lore explains that name as a corruption of Latin *divina*, or 'divine', the intimation being that the variety's qualities were recognized as long ago as Roman times. In favour of the folkloric explanation, it can be noted that the Epirotes have preserved some archaic Roman terms. Yet, if the variety is in fact of great antiquity, its name perhaps derives from some untraceable Illyrian term.

Whatever the origin of the name *debína*, it is in the vicinity of Ioannina, especially at Grammeno, whose vineyards are at present recovering from a devastating blight of a few years ago, that the variety makes its most significant southernmost appearance, while its best performance of all, in either Greece or Albania, is traditionally said to be at Zitsa. It is known from Western travelogues that several kinds of wine were made at Zitsa in the past, including a resinated white wine and one flavoured with wormwood, both of which have since been lost to local tradition, and even to the memory of Zitsa's oldest living generation. However, the wine that became dominant in local tradition, eventually largely displacing other kinds, was instead a semi-dry and more or less spritzy rosé, for which red wine varieties were used along with *debína*, and perhaps some other white varieties.

Zitsa acquired its effervescence fortuitously, when the early villagers found that their grapes could not ripen fully under local climatic conditions. Toward the end of the growing season, they would gather together the shoots of a vine and tie them upward, thereby exposing the berries directly to the sun to enhance ripening, and promote some super-maturation. The level of sugar in the resultant must was so high that it could not be entirely fermented out in the short time between the vintage, in late September to early October, and the early onset of weather cold enough, owing to air blowing off Pindos, to halt the progress of the yeasts in the must. With the coming of spring, the wine would begin to ferment again, yielding abundant carbonic gas, which the villagers learned to capture in the barrels, so that the gas would hold up until the wine was drunk off by the time of the succeeding vintage. Because it was rare for all of the sugar to be fermented out even by that time, the wine was typically semi-dry. Also, it was rosé in colour, or 'blonde-red' (*xanthokókkino*), as the Zitsiotes call it, since the *debína* was usually vinified together with the blackish *vlákhiko* and *bekári* varieties, on skins and stalks. Although it can be supposed that few villagers had reason to take the trouble of separating white from black grapes, it is also noteworthy that the Zitsiotes love the colour of their typical wine, and are quite conscious of it. There has never been a reason for them to change their ways either, since Zitsa's rosé has long been popular at Ioannina.

Zitsa's traditional reputation gained it an appellation of origin immediately following the inauguration of the Greek appellative system in 1971, but not for the rosé wine dominant in its tradition. Only white wines, either dry, dry sparkling, or semi-dry sparkling, may qualify, and only the *debína* is authorized for them. One reason for shunting the rosé aside in spite of its tradition – usually a major consideration in the awarding of appellations in Greece – is the doubtful pedigree of the *vlákhiko* and *bekári*. Presumably a dark variant of the *debína* would pass the blood test – *divina* after all – but while one is found in various places in southern Albania and regarded as a quality wine variety by Albanian viticulturalists and enologists, Greek ampelographers have yet to uncover it either around Zitsa or elsewhere in Epirus, much as they believe it must be there. Also, however, by vinifying the preferred *debína* alone, the price paid for it will be bolstered up, thereby protecting its place in the Zitsiote vineyards, which have declined in extent in recent years owing to emigration. At present, only about 100 hectares of *debína* are planted in the appellation zone, which also includes the neighbouring villages of Karitsa, Klimatia, Protopappa, Gavrisii and Ligopsa. Altogether, about 400 hectares of vines are cultivated in the area generally.

Unresinated dry white wine could not be said to be without a tradition at Zitsa, and may actually have been the premier wine, even if very little of it was made outside the walls of the Monastery of the Prophet Elias, which was at one time the leading producer of Zitsiote wine. The Monastery, now standing deserted on the conical hill cap above Zitsa, was founded at the end of the fourteenth century, just a short while before the village. During Ali Pasha's time, it was presided over by a Dionysus-devoted prior (*igoúmenos*) whose acquaintance was made by several visitors from the West:

> a man of excellent qualities . . . much more addicted to the culture of his vineyard than to that of literature . . . His reputation as a jovial spirit was established for twenty miles round the monastery. . . . The exploit on which, however, the egoumenos principally plumed himself, was the victory he had achieved [in old-fashioned play testing wine drinking stamina] over Mouctar Pasha, Aly's eldest son, who, in the matter of wine, is just as correct a mussulman as his worthy father.
>
> (Pouqueville, 1820)

Little wonder that Ali, the ever-thirsty 'Lion of Ioannina', was wont to escape his dank capital for his villa at Zitsa, where, most uncharacteristically for him – this was a man who eventually turned on and slaughtered his own sons – he remained on good terms with the Bacchic priest. Ali seems always to have fêted his Western visitors at Zitsa, including Lord Byron. On 12 and 13 October 1809, Byron stayed at the Monastery, and his travelling companion Hobhouse recorded that the *igoúmenos* served them the wine of which he was most proud, a *white* one.

It may be instructive about the style of Zitsiote white wine, that the grapes for the abbot's special wine were crushed entirely by hand.

The notion of crushing by hand was probably a legacy of ancient times, and may have predated crushing by foot:

> The god untaught, without winepress and without treading, squeezed the grapes firmly with hand against wrist, interlacing his fingers until he pressed out the inebriating issue, and disclosed the newflowing load of purple fruitage, and discovered the sweet potation: Dionysos Tapster found his white fingers drenched in red!
>
> (Nonnos, *Dionysiaca*)

Hand-crushing apparently survived as a must-extraction technique intermediate between that for *prótropon*, the sweet wine produced from a must gained just by the pressure of grapes piled on one another, and foot-crushing. Like the *prótropon* technique, hand-crushing was no doubt reserved for small batches of wine of especially fine quality, since its use reduced the yield of must from the grapes and released only their fruitiest properties. Unlike *prótropon*, however, hand-crushing was probably applied to choice well-ripened grapes, rather than to over-ripened ones. Certainly Hobhouse did not note the abbot's wine as a sweet one.

Although hand-crushing is now preserved only in Hobhouse's travelogue, youthful sweetness and freshness remain essential to the true character of Zitsiote wine. These qualities can be obtained in dry white still wines of the region by early-morning harvesting, use exclusively of free-run must, and bottling after a few months without any time in wood. I think the marks of full success include a light but well-defined aroma, which is somewhat like the smell of a fruit salad composed mainly of apples and pears, with a dash of cinnamon or cloves added for good measure. But there must be more to it than that, for such Zitsa wines do not have just that scent of apple-pie filling this description might suggest. Their acidity also runs towards appley, although there seems to be an overlap with Rauenthaler Steinmacher in this respect. These Zitsa wines are not crisply acidic in the way we generally expect of white wines, yet they are as fresh-tasting as white wine can be without that, and most aptly conform to Western notions of 'fruitiness' going back at least to Plutarch: 'no other fruit unites the fine qualities of all fruits as does the apple' (*Moralia*, 'Table-talk'). Furthermore, they are almost never without some perceptible carbonic gas, even if they only infrequently send up a few beads through their nascently greenish, straw-yellow colour to suggest it.

Wines such as I describe used to be produced and bottled by the Union of Agricultural Cooperatives of Ioannina and the private firm of Monastiri Zitsa. The latter's Cuvée de Balthazar, an appellation of origin wine, was an especially satisfying wine which, if caught young, left no doubt as to how Zitsa might have earned a good reputation for white wine. However, at present, Monastiri Zitsa's winery is as deserted as the Monastery of the Prophet Elias which sits just a little above it. The firm's activities have been picked up by Cavino, whose winery is way off at Aegion, near Patras, which is hardly an address that inspires confidence in a Zitsiote wine. Cavino produces two white still wines with the Zitsa appellation, a lesser one under the Balthazar label and a better one under the Debina label. However, Cavino may be selling its interest in Zitsa, and it is to be hoped that their successor will take over the former facilities of Monastiri Zitsa and revive that firm's fine products. As for the Union, its winery is located virtually beside the village of Zitsa, but its dry white still wine, under the Zitsa label, has recently been palpably altered in style, and seems to me to stray close to forfeiting the charming Zitsa character in a vain attempt to make a divinely dry *debína* wine. I cannot believe it was what Ali's abbot was after when he had his vintage crew set their monkish hands to work in the grapes.

The Zitsa white still wines, even when only of acceptable quality, can be commendable companions for both appetizers and main courses. Mildly flavoured hams, like the Polish and Danish sorts, and bland cow's-milk cheeses, usually gain them favour. Among main courses, veal dishes, other than ones at all tomatoey or lemony, will come to mind, and turkey can substitute for veal in many instances. Other poultry dishes to consider are creamed chicken over biscuits and Greek *kotópita* in phyllo and flavoured with nutmeg. Generally a bit of nutmeg or thyme tends to strike a resounding aromatic chord with the best Zitsa whites, and I have found that holding true from *pastítsio* to kohlrabi with nutmeg-tinged cream sauce. Other cooked vegetables to have are baked carrots and parsnips, or cauliflower topped with breadcrumbs browned in butter. As for seafood, I do not usually think of Zitsa, but two exceptions would be *sole véronique* and Greek-style mussels pilaf prepared with currants, pine nuts, parsley, and white wine.

The naturally sparkling (*afródis*) white wines bearing the Zitsa appellation are new to Zitsa's repertoire, although, of course, they grow out of the region's old penchant for CO_2. The Union currently markets its representatives under the Zitsa label, while Cavino uses the Byron label. Non-appellation wines, for which red grapes are used in addition to *debína*, have also been produced. All of the sparklers, appellation and non-appellation alike, are produced by the *cuve close* method, and have the peculiar touch of acidity under their gassiness, for which reason they are perhaps not wines for caviare canapés.

The semi-dry efferevescent rosé wine which is central to Zitsiote tradition has hardly been forgotten in the region, and indeed remains the most popular sort of wine thereabouts. Usually, it is not at all a wine for keeping, as is well illustrated by the story told by a foreigner who resided at Ioannina in 1945 and, on the basis of a bottled sample from a vendor, bought a barrel of *pétillant* Zitsa rosé, just to see it go off by the time he thought it would be ripe for drinking. The Union offers a wine of this type under the Archontissa label, that does not spend time in wood and is being made with a very little bit of *cabernet sauvignon*, now that the Sinbad of grape varieties has made it even to wild Epirus. Archontissa has a pale pink colour, very light body, and a cider-like fizziness. I much preferred Monastiri Zitsa's Kyra Frosyne, which was a fully semi-sparkling wine, produced by fermenting red and white grapes on the skins in closed vat and bottled after spending one year in oak. Maybe the next occupant of their winery will be so daring as to reproduce it.

As may be suggested by the Zitsiote expression 'blonde-red', which is habitually used to describe the traditional rosé wine, Kyra Frosyne did not offer one of those run-of-the-mill, monochromatic, barely rosy colours of the sort which gives the rosé family a bad name in our eyes. Instead, an array of light pink to orange inclinations, not quite copper or onion-skin, greeted the eye. A bouquet of sweet herbs and fruit developed during maturation, and these held up well in bottle and mouth. The semi-dry nature was countered by tannic astringency, as well as by the acidic turbulence of the bubbles. Kyra Frosyne was not a wine to be maligned out of hand, as we are usually taught to do these days with any semi-dry foaming pink wine, and to drink it with foods which feature kindred prickly sensations yet leave a coating in the mouth, such as fried aubergine (eggplant) or courgette (zucchini) sticks dipped in *tzatzíki* (cucumber-yogurt-garlic sauce), to say nothing of chopped chicken livers on crusty poppy-seeded bagels, was to rise to the sublime.

The major producers of Zitsiote wine have drawn at least three-quarters of their grapes from Zitsa itself, and the rest from the other villages of the appellation zone, especially Karitsa. At present, the Union is turning out about 4,000–5,000 hectolitres annually, of which about one-fifth is rosé. Figures for Cavino are unavailable at this time; Monastiri Zitsa used to produce about 6,000–7,000 hectolitres annually, of which 2,000–3,000 was rosé. All the commercial Zitsa wines, whether white or rosé, still or sparkling, have been at $11–11.5°$ alcohol, and it is worth noting that while this level does not necessarily preclude their 'travelling well', it is all too easy away from Ioannina to find deteriorated bottles. Historically minded wine-bibbers may appreciate knowing also that, apparently because Zitsa's rosé is so strongly identified with the area of Ioannina, the major bottlers have chosen for their wines of that type names which evoke an historical figure dear in Epirote folklore: the lady Euphrosyne, or Frosyni, Mouchtar Pasha's mistress, who was drowned in the Lake of Ioannina by Ali's henchmen for repeatedly resisting his own amorous advances. The chances are that her memory will be preserved on future labels as well.

I must also suggest trying a very different kind of bottled Zitsa wine, a rosé made by Dimitrios Siatras of Karitsa. Siatras makes his wine at home, using only purchased grapes, most of which come from the vineyards of Karitsa, and the rest mostly from the vicinity, but also from outside the appellation zone. The wine is marketed only around Zitsa and in Ioannina, Siatras having his own shop in the latter place at 91 E. Venizelos Street. It is sold in homely, outsize bottles, which are unlikely to escape one's reconnoitring eyes. Siatras's rosé harks back to an apparently earlier tradition of Zitsiote wine. Not only is it produced by a fermentation on stalks as well as skins, but it is also bottled as a still, *imíglyko*, or 'semi-sweet', wine. I do believe, though, that I have observed bottles of it refermenting on shop shelves exposed to the sun.

Even after the effervescent rosé came to the fore in local tradition, Zitsa has never lacked producers of Doric mentality who begin drinking their wine several months before spring weather rekindles the fermentation that induces the froth. A market for it persists even in Ioannina. Still Zitsiote rosé is unctuous, with a somewhat heavy, flattish initial sweetness that trails off to a dry finish, helped along by the early and sustained appearance of a tannic sensation. Moderate chilling adds rigour to the experience; cellar temperature will do. There is not a prickle of carbonic gas, and not in the least for that reason, Siatras's Imiglyko is likely to seem a most arcane taste, in its way on a par with the ear-boggling polyphonic Epirote songs. Have some nevertheless with a *mousaká* redolent of sweet spices, capped by a mighty layer of white sauce, and served tepid. For those to whom that sort of combination comes naturally, it is a match for Sauternes with *pâté de foie gras*.

METSOVO

Other than Zitsa and Grammeno, the Epirote sites whose wines are commended by natives of the region – who are just about the only source of information – are mostly towards the Albanian border. Aristi, north of Zitsa and over halfway to the border area town of Konitsa, is known for its still rosé, which is made mostly from the dominant *debína* together with *bekári*, although several whites planted to only a very small extent also play a part, such as *vótska* (a fairly common Epirote variety usually called *votzíki* elsewhere). Around Konitsa, red *broúsko* wines from *bekári* are found, but not much is grown these days. To the north-east of Konitsa, the high mountain village of Molista is mentioned very favourably for its wines of white and rosy colour, made from *debína, votzíki* (called *vóska*), *moskostáfylo* (perhaps it is the *moskhómavro* of Siatista in Macedonia), and possibly others. However, it is the village of Metsovo, east of Ioannina and nearly atop Pindos, that has become the talk of Greek wine circles lately, despite its production being not so much larger than that of many another Epirote community.

Charmingly situated in evergreen country, at about 1150 metres above sea level, Metsovo lies by the Epirote gateway to Thessaly through Pindos. It is in the heart of Greece's Vlach (*Vlakh*) country, where the inhabitants still speak a form of Latin known as Aromunian, or just 'Vlach', which is akin to Romanian, and reminiscent of the time of Roman domination of the Balkans. Through assimilation, the Vlach population has retreated into just a few enclaves, of which Metsovo is the chief bastion. The Vlachs are usually associated with pastoral pursuits, rather than viticulture, but vineyards and wine-making were very much a part of life at Metsovo in the past ('The vines [in Epirus] rise to below the peaks of the Pindus, as below Metzovo,' Ami Boué, 1840). Until about fifty years ago, the village had nearly 150 hectares in vines, which were subsequently wiped out by phylloxera and not replanted. All were abandoned, save for one small plot preserved by a man who was still cultivating it in 1983, when he was ninety-five years of age. Mr Kotanitsis was at that time the oldest living Metsovite, and attributed his age not so much to his wine drinking as to his daily hike to his vineyard to potter around in it. Fittingly, his son is involved in the task of viticultural reconstruction now underway at Metsovo, but at about fifty years of age the son may have to equal his father's longevity to see much fruit from the effort.

The driving force behind the reconstruction is the Averoff family, Metsovo's leading clan. Although of national political importance, the Averoffs always find time to lavish attention on their native ancestral community, primarily through the Tositsa Foundation, which is designed to administer funds bequeathed to Metsovo by an Italian of Metsovite origin.

After a viticultural hiatus of several decades, the Averoffs planted vines at Metsovo in 1964. The village's former tradition was in dry red wine, and the Averoffs decided to stick to tradition to that extent. However, rather than plant the old local varieties, like *vlákhiko*, the Averoffs instead imported *cabernet sauvignon*, thinking to bring glory to Metsovo's name. The first wine was produced in 1966, with the processing, cellaring and eventual bottling of it taking place in the Averoff home. Then, acting through the Tositsa Foundation, and for its benefit, the Averoffs saw to the construction of the diminutive Metsovo cellar, which was opened in 1975. The custodian of the cellar is none other than Kotanitsis the Younger, who also supervises production, under the guidance of an absentee enologist. The grapes are brought to the cellar at vintage time, which occurs between the last third of September and the first third of October. After the crushing of the grapes, the must remains on the skins for about six days before removal and a further three weeks of fermentation. The resultant wine, at 11.7°, goes into small oak barrels for about four years prior to being bottled under the Katoyi ('Cellar') label.

Katoyi has become by far the most costly of all Greek wines, although it may nevertheless be argued that the greatest expense a seeker of it will have is the time invested in looking for a bottle. It has finished well in some Western European wine competitions, and gained a number of letters and certificates of praise. None the less, for a long while I feared that I would find nothing complimentary to say about Katoyi. The vintages from 1978 to 1982, tasted from bottles in Athens and Ioannina, or from barrels in Metsovo, uniformly presented my nostrils with a dominating sulphurous smell that was never dispelled by any breathing other than my own, and my palate with a bitterish quality that appeared right away. Fortunately, I have been rescued from my dilemma by a bottle from the 1983 vintage that was brought to me at home, a long way from Pindos. It shared not at all in what I had found to be real problems with the earlier vintages I had tasted, and to my way of reckoning was very good, dark ruby-red wine, somewhat on the lightish side, with a good deal of the fruit and spice I like to see in *cabernet,* and none of the 'sweet pepper' flavour I have never taken kindly to in my glass, much as I enjoy it on my plate. I think that only a committed *cabernet* enthusiast could see much more good in Katoyi than that (though certainly there will be better vintages) and I still find it incredible when I hear the price Greeks are paying for it ('Novelty has a mighty power to make pleasure seem greater,' Athenaeus, *The Deipnosophists*).

One wishes Metsovo well with its wine-growing rejuvenation. The Averoffs have plans for Metsovo and Katoyi that are quite ambitious, considering recent statistics. In 1982, somewhat over 80 hectolitres of Katoyi were produced from fourteen tons of grapes, almost nine-tenths of which came from Metsovo, and the rest from nearby Votonossi. The Metsovo vineyards, which lie on the south-facing slopes below the village, at about 950 metres above sea level, amount to only 8 hectares or so. The Averoffs have 2.7 of them, while another 5 are in the name of the Tositsa Foundation, which now owns the vineyards formerly belonging to the Church of St Nicholas; Katoyi is indeed presented on its label virtually as a sort of estate wine of the St Nicholas property. The holdings of the Foundation are cultivated by several Metsovites, but altogether only about twenty of the villagers cultivate the thirty-odd vineyard parcels in the community. Yet neither the small output, nor the lopsided ownership pattern, nor the small number of vine-tenders daunts the Averoff vision of forming a wine cooperative. They mean it, too, for the cellar has just undergone an expansion. And it is a foregone conclusion that the Averoffs will seek an appellation of origin for their beloved home town. Anywhere else, all of this would seem laughable, but the Averoffs have a record of getting what they want for Metsovo. May we all benefit from it in the coming years.

CLASSICAL REFLECTIONS

Could anything like the effervescence of Zitsa's wine have been known during antiquity?

The ancient Greeks were as taken by the sight of foam on comestibles as we are. The naturalist Theophrastus (*Enquiry into Plants*) mentioned a kind of garlic used to prepare salads because when pounded it would foment an increase in liquid volume. He is translated as indicating 'a foaming dressing' for salad, since the adjective he used was *ekpnevmatoúmenon*, or 'imbued with breath', that is to say, inflated by intake of air. Also, the more or less sudsy beer of the ancients, *zýthos*, was named after fermentation, suggesting that the word describing this was transferred to the product through the visual carry-over of foam. Plato, too, considered effervescence in the first instance from its visual aspect, although he treated it in his discussion of tastes ('affections peculiar to the tongue'):

> a film of moisture, sometimes earthy, sometimes pure, embracing a volume of air; and thus they form capsules containing air: – in some cases the films are of pure moisture and transparent and are called bubbles; in others they are of earthy liquid which effervesces and rises all together, when the name of seething and fermentation [*zýmosin*] is given to it: and the cause of all these conditions is termed 'acid' [*oxý*].
>
> (*Timaeus*)

Although they seem to have been familiar with carbonic acid, the ancients left no record of their having made effervescent wines as such. However, they may have had some acquaintance with the phenomenon of carbonic gas as a major gustative sensation in wine:

> Into it he poured one ivy-wood cup of red drops ambrosial bubbling with foam [*afró*], then he poured in twenty measures [of water], and mingled the blood of the Bacchic god with fresh-flowing tears of the Nymphs.
>
> (Timotheus, fourth century BC, as quoted by Athenaeus)

The word *afró*, used by Timotheus, is the root of the term *afródis*, applied to sparkling wine by the modern Greeks. Nevertheless and despite their familiarity with beer, the ancients were apparently ill at ease with bubbles in wine. According to Plutarch, vintage workers were even 'afraid to pilfer the must while it is still fermenting' (*Moralia*, 'Table-talk'). It is perhaps relevant to note in that regard that the contemporary enologist Émile Peynaud calls the taste for carbonic gas 'recent and artificial' (*Le Goût du Vin*) – 'artificial' because it is urged by the mind's desire. He also mentions its sensation as 'brutal', which is altogether reminiscent of Plato on the subject of such liquids: 'a sort of frothy substance [*afródes yénos*]' which 'corrodes the flesh by burning' (*Timaeus*). Plato may also have thought the taste for it 'unnatural', having noted that 'all that is contrary to nature is painful'. It could be mentioned as well that the bubbly rosé of Zitsa came to the fore in local tradition only gradually, and with the approval of the sophisticated audience of Ioannina.

GASTRONOMIC NOTES

The maize stalk could serve as the emblem of Epirote farming. Maize's suitability as a subsistence crop on poor mountain plots led to its widespread cultivation by many of the inhabitants of the region, and in consequence one of the most characteristic Epirote foods is *bobóta*, or cornbread (maize-bread), which is largely disdained, although often known, elsewhere in Greece, exactly because of its association with the sort of grim poverty much of Epirus has known even in good times. Corn also forms the basis for a number of other traditional country foods, including: *batsarópita*, a pie of cornmeal, marrows and dripping; *rapostópita*, a pie, or rather a bread, baked in a particular kind of pastry tray; and *bólia*, boiled corn with walnuts. A diet made up of *bobóta* and other cornmeal foods would be nutritionally unsound, and invite pellagra, but when complemented by milk products can provide a more or less healthy existence. Fortunately, milk products abound in Epirus: the upland areas of the region offer an especially advantageous environment for dairy farming. The very presence of the Vlachs is testimony to that, for their ancestral occupation is the semi-nomadic herding of sheep and goats.

A significant departure from the regional dairying tradition was made with the opening of the Metsovo Dairy, founded by the Tositsa

Foundation in 1959. Because the Greek market was already saturated with sheep's-milk cheeses, it was decided not to produce traditional cheeses, but to acquire dairy cattle instead, and to look to new sorts of cheese. Cattle were distributed to farmers, who were instructed in caring for the animals. At the same time, young students were sent to Italy to learn cheese-making as it is practised there. The Metsovo Dairy consequently turns out mostly cow's-milk cheeses influenced by Italian prototypes. A *chèvre*-type cheese of sheep's and goat's milk is an exception. The premier product is *kapnistó tyrí Metsóvou* (smoked cheese of Metsovo), whose initial processing is similar to that for provolone, although in final result one might sooner think of a smoked gouda. It is much sought after by Greek cheese fanciers, some of whom perhaps drink Katoyi with it. Partisans of any Zitsiote wine can take comfort and full consolation in the *chèvre*, or even in plain *bobóta*.

A number of specialities from the Epìrote marches, as around Konitsa, feature offal. One of the best-known is *splinántero*, which consists of the offals and blood of sheep or goats, seasoned and stuffed into intestines, and then spit-roasted. *Splinántero* is well known in Ioannina, and several *rôtisseries* there serve it. The dish has the 'sweet' flavour characteristic of offal, and does well in all respects with Kyra Frosyne. More rare are *boubári* and *trímma*, which consist of special mixtures stuffed into large intestines and oven-roasted: the mixture for *boubári* includes finely chopped sheep or goat's livers, rice and pepper; that for *trímma* is made from finely chopped livers and cabbage, *croûtons* and sheep's-milk butter. *Boubári* and *trímma* are largely winter foods, and are particularly associated with the Christmas season.

A number of other unusual Greek foods are also found in the environs of Konitsa (a foretaste of what might be encountered beyond the border?). A variety of *pítes* (pies) is made in rural areas there, and they differ considerably as regards the relative lavishness of their ingredients: *patatópita* is a sort of potato purée between pastry leaves; *tziarkhópita* is a pie filled with a cooked preparation of a kind of cabbage; *rizópita* is filled with rice, leeks, onions and flour, etc. I must also mention *karidáto*, or meat stewed with walnuts, and *ghíza*, which is *myzíthra* cheese fried in oil, garlic, oregano and red pepper, the latter being a popular spice in north-eastern Epirus. A type of fish called *tsíma* is commonly caught in the streams of the

north, and sometimes baked with leek. In the vicinity of Aristi, there
is trout from the Voïdomati River.

Down around Ioannina and its lake, turtles and eels are caught
and roasted, and I have also heard of a way of preparing eels
in pastry. However, both eels and turtles are encountered rarely
nowadays. The town also has its own pastry speciality, *yanniótiko*,
which is a honey-and-nut creation incorporating both the phyllo of
baklavá and the shredded wheat of *kataïfi*. Sip some of Siatras' wine
with it. Polyphonic Epirote songs indeed!

Concerning Wine and the Greeks during Antiquity

An Essay Interpreting the Ancient Record

She brought them inside and seated them on chairs and benches, and mixed them a potion, with barley and cheese and pale honey added to Pramneian wine . . .

(Homer, *The Odyssey*, c. eighth century BC)

Although nearly three millennia separate us from the era when Greece emerged as the foremost wine producer of the ancient world, a fascination with that time still persists in our wine lore. Indeed, not even the dissuading remarks of the influential nineteenth-century writer Cyrus Redding, who in his significantly titled book *A History and Description of Modern Wines* pointedly sought to put the ancients to rest, succeeded in making any lasting headway against it. Attention has returned to the Greeks of antiquity and their wines with each new generation of enophiles; it is as if we moderns should find ourselves orphans in the realm of Dionysus and wish to know something of our never-seen parents, so as to know ourselves better.

We might easily think that ancient Greece's mystical attraction for us must derive from certain Greek wines of antiquity, such as Pramnian, Maronean, Khian, Thasian or Koan, which enjoyed such a widespread reputation in their own time that they have been much vaunted in retrospect by writers of recent centuries, several of whom may even be suspected of having gone to their graves convinced that they had never really appreciated all that wine could be because they had not known at first hand the glories of ancient Greek wine-making. We are therefore liable to overlook the circumstances that gave rise to such repute and to think that the experience of the ancients was different from our own. Yet the source of the attraction most certainly emanates from below the superficiality of ephemeral reputations in wine, and goes back to that earlier stage in the unfolding of wine appreciation at which interest in the nature and characteristics of wine was stimulated. That stage consisted of the pervasive secularization of wine, and was first reached in the Aegean world, for which reason our experience of wine is indissolubly linked to that of the ancient Greeks, and we are irresistibly and eternally drawn to theirs when considering our own.

Ancient Greek literature contains a good many reminders of the mysticism that had grown up around wine in early times, which favoured sacramentality and, in turn, priestly prerogative. We might just reflect on Athenaeus's observation that some early inhabitants of the island of Ikaria called the vine from which Pramnian wine was produced *dionysiás*, while others called it *ierá* (holy). But in the earliest days of wine, when its making occurred haphazardly, no aura of sacredness and exclusivity attached to it. It was the day of the Zorba-like satyr, at one with what nature afforded, and not in need of the supernatural explanations of priests. Plutarch noted a vestige of that epoch when he mentioned the priests of the Sun-god at Heliopolis, in Egypt, who only began to use wine during the sixth century BC:

> before that they did not drink wine nor use it in libation as something dear to the gods, thinking it to be the blood of those who had once battled against the gods, and from whom, when they had fallen and had become commingled with the earth, they believed vines to have sprung. This is the reason [said the priests] why drunkenness drives men out of their senses and crazes them, inasmuch as they are then filled with the blood of their forebears.
>
> (*Moralia*, 'Isis and Osiris')

Further evidence of the profane origins of wine-growing is that in ancient Greek lore the god of wine, Dionysus, is first identified with the dynamism of vegetative growth, as embodied in sap, and later on with all arable land. The modern Greek historian Ioannis Melas, writing of Ikaria, describes Dionysus as a 'god of the peasants, a democratic god, in contrast to the gods of the noblemen', thereby confirming in unambiguous terms Plutarch's mention of Dionysus as the first ploughman (*Moralia*, 'The Roman Questions').

Of course, the rites connected with the worship of Dionysus in ancient Greece demonstrate a residual mysticism still alive in late antiquity. In the second century AD Pausanias recorded a somewhat startling survival of magical rites from a much earlier time, when priests had instructed the laity on practices by which to gain divine favour. It concerned the inhabitants of Methana, a remote settlement on the north-eastern Peloponnesos, where a south-west wind called *lips* often wrought havoc with the budding vines:

> So while the wind is still rushing on, two men cut in two a cock whose feathers are all white, and run round the vines in opposite directions, each carrying half of the cock. When they meet at their starting place, they bury the pieces there. Such are the means they have devised against the Lips.

> (*Description of Greece*)

But this was a rare instance of such magic, one mentioned by Pausanias for the incredulous amusement of his readers. The spread of the vine around the Aegean had in fact countered the legacy of magic inspired by awe of the supernatural, and largely confined memory of it to symbolic ceremonial observances evoking earlier days. For a kind of 're-democratization' was brought about on a mature and worldly plane.

The change that took place in Greece is reflected in a once-popular legend meant to explain the original revelation of wine-making, that is to say, acquisition of knowledge of its routine. According to the story, the mythical King Icarius[1] was taught the secrets of the vine by Dionysus, on condition that they not be divulged to anyone else, which was to say persons of lower station. The god, ever mischievous, must have understood that this instruction was contrary to his own nature, and King Icarius, once he set to drinking his first wine, proved as incapable as other mortals of containing his gregariousness and preserving the exclusivity of knowledge he had been granted: he shared the wine, and the secrets of the vine, with all who happened by, without question as to *who* they were. Icarius' subjects, unable to cope with the heady effects of the drink, though in their own ignorant way no less so than the knowing royal personage (we may

---

[1] In spite of the association of the King Icarius legend with the wine tradition of Ikaria, the king's name may have originated at Attic Ikaria on the mainland, to which the island of that name was once politically tied.

understand here the dichotomy between the inexperienced laity on the one hand, and the initiated priest on the other), slew the king for it. Upon recovering themselves, they apparently thought their judgement of wine hasty and, as if deciding that it was indeed meant to be theirs, maintained the vine. Their resolve was the undoing of the exclusivity that had enveloped wine through its association with the theological bases of civilization in the eastern Mediterranean.

Greece's peculiar geographic configuration, an archipelago hemmed by continental land masses, compelled the secularization of wine which took place there. For geographic reasons, the vine was introduced only gradually around the Aegean, as is suggested by legends about Dionysus's propagating travels around that sea. Consequently, there was ample opportunity for local peculiarities to develop in wine-growing as viticulture spread. Throughout the second millennium BC, vines and wine-making notions from Egypt, Phoenicia, the Caucasus and the Black Sea areas influenced wine-growing on the adjacent areas of Greece. With the settlement of the Archipelago by the Hellenes, during the period of about 1100–800 BC, the Aegean islands were affected by several tendencies, depending on the place of origin of the settlers. Because native and imported wine-growing techniques were combined and developed in different ways at different places, the written record of the ancient Greeks indicates a wide variety of local customs in every aspect of wine-growing and wine-making. The diversity in wines was unprecedented in the ancient world, and aroused considerable curiosity among the inhabitants of the Aegean ('All this is said by way of enologizing, or talking about wines, gulping down, as it were, all the names of wines,' Athenaeus, *The Deipnosophists*).

The geographic make-up of the Aegean basin not only promoted great variety, but also fomented trade in wine, just as happened with other storable staples, such as cheese:

Some say that Salamis is foreign to Attica, citing the fact that the priestess of Athena Polias does not touch the fresh cheese made in Attica, but eats only that which is brought from a foreign country, yet uses, among others, that from Salamis. Wrongly, for she eats cheese brought from the other islands that are admittedly attached to Attica, since those who began this custom considered as 'foreign' any cheese that was imported by sea.

(Strabo)[2]

As Aegean trade developed, people learned of wines from other places and began asking for them by name. (Calling certain wines by the ancient term *xakoustós* (famous), but literally meaning 'heard of', present-day Greeks continue to recognize implicitly the sequence by which wines of the Aegean first gained renown.) The commercialization of the plethora of Aegean wines clinched the secularization of wine in Greece, because enough people became familiar with, and accustomed to having available, the myriad sorts offered in the Aegean, and would no longer settle for less ('Then did you go round all the wine-merchants of the city in turn, tasting and comparing and judging the wines?', Lucian, *Hermotimus or Concerning the Sects*).

Central to Greek civilization was the belief that what humankind devises cannot be held to an abstract standard of worthiness, that is to a standard which does not accommodate our need and virtue: 'We must treat of what is good; and not of what is absolutely good, but good for us men. We are not to deal with the good the gods enjoy' (Aristotle, *Metaphysics*). As befitted the secularization of wine which the Greeks effected, wine was not to be shackled by absolutes, but instead fell within humanity's prerogative and competence: 'Leave nectar to the Blessed [the Olympians]; and I will give mankind to heal their sorrows delicious wine, another drink like nectar self-distilled, and one suited to mortals' (Cronides speaking to Zeus, in Nonnos' *Dionysiaca*). The ancient Greeks consequently were attracted by the gamut of pleasurable possibilities wine-making afforded, and accordingly looked at wine from a variety of perspectives.

The Greeks swelled the ranks of wine, which may be categorized under the headings of *wines of origin* and *wines of type*. *Wines of origin* circulated in commerce under the name of the place where

---

[2] The Greeks' comprehension of the pivotal role of maritime activity in their civilization as a whole is revealed particularly clearly in Strabo's view, in his consideration of Plato's theory of the stages of civilization in antediluvian times, that 'the greater or lesser courage . . . in approaching the sea' is the benchmark by which the stages are recognized.

they were produced, and were entirely an outgrowth of trade, which made their names known abroad. Although the Greeks were not the only people to call wines by place-names, the unprecedented number of Greek wines in that class, in an area small enough for all the inhabitants potentially to have access to as many as were exported, caused them to embellish the idea, and indeed to anticipate the twentieth century's concept of 'appellation of origin'. The main spur was probably the threat of wine fraud. In that context we might consider the fate of Pramnian wine, whose name was borrowed over such a long span of centuries after Ikaria's economic decline that by the time Athenaeus wrote of it people generally had forgotten that the name had ever had a geographic significance. To identify their wines, wine-producing places usually devised insignias, and also distinctively designed amphorae. As early as the fifth century BC, the Thasians, who produced one of the most sought-after wines of antiquity, began protecting their name in the wine trade by law, and stamped their amphorae to convey that status. More sophisticated Greeks affected greater distinction in the expressions they used to indicate the renowned wine sites. Strabo, for example, went beyond colloquial usages such as *xakoustós*, and used the highly stylized terms *dionomasménon* and *en onómati* in reference to places having 'a name', or *ónoma*, in wine, terms which are echoed in the current Greek term for 'appellation of origin', *onomasía proeléfseos*.

The Greek *wines of type* were of four general sorts that may be identified as: *facsimile wines*; *mixed-origin wines*; *wines of process*; and *sophisticated wines*. *Facsimile wines* were those which were meant as imitations of specific wines of origin. In some cases, if not most, they may have been regarded as legitimate articles of commerce, rather than bogus ones, at least when fully identified: for example, if Lesvos, which commonly marketed wine it termed 'Pramnian', were in some way to let purchasers understand that they were taking 'Pramnian of Lesvos', rather than the original Ikariote Pramnian. Wines of that sort may have earned their name by a fortuitous similarity to the wine from the more famous, or at least earlier, location; an extreme instance is provided by the Pramnian name, which Athenaeus said was used by some of his contemporaries as 'a special term for all black wine', although the original Pramnian had long since ceased to be considered a prototype. However, facsimile wines also resulted from calculated effort. According to Athenaeus, Didymus, an earlier writer, reported that the Pramnian name was applied to all wines made from that grape, which demonstrates a certain varietal-mindedness. The adoption of grape varieties originally used to make wines of a particular area had become a commonplace way to create facsimile wines.

Mixed-origin wines were blends of two or more wines of origin, mostly prepared by merchants who dealt in a variety of wines, and there were a number of them: 'There are many . . . such blends mentioned by and known to experts' (Theophrastus, *Concerning Odours*). Judging by Theophrastus's reference to the beneficial effect of mixing Heraclean and Erythrean wines, it would appear that the habit was regarded as a skill entrusted to highly trained practitioners, analogous to the modern practice of blending compatible wines from various casks. Consequently, mixed-origin wines in Theophrastus's day, in the fourth century BC, were not at a disadvantage on the market, and did not need to be traded under names suggesting the possession of characteristics typical of wines of particular places (which is to say, too, that they were probably not usually a means of creating facsimile wines). However, the ancient record does not indicate the names used to identify mixed-origin wines; it is not possible to ascertain, for instance, to what extent certain names, or sorts of names, may have been used commercially to indicate particular customary blends. The only name to be found associated with them in the Greek literature is *alloïnia*, or 'jumble wine', which Plutarch indicated as a broad pejorative, used colloquially in the case of indiscriminate blends. His statement, from the first century AD, seems to bear witness to a degradation in the practice of mixing wines after Theophrastus' time; in Plutarch's day 'those who mix wines try to conceal the wily practice' (*Moralia*, 'Table-talk'), which suggests an additional reason for preferring single-origin wines, whether wines of origin or facsimile wines, during late antiquity.

Wines of process arose from, and were usually named for, particular techniques that had been developed: *saprías* signified a wine matured in a way meant to highlight agreeable features of *saprótita*, or 'putridity'; *prótropon* indicated a wine made from self-expressed juice, the juice 'first urged'; *omfakítis* wine owed its name to the under-ripe grapes, *ómfakes*, used with over-ripe ones in its making, etc. Wines of process could theoretically be produced at virtually any locale where wine was made, but in practice there may have been some overlap with *wines of origin*, and with *facsimile wines* as well, since certain places were sometimes recognized for, and commonly associated with, a particular wine of process. An aberrant case illustrating the identification of a wine of process with a place-name is that of Pramnian. Two centuries after Didymus reported that Pramnian, once solely a wine of origin, had become a pan-Aegean varietal wine, that is, a facsimile wine, Dioscorides noted the name only as a generic term for *prótropon* wine, a kind of wine probably unknown at Ikaria.

A particular subdivision of the wines of process category comprised *sophisticated wines*, which were distinguished by the addition of an extraneous substance, and typically named after it: *ritinítis* was called after the resin which was added to the wine; *thalassítis* was named for the sea-water added; and so on. Most wines of that class probably originated in attempts at enhancing the soundness and durability of wine, since the addition typically was made by the producers or traders. However, a desire to influence a wine's flavour in a particular way, or to gain a specific healthy effect on the human organism, may also have been an initiating factor, as is suggested by Theophrastus' indication that additions were sometimes made at the time of use also, that is, by the drinkers themselves.

It is especially to be noted about sophisticated wines that wine had no sacrosanct status among comestibles. Therefore, the addition to it of savoury substances – the effect of which on the human sensory apparatus would have been analogous to late twentieth-century AD notions of 'combining' wines and foods – had as much validity as the use of flavourings in cookery:

> Next we must endeavour to speak of those odours, and also those tastes, which are artificially and deliberately produced. In either case it is clear that improvement is always what we have in view; for that is the aim of every artificial process. Now even uncompounded substances have certain odours, which men endeavour to assist by artificial means, even as they assist nature in producing palatable tastes . . . Further one must know which odours will combine with which, and what combination makes a good blend, just as in the case of tastes; for there too those who make combinations and, as it were, season their dishes, are aiming at this same object.
>
> (Theophrastus, *Concerning Odours*)

Theophrastus' precepts explain the selectivity that producers generally exercised in preparing sophisticated wines; certain wines were traditionally deemed more suitable than others to accommodate particular substances, as, for instance, in the case of Koan wine, which was especially valued because it made a *thalassítis* that surpassed all others. By the same token, the discrediting of sophisticated wines later on, in Plutarch's time ('those who colour wine with aloes or sweeten it with cinnamon or saffron are adorning it . . . and acting as a kind of pander', Aristion, in Plutarch's *Moralia*, 'Tabletalk'), was probably a result of insouciant flavouring of wines while drinking, which itself was perhaps brought on by the outbreak of unbridled gastronomic amateurism to which Plutarch alluded ('But nowadays people correct the chefs,' *Moralia*, 'Advice about Keeping Well').

Insight into the general nature of Greek wines, as distinct from types, is provided by Athenaeus's passage concerning the Ariousian wines of Khios: 'Most pleasing is the Hiote, especially that called Ariusian. There are three kinds of it: one dry [*afstirós*]; another rather sweet [*glykázon*]; the third, a mean between these two in taste' (*The Deipnosophists*). Athenaeus's breakdown is the earliest statement of a standard European concept of a continuum of basic vinous flavour, and suggests a substantial overlap in nature between the wines of ancient Greece and those of the modern world, notwithstanding any divergences resulting from changes in technology. Indeed, the pioneering modern wine writer André Jullien, as though persuaded that the formula devised by his spiritual forebear could be superimposed on the array of modern wines that he intended to categorize and rank for posterity, found Athenaeus's typology a suitable paradigm:

Wines differ from each other principally in consistency and colour. Consistency seems to me to present three distinct types, namely: dry wines [*vins secs*], sweet ones [*de liqueur*], and the wines I characterize as mellow [*moelleux*]. . . . Dry wines are characterized by a piquant taste. . . . Sweet wines are those which . . . conserve much sweetness. . . . Wines I call mellow hold the mean between the dry wines and the sweet ones.

(*Topographie de tous les vignobles connus*, 1816)

(Jullien's mention of Khios, or Scio, shows his familiarity with Athenaeus's information on Ariousia, while the telltale evidence of Athenaeus's influence on Jullien's formulation is the French idiom 'to hold the mean between', which was exactly that used in the instance of the third Ariousian wine by Lefebvre de Villebrune in his 1789 translation of *The Deipnosophists*.)

The compatibility of Athenaeus's and Jullien's terms, and the general correspondence among the respective wines indicated by them, may be postulated primarily because, as regards vinous 'consistency' more particularly, acidity content comparable to that of modern wines can be imputed as generally characteristic of the ancients' wines, notwithstanding Greek use of the term *pakhýs*, or 'fat', to describe some of them. *Pakhýs* connoted a 'stoutness' that resides in alcohol and 'oiliness', and was an encomium because it indicated the 'heat' integral to a truly vinous nature. Nevertheless, a wine's 'stoutness' did not preclude the possibility of its possessing enlivening acidity. On the contrary, wine was expected to have a 'cold' element: '[wine] is not hot in an absolute sense, but has in it certain atoms productive of heat and others of cold' (Plutarch, *Moralia*, 'Table-talk'). That element was understood to be provided by acidity: 'acid wines cool' (Hippocrates, *Ancient Medicine*). A representation of Dionysus on a chest, described by Pausanias (*Description of Greece*), shows the god holding a golden cup and surrounded by vines, apple trees, and pomegranate trees:

> There is no extinguisher more deadly to fire than vinegar; it masters and smothers the flame best of all because of its excessive coldness. And we see physicians using *vinous* fruits [emphasis added], like pomegranates and apples, for refrigerants more than they use others.

> (Plutarch, *Moralia*, 'Table-talk')

The most significant indication of the compatibility of acidity with 'fatness' in wine is Athenaeus's mention of one wine as '*éftonos* and *pakhýs*', *éftonos* meaning 'well-toned', and corresponding to the contemporary terms 'firm' and 'vigorous', which connote emphatic acidic sensations of a healthy sort.

The ancients have also afforded more practical demonstrations of the acidity of their wines. The frequency with which they alluded to the gleam of wine must be taken as proof of levels of acidity approximating those of modern wines, since relatively low pH levels account for wine's brilliance. Furthermore, Theophrastus' statement that wine, in comparison with solid food, 'does not linger on the palate for any length of time, but merely touches it' (*Concerning Odours*) demonstates acidity sufficiently uplifting to forestall cloying.

APPENDIX I

Also, Plutarch's statement, in 'Table-talk', that 'mildly salty foods . . .
bring out the sweetness and smoothness of any kind of wine', is
readily intelligible to moderns, who know that nothing can temper
the feel of acid in wine as salt does ('The white wines are above all
known as privileged partners of the products of the sea. Their savour
effaces the salt and is enhanced by it', Émile Peynaud, *Le Goût du
Vin*, 1980).[3] Of course, acid deficiency was no doubt a problem with
some wines, proof of which are the ancient practices of adding
gypsum to them, as was done for lesser wines in Greece in recent
centuries as well, and the making of some musts in part from
unripened grapes, as in the case of the so-called *omfakítis*. Even those
practices, however, only make more apparent the ancients' feel for
the balance between 'heat' and 'cold' in wine.

The potential for acidity derived from the timely collection of
grapes, the importance of which was fully appreciated by the Greeks:
'The vine is in her prime, ripening without the sickle . . . when shall
we gather the grapes?' (Nonnos, *Dionysiaca*). The grape varieties
themselves may be considered, too. It is instructive to note that
present-day Greek varieties of verifiable ancient lineage – varieties
such as *liátiko, limnió, athíri, aïdáni* – are quite up to producing firm
wine, at least when planted in suitable places. And in fact, the
outstanding Aegean wine sites of antiquity, such as Ariousia, typically
were north-facing and relatively high, exactly the conditions modern
Greek enologists have found play the role in the Aegean that latitude
fulfils in more northerly wine regions of Europe in the development
of acidity in grapes. Perhaps the ancient wine lore that tells of
Dionysus's birth on the north-eastern promontory of Ikaria called
Drakanon once had a practical symbolic significance for the ancient
wine-grower of the Aegean.

Notwithstanding a compatibility between Athenaeus's and Jullien's comprehension of the dryness-to-sweetness continuum, some
divergence must also be presumed because Athenaeus would have
estimated the relative 'dryness', or *afstirótita*, of a wine in part by

[3] Plutarch would probably have explained the effect of salted food on wine as an
instance of that which is 'hot' overcoming that which is 'cold', since salt was
perceived by the ancients as 'oily' (*liparós*): 'Why is the sea less cold than fresh
water? . . . is it because sea-water is more greasy [*liparotéra*], and so does not
extinguish the heat? The same thing is true of other substances. For that which is
more greasy is warmer' (Aristotle, *Problems*).

reference to its alcoholic degree, as manifest in its potency; for example, he mentioned Ikariote Pramnian wine as 'neither sweet nor fat, but dry [*afstirós*], hard, and of extraordinary strength [*dýnami*]'. Dryness and potency were linked in the ancient view partly by their association with the 'heat' of wine, and partly by the observation that both increased with the ageing of wine:

> wine at first is 'sweet' [*glyký*], [but] the changes due to fermentation make it 'dry' [*afstirós*] as it ages . . . [And] ageing increases its force, the water being separated out, [so that] the wine becomes less in measure, more powerful in strength.
>
> (Plutarch, *Moralia*, 'Table-talk')

The porosity of earthen wine jars on the one hand allowed entry of air, which was perceived to 'sharpen' wine, since acidic sensations were augmented at the expense of sweetness: 'coldness [the essential quality of acid] because of its relationship to tartness [*afstiró*], when it prevails, destroys sweetness [*glyký*]' ('Table-talk'). On the other hand, the porosity of the jars also encouraged the evaporation of water to the advantage of alcohol, at least under conditions of relatively warm maturation and storage conditions. The likelihood, therefore, is that the most significant difference between ancient wines and their modern counterparts was a relatively elevated alcohol content, albeit mostly, or only, in certain aged wines.[4]

Quality, even of a kind that would be recognized as such today, may be ascribed to Greek wines of antiquity, not only because of the care with which it is apparent that many of them were made, but also

---

[4] Although such wines may have been heavily watered before they were drunk, it is not likely that they generally surpassed 16–20° alcohol, since the ancients had no spirits and would have reckoned wines like that extremely potent drinks. Among the few exceptions would have been Roman Falernian, which apparently was subjected to a special sort of processing, since Pliny reported it as 'the only wine that takes light when a flame is applied to it' (*Natural History*). Even Falernian, though, may not have had an alcohol content like that of a modern distilled beverage or been suited to flambéing, since Plutarch mentioned sea-water as flammable also, on account of the 'fat' contained in its salt (*Moralia*, 'Table-talk'). Furthermore, in addressing the composition of substances which accounts for their relative propensity towards evaporation and flammability, Aristotle observed that 'wine presents a difficulty . . . [because] there is more than one kind of liquid called wine . . . and different kinds behave differently' (*Meteorologica*).

because of what ancient writers reveal about sensory aptitude in that era. From that material, the greatest part of which pertains to the sense of smell, a comprehensive picture of wine appreciation among the ancient Greeks emerges.

The strength of the attraction that vinous smells must have exerted in pre-Homeric times is apparent in Pausanias's relation of a very old legend about the Triton, or sea monster, of Tanagra, a city along the Asopus River of north-eastern Boeotia. The monster was in the habit of waylaying small vessels, and the inhabitants finally had the idea of setting out a bowl of wine for him:

> They say that, attracted by the smell, he came at once, drank the wine, flung himself on the shore and slept, and that a man of Tanagra struck him on the neck with an axe and chopped off his head. And because they caught him drunk, it is supposed that it was Dionysus who killed him.
>
> (*Description of Greece*)

However, it was by way of foretelling a positive or negative effect on the body that the ancients took a more particular interest in the smell of wine. The nostrils, according to Theophrastus (*Concerning Odours*), and the whole of the body, according to Plato (*Timaeus*), are restored to their natural condition by 'good odours'. Moreover, the brain was thought 'cold' by nature, and therefore in need of the 'warmth' of smells: 'A highly important element of health is to put good odours to the brain' (from Alexis's *Love-lorn Lass*, as quoted by Athenaeus in *The Deipnosophists*). 'Good odours' were those thought to participate in the quality of aromatic 'lightness' (*koufót-ita*), a conception that developed from a view of odours as substances in the process of dissolution, and occupying the middle ground, so to speak, between water and air; Plato, in the *Timaeus*, said all odours were lighter than water and denser than air.[5] The more an

---

[5] Both moisture and air were thought necessary to fire, and heat as well as air was thought necessary to a manifestation of smell. Plutarch likened odour to fire, in so far as it is 'an exhalation . . . engendered by heat' (*Moralia*, 'Table-talk'), while Theophrastus wrote that an odour becomes 'more pronounced with movement; for then it becomes active and mingles more with the air' (*Concerning Odours*). How conducive such explanations are to imagining the ancients palming and swirling the drinking vessel called 'aryballos', described by Athenaeus as 'a cup that is wider at bottom, but contracted at the top' (*The Deipnosophists*).

odour had left behind the 'earthy', or 'heavy', element that makes water denser than air, the 'purer' was the smell perceived to be. Scents of that quality, Theophrastus wrote, make the body resistant to other smells that may follow, as in the case of 'certain wines [which] if they are first drunk [allow] no satisfaction in others' (*Concerning Odours*).[6]

Generally, flowers were observed to possess the 'lightness' of smell which ensured the physiological benefit of odours, for which reason floral odours occupied a particularly important place in the ancient Greek perspective on wine. Floral odours were thought most beneficial for the brain, and therefore for the whole organism, usually because of 'warming' effects that 'clean out the conduits of the organs of sense, and . . . thin and easily separate the humours without violence and shock' (Plutarch, *Moralia*, 'Table-talk'). Additionally, floral odours were deemed capable of forestalling intoxication, hence the wearing of garlands of flowers by those attending symposia:

> the exhalation of flowers . . . protects the head against drunkenness . . . for warm flowers by their gentle relaxing action open the body's ducts and give the wine a vent; and those which are soothingly cool check the fumes by their temperate touch, as for example, the garland of violets and roses.
>
> (Trypho speaking in Plutarch's 'Table-talk')

Some wines were even infused with floral smells, like one of Thasos scented with rose perfume, which came in for special praise from Theophrastus, who noted that rose perfume, on account of its 'lightness', was able to penetrate 'as no other can and fills up the passages of the sense [of smell]' (*Concerning Odours*). However, vinous odours were also thought to have an affinity to floral odours naturally, such that floral smells were expected in wines even without additions of floral essences being made:

> Fig and apple have their grace as far as the teeth; but no other plant can rival your grapes – not the rose, not the tinted daffodil, not anemone, not lily, not iris is equal to the plant of Bacchos! For

---

[6] Theophrastus was careful to include a caveat on this subject: 'To speak generally then . . . things which are least of an earthy nature have a good odour . . . But, even as many things pleasant to the taste present a certain bitterness, so many things that have a good odour have a kind of heavy scent.'

with the new-found streams of your cru
will contain all flowers: that one drink
will combine in one the scent of all the
flowers will embellish all the spring-tim
meadow.

No wonder that Euripides called Dionysus *philanthēs*, or 'flower loving', and that the ancient Greeks inaugurated the term *anthosmía*, or 'flower-smell', that is, 'bouquet', as an allusion to the preferred vinous smell of older wines, such as the *saprías* wine which the fifth-century BC poet Hermippus praised elatedly for smelling at once of violets, roses, and hyacinth.[7] The association of vinous smells with floral aromas could have contributed to Dionysus's identification as the god of wine, since his earlier identification had been with the generativeness of plant life, as represented most of all by budding and flowering.

The ancients also became well attuned to the aromatic savour of wines:

> For the two senses of taste and smell being akin to one another, each provides in a way for the enjoyment of the other: wherefore it is through things which appeal to the taste, as well as those which appeal to the sense of smell, that men try to discover fragrant odours.
>
> (Theophrastus, *Concerning Odours*)

Theophrastus's commentary on perfume-making, which draws parallels with cookery and wine-making, indicates that what is lauded today as 'complexity' of flavour was also appreciated in the fourth century BC: 'The more numerous and the more various the perfumes that are mixed, the more distinguished and the more grateful will be the scent.'

Perhaps more striking is Theophrastus's comprehension that 'harmony' was the mechanism by which such results were achieved. He

[7] Apparently because of Hermippus' description, Vasilios Logothetis (1975), ampelographer and historian of the vine, thought *saprías* was a wine to which flowers were added. In fact, no written evidence from the classical period links *saprías* with a technique of that sort – such an origin might sooner be attributed to the wine called *anthosmías* – while classical discussions of the *saprótita* concept demonstrate otherwise.

indicated that there was no dearth of cases in which the reverse effect occurred, when 'complexity' lacked the unifying element that made it praiseworthy, and instead represented disharmony and a degradation in quality. In Plutarch's 'Table-talk', Philinus made a classic statement about such instances:

> When a number of divergent qualities in food are united, essentially opposed and clashing as they are, they encounter each other prematurely and are destroyed. Like a mob of ill-assorted riffraff in a community, these elements cannot easily establish unity and harmonious order among themselves, but each pulls in its own direction, and will not come to terms with an alien kind. Wine offers a clear proof; the mixture of several wines together, the so-called *alloinia* . . .

The people of the Aegean did not suddenly acquire the deliberate sensory attentiveness that encouraged them to replace awe with joy and ritual with pragmatism in their approach to wine. For a long time their devotion was epitomized by the maenads, the women 'maniacal' from wine. Memory of those ancestors was retained by much later generations through customs such as the *oreibasia*, the biennial gathering held in heavily wooded retreats on Parnassos for purposes of ecstatic gambolling in honour of 'mountainbred Dionysus' (Nonnos, *Dionysiaca*):

> we must be especially wary of these pleasures; [music and dance] are extremely powerful because they do not, like those of taste and touch and smell, have their only effect in the irrational and 'natural' part of our mind, but lay hold of our faculty of judgement and prudence.
>
> (Plutarch, *Moralia*, 'Table-talk')

The first break with the outlook of the satyr was signalled by a switch in Muses, through which it became possible to extricate wine from hypnotic, ritualistic dance, in favour of poetry. It is above all in the poetry of the ancients that a sublimation of the visceral appeal of wine is discerned: 'a kindly spirit, a sweet Muse, and delicious wine in Boeotian cups' (Bacchylides, fifth century BC).

Athenaeus noted an apparently witty mention of the famous Phliasian (Nemean) wine by Antiphanes, a fourth-century comic poet. Poetry may also have ushered in the characteristic Greek sense of humour about wine. The Greek dramatists used humour to whittle wine down to human size, as in the case of Aristophanes' characterization of Pramnian wine as 'contract[ing] the eyebrows as well as the bowels'. The humour of the dramatists both grew from and sanctioned ordinary palaver as it touched on wine ('why, spurning the fine bouquet of mellow wine like this, do we not drink coarse, inferior wine out of the cask – wine surrounded by a choir of singing mosquitoes?' – Martion, in Plutarch's *Moralia*, 'Table-talk'). As such, it is inestimably important in the secularization of wine, since nothing else so effectively served to 'democratize' wine appreciation.

Yet ancient Greek literature offers plenty of evidence that the humour could be lost and democratization undone ('And let the wine be one and the same for all the guests – where is it laid down that he should get drunk on wine with a fine bouquet while I must burst my belly on new stuff?' – Lucian to Cronus, in his *Saturnalia*). By chance, Athenaeus recorded an instance of a tumble from that pinnacle where the enophile stood as master of wine, when he mentioned the deposition of a certain nobleman by the name of Demetrius. Brought before the court on charges of profligacy, Demetrius apparently thought to make short work of his self-defence: 'But I am living as becomes a man of breeding as it is. For I have a mistress fair, I have never wronged any man, I drink Chian wine, and in all other respects I contrive to satisfy myself' (as quoted in *The Deipnosophists*).

Demetrius in effect had reversed roles with wine, making it the subject and himself the object: a wine was to confer worth on him. He had lost touch with what was for the Greeks a self-evident truth, that things wrought by humankind could acquire 'goodness', which was synonymous with 'beauty', only through a favourable influence, and that such a result stemmed from within, much as when, after slaying King Icarius, they realized that the 'evils' of wine lie in themselves rather than in wine. 'But a pleasant and happy life comes not from external things, but, on the contrary, man draws on his own character as a source from which to add the element of pleasure and joy to the things which surround him' (Plutarch, *Moralia*, 'Virtue and Vice'). Not being wary of what he invested in things, Demetrius had absolved himself of having to rely on his senses for the perusal of vinous features – colours, aromas, flavours – and in so doing forfeited his frankness of perception and conscientiousness of judgement, and could only be a threat to the rational appreciation of wine which had been gained. In a sense, he had reverted to the mentality of the maenads:

> For the lover of fish and the fish-eater are in a way fish-mad, the lover of wine [*philoenos*] is wine-mad [*oenomanis*], and so on in similar cases; it is not strange that the word 'madness' [*mania*] is applied to them, since they err madly, and are too far removed from the truth.
>
> (Chrysippus, *On Good and Evil*, as quoted in *The Deipnosophists*)

APPENDIX II

Transliteration Key

The Latin letters by which I have transliterated Greek terms, grape variety names, and wine labels are as set out below. In the case of place-names, I have generally used the spellings most likely to be found on current maps, or else those most familiar to Anglophones. Also, I have let stand any transliterations used by other authors, as in the case of the translations of classical works, whenever I have quoted from those.

a = α	n = ν
af/av = αυ	ng = γγ
b = μπ	nk = γκ
d = δ, ντ	o = ο
dg/dz = τζ	ou = ου
e = ε, αι	p = π
ef/ev = ευ	r = ρ
f = φ	s = σ
g = γ	t = τ
i = η, ι, ει, οι, υ	v = β
iy = υγ	x = ξ
k = κ	y = υ
kh = χ	ye = γε
l = λ	yi = γι
m = μ	z = ζ

Note: In the cases of af/av, dg/dz, and ef/ev, the choice depends on the sound assimilation required by the next syllable.

APPENDIX III
Lexicon

The contribution which Greece made to the language of wine appreciation was seminal. Never before within the territorial bounds of a single language had such an array of wines been available, and the Greeks reacted by developing a precise, commonly understood terminology for differentiating among those wines, in a manner which conformed, it must be emphasized, with their general outlook:

> We, however, for our part, are convinced that the chief merit of language is clearness, and we know that nothing detracts so much from this as do unfamiliar terms; accordingly, we employ those terms which the bulk of the people are accustomed to use.
>
> (Galen, *On the Natural Faculties*)

The ancient notions concerning wine and its characteristics are more germane to us than we might imagine, for they were taken by Greek colonists to the Western Mediterranean and thereby entered all subsequent vernaculars. That influence was renewed during the Renaissance, when emulation of classical Greece was stimulated by an intimacy with its literature. Still later, during the very time when the economic bases were being laid for the modern 'great wines', the translation of important classical works into the several major Western European vernaculars put the wine terminology of the ancient Greeks at the disposition of educated Europeans who had a particular interest in wine. Were it not for that continuity of our orientational glances back at ancient Greece, the language of wine today might bear much less resemblance to its actual content, which conceptually has remained virtually homogeneous throughout Western civilization, and is not at all different in its fundamentals from what it was in the time of Athenaeus, Plutarch, Hippocrates or Theophrastus.

A special significance also attaches to the ancient Greek vocabulary of wine appreciation in relation to the subsequent evolution of Greek wine. Although the light which emanated from Greece in this respect eventually diminished, ancient sensibilities about wine were not altogether forfeited. Later Greek history, and particularly that recorded by Western visitors since the sixteenth century, amply demonstrates that whenever conditions encouraged it, or just countenanced it, outstanding wine continued to be produced on Greek territory. Facilitating the retention of that tradition, and proving it, too, was the parallel maintenance of the ancient Greek approach to wine, condensed, as though packaged for survival, in the prototypal Greek language of wine. Although additions and modifications were made during the intervening centuries, as is only to be expected in any living culture, many particulars, and all the concepts, of the still exemplary ancient vocabulary remain alive in Greek speech today. Indeed, ardent wine enthusiasts who have delved into the original language of classical Greek literature can expect their ears to prick up now and then in recognition of an unusual antique word uttered expressively by some wizened and unlettered Greek tiller of the soil out in his Aegean vineyard.

Note: the terms which follow have been selected for discussion because they are central to understanding the ancient Greeks' concept of wine and complement the rest of the text.

Unless otherwise stated, references to Plutarch are from *Moralia*, 'Table-talk', and those to Theophrastus are from *Concerning Odours*, while all references to Athenaeus are from *The Deipnosophists*.

Adjective headings are given in masculine singular form.

The terms have been transliterated according to the system found on page 270.

afstirós (ˊ) : austere

The ancients conceived of *afstirós* as the antithesis of everything sweet conveyed in either its literal or figurative sense. According to Hippocrates, sweetness participated in wetness, which in wine was manifest mostly in 'oily' texture. The comparative lack of textural sweetness in *afstirós* wine is attested to especially by some of Athenaeus's notations in which he opposes *afstirós* and its allied concepts to oily (*liparós*), and is most notable in his decription of Pramnian wine as 'neither sweet [*glykýs*], nor fat [*pakhýs*], but dry [*afstirós*], hard [*sklirós*], and of extraordinary strength'.

Hence, too, did Hippocrates (*Ancient Medicine*) mention that 'dark and harsh [*afstirí*] wines are more dry [*xirí*]' than others; he also spoke of *afstirí* white wines, though. Furthermore, Plato (*Timaeus*) mentioned the term *afstirós* as indicating a kind of rough (*trakhýs*) drying sensation, but one less drying than the sensations called astringent (*stryfnós*) or bitter (*pikrós*). From Plutarch it is known that acid was regarded as a major contributory component of the 'austere' sensation: 'coldness [the essential quality of acid as the ancients perceived it] because of its relationship to tartness [*afstiró*], when it prevails, destroys sweetness [*glyký*].' (Indeed, enologists today know that high acidity levels emphasize the feel of tannin and promote sensations of hardness and astringence. See Émile Peynaud, *Le Goût du Vin*.) The Greek term was taken by the Romans as *austerus*, and thereby became a wine term shared by various Western European cultures, although sometimes with additional connotations. Ironically, when the Greeks came under strong Venetian influence in the late Middle Ages, they adopted the Italian term for rough and sharp wine, *brusco*, or *broúskos* in modern Greek, in preference to their own ancient term. The overlap of *broúskos* and *afstirós* is apparent in a careful Greek explanation of *broúskos*: 'Astringent [*styfós*], rough [*trakhýs*], and sometimes tart [*ypóxinos* "sourish"] wine, in which the taste of alcohol and acid is stronger than that of sugar' (*Neoteron Enkyklopedikon Lexikon*).
Cross-reference terms: *glykýs, liparós, pakhýs, pikrós, sklirós, stryfnós, trakhýs, xirós*

anthosmía (˘) : bouquet
The notion of *anthosmía* was bound up in Dionysian legends [pages 264–6], and was quite specific to Greek culture. The term literally means flower-smell, and was an allusion to the smell of sound older wines. Theophrastus's comment, that 'even uncompounded substances have certain odours, which men endeavour to assist by artificial means', suggests why the ancients would have wanted a term to distinguish the vinous smell of older wines: techniques to age wine constitute artificial means that result in another quality of smell. Their empirical finding must have been that ageing causes an age-worthy wine to shed the coarse and earthy components of its smell, in a way analogous to their experience of flowers: 'The scent of flowers, too, is sweeter [*evodéstere*] when it reaches you from a distance, but if you bring them too close, their odour is not so pure and unadulterated. The reason is that much that is earthy and coarse accompanies the scent and destroys its pleasant odour when received from near by, but if from a distance, the coarse and earthy parts slip off all round and fall, while the pure and fresh part of the scent by its lightness is brought intact to the sense of smell' (Plutarch). Certainly the Greeks knew well-matured wines that smelled evocatively of various flowers, such

as the aged *saprías* wine which Hermippus described as smelling at once of violets, roses and hyacinth (Athenaeus). The term *anthosmía* must have migrated westward with Greek colonists during antiquity, but over time apparently lost its precision of meaning in Western Europe. For it was not until after the rediscovery of classical literature in much more recent times that the term bouquet acquired the specific meaning it now has, which is identical to that given to *anthosmía* by the ancients. Indeed, in his 1789 French translation of *The Deipnosophists*, Lefebvre de Villebrune failed to give *anthosmía* as bouquet, or anything else corresponding to its meaning. As late as his day, bouquet had only a general usage, in the sense of attractive smell [see page 40 for Savary's use of the term in 1788]. In twentieth-century Greece, however, the term *anthosmía* has greatly receded in use, and been virtually completely supplanted by the imported term *boukéto*, particularly among Greek enophiles. Cognizance and occasional use of the ancient and indigenous term by Greek enologists will perhaps ultimately rescue it from disappearance.

Cross-reference terms: *ápsitos, ároma, evármostos, evódis, sýnthetos, yeódis*

ápsitos (ʹ) : 'unbaked', 'immature'
This modern Greek term is used to indicate a very tart new wine, especially a red one, but sometimes also a speciality wine which has been aged for several years, but not yet sufficiently to have achieved the special character expected of the style, especially its aromatic character. The notion, which is only metaphorical, must be very old in Greece: 'And there was wine . . . dry by now [that is, "fermented out"] but still crude [*ápeptos*]' (Lucian, *Lexiphanes*). *Ápeptos* literally meant uncooked, but was used in the sense of immature or unripe, for as Aristotle explained (*Meteorologica*), ripening is the departure of cold, which was regarded a passive force, and the acquisition of heat, an active one, as in the case of fruits, which are mature when their seeds have darkened and can be propagated. It is likely that the concept influenced Greek wine storage practices, since Plutarch emphasized the importance of storing wine so as so retain its heat, when he repeated Hesiod's advice (*Works and Days*), that wine should be drunk freely at the beginning and end of a cask, where heat could not be retained, but sparingly in between, where it could be. Of course, the retention of heat required the opposite quality, coldness, which made for the sort of paradox which was so popular with some of the ancients.

Cross-reference terms: *anthosmía, pyknós*

ároma (ʹ) : aroma
The ancient Greeks usually referred to smells found in the plant world by the term *ároma*, which appears to have derived from the smell arising from the earth itself as it was being broken for cultivation: *ároura* is the

term for ploughed land and *árotron* for the plough. The smells of earth were at some very early time presumed good: 'Do you note how sweet the earth smells and the steam is coming forth with greater fragrance? It would seem that some seller of frankincense dwells in the chasm, or else a Sicilian cook' (Athenaeus). Consequently, the term *ároma* eventually took on the meaning of the term *evosmía*, or good smell, and finally replaced it in Greek parlance. That an aroma of the land might be transmitted even to a well-made wine would have been self-evident at least to Plato, who called wine a kind of water that had coursed through the plants of the earth (*Timaeus*).

Cross-reference terms: *evódis, yeódis*

drimýs (ʹ) : pungent, acrid, sharp

The term *drimýs* was among the several words the ancients found suitable to qualify a smell. It was used particularly for smells having a physical or physiological impact: 'sharp [*drimýs*] like vinegar' (Galen, *On the Natural Faculties*); 'stinging [*drimýtaton*] smoke' (Aristophanes, *The Clouds*); the root of the wild vine is 'heating and pungent [*drimý*]' (Theophrastus, *Enquiry into Plants*). However, the term's connotations were hardly all unfavourable. Indeed, the quality called *drimýs* participated in aromatic lightness (*koufótita*), which was understood as a kind of volatility: 'those [substances] which share the warmth of the mouth . . . and owing to their lightness [*koufótita*] fly upward to the senses of the head penetrating all that is in their path . . . are called "pungent" [*driméa*]' (Plato, *Timaeus*). Thus did Theophrastus (*Enquiry into Plants*) use *drimýs* to describe the smells of marjoram, savory, mustard and cress. Plato (*Theaetetus*) attributed unpleasant cases of *drimýs* smells to rough (*trakhýs*) aromatic substances, whence his idea that smells take geometric shapes.

Cross-reference terms: *efkháristos, evódis, koúfos, trakhýs*

efkháristos (ʹ) : pleasing, satisfying, gracious.

The term *efkháristos*, familiar to us because 'eucharist' can be identified in it, evokes the joyous realism which has been the hallmark of wine appreciation in Greece these many centuries. It follows in the line of Athenaeus's favourite superlative for wine, *khariéstatos*, or most pleasing, and shares with it the root *kháris*, which takes in charm as well as grace, as in charisma. Athenaeus's term was grounded in the belief, as put by Protagoras, that 'man is the measure of all things', a belief so fundamental to the Greeks that Aristotle thought it did not merit explicit statement. That is, Athenaeus's assumption was that wine exists for man, and not vice-versa. Indeed, the term *khariéstatos* did not convey a notion of 'divine perfection' in wine, but instead accommodated the palatably presented 'imperfection', otherwise known as 'character', which attracts humankind because it is their own condition. 'For men consider divine the common things which most completely supply their practical needs,' such as, for example, salt, which 'will render most [foods] harmonious [*evármosta*] and so "gracious" [*kekharisména*] to our taste' (Plutarch). Hence, some Greeks called salt charites [*khárites*], or joys/charms, much as when Plutarch noted that 'womanly beauty is called "salty" and "piquant" [*drimý*] when it is not passive nor unyielding, but has charm and provocativeness.'

Cross-reference terms: *drimýs, evármostos, kharaktír*

éftonos (ʿ) : well-strung, that is, well-toned, firm, vigorous
Éftonos was derived from the Greek verb to stretch, which demonstrates that while, like most other terms the ancients used to describe the feel of potable liquids, it drew on tactile experience, a spatial relationship was also signified, namely tension, as when a slack string is drawn to a tightness in which there is still some give. The fact that *éftonos*, virtually alone among tactile descriptions, was used to describe wine but not water, suggests that the notion was central to the ancients' identification and delineation of vinous (*inódis*) character. It denoted a particular harmony between heat and cold in wine, that is, in modern terms, between alcohol and acidity, which constitutes a kind of vinous strength, in the sense of toning or undergirding. Therefore the notion was also thought of as nerve, as when Niger argued that the filtering of wine 'cuts out its sinew [*névra*]' (Plutarch). The modern successor term is *tonotikós*, which alludes to the interplay of alcohol and acidity whereby the tongue is immediately lifted out of its humdrum existence into a feeling of what might be termed a sort of dynamic suspension.

Cross-reference terms: *inódis, nevródis, romaléos*

eklektós (ʿ) : choice; an encomium for a wine of marked vinous (*inódis*) characteristics
The term *eklektós* was derived from the verb *eklégo*, which means to select/to choose/to elect. Using the same building blocks – *ex* (out) plus *lego* (to pick) – the Romans constructed the verb *eligo*, or *elego*, which they used just as *eklégo* had been by the Greeks: 'At the vintage the careful farmer not only gathers [*legitur*] but selects [*eligitur*] his grapes; he gathers for drinking and selects for eating' (Varro, *On Agriculture*). Furthermore, just as the Greeks had derived the quality indication *eklektós* from *eklégo*, so the Romans derived *elegantia* from *eligo/elego*. Thus did Pliny (*Natural History*) mention certain vineyard areas of the Spanish provinces as being known for *elegantia* of product, as opposed to other areas known for *copia*, or quantity. Later on, however, the Romans invested *elegantia* with a descriptive function as well, rather

than just a quality indication, first for application to people, and then also to objects of human use, in order to convey the impression that the human organism is in no way taxed by the object of its delight. But the Roman authors did not apply it to wine in that way, and instead used the term *suave*, which corresponded to Greek *idýs*.

Cross-reference terms: *evármostos, evyenís, idýs, inódis*

evármostos (ʿ) : well-jointed or well-articulated, that is, harmonious, balanced; *armonikós* in modern Greek

The ancients' use of the term *evármostos* as a sensory description for application to comestibles is demonstrated by Plutarch's comment, that salt 'will render most [foods] harmonious [*evármosta*] and agreeable and so "gracious" [*kekharisména*] to our taste.' The fact that Plutarch linked the notions of harmonious and gracious indicates that the essential quality of a harmonious flavour was understood to be the absence of painful sensations. In that same vein, Hippocrates (*Ancient Medicine*) observed that when any of the 'vast number' of taste sensations is not 'compounded', that is, set off against others, it 'stands alone [and] is apparent and hurts a man', as in the case of 'highly seasoned delicacies', whereas 'well-compounded foods have nothing undiluted and strong, but form a single, simple whole'. The same principle was applicable to smells, as is seen particularly clearly in Theophrastus's discussion of perfume-making, in which he points out that 'the aim and object is not to make the mixture smell of one particular thing, but to produce a general scent derived from them all'. The notion *anthosmía*, or bouquet, very likely developed from accumulated empirical experience along that line.

Cross-reference terms: *anthosmía, efkháristos, idýs, sýnthetos*; also see pages 95–6 and 266–7

evódis/évosmos (ʿ) : sweet-smelling, fragrant

The ancient Greeks' attribution of smell to fire was taken furthest by Heracleitus (*On the Universe*), who stated that, 'If all things were to become smoke, the nostrils would distinguish them'; Theophrastus rounds out the meaning there in noting that, 'Every plant animal or inanimate thing that has an odour has one peculiar to itself.' None the less, the ancients were uniformly frustrated in trying to supply words to describe those differences. Plato, who fully anticipated twentieth-century olfactory researchers in expecting that odours take geometrical shapes which are transferred to the faculties for interpretation, despaired of closing the gap. He concluded that classificatory words for smells could not be found, since odours by their very nature are substances in the process of dissolution, which no longer constitute the original whole that might be classified could it be captured and perceived by the olfactory sense for a reading by the faculties (*Timaeus*). It was thought that, with the exception of the case of likening the smell of one thing to another, virtually all that could be said of odours is that some are good/pleasant and others evil/unpleasant in their impact on the human organism, and that such other descriptions as were in use, words such as pungent, powerful, faint, etc., prove to be equally applicable to good and evil smells.

Cross-reference terms: *ároma, drimýs, evármostos, idýs, sýnthetos*

evyenís (ʻ) : noble; used by modern Greeks to indicate wines of the highest quality, that is, ones which possess all properly vinous essentials, as well as character of their own, all in a way that is generally found most pleasing

It seems to be a unique case that in this instance the ancient written record affords an indication of the approximate time at which the notion began to be applied. Since Plato once used the term *yennéa*, which corresponds to generous and chivalrous in modern Greek, to indicate choice grapes and figs, and qualified it with the phrase 'now so called', it must be presumed that it was a new use of the term, which apparently entered speech only during his lifetime, and therefore probably in the early fourth century BC. Athenaeus said Plato had meant it as well-born or high-bred, that is, *evyenís*, which corresponds to noble and polite in modern Greek. However, the notion seems to have been used only rarely by ancient writers: Plutarch said that *yennéous karpoús*, or noble crops, might be had even from difficult land if care were taken; Columella referred to the mention of *nobilem vitem* by one Julius Graecinus, in advising the planting of superior vines; Athenaeus called one wine *evyenís*, but without suggesting its superiority over numerous others which he praised in other terms. The shared contextual meaning seems to have been no more – but no less, either – than the now outclassed 'excellent', which in fact was the word used by Lefebvre de Villebrune (1789) in rendering Athenaeus's term *evyenís* in the last cited instance.

Cross-reference term: *inódis, spoudéos*

glykýs (ʻ) : sweet

The ancients resorted to either of two words to indicate a sweet taste experience: *glykýs* or *idýs*. The two may at some very early time have been nearly interchangeable for reference to wine, since the term *meliïdýs* ʻ, or honey-sweet, was an encomium for wine in Homeric times and suggests a closeness in concept between literal and figurative sweetness. The two terms overlapped considerably later on as well. However, the general tendency was for *glykýs* and *idýs* to diverge in usage, with *glykýs* being taken as the term for sweet in its literal sense, that is, as a taste *per se*, and therefore perceived as residing in the first place in the wine, rather than in the taster's emotional reaction to it. Nevertheless, *glykýs* did not necessarily

indicate something extremely sugary. Nor did it even suggest an absence of 'harsh' sensations of touch. Notably, Theophrastus's mention (*Enquiry into Plants*) of the root of the male-fern as *glykýstryfnos*, or sweet astringent, demonstrates that a certain austerity was possible even in the presence of more or less apparent sugar content; indeed, the successor term in modern Greek, *glykóstyfos*, is used as a wine description. Necessary to *glykýs* wines was, instead, the gliding, glycerine-like texture of a sweet liquid, that is, one which participates in oiliness. The latter quality was perceived as primarily responsible for the wet quality of a liquid (olive oil was regarded as quintessentially liquid), and therefore the opposite of dry.
Cross-reference terms: *afstirós, idýs, liparós, moskhátos, stryfnós, trakhýs, xirós*

idýs (΄) : delightful
The overlap in usage between *idýs* and *glykýs* is clear in the usual translation of *idýs* into modern Greek as *glykópioto*, or sweet-drinking, in instances concerning wine. The divergence is equally clear in Plutarch's explanation that ' "pleasantness" [*idýn*] differs from "sweet" [*glyký*], for wine at first is "sweet" and becomes "pleasant" when the changes due to fermentation make it "dry" [*afstirós*] as it ages'. The term *idýs* essentially implied the antithesis of pain, for its root is in *ídos*, which is the source of the word hedonism; the modern Greek verb *idýno* can be used as 'to alleviate', and *idýs* itself still connotes clement or balmy, in which connection it is also worth noting that the Greek for the plant mint is *idýosmos*, or *dyósmo*, that is, '*idýs*-smelling', which was anciently also a wine description. *Idýs* consequently moved ever further towards the figurative sense of sweet, rather in the way of signifying a mood, that is, an emotional response to a taste, and therefore a condition more of the taster than of the wine. Thus did the commonly used expression *idýs ínos* (*oenos*) evolve towards use in some contexts as modern enophiles would use 'fine wine', an early example being provided by the fifth-century BC poet Bacchylides: 'a kindly spirit, a sweet Muse, and *ínos idýs* in Boeotian cups'.
Cross-reference terms: *efkháristos, eklektós, glykýs, moskhátos*

inódis (΄) : winy, vinous
Inódis [*oenodis*], properly speaking, was a conception of Aristotelian proportion: 'being essentially a particular thing, distinct and separate in place or form or thought' (*Metaphysics*). That is, it encompassed all properties appropriate to wine, but arranged in a configuration, or ensemble, of sensations such as not to permit mistaking in any way for anything other than wine. Moulding the notion was a certain abstract idea of roundness, the round form being thought the one most appropriate to

the universe, since, as Aristotle explained it, that shape indicates a completeness of kind that is to be reckoned 'the best of things.' In the Greek view from Aristotle onwards, it is only from wines *inódis* in that sense that superlatives of praise have generally been thought merited; as one Greek long resident in New York sums up the term, it is the equivalent of the expression 'the coffier coffee'. Since the ancients considered heat to be the essential property of wine distinguishing it from water, we can know that early Aegean wine-drinkers esteemed alcohol in wine more than we generally do today, which is to say that their perception of balance would have centred about the strength provided by alcohol, rather than the sharpness of acidity, whose 'coldness' belonged more to water.

Cross-reference terms: *éftonos, kharaktír, opós, pakhýs, pikrós, romaléos, trakhýs, yeódis*

kharaktír(as) (ˊ) : character

The term *kharaktír* literally means a notching, and so by extension signifies identifying mark(s). As a sensory concept, it probably came into use as a colloquial way of expressing what Greek thinkers were wont to call *idéa* ˊ: 'Of odours some are, as it were, indistinct and insipid, as is the case with tastes, while some have a distinct character [*idéas*]' (Theophrastus). It may have been that people generally were confused, intimidated, or put off by the abstract connotations which 'idea' carried with it when it came to the matter of their daily bread. Certainly in the Greek usage, *kharaktír* has a popular nature, in that, for example, while they can agree with Theophrastus' statement that 'Every plant animal or inanimate thing that has an odour has one peculiar to itself', true sensory character is recognized only in smells, and tastes, whose peculiarity is apparent even to non-experts not used to distinguishing among members of a class. Not surprisingly, it has remained one of the most valued attributes of wine in Greece, indeed perhaps second only to *inódis*/vinous.

Cross-reference terms: *efkháristos, evármostos, inódis, trakhýs, yeódis*

khondrós (ˊ) : coarse

The modern Greeks use the term *khondrós* to connote a wine deficient in vinous character on account of rough but loose texture, in a way analogous to 'mealy'. Indeed, the adjective *khondrós* is very close to the noun *khóndros*, meaning grain and grit. It is particularly instructive to note that the latter term was that by which the ancient Greeks called gruel [page 00]: the description *khondrós* was perhaps originally a way of indicating a wine whose taste recalled the more or less liquid grain foods and dilute grain drinks that were usual in the ancients' diet. The likelihood of such an origin is strongly suggested, too, by the ancients' use of the term *synkomistós* in the case of solid foods. *Synkomistós*, which is somewhat obscure to classicists and has been lost to Greek speech, derived from the term for bread of unbolted meal and was mentioned by Hippocrates (*Regimen*) in his arrangement, apparently according to incremental degrees of dryness, of the several words commonly used to connote the harsh sensations of touch; *synkomistós* may have approximated to 'chafing'.

Cross-reference terms: *stryfnós, trakhýs, xirós, yeódis*

koúfos (ʹ) : light

Koúfos was used by the ancients on the one hand in the sense of light-bodied: 'practically everybody knows that what is lightest [*koufótato*] is so because of the looseness [sparseness] of its elements, whereas the dense [*pyknós*] and compact, because of its weight sinks below the rest' (Plutarch). On the other hand, it was also used to connote a delicate smell, in Theophrastus's sense of a swift but soft penetration of the nasal passages, up to what might be thought of as the upper register of smell sensors: 'the souls of the dead change into beings and mount upwards to the higher and purer regions since they share in the quality of lightness [*koufótita*] (Athenaeus). The term has been replaced in modern Greek by *elafrós* ʹ, which seems to have been a secondary term for the same sensations during antiquity, or else perhaps a term only less frequently used by ancient enophiles; Athenaeus described one wine as 'very light [*koufós*]' and delicate', which the translator Evangelos Fotiades has rendered into modern Greek as 'very *elafrós* and delicate'.

Cross-reference terms: *drimýs, pyknós, tryferós*; also see pages 264–5

liparós (ʹ) : oily

Oiliness was perceived by the ancients to contribute to heat and strength in wine, and consequently could enhance vinous character. At the same time, however, its feel, which was presumed to derive from rounded particles, was considered responsible for the wet quality of liquids, and therefore the opposite of dry [*afstirós*]. Because olive oil silently spills on to, rolls over, covers and fills in any surface to which it is given access, it was thought to be composed of the most rounded particles, and therefore the quintessential liquid (Plutarch). However, judging by Theophrastus's mentions of oil in connection with its use in perfume-making, it would seem that oiliness would also have been valued as a quality which facilitated a wine's capacity to bear and project aromatic material. Yet the earliest impetus for calling wine *liparós* may have come through visual perception: the early poet Pindar wrote of 'gleaming [*lipará*] Naxos' (*The Pythian Odes*), by which he seems to have meant something approximating to 'slick', much as when Plutarch noted of oil, that 'visually it is the clearest reflection, having no unevenness to distort the reflection'.

APPENDIX III

Cross-reference terms: *afstirós, glykýs, myelódis, pakhýs, sklirós, strongylós, xirós*

moskhátos (ʻ) : sweet-smelling (literally, musky)
Greek acquaintance with the East and the Persian word *moushk*, or 'musk', resulted in a number of popular Greek terms based on it, all connoting a sweetly attractive smell. The term *moskhátos* was applied to fruits, and thence as a proper name for the highly scented muscat varieties of grapes, for which reason the ancient name(s) of those varieties cannot be ascertained from classical literature [pages 19, 48]. Similarly, the term *moskhovolistós* (literally, musk-casting) is used in reference to sweet smells in wine, especially those evoking spices such as allspice, cinnamon, nutmeg, etc., which can be explained by the fact, demonstrated by gas chromatography, that the muscat varieties of grapes are generally characterized by their overlap with the smell of coriander; however, the term is hardly restricted to use for muscat wines, and on the contrary is more frequently used in the case of well-matured dry red non-muscat wines. The *moskhátos/moskhovolistós* sort of terminology apparently replaced the ancient term *idýs* ('delightful') for application to smells. For while Epictetus reported that Socrates was said to have smelled *idýs*, an old Aegean serenade of modern times sings, 'Alas! two apples joined together are not to be found, like the breath of your body so *moskhomiris-ména* [literally, "smelling of musk"]!'
Cross-reference terms: *evódis, idýs*

myelódis (ʻ) : mellow (literally, marrowy)
Although there is no instance of its application to wine in extant ancient literature, the textural description *myelódis*, which alludes to the 'gliding' feel of marrow (*myelós*) was probably in use among the Greeks of antiquity. Certainly it was a sensory description, since Aristotle (*Historia Animalium*) speaks of the *myelódis* look of a liquid; Aristotle's usage suggests that the term may have originated from visual perception, much as is the case with the related term *liparós/*oily. Furthermore, the Greeks characterized marrow as oily and soft, while Plato (*Timaeus*) explained that it was formed from 'such of the primal triangles as were unwarped and smooth'. From the ancient viewpoint, since marrow participates in the oiliness inherent in sweetness, it displays a degree of the wet quality distinguishing sweetness from dryness. Quite in line with that, the early modern wine writer André Jullien marked *vins moelleux* (literally, marrowy wines) as those which 'without having a sugary taste, or a flat one, have a certain consistency, and are rather sweet than dry and piquant' (*Topographie de tous les vignobles connus*, 1816). Hence Jullien found

Burgundy 'more *moelleux*' than Bordeaux, that is, closer to the transition between the truly sweet and the only figuratively 'sweet' wines.
Cross-reference terms: *glykýs, liparós, xirós*

nevródis (´) : firm (literally, 'nerved')
The antiquity of this notion is apparent from the debate, recorded by Plutarch, in which Niger argued that filtering wine 'cuts out its sinew [*névra*]'. Its meaning is confirmed by the French tasting term *nerveux* (nerved), which no doubt is a direct offshoot of it, probably attributable to ancient Greek colonists who settled Massalia (Marseilles) and the lower Rhône valley, to which they brought viticulture. A reason for thinking so is that the notion of vinous nerve was well suited to colloquial expression, and so also to the busy commercial culture of what was at the time only an outpost of Greek civilization. The primary, or at least the formal and literary, expression for the idea was *éftonos* (see that heading).

opós (´) : sap
Although not used as a description of individual wines, this term was at the core of the Greek approach to wine. Indeed Plato (*Timaeus*) classified wine as a sap, a category which he defined as a kind of water that had coursed through plants. The association of wine with sap must have originated much earlier, however, since Dionysus himself was identified with it; that association probably originated in river environments where the wild vine grew profusely, since Plutarch mentioned Dionysus and Poseidon as the gods with control over the moist and generative. Identification of wine as a sap provided an explanation as to why wine should be distinct from water in spite of sharing certain features with it: namely, it had picked up colouring and flavouring matter of a different sort along its journey through the vine. Thus Plutarch mentioned 'wine-like bitter [*afstrés*] roots', since harsh but palatable tastes were in part a manifestation of what we would call extract material today.

Actually, a number of conceptions about wine, as represented by certain descriptive terms, may have originated in the identification of wine as a sap. Notably, *afstirós* wine was by its nature heating and drying rather in the way Theophrastus (*Enquiry into Plants*) meant when he described the root of the wild vine as 'heating and pungent [*drimý*]'. Also, the term *liparós*, or oily, could have that origin, since Theophrastus mentioned 'a sticky [*liparón*] juice [*khylón*]; juice/pulp, or *khylós*, which came from the verb to pour (*khýno*), was the final metamorphosis, so to speak, of sap, as the usable issue of fruit. (The related term *khýma* is still commonly used in Greece, in the expression *krasí khýma*, in reference specifically to 'unbottled wine'.) Perhaps even the idea of wine being sinewy (see the heading *nevródis*) was born of wine's association with sap, by reason of the flow of juice – the latent must – through *fibrous* plant tissue. What is more, there is reason to think that the characteristic equanimity which the Greeks brought to the appreciation of various kinds of wines, that is to say, various sorts of harmony, was attributable to the wine/sap connection: 'The natural qualities of roots, fruits and juices have many virtues of all sorts, some having the same virtue and causing the same result, while others have opposite virtues' (Theophrastus, *Enquiry into Plants*). In light of the ancient Greek perceptions on this matter, the French tasting term *sève*, or sap, probably ought not to be thought of as a spontaneous development, but rather a logical local evolution of ancient conceptions about wine that were spread with the vine itself.

Cross-reference terms: *afstirós, drimýs, inódis, romaléos, yeódis*; also see pages 35–6

pakhýs (ʿ) : fat

The term *pakhýs* is one of the oldest terms the Greeks have for describing wines, and indicates one of the most esteemed of specifically vinous qualities. It encompasses both the aromatic and the 'mouth-feel' components of flavour sensation. That is, 'fat' indicated wine that was both dense (*pyknós*) and oily (*liparós*), and therefore one possessed of a marked capacity for aromatic flavour, but also wine having ample vinous force. A curious confirmation of the latter aspect of the notion is in the name of the ancient Greek settlement of Pachino in south-eastern Sicily, which is still known for its heady vintage; the name is a contraction of the ancient Greek expression *pakhýs ínos* (*oenos*), and has come down in local lore as signifying *vino forte*, that is, strong wine. Perhaps, therefore, the term *pakhýs* demonstrates that the ancients had an intuitive comprehension of alcohol's influence on vinous texture.

Cross-reference terms: *inódis, liparós, pyknós*; also see pages 261–2

pikrós (ʿ) : bitter

Plutarch's statement (*Moralia*, 'Advice to the Bride and Groom'), that 'the acerbity of the mistress, like that of wine, ought to be salutary and pleasant, not bitter [*pikrón*] like that of aloes, nor suggestive of a dose of medicine', gives point to Aristotle's description of wine as 'a mixture of bitter and sweet flavour' (*Problems*). The mark of true bitterness was a relentless drying sensation: 'desiccant in action what is bitter in taste' (Plutarch). In wine, the tendency towards that extreme was expected to reach only to harsh (*afstirós*) and astringent (*stryfnós*) sensations, that is, palatable ones. Thus, when Theophrastus wrote that wine overpowers the 'astringent and somewhat bitter [*ypópikron*]' perfumes added to it, and that 'wine indeed . . . has a special property of assimilating odour', he could have added, based on Galen's instruction (*On the Natural Faculties*), that only things which share properties can be successfully mixed; that it is wine's own tendency towards the desiccant that enables the accommodation. Plato (*Timaeus*) attributed bitterness, which he considered a species of 'roughness', to the excessive drying action of 'earthy particles'.

Cross-reference terms: *afstirós, stryfnós, trakhýs, xirós, yeódis*

pyknós (ʿ) : thick, dense

Plato (*Timaeus*) explained that the densest material is formed of the finest and most uniform particles, for which reason density was considered the main factor accounting for weight. Since, among liquids, oil possessed density in the greatest degree – it was the quintessential liquid – wine could hardly be considered 'dense' in an absolute sense; on the contrary, Aristotle (*Meteorologica*) actually mentioned wine as one of the 'watery liquids'. However, one wine could be called denser than another, and the relatively denser wine of any particular type generally would have been deemed superior because of its greater 'fatness' and ageing capacity. In the latter regard, it is to be noted that relatively greater density was observed to enable a wine to retain its heat – the essential quality for wine – longer, much as when Theophrastus explained that 'close [*pyknós*]' materials such as lead and stone were for that reason used to store perfumes.

Cross-reference terms: *koúfos, pakhýs, sklirós, strongylós*

romaléos (ʿ) : robust

The modern Greeks use the term *romaléos* to indicate a wine whose vinous force is felt immediately upon the soft palate. The antiquity of the notion is effectively demonstrated by Plutarch in his recording of Niger's statement 'that wine . . . ought to be drunk straight from the winejar . . . with all its natural power [*rómin*] and strength [*dýnamin*]'. 'Power' and 'strength' may be understood as having connoted, respectively, the physical impact in the mouth attributable to the outward manifestation of a high alcoholic degree, virtually as 'throw-weight', and the physiological impact of it, as manifest in headiness. It is tempting to think that it was all intertwined with the nature of Dionysus. For in ancient Greek mythology, Dionysus's favourite was a particularly beautiful satyr possessed of spirit and vigour, Ampelos, who was especially fond of riding a very wild bull. When one day he was thrown and killed, Dionysus, inconsolable, intervened before Ampelos could reach the underworld, and asked Zeus to transform the satyr into a plant. Thus was Ampelos transformed into the plant of the same name, *ámbelos*, or 'vine', which Dionysus loved as much as he had the satyr himself.

Cross-reference terms: *inódis, opós*

saprós (ʿ) : mellow (literally, putrid/rotten); see pages 64–6 *sklirós* (ʹ) : hard

The ancients attributed the sensation called *sklirós* to particles which are rough (*trakhýs*) because of their irregular, that is, unrounded, shapes: ' "Hard" is the name given to all things to which our flesh yields; and "soft" [*malakón*] to those which yield to the flesh . . . Those which yield are such as have a small base of support; and the figure with square surfaces, as it is the most firmly based, is the most stubborn form' (Plato, *Timaeus*). It may be said that stubbornness was associated with a straight-edge quality, which Plato described as *oxý*, that is, keen/sharp. He said the quality was most apparent in fire, the element to which wine essentially belonged. None the less, acid, in spite of its essential participation in the element of water, was understood to partake of it also, and indeed was named *oxýs*. This may have been because air was known to sharpen the taste of things, other than dense and practically impenetrable oil, and understood to permeate water, whose coldness linked it with rigidity and therfore hardness. (It will be seen that in storing wine, the ancients made practical use of the paradox that density, the guardian of a substance's intrinsic heat, is so often associated with hardness, which was essentially an attribute of coldness.) In this nexus may be reconciled ancient Greek thought regarding the heat and cold of wine, keeping in mind Plato's categorization (*Timaeus*) of wine as a kind of water filtered through the plants of earth, that is, a sap.

Cross-reference terms: *éftonos, inódis, opós, pyknós*

spoudéos (ʹ) : excellent (literally, serious/important)

The origin of this term, which today is used only by versed Greek enophiles, may have been as much in social as in taste distinctions. Its use is found only in Plutarch's relation (*Lives*, 'Caius Marius') of a plebeian's concealment of the patrician orator Marcus Antonius. The host wished to provide for his high-ranking guest in due manner, and so sent his slave to the nearby inn for especially good wine. 'As the slave tasted the wine more carefully than usual and ordered some of better quality, the inn-keeper asked him what was the reason he did not buy the new and ordinary [*dimotikón*/of the demos] as usual, instead of wanting some that was choice [*spoudéon*] and expensive?' It may not have been coincidental that the circumstances and the relation of the incident occurred relatively late in antiquity, since Plutarch and other authors then make numerous comments indicating endemic decadence and rampant palatal elitism. For example, in his 'Laws for Banquets', Lucian (*Saturnalia*) lays down the principle that 'All shall drink the same wine, and neither stomach trouble nor headache shall give the rich man an excuse for being the only one to drink the better quality.' (The inn-keeper's observation, incidentally, proved the undoing of Marcus Antonius's concealment.)

Cross-reference terms: *efkháristos, evyenís, idýs*

strongylós (´) : round
No documentary evidence proves the use of the term *strongylós* as a wine description during antiquity. None the less, classical literature allows that inference. *Strongylós* was the only one of the several terms which the Greeks had for 'round' – the others being *sferoïdís*/spherical, *kykloterís*/circular, and *periferís*/having a periphery – that necessarily implied volume as well as shape. In that sense it would have connoted 'compact', since Plato (*Timaeus*) explained roundness of shape as due to regular, or uniform, particles, and said also that such particles make for the greatest density, since they pack together more closely. However, round was not identical with dense, since it necessarily implied a time dimension; Plato mentioned the universe, which exists in time as well as space, as 'rounded and spherical'. Consequently, *strongylós* would also have indicated 'full', in the sense of concentrated and long flavour, that is, a harmonious opening, progression and close of vinous flavour. The fact that in Greece today even untutored wine-growers in remote places have that sense of *strongylós* – a term which they themselves use – is an indication of the term's antiquity as a wine description: it must have been ages ago that such an abstract gustative notion became so deeply ingrained in the popular culture.
Cross-reference terms: *evármostos, inódis, pakhýs, pyknós*

stryfnós (´) : astringent
The ancients' writings demonstrate that astringence was as close as they thought wine ought to come to the ultimate dryness represented by true bitterness. The approach of astringence to bitterness in the ancients' conception is demonstrated by Theophrastus' phrase linking the two: 'astringent [*stryfnón*] and somewhat bitter [*ypópikron*]'. Further, Hippocrates' (*Regimen*) placement of *stryfnós* in his arrangement of apparently progressively more intense austere sensations may be cited: 'things acid [*oxéa*], sharp [*driméa*], harsh [*afstirá*], astringent [*stryfná*], *synkomistá* [see *khondrós*], and dry [*xirá*]'. The Greeks today generally use the synonym *styfós* for the same sensation, and also have the idiom 'to scrape the throat' for such instances: 'Suddenly the woman stretched out her hand and filled two glasses to the brim with wine . . . a red throat-scraper from Kissamos' (Kazantzakis, *Freedom or Death*). Non-Greeks will take note that a synonym for *stryfnós* was *styptikós*, or styptic, and that in Greek folk culture today *stypsátiko* is a name for press wine (as apposed to wine made from free-run juice), which in the case of red wine is almost invariably marked by this characteristic under village conditions.

APPENDIX III

Cross-reference terms: *afstirós, drimýs, khondrós, pikrós, sklirós, trakhýs, xirós, yeódis*

sýnthetos (') : complex
'Some sense-experiences,' wrote Theophrastus, 'are simple [*ámikta*/un-mixed], some compound [*miktá*/mixed or composite] . . . [the simple] cannot be resolved into two components.' The term *sýnthetos*, in which we can recognize synthetic, may have come into use out of observing the compounding of ingredients in perfume-making, since Theophrastus referred to *sýntheton osmín* (compound perfume), that is, a man-made fragrance achieved by mixing various substances. The *sýnthetos* concept was valued, not for its own sake, Theophrastus noting that mixtures could fail in result, but rather because the combining of substances so as to set off one quality against another created, paradoxically, a kind of unity of aromatic character: 'The aim and object is not to make the mixture smell of one particular thing, but to produce a general scent derived from them all.' The notion of unity is further demonstrated by the related term *sýmplektos*, which means woven together, as does its latinized form, complex. Unity of aromatic character brought with it staying power, as confirmed by stability of perception. Theophrastus also instructed that it is only through such mixtures, to whatever degree, that smells arise at all, a principle he derived from the observation that only earth among the four elements can have an odour, since it is the only one which even in its isolated form is an impure substance.
Cross-reference terms: *anthosmía, ároma, evármostos, yeódis*; also see pages 266–7

trakhýs (') : rough
As a sensory term, *trakhýs* was used by the ancient Greeks primarily to indicate the opposite qualities to oiliness: 'roughness is due to hardness and irregularity [of particles], smoothness to regularity and density' (Plato, *Timaeus*). To roughness were attributed all 'drying' taste sensations: 'For whenever earthy particles enter in by the little veins [tastebuds] which are a kind of testing instruments of the tongue, stretched to the heart, and strike upon the moist and soft parts of the flesh, these particles as they are being dissolved contract and dry the small veins; and if they are very rough they are termed astringent [*stryfnós*]; if less so, harsh [*afstirós*].' The role of roughness in vinous nature is apparent from Aristotle's (*Problems*) description of wine as 'a mixture of bitter and sweet flavour', bitter (*pikrós*) being the polar condition of drying taste sensations and therefore the archetype of roughness, while sweet (*glykýs*) participates in oiliness. It may be inferred that sensations of impact and irritation were considered integral to vinous nature, and that indeed the lack of such was not viewed

as harmony, but rather insipidness, or lack of character; it was very likely
for that reason that Aristotle thought the sweetest wines generally were
not truly wines [page 95]. Consciousness of the vinous virtue of roughness
persisted at least up to the time of Jullien (*Topographie de tous les
vignobles connus*, 1816), who defined the French tasting term *grain* as 'a
kind of harshness [*âpreté*] . . . without having anything disagreeable', and
said further that even 'delicate' wines, which to him meant 'harmonious'
ones, may have 'a certain *grain*', provided that it is 'well-combined' and
not dominating.
Cross-reference terms: *afstirós, evármostos, glykýs, inódis, kharaktír,
liparós, sklirós, stryfnós, xirós, yeódis*

tryferós (ʻ) : mild
By the term *tryferós* the ancients indicated an overall 'mouth-feel' that is
vinous in a most restrained way. Sometimes they used it in a way similar
to the modern notion 'elegance'. In describing one wine as 'very light
[*koúfos*] and delicate [*tryferós*]', Athenaeus sounds very much like
H. Warner Allen (*The Romance of Wine*, 1932) describing the 1877
Bordeaux wines: 'light, stylish wines, gifted with finesse and a delicate
elegance'. The translator Evangelos Fotiades gives *tryferós* as *apalós* in
modern Greek in his rendering of Athenaeus's description. The term
apalós was also in circulation during antiquity as a gustative description,
Theophrastus (*Enquiry into Plants*) mentioning a kind of lettuce that was
'sweeter and tenderer [*apalotéra*]'. However, Greek enophiles today are
apt to use the imported term *finétsa* (finesse).
Cross-reference term : *koúfos*

varýs (ʻ) : heavy
The notion of weight in liquids was hardly an abstracton originally: water
from Eulaeus (Evlaion) was reported by Strabo to be 'so far the lightest
[*elafrótaton*] of all waters that an Attic cotyle of it weighs a drachma less
than other waters'. It was probably through the fact that liquids, including
some waters, were perceived, whether visually or by taste, to contain more
or less palpable solid matter, that the more abstract notion 'bodied'
(*somatódis/*ʻ) came into use. At that point, weight became closely associated with the notion of density: 'Practically everyone knows that what is
lightest [*koufótato*] is so because of the looseness of its elements, whereas
the dense and compact because of its weight [*város*] sinks below the rest'
(Plutarch). However, since smells could also be characterized as heavy,
the aromatic component of vinous force was also brought into the notion
of weight, in a favourable sense of 'heft'.
Cross-reference terms: *koúfos, pyknós, romaléos, yeódis*

xenólogo (ʻ) : an alternative name for malvasia/malmsey formerly in use on

Santorini [see pages 77, 87] to connote the use of various kinds of grapes in making that wine (literally, 'alien kind')

Central to the concept behind the name *xenólogo* is the word *loyí*, or kind/sort, which came from the ancient verb *légo*/to gather. *Loyí* finds its way into Greek terms and expressions meant to convey a sense of heterogeneity, as in the case of the *loïsima* ('mottler') synonym of the *roméïko* grape variety [page 72]. It is apparent from such usages that the term *xenólogo* followed in the line of the ancients' term *allófilon*, which means 'different breed' and was recorded by Plutarch as indicating what is diverse and separate, that is, what is alien to each other, in the gustative realm: 'When a number of divergent qualities in food are united, essentially opposed and clashing as they are, they . . . cannot easily establish unity and order among themselves, but each pulls in its own direction, and comes to terms with an alien kind [*allófilon*]. Wine offers a clear proof; the mixture of several wines together, the so-called *alloïnia* [approximating "jumble-wine"].' Plutarch was confronting the core complex of notions from which have sprung most gastronomic practices, among which in wine are found those ranging from *xenólogo*/malvasia to *alloïnia*, as differentiated by the stage at which the telling mixture is accomplished: in the vineyard for *xenólogo*/malvasia; in the merchant's shop for *alloïnia*. The intermediate stage would be represented by the *cuvée* concept, the final product in that case being determined by an early blending of the product of different vats. Francophone enophiles may in that regard all the better appreciate their colloquial usage of the term *cuvée* as kind/sort.

Cross-reference terms: *evármostos, sýnthetos*

xirós (ʿ) : dry

For the ancients, dryness was not so much the opposite of sweetness, as of wetness; liquid was perceived to be 'anything which has no ingredient of dryness in it; and that is the case with oil' (Plutarch). They therefore associated it mostly with a wine's physiologically heating and drying effects, which were a result of tannic substances and alcohol, while the actual taste sensations that accompanied dryness went by names like *afstirós*/harsh, *trakhýs*/rough, etc. Hence Hippocrates's statement (*Ancient Medicine*): 'Water is cooling and moist. Wine is hot and dry [*xirón*]. Dark and harsh [*afstirí*] wines are more dry. They dry by reason of their heat, consuming the moisture out of the body.'

Cross-reference terms: *afstirós, liparós, pikrós, stryfnós, trakhýs, yeódis*; also see pages 262–3.

yeódis (ʿ) : earthy

The ancient Greeks used the term *yeódis* in reference to either the feel or the smell of a wine. Because the origin of the term was in water that is full of particles of earth, the notion first came to allude to solid matter generally, even when the particles were so small as not to be palpable as such. Their manifestation was then seen instead in weight, roughness and dryness: 'When water, wine, and the other liquids with their high proportion of muddy, earthy matter encounter fire, they rend it apart and by their roughness and weight crush and extinguish it' (Plutarch). However, it was also recognized that smell could be a manifestation, especially in the case of some distinctive soils, in which connection it is noteworthy that Theophrastus said that 'earth is the only elementary substance which has a smell'. Thus, while *yeódis* was probably most often used in a negative way, that was not always the case: 'To speak generally then . . . things which are least of an earthy [*yeódi*] nature have a good odour . . . But, even as many things pleasant to the taste present a certain bitterness, so many things that have a good odour have a kind of heavy scent' (Theophrastus).

Cross-reference terms: *ároma, kharaktír, khondrós, opós, pikrós, trakhýs, varýs, xirós*

APPENDIX IV

Prominent Greek Grape Varieties

___

Note: AO signifies Appellation of Origin; VP signifies *Vin de Pays*/Country Wine.

Variety	Major Growing Areas	Significance
aïdáni áspro	Cyclades	For dry and sweet white and rosé wines; authorized for AO Santorini wines; formerly important in malmsey/malvasia production
asýrtiko	Santorini, Khalkidiki	For dry and sweet white wines; chief variety of Santorini, authorized for AO wines; recently transplanted to Khalkidiki and required for AO Playies Melitona and VP Ayioritiko (Athos) white wines
athíri	Dodecanese, Cyclades, Crete, Khalkidiki	For dry and sweet white wines; chief variety of Rhodes, providing varietal dry white AO wines; on Santorini, authorized for AO wines, dry or sweet; recently transplanted to Khalkidiki and required for AO Playies Melitona and VP Ayioritiko (Athos) dry white wines; formerly important in malmsey/malvasia production
ayioryítiko synonyms: mávro neméas mavroúdi neméas	North-eastern Peloponnesos	For dry and sweet red wines; provides varietal red AO wines of Nemea

Variety	Major Growing Areas	Significance
debína	Inland Epirus	White variety used in white and rosé wines; produces varietal AO Zitsa white wines – dry still, dry sparkling, and semi-dry sparkling
filéri	Central, western, southern Peloponnessos	Red variety, generally used for dry wines, either reddish or white in colour
goustoulídi synonyms: *vostilídi* *avgoustelídi*	Ionian Islands, west coast of mainland	White variety for dry and sweet wines, especially on Zakynthos
kakotríyis	Ionian Islands, coastal Epirus	Red and white variants, both for dry wines, above all on Corfu
korífi synonyms: *mávro arakhóvis* *galanó*	Boeotia (Central Greece)	Red variety for dry wines, especially at Arakhova; not currently of commercial importance
kotsifáli	Central Crete	Red variety for dry wines; required for AO Arkhanes and Peza dry red wines
krasáto	Northern Thessaly, western Macedonia	Red variety, generally for dry wines; authorized for AO Rapsani (Thessaly) wines
liátiko synonyms: *mavroliátis* *liátis*	Central and eastern Crete, Cyclades	Red variety for dry and sweet wines; provides varietal red AO wines of Dafnes and Sitia on Crete; formerly important in malmsey/malvasia production
limnió synonyms: *limnióna* *kalabáki*	Limnos, Thessaly, Khalkidiki	Red variety for dry wines; required for AO Playies Melitona and VP Ayioritiko (Athos) dry red wines
mandilariá synonyms: *mandilári* *amoryianó* *koundoúra mávri*	Dodecanese, Crete, Cyclades, Eastern Sporades (variants); one of the most widespread varieties in the Aegean area	Red variety for dry and sweet red wines; provides varietal dry red AO wines of Rhodes; required for AO Arkhanes and Peza wines on Crete

Variety	Major Growing Areas	Significance
dombréna *mávri* *mávri korinthiakí* synonyms: *stafída* *lianorrógi*	Northern and western Peloponnesos, Ionian Islands	Red variety used primarily for drying as currants, but also in fresh state for wine, especially sweet wines in Akhaïa (Peloponnesos) and Zakynthos (Ionians); authorized up to 50 per cent for AO Mavrodaphne of Patras sweet red wine
mavrodáfni	North-western Peloponnesos, Ionian Islands	Red variety for sweet and dry wines; provides AO sweet red wines of Patras (Peloponnesos) and Cephalonia (Ionians)
mávro *mesenikóla*	Western Thessaly	Red variety for dry red and rosé wines, especially near Karditsa
monemvasiá synonyms: *monovasiá* *monemvasítiko*	Cyclades, south-eastern Peloponnesos	White variety for dry and sweet wines; required for AO Paros dry red wines; formerly important in malmsey/malvasia production
moskháto *alexandrías*	Limnos	White variety used for sweet and dry wines; provides varietal AO muscat wines of Limnos
moskháto *amvoúrgou*	Thessaly	Red variety, primarily for dessert grapes, but also vinified; especially for dry and sweet red wines around Karditsa and Tyrnavos
moskháto áspro synonyms: *moskhoúdi* *moskhostáfylo*	Samos, Dodecanese, Crete, Ionian Islands, Peloponnesos	White variety for sweet and dry wines; provides varietal AO muscat wines of Samos, Patras (Peloponnesos) and Rion of Patras (Peloponnesos); required for AO muscat wine of Rhodes
moskhofílero	Central and southern Peloponnesos	Red variety for dry and sweet white wines; authorized for AO Mantinia wines
moskhómavro synonym: *moskhógaltso*	Western Macedonia, western Thessaly	Red variety for vinification; basis of sweet white wine of Siatista (western Macedonia); not currently of commercial importance

Variety	Major Growing Areas	Significance
negóska	North-central Macedonia	Red variety for dry wines; required for AO Goumenissa dry red wines
petrokóritho synonyms: *koríthi kókkino*	Ionian Islands, west coast of mainland	Red variety for dry red and rosé wines, especially on Corfu
robóla synonym: *asprorobóla*	Ionian Islands, west coast of mainland	White variety for dry and sweet wines; provides varietal dry white AO Cephalonia wines
roméïko synonyms: *mávro roméïko, loïsima*	Western Crete, southern Peloponnesos	Red variety used for dry red, rosé, and white wines, especially in Kissamos region (Crete)
rodítis synonyms: *roïdítis rodomoúsi kokkinári violedó*	Peloponnesos, Central Greece, Cyclades, Ionian Islands; found virtually throughout Greece	Reddish or white variety for dry wines of rosy or white colour, often as varietal wine; provides varietal dry white AO Ankhialos (Thessaly) and Patras (Peloponnesos) wines; frequently used for coloured resinated wines in Central Greece and Peloponnesos; authorized for VP *retsína* (white) and *kokkinéli* (reddish) resinated wines of Attica, Boeotia, and Euboea
rozakí	Crete, Dodecanese	White table grape variety, used in dry and sweet mixed-varietal wines
savatianó synonyms: *savathianó stamatianó sakéïko koundoúra áspri dombréna aspri*	Central Greece, Peloponnesos, Cyclades; among the most widespread varieties in Greece	White variety for dry and sweet wines, often resinated in the case of dry; provides unresinated varietal dry white AO Kantza (Attica) wines; authorized for VP retsina resinated wines of Attica, Boeotia, and Euboea
soultanína	Central Crete, Dodecanese	White variety primarily for drying as raisins, but also in dry and sweet mixed-varietal wines

APPENDIX IV

Variety	Major Growing Areas	Significance
stavrotó synonym: *ambelakiótiko* *tráni*	Thessaly, western Macedonia, Euboea Dodecanese	Red variety for dry red and rosé wines; authorized for AO Rapsani (Thessaly) dry red wines White variety for sweet muscat wines; required for AO Rhodes muscat wines
vertzami synonyms: *martzaví* *lefkadítiko*	Ionian Islands, west coast of mainland	Red variety, primarily for blending wine on Lefkas (Ionians)
vilána	Central and eastern Crete	White variety for dry or sweet white wines; provides varietal dry white AO Peza wines; formerly important in malmsey/malvasia production
xynómavro synonyms: *mávro naoúsis* *niaoustinó* *xynógaltso* *popólka*	Central Macedonia, northern Thessaly	Red variety for dry wines; provides varietal AO wines of Naousa and Amyntaion (central Macedonia); required for AO Goumenissa (central Macedonia) wines; authorized for AO Rapsani (Thessaly) wines

Of special note is that various grape varieties in Greece are called *asproúda/a-sproúdi* ('whitey') or *mavroúdi* ('blackie') locally. In order positively to identify such varieties, either a synonym must be known, or the *asproúda/ma-vroúdi* name must be further qualified in some way. For instance, there is the *mavroúdi neméas* synonym for the *ayioryítiko* variety.

APPENDIX V

Note to Researchers

At times, one must tread carefully in the source material. In the case of the travelogues, which in general are indispensable to a study of the history of Greek wine, as of Greece itself, in recent centuries, it will be apparent that they are sometimes inaccurate or contradictory. For example, Tournefort inexplicably confused the south-western Khian settlement of Mesta for Ariousia. While conflicting statements are sometimes the result of their having been written in different periods, when different circumstances held, at other times they are due to the difference in the extent of contact which the authors had. But it is also possible to fault statements made by Greek wine professionals in certain instances, at least when it comes to matters not entirely grounded in measurable data. For example, statements made by enologists regarding wine traditions at particular places do not always tally with what one learns on site or in more extensively researched ethnographical studies. Or again, as concerns ampelography, the division between grape varieties and clones is not in all cases settled, and finds expression in differences of opinion over names and synonyms. Lastly, researchers who go through the ancient material in the expectation of conveniently gathering the ancients' views on wine ought to keep in mind a statement made by the classicist W. H. S. Jones in his introduction to his translation of Hippocrates's *Nature of Man*: 'To a modern it appears somewhat strange that a writer should be intentionally obscure. . . . But in ancient times the public taste was different; the reader, or hearer, was not always averse to being mystified, and authors tried to satisfy this appetite for puzzles.'

Bibliography of Principal Sources

Note: Titles of Greek-language sources are given in English and marked by (G). *HOC* refers to *Hellenica Oenologica Chronica*, the bulletin of the Greek Wine Institute. Titles of *HOC* articles are as given in the English-language summaries.

A. ENOLOGY AND AMPELOGRAPHY

Davidis, Ulysses. *Greek Viticulture*, III, *Ampelographic Elements*, Athens: Superior College of Agriculture, 1982 (G).

Di Stefano, Nicolo, 'Analisi della Viticultura e dell'enologia della Grecia', *Quaderni di Ricerca e Esperimentazione*, 10, 1968, pp. 29–46

Georgakopoulos, G. 'The Composition and Quality of the Wines of Macedonia', Athens: Wine Institute, 1957 (pamphlet, 13 pp.) (G)
'Stabilisation des Vins Doux: Grèce', *IXe Congrès International de la Vigne et du Vin*, III, Paris: OIVV, 1959 (pp. 85–101)
'The Wines of Attica', Athens: Wine Institute, 1957 (pamphlet, 13 pp.) (G)

Harvalia, Antigone, and Eirini Bena-Tzourou. 'The Colour of Red Wines of Various Varieties and Regions of Greece', *HOC*, 1, 1981, pp. 3–23 (G)

Kourakou, S. 'Degré de maturité optimale du raisin selon le type de vin à éláborer', *Bulletin de l'OIV*, 50–559, Sept. 1977, pp. 617–39
'La Grèce viti-vinicole', *Bulletin de l'OIV*, 51–573, Nov. 1978, pp. 914–59

Kourakou-Dragona, Stavroula, and Antonis Popolanos, 'Peculiarities of Wine Production in the Vineyards of the Aegean: 1. Paros', *HOC*, 3, 1983, pp. 1–38 (G)

Kourakou-Dragona, Stavroula, and Sotiris Sotiropoulos. 'Enological Aspects of Red Vine Varieties in Greece', *HOC*, 4, 1985, pp. 67–93 (G)
'Quality Potential of White Vine Varieties in Greece', *HOC*, 4, 1985, pp. 39–64 (G)

Krimbas, Vas. *Greek Ampelography*, I–III, Athens: Ministry of Agriculture,

1943 (I), 1944 (II), 1949 (III). (Vol. I carries grape variety descriptions in Greek and French, with fuller information in Greek. Vol. II is in Greek only. Vol. III has descriptions in Greek, French, and English) 'Le Vin et les cépages malvoisie', *Bulletin de l'OIV*, 20–193, March, 1947, pp. 23–53

Logothetis, Vasilios. *The Contribution of the Vine and Wine to the Civilizations of Greece and the Eastern Mediterranean*. Thessalonica: University of Thessalonica, 1975 (G)

The Malvazias. Thessalonica: University of Thessalonica, 1965 (monograph, 44 pp.) (G)

Popolanos, Antonis. 'Problems of Wine Production in the Viticultural Zone of Amintaion', *HOC*, 1, 1981, pp. 29–56 (G)

Pyrlas, P. 'Les Vins résinés de Grèce', *Le Progres Agricole et Viticole*, 23, no. 11, March 12, 1911, pp. 321–6. (The article appeared in Greek, with a few added comments, in the *Bulletin of the Greek Agricultural Society*, 3, no. 4, April 1911, pp. 114–120)

Sotiropoulos, Sotiris, 'The Appellation of Origin "Côtes de Meliton" ' *HOC*, 1, 1981, pp. 61–78 (G).

B. REGIONAL STUDIES

Bounias, Ioannis. *About Corfu*, Athens, 1954 (G)

Danezis, Michail A., ed. *Santorini*, Athens, 1971 (G)

Debonos, Angelos-Dionysis. *The Historical Cycle of Cephalonian Wines*, unpublished study, commissioned by the firm of Inoexagoyiki, Argostoli, 1985 (76 pp.) (G)

Hatzisotiriou, Yeoryios D. *History of Paiania, and the Areas East of Hymettus*, Athens, 1973 (G)

Melas, Ioannis. *History of the Island of Ikaria*, Athens, 1955 (G)

Palamiotis, G. 'Samos', *Bulletin of the Greek Agricultural Society*, Nov.–Dec. 1914 (G)

Romas, Dionysios. *About Zakynthos*, Athens, 1957 (G)

Salvator, Ludwig. *Zante*, Prague, Heinr. Mercy Sohn, 1904.

C. GENERAL HISTORY

Alivizatos, Babis. *The State and Agricultural Policy*, Athens: Ethnikos Typografos, 1938 (G)

Geanakopulos, Deno John. *Byzantium*, Chicago: University of Chicago Press, 1984

Laiou-Thomadakis, Angeliki E. *Peasant Society in the Late Byzantine Empire*, Princeton, N.J.: Princeton University Press, 1977

Vacalopoulos, Apostolos, E. *The Greek Nation, 1453–1669*, New Brunswick, N.J.: Rutgers University Press, 1976

Vickery, Kenton Frank. 'Food in Early Greece', *University of Illinois Bulletin*, XXXIV, no. 7, 1936

Zografos, Dimitrios L. *History of Greek Agriculture*, Athens: Akropolis Press, 1921 (G)

D. TRAVELOGUES, etc.

Bent, James Theodore. *Aegean Islands: The Cyclades, or: Life among the Insular Greeks*, Chicago: Argonaut, Inc., 1966 (Reprint. First published, London: Longmans, Green & Co., 1885)

Boué, Ami. *La Turquie d'Europe*, Paris: Chez Arthus-Bertrand, 1840

Davy, John. *Notes and Observations on the Ionian Islands and Malta*, London: William Blackwood and Sons, 1881

Dodwell, Edward. *Tour through Greece*, London: Rodwell and Martin, 1819

Leake, William M. *Travels in Northern Greece*, London: J. Rodwell, 1835

Napier, Charles. *The Colonies*, London: Thomas and William Boone, 1833

Pouqueville, François. *Travels in Epirus, Albania, Macedonia, and Thessaly*, London: Sir Richard Phillips and Co., 1820.

Voyage de la Grèce, Paris: Chez Firmin Didot, 1826

Tournefort, Joseph. *Relation d'un voyage du Levant*, Paris: Imprimerie royale, 1717. (Also appeared in English, as *A Voyage into the Levant*, London: D. Browne, 1718)

Turner, William. *Journal of a Tour in the Levant*, London: John Murray, 1820

Walpole, Robert, ed. *Travels in Various Countries of the East*, London: Longman, Hurst, Rees, Orme and Brown, 1820. (Contains unpublished papers of Thomas Raikes, John Sibthorp, et al.)

Index